Twenty Cases Suggestive of Reincarnation

Twenty Cases
Suggestive of Reincarnation

Second Edition, Revised and Enlarged

Ian Stevenson, M.D.

University Press of Virginia

Charlottesville

The University Press of Virginia
Second edition, revised and enlarged, copyright © 1974
by Ian Stevenson
First edition, copyright © 1966 by the American Society
for Psychical Research

Second paperback printing 1988

This book was first published as Volume 26 (1966)
of the *Proceedings* of the American Society
for Psychical Research.

ISBN: 0-8139-0872-8
Library of Congress Catalog Card Number: 73-93627
Printed in the United States of America

Contents

Foreword by C. J. Ducasse   vii

Preface to the Second Edition   ix

Acknowledgments   xi

Acknowledgments for the Second Edition   xv

I.   Introduction   1

II.   Seven Cases Suggestive of Reincarnation in India   15

III.   Three Cases Suggestive of Reincarnation in Ceylon   128

IV.   Two Cases Suggestive of Reincarnation in Brazil   181

V.   Seven Cases Suggestive of Reincarnation Among the Tlingit Indians of Southeastern Alaska   216

VI.   A Case Suggestive of Reincarnation in Lebanon   270

VII.   Discussion of Results Obtained in Follow-up Interviews   321

VIII.   General Discussion   331

Index   389

Foreword

PROMINENT among the questions with which psychical research has concerned itself from its very beginnings has been that of survival of the human personality or of some part of it after the body's death. The *prima facie* evidences of survival which psychical research has considered have been mostly such occurrences as hauntings and apparitions of the dead, out-of-the-body experiences, and communications received through mediums or sensitives and purporting to emanate directly or indirectly from some person whose body had died but whose mind or personality survived.

The conception of survival to which evidence of these kinds is relevant would be discarnate survival. Conceivably, however, survival, if it occurs, might take the form of reincarnation either immediately after death or perhaps after an interval of discarnate existence. This conception has not been widely entertained in the West, but its reasonableness has commended it to some of the most eminent thinkers there who have given it attention. Among them in antiquity have been Pythagoras, Plato, Plotinus, and Origen; and in modern times Hume, Kant, Fichte, Schopenhauer, Renouvier, McTaggart, Ward, and Broad.

In 1860 a monumental work, *A Critical History of the Doctrine of a Future Life*, was published by a learned Unitarian clergyman, the Rev. W. R. Alger. In it, he considers among other conceptions of survival "the notion that when the soul leaves the body it is born anew in another body, its rank, character, circumstances, and experience in each successive existence depending on its qualities, deeds, and attainments in its preceding lives." He states that in the East the adherents of this idea numbered at the time over six hundred million. And, as accounting for "the extent and the tenacious grasp of this antique and stupendous belief," he points out in 1880, in the enlarged tenth edition of his work, that the "theory of the transmigration of souls is marvellously adapted to explain the seeming chaos of moral inequality, injustice, and manifold evil presented in the world of human life" (p. 475).

Obviously, however, these virtues of the reincarnation hypothesis are not evidence that it is true; for the world may really be as full of injustice, inequality, and evil as it appears to be.

If, then, one asks what _would_ constitute genuine evidence of reincarnation, the only answer in sight seems to be the same as to the question how any one of us now knows that he was living some days, months, or years before. The answer is that he now _remembers_ having lived at that earlier time, in such and such a place and circumstances, and having done certain things then and had certain experiences.

But does anybody now claim similarly to remember having lived on earth a life earlier than his present one?

Although reports of such a claim are rare, there are some. The person making them is almost always a young child, from whose mind these memories fade after some years. And when he is able to mention detailed facts of the earlier life he asserts he remembers, which eventual investigation verifies but which he had no opportunity to learn in a normal manner in his present life, then the question with which this confronts us is how to account for the veridicality of his memories, if not by supposing that he really did live the earlier life he remembers.

The twenty cases of such apparent and mostly verified memories, which Dr. Stevenson personally investigated, reports on, and discusses in the present _Proceedings_ of the American Society for Psychical Research, are not claimed by him to settle that question; but they do put it before the reader sharply and, because of this, are fully as interesting and important as are the more numerous cases suggesting discarnate survival, to which psychical research has given close and lengthy attention.

C. J. Ducasse,
Chairman, Publications Committee
American Society for Psychical Research

Preface to the Second Edition

THIS book was originally published in 1966 as Volume 26 of the *Proceedings* of the American Society for Psychical Research. It was and still is addressed primarily to scientists of any discipline who may find the contents of interest and value. But a larger public has manifested a growing interest in the work and to meet this demand a new edition has been prepared with the present publishers.

The publication of a new edition has provided the opportunity of including material derived from follow-up interviews with eighteen of the twenty subjects. These later interviews took place at varying intervals after the original investigations, but in every one of the eighteen cases followed up at least one interview has been held not less than eight years after the original ones. For some, the latest follow-up interview occurred more than ten years after the original interviews.

This edition also contains new information permitting a better understanding of the recitative xenoglossy of Swarnlata Mishra. At the time of publication of the first edition of this book the songs and dances of Swarnlata had not been definitely identified; but this has now been done (at least for two of the songs) and I have provided a fuller account of the songs and dances and of the possibilities existing for Swarnlata to have learned them normally.

The text of the first edition of this book was read by a number of persons directly connected with the cases either as subjects, members of the subjects' families, or as interpreters for me in the investigation of the cases. I am happy to record that none of these readers has pointed out any major flaw in my reporting of the cases with which they were concerned. Nevertheless, they have drawn to my attention (or I have discovered myself) a number of minor errors in the spelling of names or other details. I have corrected all these in the present edition.

As regards the interpretation of the cases, I have little to add to what I said earlier in the section of General Discussion. What I can add will be best reserved for the section of Discussion in a new book of case reports now in preparation. Nor do I have anything to retract. I would only here reiterate that I consider these cases *suggestive* of reincarnation and nothing more. All the cases have deficiencies as have all their reports. Neither any case individually nor all of them collectively offers anything like a proof of reincarnation. My most important single conclusion about them is of the need for further study of similar cases. If anyone takes up this task I shall consider my efforts amply rewarded.

I. S.

Division of Parapsychology,
Department of Psychiatry,
University of Virginia,
Charlottesville, Virginia 22901
August, 1973

Acknowledgments

DURING the years of preparation of this monograph I have incurred many debts for generous assistance from colleagues.

Some persons have contributed in a general way to all of the investigations. For early financial assistance and much encouragement I am grateful to Mrs. Eileen J. Garrett, President, Parapsychology Foundation. Final revisions of the material were completed during my tenure of a Fellowship in Zurich, Switzerland, provided by the Commonwealth Fund to whose directors I am grateful for this support. To Mr. Francis Story I am indebted for much helpful exchange of information about cases and for his important contributions to the results of my first visit to Ceylon and my second visit to India on which occasions he accompanied me during my investigations of cases and added greatly to the gathering of data and their analysis. I am hardly less indebted to Dr. Jamuna Prasad, Deputy Director of Education, Uttar Pradesh, who acted as chief interpreter during my second visit to India and who with his associates took extraordinary pains to make the translations as accurate as they could be. Dr. Karl Müller and Professor P. Pal sent me much helpful information and ideas about cases of the reincarnation type which they had studied. I have profited greatly from the suggestions and counsel of Dr. Karlis Osis and Mr. Arthur W. Osborn. Dr. Robert W. Laidlaw has contributed much helpful encouragement. Señor José Martín and M. Reşat Bayer have assisted me in the study of as yet unpublished cases which have added to my store of knowledge on cases of the type here considered and thus to the present monograph.

The publication of this monograph owes much to the encouragement and assistance I have received from the beginning of my investigations from Professor C. J. Ducasse. The Foreword which he has written has put me even more in his debt. I thank him also for further suggestions made after a complete re-reading of the manuscript. I am indebted to Dr. Gardner Murphy, who has read the manuscript both in an early draft and in the final revision and given many valuable suggestions. His persistent and constructive interest in my work has been the more appreciated because he has sometimes differed with me in the interpretation of the data. Dr. J. G.

Pratt has read the entire manuscript and provided many comments of which I have taken advantage.

For conscientious care in many revisions of the manuscript I wish to thank my research assistant, Mrs. Betty Heavener. And to Mrs. Laura A. Dale, editor of the publications of the American Society for Psychical Research, I express my warm appreciation for her careful editorial work in the final steps of publication.

My thanks go also to the subjects of the cases and the numerous members of their families and other witnesses who cooperated so well in my inquiries and whose frequent and generous hospitality I can only partly repay by trying to record as truthfully as I can what they told me about their experiences.

Finally, I cannot refrain from thanking two persons whose wish to remain anonymous will not prevent me from expressing gratitude for assistance and encouragement without which I could not have completed this work.

Some of those already named as well as many other persons have contributed to the work reported in particular sections of this monograph, as follows:

India

I am grateful to Professor P. Pal, Itachuna College, West Bengal, both for making available his reports on the cases of Sukla and Swarnlata and for assisting me on the second day of my investigation of the case of Sukla; to Mr. Sudhir Mukherjee, Meerut, U.P., India, for assistance as interpreter during ten days of my investigations in India in 1961; to Mr. Subash Mukherjee for coordination in India of certain aspects of the investigations and translations of relevant documents; to Professor B. L. Atreya, Emeritus Professor of Philosophy, Benares Hindu University, Benares, U.P., India, for having placed at my disposal correspondence and affidavits concerning the cases of Parmod Sharma and Ravi Shankar; to Mme Robert Gaebelé, Conservateur de la Bibliothèque Publique et des Archives, Pondicherry, India, for having made available to me information concerning the case of Mallika and for arranging my interviews with persons concerned in that case; to Mr. H. N. Banerjee, Department of Parapsychology, University of Rajasthan, Jaipur, who acted as interpreter for me in my study of the cases of Jasbir and Prakash in 1961 and kindly placed at my disposal documents and notes which he had made or collected for the case of Swarnlata; to Dr. Jamuna Prasad, Deputy Director of Education, U.P., who acted as chief interpreter during my study of three of the cases in 1964; to Mr. R. S. Lal, Mr. Vishwa Nath, Mr. Chandra Prakash, Mr. Ram Deo and Mr. S. K. Singh, all of the Bureau of Psychology, directed by Dr. Prasad, who acted as assistant interpreters for the study of some cases in 1964. Mr. Jagdish Chandra has kindly placed much valuable material about older Indian cases at my disposal.

Ceylon

I wish to thank Mr. E. C. Raddalgoda, Kotte, Ceylon, for acting as interpreter during interviews conducted with Sinhalese witnesses; Dr. William A. Coates, formerly Fulbright Professor of English, University of Ceylon, Peradeniya, Ceylon (later at the Department of Modern Languages and Linguistics, University of Rochester) for much assistance during my investigations in the summer of 1961; Venerable Ananda Maitreya, Professor of Buddhist Philosophy, Vidalankara Pirivena, Colombo, for sharing information about the case of Wijeratne and facilitating my interviews with witnesses in this case; Mr. Siri Perera, Colombo, for procuring a certified copy of the court transcript of the trial of Ratran Hami in 1928; Venerable Piyadassi Thera for sharing with me information about the case of Gnanatilleka.

Brazil

I am grateful to Mr. Waldomiro Lorenz of Porto Alegre, Rio Grande do Sul, who arranged for my interviews with witnesses of the two cases here described. He often himself acted as interpreter and placed his notes on the case of Marta at my disposal. Mrs. Cordelia Anuda of São Paulo enabled me to talk with Mrs. Ema Bolze Moreira in São João Novo and acted as interpreter for that interview.

Alaska

Dr. Louisa E. Rhine and Mrs. Sydney Loosli communicated information to me about the first case of the group reported in this section. Mrs. Loosli, Mr. Cyrus Peck (Secretary of the Alaska Native Brotherhood), Mr. Charles Klevgard (of the Social Service Department, Mt. Edgecumbe Native Hospital, Sitka, Alaska), and Mr. George Hall (former Park Historian, Sitka and Glacier Bay National Monuments, Sitka, Alaska) assisted me greatly in the arrangements for my interviews in Alaska. To Mr. Hall, Dr. Marius Barbeau (National Museum of Canada, Ottawa, Ontario), Dr. Erna Gunther (Department of Anthropology, University of Washington, Seattle), Dr. Frederica de Laguna (Department of Anthropology, Bryn Mawr College, Bryn Mawr, Pennsylvania), Mr. Robert Pace (Department of Sociology and Anthropology, Wake Forest College, Winston-Salem, North Carolina), and Mr. William L. Paul, Sr. (President Emeritus of the Alaska

Native Brotherhood) I am also indebted for much useful material about the history, customs, and beliefs of the Tlingit Indians and their neighbors. Thanks are due also to Mrs. Olga Podtiaguine for translating (from Russian into French) extracts from Veniaminov's report on Alaska and the Tlingits.

Lebanon

Dr. Sami Makarem (Department of Arab Studies, American University of Beirut) assisted me greatly by acting as my interpreter in August, 1964, and furnishing helpful information about the Druse religion and people. Mr. Clement Abushdid and Mr. Wadih Rabbath acted as French-Arabic interpreters during my investigations in March, 1964. Dr. Mustafa Khalidy kindly arranged some helpful introductions in Lebanon for me to members of the Druse community in Beirut. His Eminence Sheikh Mohammed Abu-Shakra, Dr. Naif Hassan, and Mr. Anis S. Rawdah also furnished me with additional information about the Druse religion.

I. S.

June, 1966

Acknowledgments
of Assistance in the Preparation of
the Second Edition

MANY of the persons whom I have mentioned above continued to assist me in the years following the original work on which this book was based. I continue to feel gratitude to them, but will not repeat their names here. In addition, however, several other persons have assisted in the follow-up interviews or contributed in other ways to the preparation of the second edition. In this connection I wish to mention particularly the following persons:

India

Dr. L. P. Mehrotra, Mr. K. S. Rawat, and Mr. Parmeshwar Dayal, all of whom acted as interpreters and research assistants for me.

The investigation of Swarnlata's songs and dances took almost as much time and effort as the study of a new case. So I feel justified in mentioning again the name of Professor P. Pal, who tirelessly aided in collecting information that would help in the evaluation of these important aspects of Swarnlata's case.

Ceylon

Mr. Godwin Samararatne and Mr. Amaraseeri Weeraratne who acted as interpreters for me; Mr. V. F. Guneratne who assisted generously in facilitating my follow-up interviews with Wijeratne and in keeping me in touch with developments in his case; the late Professor K. N. Jayatilleke, Mr. H. S. S. Nissanka, and Dr. G. Karunaratne who assisted in the follow-up interviews with Gnanatilleka.

Alaska

Mrs. Betty Hulbert who conducted on my behalf a second follow-up interview with Henry Elkin.

It is a pleasure as well as an obligation to repeat my thanks to Mrs. Laura A. Dale, the editor of the publications of the American Society for Psychical Research, who has interested herself as much and as competently in the preparation of the second edition of this book as she did in that of the first edition.

Finally, I wish to thank my secretaries, Mrs. Carole Harwell and Mrs. Cynthia Henderson, for tireless application to the task of typing and retyping the additions and corrections for the second edition.

Twenty Cases Suggestive of Reincarnation

Introduction

I N 1960 I published a review and analysis of cases suggestive of reincarnation.[1,2] Most of the cases considered in those articles had already been published in one form or another, and I was able to include details of only one case which I myself had investigated, the case of Henriette Weisz-Roos. In these articles I expressed the hope that the study of further cases of this kind might contribute to the knowledge of psychical research bearing on the survival of physical death by human personality. Since then I have had opportunities to study alone and with colleagues many cases of persons who claim to remember a previous life. I am here presenting some of the results of these studies.

In the international census of cases suggestive of reincarnation which I have undertaken, I now have nearly six hundred cases listed.[3] Of these my colleagues and I have personally investigated about a third and have derived information about the others only from previously published reports or other communications. The twenty cases presented in this volume provide a representative sample of the cases I have investigated at first hand. In this collection I have included examples of nearly every sub-type of the rebirth cases. I have included some cases which I have examined thoroughly and rather soon after the main events of the case occurred; and I have included other cases not so thoroughly studied so far for one reason or another. I have included cases rich in detail and others in which only a few fragmentary apparent memories have occurred. Similarly, readers will find some of the

---

[1] I. Stevenson. "The Evidence for Survival from Claimed Memories of Former Incarnations, Part I. Review of the Data." *Journal* A.S.P.R., Vol. 54, April, 1960, 51–71.

[2] I. Stevenson. "The Evidence for Survival from Claimed Memories of Former Incarnations, Part II. Analysis of the Data and Suggestions for Further Investigations." *Journal* A.S.P.R., Vol. 54, July, 1960, 95–117.

[3] In this connection, I hope readers will continue to send me accounts of cases suggestive of reincarnation, especially concerning persons willing to participate in a scrutiny of detail about their experiences. I can assure the subject of any such study that I will maintain his anonymity if he wishes. At the time of preparing the second edition of this book (1973) the number of cases in the collection had increased to twelve hundred. Also a much larger proportion of the total has received investigation by myself or my associates.

cases presented rather fully authenticated by many witnesses, while for others I have found only one or two witnesses as to the alleged facts. But I deliberately present these weaker cases as well as the stronger ones in order to give the reader a picture of the range of cases which *suggest* reincarnation. In my discussion at the end I argue that *some* of the cases do much more than suggest reincarnation; they seem to me to furnish considerable evidence for it. But I do not say this of all the cases and I am well aware that some are weak in both detail and authentication.

Of the remaining cases in the whole collection, about thirty others are as rich in detail and as well authenticated as the ten best cases of the present group. The remainder are minor cases in that they lack as abundant detail or as high authenticity as the former group of cases. The geographical distribution of the cases is roughly as follows: About half of all the approximately six hundred cases come from southeastern Asia (i.e., India, Ceylon, Thailand, and Burma). Most of the remainder come from western Asia (i.e., southeastern Turkey, Syria, and Lebanon), Europe, and Brazil. A few only come from the United States and Canada, apart from Alaska where numerous cases occur.

This means then that the incidence of reported cases varies widely between different cultures. It does not *necessarily* mean, however, that cultural influences alone account for the data of these cases. I believe that many of these cases minimally call for *some* paranormal interpretation of the data. This statement gives my own opinion ahead of the presentation of the data, something I excuse only by the great efforts I have made to present the data in the case reports separate from my conclusions; this, I hope, will leave the reader free to provide his own interpretation of the material. But I do not wish to overlook the important relations between cultural influences and the reported cases, a topic which I shall develop further as I study and report additional cases of this type.

Among the cases still under investigation, I have other examples of every type of case here included, although I have more examples of some types than of others. I have under investigation now only one other case of an "exchange incarnation," if I may apply this expression to the case of Jasbir (see pp. 34–52 below).

So far, most of the best evidence bearing on reincarnation has come from spontaneous cases. Relevant material does not often arise in the laboratory under circumstances where we can exert even moderate control. Some of the earliest and most thorough investigators of the evidence for reincarnation used hypnosis to regress subjects back in time to supposed "previous lives." De Rochas [4] and later Björkhem,[5] to mention two investigators only, each

---

[4] A. de Rochas. *Les vies successives.* Paris: Chacornac Frères, 1924.
[5] J. Björkhem. *De Hypnotiska Hallucinationerna.* Stockholm: Litteraturförlaget, 1943.

published reports of a series of such experiments. Unfortunately, the results of these experiments, although provocative, have proved inconclusive and, on the whole, disappointing chiefly due to the difficulty of controlling the subject's access to the information embodied in the "previous personality." The "personalities" usually evoked during hypnotically-induced regressions to a "previous life" seem to comprise a mixture of several ingredients. These may include the subject's current personality, his expectations of what he thinks the hypnotist wants, his fantasies of what he thinks his previous life ought to have been, and also perhaps elements derived paranormally.

When we think we have identified definite paranormal elements in the "previous personality" evoked under hypnotic regression we have still to decide, if we can, whether we can best account for these by our concepts of telepathy or clairvoyance, by an influence of some discarnate personality, or by reincarnation. (These decisions face us also in the spontaneous cases among children.) The plausibility of the behavioral features of the "personality" evoked gives no sure guidance to the origin of the personality or its different components. And, except in very small children or in the case of the communication of information of an extremely recondite kind, we experience the greatest difficulty in excluding normal sources of information for the contents of the "previous life." Nevertheless, some of the cases developed through hypnosis include material or behavior which we cannot easily account for except on some paranormal hypothesis. I have myself investigated one case of this type in which the subject spoke a foreign language which, according to all the evidence, she could not have learned by normal means.[6] And future experiments, especially with children and resulting in the exhibition of unusual and unlearned skills such as foreign languages, could make a valuable contribution to this subject.

In the meantime, the most promising evidence bearing on reincarnation seems to come from the spontaneous cases, especially among children. However, the study and evaluation of such cases is as difficult as with other kinds of spontaneous cases in psychical research and is naturally exposed to the same kinds of criticisms.[7]

[6] I. Stevenson, "Xenoglossy: A Review and Report of a Case." *Proc.* A.S.P.R., Vol. 31, 1974, 1–268. (Also published by The University Press of Virginia, Charlottesville, 1974.)

[7] For criticisms of spontaneous case material see: D. J. West. "The Investigation of Spontaneous Cases." *Proc.* S.P.R., Vol. 48, 1948, 264–300; E. J. Dingwall. "British Investigation of Spontaneous Cases." *International Journal of Parapsychology*, Vol. 3, 1961, 89–97; M. Scriven. "New Frontiers of the Brain." *Journal of Parapsychology*, Vol. 25, 1961, 305–318. And for criticisms of the criticisms, see: W. H. Salter. "A Commentary on 'The Investigation of Spontaneous Cases.'" *Proc.* S.P.R., Vol. 48, 1948, 301–305; H. Carrington. "The Investigation of Spontaneous Cases." *Journal* S.P.R., Vol. 34, 1948, 306–307 (correspondence); W. F. Prince. "Human Experiences." *Bulletin*, Boston Society for Psychic Research, No. 14, 1931, and No. 20, 1933; I. Stevenson. *Journal of Parapsychology*, Vol. 26, 1962, 59–64 (correspondence); I. Stevenson. "The Substantiality of Spontaneous Cases." *Proc.* Parapsychological Assoc., Vol. 5, 1968, 91–128

Methods of Studying Spontaneous Cases of the Reincarnation Type

In studying spontaneous cases, psychical researchers have for decades used essentially the methods of the historian and the lawyer, and sometimes the psychiatrist, to reconstruct past events. In most spontaneous cases, the main events have already occurred by the time an investigator reaches the scene. Once he arrives there, much depends upon his skill as an interviewer in eliciting and analyzing the testimony. The skill of the interviewer should never be casually assumed in such inquiries.

Granting, however, sufficient skill in the interviewer, a central difficulty of all such inquiries lies in the unreliability of the memories (and even perceptions) of the experients and the witnesses, who may omit or import various details of the case and thus alter it, sometimes immeasurably, from an accurate representation of actual events. Such alterations of memory may arise from deficiencies of intelligence in the reporting person or from errors motivated by his wishes or fears when confronting something of emotional significance to him. But if we ask how we detect such errors in relation to the "real events" in any inquiry, we have to acknowledge that we do this by comparing what one informant said with what some other informant said or wrote about the same event. We can never escape in science, even in the laboratory, from human testimony of some kind, and the task is that of testing and improving rather than discarding such testimony. Lawyers and historians try to reach documents written at the time or shortly after the events concerned. They know, however, that writing confers no authenticity on a document beyond the qualities of the writer, and a document written by an unreliable witness has less value than the verbal testimony of a reliable one. But for this fact, historians and lawyers would have little to do.

In the study of the present cases I have tried to follow these traditional methods of law, history, and psychical research. Unfortunately, two weaknesses of many previously investigated cases of this type have occurred in the present series. First, with two exceptions (Swarnlata Mishra and Imad Elawar), the statements of the subjects (usually children) were not written down prior to attempts at verification. Secondly, the recognitions by the child of people and places of the supposed previous life were not observed (with few exceptions, e.g., in the case of Imad Elawar) by persons unconnected (that is, independent in attitude) with the two families concerned. In the frequent absence, then, of opportunities for direct observation of the important past events of the cases, I have gathered testimony from as many witnesses of these events as I could interview. And I have often interrogated the same witnesses at intervals of one to several years. Sometimes also I have been able to compare the results of my inquiries with those of other independent persons who had previously studied a case and in whose competence to do so I had confidence.

After gathering all this testimony, I became able to compare the statements made by different persons of one family or community with each other and with the statements relating to the same events made by members of the other family or community. I could also compare the statements of one person at one time with his statements made at another time to myself or to another investigator. This leads to the question of the reliability of the information thus gathered, an important topic which I shall discuss further shortly. But here I wish to add and emphasize that verbal information constituted only one portion of the data available on these cases. For I have rather often had the opportunity to observe directly the *behavior* of the subject himself and of the persons surrounding him in his family, and that of the persons in the family of the previous personality. I may also point out here that the behavior of the child corresponded in these cases very well with what the witnesses told me about his or her behavior. This increases my confidence in what they told me about the informational aspects of the cases; that is, what the child claimed to remember, which statements I could not usually hear from the subject at first hand, but could only learn about from the parents and other witnesses. The identification by these children with the previous personality seems to me one of the most important features of these cases. Such personation, with components of strongly emotional behavior, transcends the simple recital by the child of information about another person who lived before. In my opinion, these behavioral features of the cases both add considerably to their authenticity and greatly increase our opportunities for studying human personality.

Detection and Disposition of Possible Errors in Collecting Data

Since the value of cases of this type depends, however, on the accuracy of the testimony of the witnesses and of the reporting of what they said they saw or heard, I have given much attention to the assessment of this accuracy in the witnesses of the cases I have studied.

In the absence of written records, we count on the accumulation of corroborating testimony from several witnesses who try to remember the same or related events. I have, therefore, tried to find as many different witnesses for the cases as I could. In correlating the testimony of different witnesses or of the same witness at different times, I have found that discrepancies occur in about ten per cent of all the statements made to me. This incidence, rather lower than I had expected when I began these studies, increases my confidence in the general accuracy of the informants since, on the whole, the accounts they give of the events of the cases agree very well. The discrepancies occur, moreover, nearly always with regard to accessory details rather than main events. Witnesses may agree, for example, that a child recognized a particular debtor who owed money to the previous personality, but disagree about the sum owed. Or they may agree about the mode of death of a person, but disagree about when it occurred. Some details are crucial, however, and I do not mean to imply that we can overlook all discrepancies in details. I merely want to emphasize that most discrepancies occur in details rather than in the main outlines of events.

Nevertheless, the handling of discrepancies in testimony about cases of this kind poses a difficult problem. On the one hand, certain witnesses quickly (or slowly) prove themselves unreliable by pretending rashly to a knowledge of the facts which in fact they do not have; it seems unfair to allow the testimony of such a person to cancel out that of an obviously more reliable informant just because it offers a discrepancy. On the other hand, I would not be fair to the reader if I suppressed all discordant testimony since I might thereby, however unconsciously, give some bias to the reported data of the case. It has seemed to me, however, that the total elimination of some few items in which discrepant testimony occurred would act in nearly every instance toward weakening the evidence of paranormality in the cases, and that to add such discrepant items to those consistently witnessed to could spuriously make the cases seem richer than they are. I have concluded, therefore, that I could safely eliminate completely most of the items in which discrepant testimony occurred. But I have retained some, in each instance offering a comment on the discrepant testimony.

Recently I have paid much more attention to the analysis of individual discrepancies than I had earlier and found it instructive to trace the explanation for each as far as I could. This became easier with two interpreters than it had been when I had only one interpreter. I then found that some discrepancies occurred through slips in interpretation, the translation coming through in a slightly (or seriously) different form on different occasions. Other discrepancies occurred because the witness had not understood a particular question and responded to a mistaken idea of what he had been asked. Still other discrepancies occurred through deficiencies of attention or memory on the part of witnesses. The analysis of discrepancies during or shortly after the interviews has enabled me to "save" some important items which would otherwise have been lost and this has increased my conviction that the elimination of such discrepant items as I have dropped has diminished rather than strengthened the cases.

With rare exceptions, all the testimony recorded derives from firsthand witnesses. Occasionally I have retained the testimony of secondhand witnesses, but have always noted these occasions in the case reports.

I shall next give some particular details of the three main possible sources of error in the reports and the measures taken to reduce or discount them as important weakening factors in the case reports.

Translations and Possible Errors of Interpreters

I know French and German rather well and some Spanish and Portuguese. I pretend, however, to no working knowledge of Asian languages such as Arabic or Hindi. The major possible occasions for undesirable influence of the records by interpreters occurred in some of the cases in India, Ceylon, and Lebanon.

Of the seven Indian cases, I needed interpreters for the study of five. (In the case of Swarnlata nearly all the witnesses spoke English and in the case of Mallika they chiefly spoke French.) For these five cases I had at least two and sometimes three interpreters. In 1964 I had two interpreters assisting me simultaneously: one translated while I made notes in English; the other checked the translation and also made notes in Hindi which we later compared with my notes in English.

For the three Ceylonese cases, I had two interpreters (simultaneously) for one case (Wijeratne) and one interpreter for the other two, although in one of these two cases (Gnanatilleka) one of the main witnesses spoke English.

For the case of Imad Elawar in Lebanon, I had three interpreters at different times.

In summary, for nine of the eleven Asian cases in which I required interpreters, I had at least two interpreters, often working with me at different times. I have detected some discrepancies attributable to errors of translation, but am confident such errors affect a small and insignificant group of all the items of the cases.[8]

Methods of Recording and Possible Errors

Other errors may have crept into the records during the process of recording the statements of the witnesses or my observations of their behavior. It is my practice to make written notes as the witness or interpreter talks. I prefer this method to the use of tape recorders in these investigations because (a) a tape recorder frequently leads to an initial inhibition on the part of the witness, who may become forgetful or guarded in its presence until he has become used to it; and (b) since one can rarely have completely private interviews in the East (several persons usually assembling to give their testimony at once), a tape recorder sometimes fails to give adequate information with regard to who actually said what, a point to which I attach much importance. In listening to the tape afterwards, it may be quite im-

---

[8] I have provided some further details about the investigation of the cases, including the use of interpreters, in the reports which follow.

possible to remember correctly the ownership of different voices. Further-more, tape recordings do not furnish the correct spelling of names and in various ways, e.g., if a voice suddenly drops in volume, one can often lose details of information with them. In my opinion, written notes are therefore in any case essential, and I see no reason why they should not be relied on altogether provided the notes are made as the witness talks. (In a few in-stances—as, for example, when a witness talked in an automobile—circum-stances have interfered with doing this and I have had to make my notes upon returning to my hotel some hours later or, rarely, the next day.)

My confidence in the accuracy of my notes made during interviews was strengthened by some experiences in Turkey. During the study of some cases there in March, 1964, I took notes as usual, trying to capture as many details as possible. At the same time, M. Reşat Bayer, who assisted me as interpreter there, also recorded the interviews (with a few exceptions) on a portable tape recorder. Afterwards, I sent M. Bayer copies of all my notes and he carefully compared them as to details retained or altered with the material on the tapes of the interviews. This comparison showed that I had made no important errors in my notes and M. Bayer found only a small number of minor discrepancies in details. The most serious of these was that I had recorded the age of a child as between two and a half and three years when, according to the tape, it should have been between two and two and a half. I had dropped some details picked up on the tapes, no doubt, because I was in the act of writing down what had just been said when the interpreter went on to say something else. But the most important point of this comparison was that I had not included any detail in my notes addi-tional to those recorded on the tapes.

In the important work of interrogating the witnesses, assessing their re-liability, and detecting important omissions or discrepancies, I was most fortunate in having the assistance of Mr. Francis Story,[9] who accompanied me in Ceylon in 1961 and in India in 1964. His active participation in the case studies provided the opportunity for a discussion of the testimony and any discrepancies or other doubts it presented while the material remained fresh. And I think this collaboration reduced the chances of my overlooking or failing to record any important points developed during the interviews.

The Apparently Precocious Language Attributed to the Subjects

Some readers of the first edition of this book have voiced skepticism con-cerning the ability of small children to express themselves in sentences as long and complex as some of those attributed to them by their parents and

---

[9] The death of Francis Story in April, 1971, deprived these investigations of an indefatigable participant who combined enthusiasm for the studies in general with a remarkable ability to examine individual cases critically.

recorded by me here. Some explanation of this seems in order. I think there are two main reasons why a subject's statements sometimes seem to be longer and more complex than what one would expect of a child of his age.

First, many of the subjects are precocious in speaking—both in their ability to articulate and in the richness of vocabulary—and some of them have quite startled their parents by the unusual words and phrases which they have uttered at a remarkably young age.

Secondly, however, in other instances the parents have given me the fully developed statement of a child that he may only have made after he acquired ample powers of speech. Let us suppose that a subject begins to speak short phrases between the ages of one and two years, as do most children. Many of the subjects of these cases then try to describe the previous lives they remember almost as soon as they begin to communicate in words, but before they have sufficient skill to transmit their ideas accurately. They often mispronounce words, use gestures to supplement what they want to say, or incorrectly apply some word they know to an object for which they do not know the correct name. Imad Elawar's first pronunciation of Khriby as "Tliby" and his use of two fingers held out together to indicate a double-barreled shotgun are examples of the first two types of expression. Marta Lorenz's reference to "goats, but they were not goats" is an example of the third type. As the child develops fuller powers of speech, say between the ages of two and four or five, he nearly always repeats (often many times) what he tried to say earlier, but can at last express more clearly. The parents have usually given me these later statements of the child. So although the subject may have started to talk about the previous life at a very early age and made or tried to make some utterances about it then, the statements I have recorded will in many cases derive from the subject's later more competent expression of the same ideas. In citing the subject's statements I have sometimes used quotation marks. It should be understood that these quotation marks surround a translation (in most instances) of what the parent (or other informant) stated the child had said. The reader should, however, add to himself some phrase such as "or words to that effect" when he reads such quotations.

Errors of Memory on the Part of Witnesses

We come next to the most important factor of the reliability of the informants' memories. Supposing that we find a large measure of agreement among different witnesses on the main facts of a case (as we have in the present cases), what confidence can we then have that the witnesses reached this agreement independently and did not become victims of a culturally endorsed wave of credulity, elaborating a lengthy story from a small nucleus of childish behavior? Possibly everyone of the group agrees without much thought that they heard or saw events which they had not, rather as the

Emperor's clothes became imposed by fear and credulity on his populace; or to take a real example, as it became the fashion to wear cuffs on trousers when the valet of King Edward VII one day inadvertently forgot to roll down the King's trousers (after polishing his shoes) before the King went out; men of fashion shortly found it pleasant or at least expedient to wear turned-up cuffs on their trousers.

In short, we have here a theory of *motivated* errors of memory and reporting. I should say the main argument against the likelihood that this kind of mass (or even localized) infection of ideas occurred lies in the markedly different attitudes of the various witnesses toward the events concerned. In the West uninformed critics commonly believe that since everyone (or nearly everyone) in the East believes in reincarnation, no one has immunity to acceptance of any story with a reincarnationist flavor, however improbable it may seem to others. Now it is perfectly true that a belief in reincarnation is widespread in the Orient and also that credulity about it often occurs there. But when you come down to specific cases, you find that the different people concerned often adopt quite different attitudes. In the first place, there exists a widespread belief that the remembrance of previous lives fates one to die young and parents often apply strenuous and sometimes cruel measures to suppress a child from talking about a previous life. Beyond this, however, a child who represents himself as really belonging to another village where he would live more happily, or one who shows habits of behavior quite alien to those of his family, presents a serious problem to his family and to himself. And we should make no mistake about the fact that many of these children threaten to run off to the other home, and some occasionally actually do so (e.g., Prakash and Parmod). Sometimes the child and parents have enjoyed some of the publicity often associated with a claim to remember a previous life. But more often they find the publicity a terrible bore and an expense; they gain nothing and lose much of their privacy as a result. Confirmation of the parents' reluctance to seek publicity for the case often comes from other witnesses, e.g., neighbors who remember how old the child was when he first began to talk of a previous life. On the average, a gap of three to five years separates the period of the child's first utterances (see the tabulation on pp. 326–327) and the development of publicity for the case outside the immediate circle of the family. Repeatedly I found that the parents had resisted (sometimes for years) the importunate pleading of the child to be taken to the other village where he claimed to have lived before. If we consider all these circumstances which can influence the motives of the witnesses to the cases, we must reject a theory which suggests that all the agreement of evidence favoring paranormal explanations of the cases derives from motivated errors of memory in the witnesses. For the motives of many of the witnesses work to distort their reporting of the events in the direction opposite to the paranormal or reincarnationist explanations. Often the witnesses force themselves to testify to something a child has said which they know carries with it the possibility that the child will leave them, or at least prefer to live in some other family.

Two other recurrent features of the testimony seem to me to strengthen confidence in it. First, if the witnesses were distorting the accounts markedly and separately, we should expect a much greater incidence of discrepancies between the testimonies of different witnesses. Why, for example, should witness A, if he is elaborating the story, restrict his elaboration so that it happens to conform almost exactly with the story of witness B, not to mention C, D, and others? The proposal that the witnesses have influenced each other makes more sense than the suggestion that they have individually elaborated accounts and accidentally stopped at the same place. But on this point, it is clear that although *some* of the witnesses could (and almost certainly did) influence each other, in other instances the witnesses could not possibly have done this (as in the cases of Swarnlata and Imad), or almost certainly did not do so because they stood on opposing sides of an issue (as in the cases of Prakash and Ravi Shankar). Moreover, the existence of *some* discrepancies points away from any complete contrivance of the accounts. Secondly, the witnesses were just as candid in telling us about mistakes and confusions on the part of the child as in telling us about his successes. (See especially the cases of Swarnlata and Imad for examples of such mistakes.) In conclusion, I do not say motivated errors of testimony have not occurred in these cases, but I do say these errors cannot account for all the agreement (or discrepancies) I have found in the testimonies of different witnesses.

Information from Follow-up Interviews with the Subjects and Their Families

Out of interest and friendship I kept in touch with some of the subjects of these cases following my initial investigations in the years 1961–64. Then in preparation for the new edition of this book I tried to visit as many of them as I could to obtain firsthand information about the further development of the subjects who had been children when I first met them or about the further courses in life of those who had been adults. In the end I was able to meet again all but two of the subjects, most of them in the years 1970–73, but one (Sukla Gupta) in 1969. Mallika Aroumougam had moved away from Pondicherry and my inquiries about her new address have not led to her being traced. The parents of William George, Jr. were unwilling to cooperate with further inquiries. All the other subjects and their families seemed genuinely glad to renew acquaintance with me and with their usual patience answered my questions most helpfully.

The interval elapsing between the initial investigations of the cases and the follow-up interviews varied. The shortest interval, eight years, occurred in the case of Sukla Gupta. The longest, twelve years, occurred in the case of Wijeratne. For the other cases the interval between my first and latest (before the preparation of this edition) interviews was between nine and ten years. In a number of cases I had additional interviews with the subjects and members of their families during the years between the first and latest interviews with them.

Method of Presentation of Data in These Reports

In the reports of the cases which follow, I have necessarily summarized and combined certain of the information given by different witnesses. Thus I have usually introduced the report of a case by a short history of its development. In preparing these summaries, I have combined and paraphrased the testimony of a number of witnesses. But when it comes to the detailed tabulations of what witnesses said about the statements or recognitions made by the subjects, and what other witnesses said about the verification of these first items, I have put down exactly what the witnesses reported. I do not mean that I have used their exact words, for I have tried to state these items briefly and also some witnesses used different words to describe the same event. But I do mean that for every item thus listed in these tabulations, I have a note (nearly always made contemporaneously) that the witness listed made a statement corresponding exactly to the item listed. And since, as already mentioned, several people nearly always attended interviews, other witnesses gave silent or vocal consent to what the main witness said, or sometimes disagreed with it. Thus, in general, I could have listed additional witnesses for each item recorded, but I have preferred to focus attention on the main witnesses who seemed to me in the best position to observe the events they reported. I will make available my original notes on the cases to any serious inquirer who wishes to compare these with the material here printed.

For each of the cases I have provided (in the case reports) some information and comments bearing on the likelihood of transmission of information to the subject through normal means of communication, including fraud and cryptomnesia. I have reserved a general discussion of paranormal hypotheses relevant to these cases for a final section at the end of the case reports. But I have thought it best to comment on some important points while the reader has the details of each case report in mind, even though some repetition occurs in the General Discussion at the end of the case reports.

Descriptions of roads and other communications between places concerned in the cases, and remarks based on these, derive from conditions pertaining in 1961–64. Since that period the means of communication have been improved in some of the places mentioned.

I have placed the information derived from the follow-up interviews in separate sections of each case report following the comments I have offered about the case. This will permit the reader to assess the case (with whatever help my comments offer) on the basis of the original investigation without regard to the information contained in the follow-up reports.

In the case reports which follow I use the phrase "the previous personality" in most instances when I wish to refer to the deceased person with whom the subject of the case claims an identification. This phrase seems less clumsy than others such as "the supposed previous personality" or "the alleged previous personality." At the same time it does not imply any commitment to the child's claim that his personality is in fact continuous with that of "the previous personality." This is the central question posed by the data and I shall grapple with it later in the General Discussion. Similarly, I usually refer to the statements attributed to the child simply as his "memories" rather than his "ostensible memories of a previous life." The statements attributed to the subject are memories of some kind and the question is whether they are memories of what he has heard or learned normally, of what he has experienced paranormally, or of what he has experienced in a previous life.

I have changed all the names to pseudonyms of the subjects and witnesses of the Alaskan cases to protect them from possibly undesirable publicity. But in all other sections I have changed only one name (in the case of Imad Elawar) and left all the other informants to testify by their real names.

Plans for Future Investigations and Reports

I hope the foregoing review of difficulties in studying these cases and attempts made to overcome them will leave no one believing that I am satisfied with the present methods. I feel strongly an obligation to improve the study of these cases in every way I can. Apart from improving methods, I should much prefer to study cases when they are fresher than most of those here reported were when I reached them. For this, obstacles remain since, as already mentioned, the families having a child of this type usually wish to avoid all publicity and hence only reluctantly notify other people about the statements of the child. Rarely do they do this before they themselves have tried to verify the child's statements. I hope, nevertheless, through improved detection of cases, to learn of some which I may then investigate immediately after the child has made his statements, and before their verification. In the present collection of cases, written notes were made before verification in two cases, those of Swarnlata and Imad. In one other case (Prakash),

I reached the scene of the main events within weeks of the verifications and could begin study of them when they were quite fresh. But in the other cases I came to study the testimony months or years after the original events.

The obvious limitations for studying cases of this type, even under the most favorable circumstances, should make us also turn to other ways of developing additional relevant evidence. I have already mentioned the possibilities for the future of further and better controlled experiments with hypnosis, especially using children as subjects. In addition, I have begun to study the patterns of recurring features in large numbers of spontaneous cases of the reincarnation type. I plan to evaluate all the cases in my collection for authenticity. I then propose to compare the characteristics occurring in the less thoroughly investigated cases with those occurring in the cases of whose authenticity I am more confident, applying a method originally devised by Hart for the study of apparitional cases.[10] If I find that patterns occurring in well-authenticated cases occur repeatedly in less well-authenticated ones my confidence in information contained in the latter cases will increase. I shall then draw on the larger number of cases in beginning to delineate patterns and make inferences from all the material available. On the other hand, if this analysis fails to show significant similar patterns between the more and the less well-authenticated cases, I may then have a basis for future discriminations in studying cases.

I shall also continue efforts to evaluate cases of this type by trying the fit of the cases to the various theories which compete for their explanation and by trying to imagine new theories which the data may suit better than they do any of the current hypotheses. And I shall continue trying to imagine and describe ideal cases which, if found, would permit definite judgments between rival theories, and trying also to find and study such crucial cases.

[10] H. Hart. "Six Theories About Apparitions." *Proc.* S.P.R., Vol. 50, 1956, 153–239.

II

Seven Cases
Suggestive of Reincarnation
in India

Introduction

THE idea of reincarnation forms an important principle in the religion of Hinduism adhered to by the great majority of the inhabitants of India. Hinduism is the oldest surviving religion of the world since its origins can be traced back to the fourth millennium B.C. Its doctrines and practices do not differ much today from what they were thousands of years ago.[1] The persuasions of Muslim and Christian conquerors and missionaries have had little impact on the continuing belief of nearly all Indians in the basic ideas of Hinduism. I have in the Introduction to this monograph alluded to the complex relationships which must connect the belief in reincarnation in particular cultures and the occurrence of cases seeming to provide evidence justifying such belief. Here I shall only add that the viability of Hinduism today may be due to the rather frequent reporting in India of experiences which seem to offer evidence for reincarnation. Cases of the kind I shall describe seem to have occurred for centuries in India. Their existence is assumed or hinted at throughout many of the Hindu scriptures and myths. Since we know that many cases of the reincarnation type occur in India today, it seems at least possible, and is perhaps likely, that such cases have occurred as frequently for centuries. Whatever may be the merits and proper interpretation of these cases, their mere *existence* has provided a continuing stream of apparent empirical support for the religion of Hinduism, and for Buddhism also.

The first investigation of a case in India known to me occurred early in the eighteenth century. The Emperor Aurangzeb heard of a case and, al-

[1] Readers will find information and bibliographies about Hinduism and Hindu beliefs in the following: S. Radhakrishnan. "Hinduism," in *The Legacy of India* (Ed., G. T. Garratt). Oxford: Oxford University Press, 1937; A. N. Coomaraswamy. *Hinduism and Buddhism.* New York: Philosophical Library, n.d.; K. M. Sen. *Hinduism.* Harmondsworth: Penguin Books, Limited, 1961; Swami Nikhilananda. *Self-Knowledge: An English Translation of Sankaracharya's Atmabodha with Notes, Comments, and Introduction.* New York: Ramakrishna-Vivekananda Center, 1946; Swami Prabhavananda with the assistance of F. Manchester. *The Spiritual Heritage of India.* New York: Doubleday and Company, Inc., 1963; *Bhagavad-Gita* (trans. by Swami Prabhavananda and C. Isherwood). Hollywood: The Marcel Rodd Co., 1944. (The last-named book is generally regarded as a gospel of Hinduism. It provides an ancient and authoritative exposition of Hindu ideas about reincarnation.)

though himself a Muslim, became interested in it and had the witnesses brought before him so he could interrogate them. The case had features, such as birthmarks, which I have found in the modern cases.[2] From the beginning of the twentieth century isolated cases and occasionally small series of cases have received investigation, sometimes of a rather careful kind. The systematic investigation of cases suggestive of reincarnation in India, however, has only begun in recent years.

In the summer of 1961, I visited India and Ceylon for the purpose of studying cases suggestive of reincarnation in these countries. On that visit I investigated to varying extents some eighteen such cases in India. Of these cases four are comparatively old, the relevant apparent memories and original investigations having occurred from twenty to thirty years ago. I hope to publish the investigations of these older cases with information about the later lives of the subjects in a separate report. In several other cases insufficient details have prevented verification of the apparent memories. In some other cases the data available seem insufficient for any reasonable judgment. And in still another group of cases investigations continue and will be reported later.

In 1964 I returned to India and rechecked thoroughly with two new interpreters and a second observer the cases of Prakash, Jasbir, Ravi Shankar, and Parmod. During this second visit to India I also investigated some additional new and old cases, reports of which will follow in later publications.

The present report describes seven rather recent and, with regard to the behavior of the children, still current cases. Most of these cases are the richest in detail, the best witnessed, and in my opinion the most thoroughly investigated of recent cases suggestive of reincarnation occurring in India. They are not essentially different from many older cases previously published, some of which I have already reviewed.[3] Their value lies in the more thorough investigation accorded to them and this has, I believe, made it possible to discuss the various hypotheses with assurance that one has available for the discussion most of the obtainable facts of a particular case relevant to the choice among these hypotheses.

Usual History of Cases Suggestive of Reincarnation

So far, the history of cases suggestive of reincarnation in India (and elsewhere) follows an almost conventional pattern. The case usually starts

---

[2] This interesting case is not, however, the earliest claim to remember a previous life known to me from India. Tulsi Das, the Hindi poet of the Ramayana, mentions in his great work a claim to remember a previous life with a few (unverified) details. *The Ramayana of Tulsi Das* (trans. by F. S. Growse) . 7th ed. Allahabad: Ram Narain Lal, 1937, p. 652.

[3] I. Stevenson. "The Evidence for Survival from Claimed Memories of Former Incarnations, Part I. Review of the Data." *Journal* A.S.P.R., Vol. 54, April, 1960, 51–71; and "The Evidence for Survival from Claimed Memories of Former Incarnations, Part II. Analysis of the Data and Suggestions for Further Investigations." *Journal* A.S.P.R., Vol. 54, July, 1960, 95–117.

when a small child of two to four years of age begins talking to his parents
or siblings of a life he led in another time and place. The child usually feels
a considerable pull back toward the events of that life and he frequently
importunes his parents to let him return to the community where he claims
that he formerly lived. If the child makes enough particular statements
about the previous life, the parents (usually reluctantly) begin inquiries
about their accuracy. Often, indeed usually, such attempts at verification do
not occur until several years after the child has begun to speak of the
previous life. If some verification results, members of the two families visit
each other and ask the child whether he recognizes places, objects, and
people of his supposed previous existence. On such occasions the case usually
attracts much attention in the communities involved and accounts reach the
newspapers. In the past only a few cases, e.g., that of Shanti Devi,[4, 5] have
received investigation by independent persons outside the immediate families of the subjects.[6] I have tried to remedy this deficiency by conducting
the international census of cases suggestive of reincarnation mentioned above
and by arranging whenever possible for firsthand investigations of the cases
by persons familiar with the methods of psychical research.[7] I hope to have
the opportunity of investigating more cases in which the child's family has
not yet attempted any verification so that the case may be observed before,
during, and after verification of the main statements made by the child. The
cases of Swarnlata (in the present group) and Imad Elawar (in Lebanon)
approach this ideal partially.

Methods of Investigation

Since I have already described my general methods of investigation in the
Introduction, I shall not repeat this description here, but merely give some
additional details in relation to the specific cases. I give next details of the
time I spent in interviewing witnesses of the cases. These figures do not include the development of considerable information about some of the cases,
e.g., Swarnlata, Sukla, and Ravi Shankar, by correspondence before and
after my visits to the scenes of the cases.

[4] L. D. Gupta, N. R. Sharma, and T. C. Mathur. *An Inquiry into the Case of Shanti Devi.*
Delhi: International Aryan League, 1936.

[5] S. C. Bose. *A Case of Reincarnation.* Ligate, Sat' ing, S.P., 19 2.

[6] Yet I think it important to note that several reports of investigations by independent persons
of Indian cases suggestive of reincarnation appeared during the 1920s and '30s. See, for example
(in addition to references 4 and 5 above): I. Sen. "Kumari Shanti Devi and Reincarnation."
Chitrapat, July 4, 1936, Delhi; I. Sen. "Shanti Devi Further Investigated." *Proceedings Indian
Philosophical Congress,* ca. 1937; K. K. N. Sahay. *Reincarnation: Verified Cases of Rebirth After
Death,* privately published, Bareilly, ca. 1927 (contains a report of the case of the author's own
son and six other cases occurring in other families which he investigated); R. B. S. Sunderlal.
"Cas apparents de réminiscences de vies antérieures."*Revue Métapsychique,* July–August, 1924,
302–307.

[7] I. Stevenson. "Criteria for the Ideal Case Bearing on Reincarnation." *Indian Journal of
Parapsychology,* Vol. 2, 1960, 149–155.

1. *Case of Prakash*

In 1961 I spent two days studying the case with Sri H. N. Banerjee assisting me as interpreter. In 1964 I rechecked the case, spending another two days interviewing previous and new informants. During the main interviews in 1964 conducted in Kosi Kalan and Chhatta, Dr. Jamuna Prasad acted as chief interpreter and Sri Chandra Prakash as assistant interpreter. In one interview in New Delhi, Sri Inder Datt acted as interpreter.

2. *Case of Jasbir*

In 1961 I spent a day investigating this case with Sri H. N. Banerjee acting as my interpreter. In 1964 I rechecked the case, spending three days and a half on it. On this occasion Dr. Jamuna Prasad acted as chief interpreter, with Sri R. S. Lal assisting as a second interpreter and note-taker.

3. *Case of Sukla*

Professor P. Pal investigated this case extensively in 1960. I spent two days investigating it in 1961. On the first day, an Indian government tourist guide, Sri S. K. Daw, acted as interpreter for me. On the second day, Professor Pal joined me and acted as interpreter. Professor Pal has continued to keep in touch with the case, and has kindly sent me additional information about some of its details.

4. *Case of Swarnlata*

In 1961 I spent four days investigating this case. For most of the interviews I needed no interpreters as the main witnesses spoke English well. In the case of a few witnesses, Sri M. L. Mishra, father of Swarnlata, acted as interpreter. Professor P. Pal studied the case in 1963 and has kindly placed his extensive notes at my disposal.

5. *Case of Ravi Shankar*

My information on this case was first developed in 1961 during a visit to Professor B. L. Atreya in Benares. Professor Atreya had not interrogated the people concerned in the case at first hand, but he had collected written affidavits through correspondence with a considerable number of witnesses (listed below in the report on the case). Dr. Jamuna Prasad and Sri R. S. Lal (with Sri H. N. Banerjee) spent a day investigating the case at first hand in 1962. Sri Lal has kindly placed his notes of the interviews then conducted at my disposal. Afterwards I corresponded directly with the father of the deceased boy with regard to certain details of the case. In 1964 I investigated the case at first hand, spending a day and a half on its study. Sri Ram Deo acted as chief interpreter, with Sri S. K. Singh assisting.

6. *Case of Mallika*

The case was investigated in 1960–61 by Mme Robert Gaebelé, who lived in Pondicherry and was in frequent touch with the people concerned in the case. I spent a day in Pondicherry in 1961, half of it devoted to a study of this case, for which there were few witnesses. I spoke French with Mme Gaebelé and with one of the other witnesses. This witness interpreted for a Tamil-speaking witness who could not speak French or English.

7. *Case of Parmod*

For this case I have available some written testimony lent me by Professor Atreya, some of which Sri Subash Mukherjee translated. In 1961, his brother, Sri Sudhir Mukherjee, acted as interpreter for me during my study of the case on which I then spent two days. In 1962, Sri Subash Mukherjee collected further testimony from some of the witnesses of the cases which he kindly translated for me. In 1964, I spent a day and a half on the case with the assistance of Dr. Jamuna Prasad as chief interpreter and Sri Vishwa Nath as assistant interpreter.

In addition to having two interpreters in the 1964 studies of the cases of Jasbir, Ravi Shankar, Prakash, and Parmod, I was, as already mentioned, fortunate in having the collaboration of Mr. Francis Story, who had accompanied me during my investigation of cases in Ceylon in 1961. Mr. Story critically observed the witnesses and interpreters (as well as myself) and sometimes directed the questioning to neglected important topics. During the interviews I took notes in English as the translations were made and the assistant interpreter took notes in Hindi. Afterwards we compared our notes and thoroughly discussed the details of the case, including any detected discrepancies which had occurred. This procedure enabled us to check further the doubtful or important points before leaving the area.

Mr. Story and Dr. Jamuna Prasad have reviewed my reports of the four cases which they assisted me in 1964.

Case Reports

The Case of Prakash

Summary of the Case and its Investigation. In April, 1950, a boy of ten named Nirmal, son of Sri Bholanath Jain, died of smallpox in his parents' home in Kosi Kalan, a town in the District of Mathura, Uttar Pradesh. On the day of his death he had been delirious and irritable. He said twice to his mother: "You are not my mother. You are a Jatni. I will go to my mother." As he said this he pointed in the direction of Mathura and another smaller town in the same direction called Chhatta, but he did not mention either town by name. (Chhatta lies six miles away from Kosi Kalan on the road from Kosi Kalan to Mathura.) Shortly after making these strange remarks, he died.

In August, 1951, a son was born to the wife of Sri Brijlal Varshnay in Chhatta whom they named Prakash. As an infant Prakash was noted to cry much more than other children, but otherwise he showed no unusual behavior until the age of about four and a half. At that time he began waking up in the middle of the night and running out of the house to the street. When stopped, he would say he "belonged in" Kosi Kalan, that his name was Nirmal, and that he wanted to go to his old home. He said his father was Bholanath. He woke up and started to run away like this four or five nights in a row and then somewhat less frequently, but continuing to do so for a month altogether. He importuned his family to take him to Kosi Kalan so strongly that one day in 1956 (in the hope of quieting him) his paternal uncle took him on a bus going away from Kosi Kalan, i.e., in the direction of Mathura. Prakash, however, immediately pointed out the error and cried to go to Kosi Kalan. His uncle then put him in the correct bus and took him to Kosi Kalan. He went to the shop of Sri Bholanath Jain, but did not recognize Sri Jain's shop, perhaps because the shop was closed at the time due to Sri Jain's absence. And for this reason also he did not meet the Jain family during that visit. The Jain family did learn, however, of his visit to Kosi Kalan.

At this time, in 1956, when he was about five years old, Prakash's apparent memories of life as Nirmal were extremely vivid. He recalled the names of Nirmal's relatives and friends which on his second visit to Kosi Kalan five years later he no longer remembered. After returning from Kosi Kalan the first time, he continued to trouble his family with his desire to return there. They adopted various measures in an effort to make him forget about Nirmal and Kosi Kalan. These included turning him counter-clockwise on a potter's wheel, supposedly to impair memory, and eventually they beat him. After some time he seemed to forget, or at least no longer spoke openly of his wish to return to Kosi Kalan.

In the spring of 1961, one of Sri Bholanath Jain's younger sons, Jagdish (older brother of Nirmal), lost by death one of his sons, a boy of three and a half. Sri Jagdish Jain shortly afterwards moved back to Kosi Kalan from Delhi, where he had been living. In Kosi Kalan he heard about the boy in Chhatta who said his name was Nirmal and that he was the son of Bholanath Jain. In the early summer of 1961, Sri Bholanath Jain was in Chhatta on business with his daughter Memo. There he met Prakash, who recognized him as his "father." Prakash also partially recognized Memo, mistaking her for another sister of Nirmal named Vimla. He begged Sri Bholanath Jain to take him to Kosi Kalan. He went down to the bus station as Sri Jain and Memo were leaving and pleaded to go with them. Some days later, Nirmal's mother, older sister Tara, and brother Devendra visited Prakash in Chhatta. Prakash wept with joy when he saw Nirmal's older sister Tara. He begged his father to take him to Kosi Kalan. The Jain family persuaded Prakash's parents to consent to his visiting Kosi Kalan again. Prakash led the way from the bus station to the home of the Jains in Kosi Kalan. Arrived there, he hesitated at the entrance, which had been radically altered since the death of Nirmal. At the house, Prakash recognized Nirmal's other brother, two aunts, and some neighbors, as well as various parts of the house where Nirmal had lived and died.

Nirmal's family became convinced that he had been reborn as Prakash. Unfortunately, the second visit to Kosi Kalan and the meeting with members of the Jain family thoroughly re-activated Prakash's longing to go to Kosi Kalan. He again began running away from home and his father again beat him to make him forget this idea, or at least its execution.

I was fortunately able to investigate this case first in July, 1961, within three weeks of Prakash's second visit to Kosi Kalan, when the events still remained fresh in the minds of the informants. Feelings in both families still ran high. Some members of the Varshnay family conceived the idea that the Jain family wished to take Prakash for permanent adoption. On my first visit to the two towns, Sri Jagdish Jain from Kosi Kalan accompanied me as a guide to the Varshnay family in Chhatta. But his presence in my party identified us with the Jain family and aroused considerable animosity against us in Chhatta. On this occasion, when Prakash first saw Sri Jagdish Jain, he smiled with pleasure and enjoyed being carried through the streets by Jagdish to his home. (Still a smallish boy, he could be easily carried.) But after questioning the adults of the Varshnay family, when I turned to talk with Prakash, I found him strangely uncommunicative. I suspected his father had instructed him to tell us nothing and the next day when I returned for a second conference with Sri Varshnay he confirmed this inference.

In 1964, the Varshnay family received me much more cordially, perhaps partly because I was familiar to them and partly because the strong emotions connected with Prakash's earlier threats to run away had partially abated. The family opened itself much more to my inquiries and I was able to listen to the testimony of Prakash's mother, whom I had not interviewed in 1961. In 1964, however, I did not have an opportunity of seeing the behavior of Prakash and his family in the presence of members of the Jain family as I had in 1961.

Relevant Facts of Geography and Possible Normal Means of Communication Between the Two Families. Kosi Kalan and Chhatta are towns about six miles apart, both on the main road between Delhi and Mathura. Chhatta (approximate population 9,000) is the administrative center of the area, but Kosi Kalan (approximate population 15,000) is the commercial center. Both the Jain family and the Varshnay family had often been in each other's town, but the members of each family denied having any previous acquaintance with the other family or knowledge of it prior to the first visit in 1956 of Prakash to Kosi Kalan. And as already mentioned, the families did not actually meet on that occasion. Sri Varshnay assured me that Prakash had never been out of Chhatta prior to the first visit to Kosi Kalan in 1956. I learned also that Nirmal during his life had only once visited Chhatta and on this occasion only passed through when he went to Mathura on a sightseeing trip. The Jain and Varshnay families are of slightly different subcastes and this would make more unlikely their having acquaintanceship or mutual friends.

Persons Interviewed During the Investigation.[8] In Kosi Kalan I interviewed:

Sri[9] Bholanath Jain, father of the deceased Nirmal (Interviewed only in 1961. Deceased in 1963.)
Srimati Parmeshwari Jain, mother of Nirmal
Memo, younger sister of Nirmal
Sri Jagdish Jain, older brother of Nirmal
Devendra, younger brother of Nirmal
Sri Ramesh Jain, neighbor of the family of Sri Bholanath Jain
Sri Basantlal Chaudhari, ex-mayor of Kosi Kalan
Sri Chandra Bhan, neighbor of the family of Sri Bholanath Jain
Sri Jaswant Singh
Sri Chiranji Lal, brother of Sri Basantlal Chaudhari, businessman of Kosi Kalan
Sri Tek Chand, businessman of Kosi Kalan

Testimony was obtained from Sri Harbans Lal of Kosi Kalan in an interview with him conducted (December, 1964) by Sri Chandra Prakash, District Psychologist of Agra.

[8] Western readers may note that women, e.g., the mothers of the subjects, who might be expected to know what they say at an early age, often play a minor part in the testimony of these cases. In India and Ceylon, however, it is often difficult to interview women who are unused to the society of men outside their families. Accordingly, I have often had to rely on the evidence of male members of the families, although whenever possible I also interviewed the women members.

[9] "Sri" is an honorific title for adult men in India, roughly equivalent to "Mr." "Srimati" for married women corresponds to "Mrs." Unmarried girls and women are called "Kumari" and boys are called "Kumar."

In Chhatta I interviewed:

Sri Brijlal Varshnay, father of Prakash
Srimati Brijlal (Shanti Devi) Varshnay, mother of Prakash
Sri Ghan Shyam Das Varshnay, older brother of Sri Brijlal Varshnay
Prakash, son of Sri Brijlal Varshnay

In Delhi I interviewed:

Srimati Tara, wife of Sri Daya Chand Jain and older sister of Nirmal
(Interviewed only in 1961.)
Srimati Omvati Devi, older married sister of Prakash

All the above informants were interviewed in 1964 except as indicated, and many were also interviewed in 1961.

Statements and Recognitions Made by Prakash. In the tabulation below I give a summary of the statements and recognitions Prakash made with regard to his claim to be Nirmal reborn. Although I have indicated some of the relationships of the various informants in the tabulation, readers should refer to the list of informants and to the summary of the case already given when reading this tabulation and also the ones I shall give later for other cases.

Of the foregoing items, 1–8 occurred before any attempts at verification. Items 9–12 occurred on the occasion of the first visits by Nirmal's family to Chhatta in 1961. Items 13–34 occurred on the occasion of Prakash's second visit to Kosi Kalan a few weeks later.

Relevant Reports and Observations of the Behavior of the People Concerned. Prakash had a strong identification with the supposed previous personality of Nirmal; indeed, a stronger identification with a previous personality than has occurred in most of the other Indian cases I have studied. The Varshnay family testified vividly to this identification which seriously bothered them, especially Prakash's efforts to run away to Kosi Kalan. Prakash insisted on being called Nirmal and sometimes would not respond when called Prakash. He told his mother she was not his mother and complained about the mediocrity of the house they lived in. He talked of "his father's" shops, his iron safe, and the members of the previous family. Often he would weep abundantly and go without food during the period of his pleadings to go to Kosi Kalan. One day Prakash took a large nail and started off in the direction of Kosi Kalan. Members of the family went in search of him and found him half a mile away, in the direction of Kosi Kalan. When asked what the nail was, Prakash replied: "This is the key of my iron safe."

Similarly, the Jain family also noted this strong identification in Prakash's

TABULATION

Summary of Statements and Recognitions Made by Prakash

Item	Informants [1]	Verification [1]	Comments
1. His name was Nirmal and he lived in Kosi Kalan.	Brijlal Varshnay, father of Prakash Omvati Devi, older sister of Prakash Shanti Devi Varshnay, mother of Prakash	Bholanath Jain, father of Nirmal Jagdish Jain, older brother of Nirmal	
2. His father was called Bholanath.	Omvati Devi Brijlal Varshnay	Bholanath Jain	
3. He had a sister called Tara.	Omvati Devi Brijlal Varshnay	Tara Chand Jain, older sister of Nirmal	
4. He had neighbors called Tek Chand, Ramesh, and Narain in Kosi Kalan.	Jagdish Jain (not mentioned by Varshnay family)	Jagdish Jain	Narain had died about the time Nirmal did, so this item was not likely to be current information readily picked up by normal means.
5. His house in Kosi Kalan was "pukka" in contrast to present "kachcha" house.	Shanti Devi Varshnay	The differences verified by myself on visits to Kosi Kalan and Chhatta.	The house of the Varshnay family in Chhatta was of mud walls (kachcha), whereas that of the Jain family in Kosi Kalan was of brick (pukka).
6. His father had four shops including a grain shop, a cloth shop, and a general merchandise shop.	Shanti Devi Varshnay	Jagdish Jain	The Jain family had four shops, namely, one cloth shop, one general merchandise store where they sold stationery, and two grocery shops. Sometime after the death of Nirmal, the Jain family disposed of two shops and retained two.
7. His father in Kosi Kalan sold shirts.	Bholanath Jain (not mentioned by Varshnay family)	Bholanath Jain	Sri Bholanath Jain had a store for general merchandise, including shirts.
8. He had an iron safe.	Brijlal Varshnay	Jagdish Jain	Each brother of the family had a drawer in the safe with his own key to his

	Informants	Verification	Comments
8. (continued)			drawer. Sri Jagdish Jain said that on one of his visits to Kosi Kalan Prakash brought with him a nail which he said was the key to his drawer in the safe. This occurred in Chhatta. There is some discrepancy in the testimony as to the occasion when Prakash recognized "his" father, but the accounts agree that he did do this.
9. Recognition of father of Nirmal as "his" father.	Bholanath Jain Memo Jain, younger sister of Nirmal		
10. Recognition of Memo, sister of Nirmal, as Vimla.	Bholanath Jain Memo Jain	Incorrect as to Memo's name, but Vimla correct name of another sister	Memo had not been born when Nirmal died. Confusion possibly due to fact that Memo was at that time about the same age as Vimla had been when Nirmal died. Discrepancies occur in the testimony with regard to how Prakash was introduced to Memo. Memo herself testified in 1964 that after Prakash had recognized her (and Nirmal's) father, Sri Bholanath Jain turned to her and said: "He is your brother." Thereupon Prakash took Memo by the hand and said, "Vimla sister."
11. Asked Memo about Jagdish and Tara, brother and sister of Nirmal.	Memo Jain	Memo Jain	
12. Recognition of Nirmal's mother.	Parmeshwari Jain, mother of Nirmal		When Srimati Parmeshwari, along with Tara and Devendra, visited Prakash in

[1] In this and succeeding tabulations, the *Informants* column lists the witnesses of what the subject did or said related to the previous life. The *Verification* column lists the informants verifying the accuracy of what the subject said or did with regard to the previous personality. In citing recognitions I have usually left the *Verification* column blank since the person who was the informant for the recognition (nearly always himself a witness of this recognition) either knew that the recognition was correct at the time it occurred or later verified its accuracy. Whenever possible, I have asked a person who was recognized by the subject about the details of the recognition, including circumstances, other persons present, and whether there were leading questions put or simply requests to name the person to be recognized. I have included information on these matters under *Comments* in the right-hand column. This column also contains some other information or explanatory material. Unless specifically noted to the contrary, the statements and recognitions made by the subject were verified as being correct or appropriate for the previous personality.

Item	Informants	Verification	Comments
12. (continued)			Chhatta he sat on Tara's lap, wept and said, indicating Srimati Parmeshwari: "This is my mother."
13. Called Nirmal's elder sister Tara by name when he saw her.	Tara Chand Jain	Tara Chand Jain	Name given and appropriate emotion of weeping shown.
14. Recognition of Devendra, younger brother of Nirmal.	Devendra Jain, younger brother of Nirmal		This recognition took place in Chhatta. "Devendra" was a pet name in the family, but also the name by which this boy was known in the community. Prakash was asked: "Do you know him?" and said: "My younger brother, Devendra."
	Devendra Jain		
15. Recognition of the way along route from bus station to house of Sri Bholanath Jain.	Tara Chand Jain Brijal Varshnay		Distance about a half mile with many turns. Srimati Tara Jain tried to mislead Prakash by suggesting wrong turns to him. In 1964, Srimati Omvati Devi, Prakash's sister who accompanied him on this route, denied that Prakash had led the way on the grounds that the brother of Nirmal (Devendra) was accompanying the party. Srimati Tara Jain in 1961, a few weeks after the event, believed that Prakash had led the way. So did Sri Brijal Varshnay, also a member of the party, in his testimony of 1964.
16. Hesitation at entrance to house of Jain family.	Devendra Jain		The entrance to the house had been markedly altered since Nirmal's death, so that the main entrance to the house used by the family was displaced considerably to one side of where it had been during Nirmal's life.

17. Recognition of Jagdish, brother of Nirmal.	Jagdish Jain	Prakash recognized Jagdish in a crowd of persons (at the Jain house) by saying, "This is my brother." In 1964 Sri Jagdish Jain said that Prakash also gave his (Jagdish's) name; but in 1961 he had not remembered this detail. Members of the Varshnay family consistently stated that Sri Jagdish Jain had come early to Chhatta and been recognized there by Prakash, but he (and other witnesses in Kosi Kalan) insisted Prakash recognized him in Kosi Kalan and that he only went to Chhatta later.
18. Recognition of Sri Ramesh Jain as neighbor who ran a small shop "in front of ours."	Ramesh Jain Jagdish Jain	A group of neighbors went to see Prakash at the Jain house. Sri Bholanath Jain pointed to Ramesh and asked Prakash: "Who is he?" Prakash replied: "Ramesh." When asked: "Where is his shop?" he replied: "His shop is a small shop in front of ours." In 1964 Sri Ramesh Jain still owned his small shop almost opposite the Jain shop, but for some years had not regularly visited his shop and moreover spent most of his time in Bundi, Rajasthan, a town far away. Thus it would be difficult for any current resident of Kosi Kalan to associate Sri Ramesh Jain with this shop. Sri Ramesh Jain happened to be in Kosi Kalan when Prakash visited it in 1961, and also when I did later in 1964.
19. Knowledge of location of shop of Sri Chandra Bhan.	Chandra Bhan Jagdish Jain	According to Sri Chandra Bhan himself, Prakash recognized him as one "of our neighbors of the shop," but did not give his name. According to Sri Jagdish Jain, Prakash did not recognize Sri Chandra Bhan but did give the correct location of

Item	Informants	Verification	Comments
19. (continued)			his shop. Sri Chandra Bhan's shop was adjacent to one of the Jains' shops.
20. Recognition of the shop of Nirmal's Uncle Narain.	Jagdish Jain		This shop was near the main Jain shop, but Narain, who had owned it, had died at the time of Prakash's recognition.
21. Recognition of Sri Chiranji Lal and statement of his occupation.	Chiranji Lal, businessman of Kosi Kalan		Prakash spontaneously greeted Sri Chiranji Lal as if he knew who he was. Sri Chiranji Lal then said: "Do you know who I am?" Prakash said: "You are Chiranji. I am the son of Bholaram" (sic). Sri Chiranji Lal then asked Prakash how he recognized him and Prakash said he used to purchase sugar, rice, and flour from his shop. Sri Chiranji Lal no longer had a retail grocery business at the time of this meeting, but formerly did have and Nirmal had made purchases there.
22. Knowledge of location of the shop of Sri Tek Chand.	Tek Chand, businessman of Kosi Kalan Jagdish Jain		Prakash said in the presence of Sri Tek Chand: "Adjacent to our shop was the shop of Teku." Sri Tek Chand's shop was formerly adjacent to Sri Bholanath Jain's shop, but he had moved his shop to another quarter not long before the death of Nirmal. Sri Jagdish Jain stated that Prakash had also recognized Sri Tek Chand, but the latter did not think so.
23. Recognition of Chameli, Nirmal's aunt.	Parmeshwari Jain Memo Jain		Recognized as "aunt"; not called by name.
24. Recognition of Chiranji, Nirmal's aunt.	Memo Jain		Not recognized by name but also identified only as "aunt." However, Prakash did enquire about Chiranji Lal's mother-in-law whose name (Dadi) he gave. Dadi had played with Nirmal. "Dadi" is

24. (continued)

No.	Item			Comments
24. (continued)				actually a general name meaning a paternal grandmother, but Indians sometimes use such general names in talking to and about each other, even when the word used does not accurately describe the speaker's relationship with the person mentioned.
25.	Recognition of room where Nirmal had slept in the Jain house.	Bholanath Jain Jagdish Jain	Bholanath Jain	
26.	Recognition of room where Nirmal had died in the Jain house.	Bholanath Jain Jagdish Jain	Bholanath Jain Parmeshwari Jain	Nirmal had been moved into this room from his usual sleeping quarters just before he died.
27.	Recognition of latrines on roof of Jain house.	Bholanath Jain Jagdish Jain	Bholanath Jain	Characteristic feature of two-story houses in Kosi Kalan, but not of smaller houses in Chhatta. Children use the roofs of such houses as latrines. On the roof of the Jain house, Prakash pointed to a corner and said, "This is where I used the latrine."
28.	At the Jain shop said there was a black wooden box for keeping money which had been brought from Agra.	Bholanath Jain Jagdish Jain	Bholanath Jain	In 1964, Jagdish Jain could not remember whether this box had been "black" or only "dark." The Hindi word "kala" is sometimes translated to mean "dark" and sometimes to mean "black" so a shift in translation may account for the possible discrepancy.
29.	Recognition of Nirmal's drawer in the family safe.	Jagdish Jain		See comment for item 8.
30.	Recognition of a chain of diamonds as belonging to Nirmal's grandfather.	Jagdish Jain		When shown the chain of diamonds Prakash said: "This belongs to my grandfather."

Item	Informants	Verification	Comments
31. He had two undershirts.	Jagdish Jain		In fact the Jain family had preserved two undershirts and some other clothing which had belonged to Nirmal.
32. Recognition of a small cart in the Jain house.	Parmeshwari Jain		Prakash said: "I used to play with this." Nirmal used to play with this cart.
33. Recognition of Sri Harbans Lal as tax collector.	Harbans Lal		Sri Bholanath Jain pointed to Sri Harbans Lal standing in a crowd and said: "Do you know him?" Prakash said: "Yes, he used to come to collect money." Information and written statement obtained from Sri Harbans Lal by Sri Chandra Prakash, District Psychologist, Agra, during an interview in December, 1964.
34. Recognition of the Jain family physician.	Brijlal Varshnay		This man came to the Jain house and when Prakash saw him, he said: "He is the doctor." Item not mentioned by witnesses of the Jain family.

tears when he was with them and in his pleadings with Sri Bholanath Jain to take him back to Kosi Kalan. After 1961 the animosity between the two families, aroused by fears of the Varshnay family that the Jain family might somehow adopt Prakash, gradually diminished. Relations improved and the two families exchanged gifts. The Varshnays then permitted some visiting by Prakash to the Jain family in Kosi Kalan. In 1964 they thought that Prakash had stopped visiting Kosi Kalan, but I learned there that he had continued visits surreptitiously. He would slip away from school and come by himself on a bus. He was fully accepted and welcomed in the Jain family on his visits to Kosi Kalan.

I observed the joy in Prakash's face when he saw Jagdish, Nirmal's older brother, on the occasion of my visit to Chhatta in 1961, and the change in him when he became taciturn after his father warned him against talking with us. And I saw also the strong emotions of the Varshnay family with regard to the suspicions, especially on the part of Prakash's grandmother, that I was promoting the adoption of Prakash by the Jain family. This lady even proposed that the villagers should beat up my party because of our supposed alliance with the Jain family in the matter of the transfer of Prakash to them. The Jain family also described the antagonism of the Varshnay family to the visits between the families. The Varshnay family resisted verification all along and only yielded finally to quiet the pleadings of Prakash. The Jain family for their part remained indifferent to verification for five years after they first heard about Prakash's claims on the occasion of the first visit to Kosi Kalan in 1956. Their interest in meeting him only revived in 1961 after an accidental meeting with Prakash in Chhatta. All these behavioral features of the case, many of which I witnessed myself, seem quite inconsistent with the hypothesis that either family arranged the case as a hoax. So are the gaps in the information furnished by Prakash and the occasional slips and inconsistencies of the informants which would, if included to enhance the natural effect of a fraud, require a high degree of acting and stage management beyond the skill of these people. Moreover, on my visits to Kosi Kalan large crowds of townsfolk surrounded my party and quickly learned of our interest in the case. The whole case was obviously a matter of public knowledge and public business. Anyone knowing of a hoax or even that the families had been acquainted earlier could easily have come forward to tell of their suspicions, but none did. In 1964 I found no more evidence of direct communication between the two families prior to 1961 than I had found on my first visit.

Comments on the Evidence of Paranormal Knowledge on the Part of Prakash. Setting aside for the moment the emotional elements in Prakash's behavior, we may ask ourselves about the likelihood that a boy of ten might pick up through normal means the kind of information he showed both when the Jain family visited Chhatta and when he visited Kosi Kalan. One can suppose that on the difficult way through the streets from the bus station to the Jain home in Kosi Kalan the murmurs of the attendant crowd guided him. We have no evidence of this, however. On the contrary, we have testimony of attempts by his sister to mislead him. More difficult to explain are Prakash's correct recognitions of numerous members of the Jain family and their neighbors, sometimes giving proper names as well as correct relationships or other identification. Two of the persons recognized were ladies in purdah.[10] Prakash, moreover, had information about the rooms of the Jain house and their objects and uses. Further, he showed knowledge of the house and of some shops accurate for the time of the life of Nirmal, but out of date at the time of his visit to Kosi Kalan. Such items, and his error in mistaking Memo (who had not been born when Nirmal died) for Nirmal's other sister Vimla, suggest previously acquired knowledge of past events rather than recently acquired knowledge as the source of Prakash's information about people and places in Kosi Kalan.

The Later Development of Prakash. I did not meet Prakash between 1964 and 1971. In November, 1971, I met him again in Aligarh, U.P., at the home of his maternal uncle.

Prakash was then about twenty years old. He had continued in school up to 1971, but as he failed the tenth class twice he dropped out of school and moved (in the summer of 1971) from Chhatta to Aligarh where he was living under the supervision of his maternal uncle, although not actually in his uncle's home. He was working as a salesman. Prakash has always impressed me as an intelligent person and I believe, without being able to document this conviction, that he was quite capable of completing secondary school, but he had not received the encouragement that seems minimally necessary to keep young persons of his age in school and applied to their studies. His health was generally good. He had not, incidentally, had smallpox, the disease from which Nirmal, the related previous personality of this case, had died. (Smallpox is still widespread in India.) His mood seemed to me a little downcast, or at least serious.

He said that he did not spontaneously think about the previous life any longer, but only when questioned or when he had some particular reason for being reminded of it. (A visit to Kosi Kalan would naturally be one such stimulus.) He said he still remembered what he had previously recalled about the previous life. In short, he claimed that his memories of the pre-

---

[10] Women practicing purdah are only seen by their husbands, children, and close female relatives. They are hidden from the public gaze, either by domestic seclusion or, if they do go out of the house, by veils. Their features are therefore unknown to strangers and the recognition of these virtually impossible for persons outside the immediate family.

vious life had not faded. I questioned him a little about various names related to Nirmal and he gave correct answers. He did not remember the name of Nirmal's mother, but her name had not figured in his memories as a small child (see Tabulation above). The correctness of Prakash's answers, however, did not offer support for his statement that his *original* memories had not faded because he had continued to visit Kosi Kalan quite frequently. In fact, he said he went to Kosi Kalan about once or twice a month. Since he had moved to Aligarh, four months earlier, he had gone to Kosi Kalan each time he had returned to Chhatta to visit his family. Nirmal's parents had both died and Prakash went to Kosi Kalan mainly to visit Jagdish Jain, Nirmal's older brother, who continued in business there. Prakash had been to visit him just two weeks before my meeting with him at the time of the great Diwali festival, an important Hindu religious occasion held every autumn. Such frequent visits to Kosi Kalan would certainly tend to keep alive Prakash's memories, at least of the names of the family members who would often be talked about, even if not actually met, during these visits.

It occurred to me that perhaps Prakash's visits to Kosi Kalan had interfered with his studies at school. But this seemed unlikely because he said he only spent two or three hours in Kosi Kalan each time when he visited Nirmal's family there.

I asked Prakash where, if he had the chance and the choice, he would like to be reborn. He said he would not like to be reborn. (In the West such a remark might be interpreted as indicative of a clinical depression accompanied by a wish to die; but in India the wish not to be reborn is almost universal and indeed a positive aspiration of devout Hindus.) When I then asked him whether, if he had to be reborn, he would prefer to be reborn in Chhatta or Kosi Kalan, he said Chhatta. It is difficult to evaluate this response since I put the question in the presence of Prakash's maternal uncle and it might have embarrassed him to say openly that he preferred the family in Kosi Kalan to that in Chhatta. The reply may, however, indicate Prakash's true feelings. It will be recalled that Nirmal, as he was dying, rather bluntly rejected his mother in Kosi Kalan and indicated that he was going to be reborn to "my mother." As he said this he gestured in the direction of Mathura and Chhatta (which lies between Kosi Kalan and Mathura). There is no reason to doubt that Prakash was loved in his own family. It is equally clear, however, that he felt and continued to feel in 1971 a strong attachment to Nirmal's family in Kosi Kalan. From the remarks and attitudes of his uncle in Aligarh, including the fact that Prakash was not actually living in the seemingly ample house of the uncle, I formed the impression that perhaps Jagdish Jain was taking a more lively and affectionate interest in Prakash as he passed from adolescence to independent manhood than his own uncle was. If so, this could well account for Prakash's continuing attachment to the family in Kosi Kalan apart from any residues of affection derived from the previous life.

The Case of Jasbir

Summary of the Case and its Investigation. In most cases of the reincarnation type, the previous personality had died some years before the birth of the present personality. The interval varies, but averages, in Indian cases, about five years. The present case has the unusual feature that the previous personality with which the subject became identified did not die until about three and a half years *after* the birth of the "physical body of the present personality." This central fact of the case needs to be remembered in reading my report. I shall return to this point later in the General Discussion when I shall also mention some other related cases.

In the spring of 1954, Jasbir, three-and-a-half year old son of Sri Girdhari Lal Jat of Rasulpur, District Muzaffarnagar, Uttar Pradesh, was thought to have died of smallpox. Jasbir's father went to his brother and other men of the village proposing that they assist him in burying his "dead" son.[11] As it was then late at night, they advised postponing burial until the morning. Some few hours later Sri Girdhari Lal Jat happened to notice some stirring in the body of his son which then gradually revived completely.[12] Some days passed before the boy could speak again, and some weeks before he could express himself clearly. When he recovered the ability to speak he showed a remarkable transformation of behavior. He then stated that he was the son of Shankar of Vehedi village and wished to go there. He would eat no food at the home of the Jats on the grounds that he belonged to a higher caste, being a Brahmin. This obstinate refusal to eat would surely have led to a second death if a kindly Brahmin lady, a neighbor of Sri Girdhari Lal Jat, had not undertaken to cook food for Jasbir in the Brahmin manner. This she did for about a year and a half. Jasbir's father supplied the materials for the food she prepared. But his family sometimes deceived Jasbir and gave him food not prepared by the Brahmin lady. He discovered the deception and this realization, together with pressure from his family, led him gradually to abandon his rigid Brahmin dietary habits and join the rest of the family in their regular meals. The period of resistance lasted under two years altogether.

Jasbir began to communicate further details of "his" life and death in the village of Vehedi. He particularly described how during a wedding pro-

[11] Although adult bodies are cremated by Hindus in India, bodies of children under the age of five are usually buried in pits. The bodies of all persons dying of infectious diseases such as cholera and smallpox are not burned, but either buried or thrown in rivers.

[12] I inquired of the villagers at Rasulpur about their methods of ascertaining when death had occurred. They rely on the cessation of breathing, the opening of the jaw, and the cooling of the body.

cession from one village to another he had eaten some poisoned sweets and alleged that a man to whom he had lent money had given him these sweets. He had become giddy and had fallen off the chariot on which he was riding, suffered a head injury, and died.

Jasbir's father told me he tried to suppress information of Jasbir's strange claims and behavior in the village, but news of it leaked out. The special cooking for Jasbir in the Brahmin style was naturally known to the other Brahmins of the village and eventually (i.e., about three years later) came to the attention of one of their group, Srimati Shyamo, a Brahmin native of Rasulpur who had married a native of Vehedi, Sri Ravi Dutt Sukla. She on rare occasions (at intervals of several years) returned to Rasulpur. On one such trip in 1957 Jasbir recognized her as his "aunt." [13] She reported the incident to her husband's family and to members of the Tyagi family in Vehedi. The details of "his" death and other items narrated by Jasbir corresponded closely with details of the life and death of a young man of twenty-two, Sobha Ram, son of Sri Shankar Lal Tyagi of Vehedi. Sobha Ram had died [14] in May, 1954 in a chariot accident as related by Jasbir and in the manner described, although the Tyagi family knew nothing of any alleged poisoning or any debt of money owed Sobha Ram before they heard of Jasbir's statements. Afterwards they entertained suspicions of poisoning.

Later Sri Ravi Dutt Sukla, husband of Srimati Shyamo, visited Rasulpur and heard reports of Jasbir's statements and met him. Then Sobha Ram's father and other members of his family went there and Jasbir recognized them and correctly placed them as to their relationships with Sobha Ram.

[13] In India persons not related, but of the same village, may be addressed with titles of relationship. Thus an older female friend of the family could appropriately be called "aunt" familiarly by a younger person of the same village.

[14] As few written records of births and deaths are kept in most Indian villages, it has not been possible to ascertain accurately the interval between the death of Sobha Ram and the revival from "death" and transformation of personality of Jasbir. A written record in the Tyagi family of Vehedi fixed the death of Sobha Ram at 11:00 P.M., May 22, 1954. The diligence of Dr. L. P. Mehrotra led to a further verification of this date with a small discrepancy. In 1972 Dr. Mehrotra traced the family of the bride in Nirmana in whose wedding Sobha Ram had participated. They had recorded the date of the wedding in the Register of Invitations as Friday, May 21, 1954. Informants said that Sobha Ram had died on the third day of the wedding at 8:30 P.M. This would give the date of his death as May 23, not May 22 as recorded by his family. But I do not think the date of Sobha Ram's departure from the wedding was noted in writing by the bride's family, so for that we are relying on their memories. They were also not firsthand witnesses of the exact time of death of Sobha Ram. There was no record of Sobha Ram's death at the hospital in Vehedi because he had expired by the time he reached there and was not admitted. But the near concordance of these independent records made by two families allows us to feel reasonably certain that Sobha Ram died on May 22 or May 23, more probably, in my opinion, on the former date.

Unfortunately, the Jat family had no corresponding written record of the date of the presumed death and transformation of Jasbir. The best testimony placed this event in April or May, 1954, but I could not obtain a more precise date or even agreement among all witnesses about the month.

A few weeks later, at the instigation of the manager of the sugar mill near Vehedi, a villager from Vehedi, Sri Jaganath Prasad Sukla, brought Jasbir to Vehedi where he put him down near the railway station and asked him to lead the way to the Tyagi quadrangle.[15] This Jasbir did without difficulty. Later Jasbir was taken to the home of Sri Ravi Dutt Sukla and from there led the way (a different route) to the Tyagi home. He remained some days in the village and demonstrated to the Tyagi family and other villagers a detailed knowledge of the Tyagi family and its affairs. He enjoyed himself greatly in Vehedi and returned to Rasulpur with great reluctance. Afterwards Jasbir continued to visit Vehedi from time to time, usually for several weeks or more in the summer. He still wanted to live in Vehedi and felt isolated and lonely in Rasulpur.

In the summer of 1961, I visited both Rasulpur and Vehedi and interviewed thirteen witnesses of the case. I returned in 1964 and restudied the case with new interpreters, interviewing most of the previous witnesses and some new ones.

Relevant Facts of Geography and Possible Normal Means of Communication Between the Two Families. Rasulpur (population 1,500) is a small village twelve miles southwest of the District town of Muzaffarnagar, Uttar Pradesh. Vehedi (population 2,000) is another small village eight miles north of Muzaffarnagar. Both villages lie off the main highways and are accessible only by dirt roads. Members of each village would attend the district town, but ordinarily would have no occasion to go to the other village. Transportation for a distance of twenty miles is much restricted in such villages. Caste differences between the two families concerned further reduced the likelihood of contact. The members of each of the families concerned in this case testified that they knew absolutely nothing of the other family prior to the verification of Jasbir's statements. Indeed, they and other villagers asserted that they had barely heard of the name of the village of the other family. I was able to learn about only two people in Vehedi who had been to Rasulpur before Jasbir's change of personality. These were Sri Ravi Dutt Sukla and his wife Shyamo who, as already mentioned, came from Rasulpur. They were, it will be recalled, the first persons of Vehedi to learn of Jasbir's transformation and claim to be Sobha Ram reborn. I learned that although Shyamo came from Rasulpur, everyone in her family (except for one member, a distant relative) had died. She therefore rarely visited Rasulpur and had not in fact been there for five years prior to the visit in 1957 when Jasbir recognized her. Jasbir's transformation had occurred three years before this visit, in 1954. Sri Ravi Dutt

[15] In Indian villages and towns, families of means have, in addition to a home, a "quadrangle" which consists of one or more sheltered rooms used as a gathering place and open living room by male members of the family. The quadrangle may be some distance from the family home.

Sukla's visits to Rasulpur were even rarer than those of his wife and he also had not visited Rasulpur for at least five years prior to 1957. I learned that Sobha Ram had visited Nirmana from time to time, a village just three miles north of Rasulpur where the Tyagis had relatives; and it was while returning from Nirmana that he had fallen off his chariot and received his fatal head injury. Since Nirmana lies near Rasulpur (much nearer than Vehedi) it is altogether possible that some people of Rasulpur, visiting in Nirmana, might have met Sobha Ram there; but I did not learn of any such contacts.

In Rasulpur I was able to find only two men who had actually been to Vehedi. One of them had lived in Vehedi many years previously and had known Sobha Ram, but did not hear of his death until about four or five months after it occurred and therefore well after Jasbir had begun to make his claims to have been Sobha Ram. He had not heard of Jasbir's change of behavior at the time he first learned of Sobha Ram's death. This informant (Sri Niran Jan) had continued to visit Vehedi after returning to live in Rasulpur at intervals of six to twenty-four months and he was a friend of Sri Girdhari Lal Jat, Jasbir's father. He denied ever having talked with the Jat family about Sobha Ram.

Another elderly inhabitant of Rasulpur had visited Vehedi and heard of Sobha Ram, but did not know him personally; he had not heard of Sobha Ram's death until after Jasbir's change. Nor did he have any close contact with Sobha Ram's family.

The fateful wedding party attended by Sobha Ram and the accident on the way back occurred nearer Muzaffarnager than Vehedi. But Sobha Ram did not die until the party had returned to Vehedi a few hours later. There is no reason to think that the news of his death (then considered entirely accidental) would have spread into surrounding villages. The Jat family and others of Rasulpur claimed to have known nothing of Sobha Ram until Jasbir began to make his extraordinary statements.

Persons Interviewed During the Investigation. In Vehedi, the village of Sobha Ram, I interviewed:

Sri Shankar Lal Tyagi, father of Sobha Ram
Sri Raghbir Singh Tyagi, uncle of Sobha Ram
Sri Santoshi Tyagi, uncle of Sobha Ram
Sri Mahendra Singh Tyagi, younger brother of Sobha Ram
Sri Surajmal Tyagi, younger brother of Sobha Ram
Sri Baleshwar Tyagi, son of Sobha Ram

In Rasulpur, the village of Jasbir, I interviewed:

Jasbir, son of Sri Girdhari Lal Jat
Sri Girdhari Lal Jat, father of Jasbir

Srimati Rajkali, wife of Sri Girdhari Lal Jat, and mother of Jasbir

Sri Paltu Singh, brother of Sri Girdhari Lal Jat, and uncle of Jasbir

Sobha Singh, older brother of Jasbir

Sri Mahipal Singh, cousin of Jasbir

Angan Pal, cousin and playmate of Jasbir, son of Sri Paltu Singh

Sri Bhim Sen, villager, unrelated to Jat family, son of the Brahmin lady who used to cook for Jasbir

Sri Ved Pal Varma Shastri, villager, unrelated to Jat family

Inder Pal, older brother of Jasbir

Sri Niran Jan

Sri Asha Ram, headman (village mayor) of Rasulpur

Sri Hridaya Ram, former headman of Rasulpur

In Muzaffarnagar, I interviewed:

Sri Ravi Dutt Sukla, formerly of Vehedi and widower of Srimati Shyamo, a native of Rasulpur

In Kudda, I interviewed:

Sri Jaganath Prasad Sukla, nephew of Sri Ravi Dutt Sukla

All the above were interviewed in 1964; many were also interviewed in 1961.

Sri R. S. Lal interviewed and obtained testimony from Sri Birbal Singh Tyagi, cousin of Sobha Ram, in January, 1965.

Statements and Recognitions Made by Jasbir. I give below in the tabulation a summary of the statements and recognitions made by Jasbir with regard to the life of Sobha Ram.

Items 1–12 derive from statements made by Jasbir before there was any attempt at verification or other contact between the Tyagi and Jat families; items 13–27 derive from statements made to or about various members of the Tyagi family of Vehedi village who visited Rasulpur; items 28–38 derive from statements or behavior of Jasbir on his first visit to Vehedi. I do not know when item 39 occurred, but it took place after the two families had had some contact.

Relevant Reports and Observations of the Behavior of the People Concerned. As already mentioned, when Jasbir first underwent a change of personality after recovering from his apparent death he refused to eat food with the Jat family. A kindly Brahmin lady prepared food from materials supplied by Jasbir's father for a year and a half. But after this period, Jasbir gradually became less rigid about his dietary habits and began to eat with the family again. In other respects Jasbir's identification with Sobha Ram seemed equally strong. He would use the present tense in his declarations, e.g., "I am the son of Shankar of Vehedi."

Sri Girdhari Lal Jat stated that when Jasbir began to speak after his illness, they noted a change in his vocabulary. For example, he would say "haveli" and not "hilli" for a house and "kapra" and not "latta" for clothes. The higher levels of society, e.g., Brahmins, use the former words and the lower levels the latter ones. The former words are more "aristocratic," so to speak.

Jasbir felt (and still felt in 1964) a strong attachment to the Tyagi family in Vehedi. He threatened to run away from Rasulpur to Vehedi on at least one occasion. He seems to have thought of himself very much as an adult and at first talked freely in Rasulpur of having a wife and children. Later, teasing and scolding led him to control his utterances. But still it seemed natural for him to think of Vehedi and his possessions there. Once when Jasbir was about six, his mother fell ill and Jasbir said if the family needed money for treatment he had money in his coat in Vehedi.

Jasbir showed affection for all the Tyagi family, but his behavior toward them was perhaps most noticeable in regard to Baleshwar, the son of Sobha Ram. When Jasbir visited in Vehedi, he and Baleshwar slept together on the same cot, something unusual for strangers to do, but appropriate for a father and son. When Baleshwar went to school in the morning, Jasbir complained. If someone in Vehedi gave a gift to Jasbir, he passed it on to Baleshwar.

Both the Tyagi and the Jat families agreed that Jasbir was happy at Vehedi. When someone from Rasulpur called at Vehedi to take him back to Rasulpur after a visit with the Tyagis he resisted and sometimes cried. In Rasulpur, on the other hand, Jasbir was lonely and something of an outcast. During my visit in 1961 I easily noticed that he did not play with the other children, but stayed aloof and isolated. Yet he talked willingly with the interpreter, although always wearing a sad expression on his quiet, pockmarked, but handsome face. Sri Girdhari Lal Jat stated during this visit that before his change of personality Jasbir had been fond of toys and of play, but afterwards became disinterested in these.

In 1964, Jasbir's isolation had not diminished and he seemed, if anything, even more depressed. His facial expression lacked animation. Although on this occasion he talked more than in 1961, he did not seem particularly eager to do so and remained a bystander in our interviews, even those with him, rather than an active participant.

Members of the Jat family acknowledged that when Jasbir first made statements about the previous life in Vehedi, they had disbelieved him and some of them had even scolded him. Jasbir's withdrawal from his family, especially from their food, and his disdain for them as members of a lower caste must have contributed to the alienation. It seems that after the verifica-

TABULATION
Summary of Statements and Recognitions Made by Jasbir

Item	Informants	Verification	Comments
1. He was the son of Shankar of Vehedi.	Girdhari Lal Jat, father of Jasbir Rajkali, mother of Jasbir	Shankar Lal Tyagi of Vehedi had lost a son about the time Jasbir made this statement.	
2. He was a Brahmin, not a Jat.	Girdhari Lal Jat Rajkali		The Tyagi family of Vehedi are Brahmins. Jats belong to a lower caste. Most Brahmins are strict about dietary habits governing the food eaten and its mode of preparation. Jasbir would probably have starved if acceptable food had not been provided.
3. His name was Sobha Ram.	Girdhari Lal Jat Angan Pal, cousin of Jasbir	Shankar Lal Tyagi	Jasbir does not seem to have mentioned the actual name of the previous personality to any other witnesses.
4. There was a culvert in the village where he belonged.	Paltu Singh, uncle of Jasbir	Seen by myself on visits to Vehedi.	A culvert in Vehedi carries water under the railway tracks. Rasulpur has no such culvert.
5. There was a peepal tree in front of his house.	Paltu Singh	The place where the peepal tree had been was pointed out to me in Vehedi.	A peepal tree had formerly grown just outside the Tyagi home in Vehedi. It had been cut down about 1962. But the item is not fully specific (in contrast to the preceding) since peepal trees grow also in Rasulpur.
6. The wife of Sobha Ram belonged to the village of Molna.	Shankar Lal Tyagi, father of Sobha Ram	Shankar Lal Tyagi	Sobha Ram's widow returned to her father's village of Molna after Sobha Ram's death.
7. He had a chariot he used for attending weddings.	Paltu Singh	The chariot, standing in a shed at the Tyagi home, was pointed out to me on my visits to Vehedi.	In 1964 the Tyagi family still possessed the chariot used by Sobha Ram and other members of the family to attend weddings.

8. He had died while returning from Nirmana in a marriage party.	Mahipal Singh, cousin of Jasbir Jasbir	Santoshi Tyagi, Sobha Ram's uncle	Sobha Ram had gone to Nirmana to fetch the bride for the wedding and was returning toward the groom's village when he fell off his chariot. Nirmana is a village about three miles north of Rasulpur.
9. He was poisoned at the wedding party, the poison being given in some sweets he ate.	Mahipal Singh Rajkali Jasbir	Unverified (see comment)	The Tyagi family had some suspicion of poisoning but no definite evidence that Sobha Ram had been poisoned at the wedding party. Jasbir even named the alleged murderer, but I have not included this name. Further, the Tyagi family did not know whether Sobha Ram had eaten sweets before dying, but did state he had taken some betels.
10. He died after falling down from the chariot.	Mahipal Singh Ved Pal Varma Shastri Hridaya Ram, former headman of Rasulpur	Santoshi Tyagi	The generally accepted cause of Sobha Ram's death was the head injury he sustained when he fell from the wedding chariot on returning from Nirmana in the wedding party.
11. The chariot in which he was returning from Nirmana in the wedding party had one white and one black ox.	Hridaya Ram Mahipal Singh	Shankar Lal Tyagi	Sri Mahendra Tyagi offered discrepant testimony here by asserting that both bullocks had been white.
12. Recognition by Jasbir of the road to Vehedi.	Rajkali		When he was only about four years old, Jasbir was with his mother near Muzaffarnagar and pointing in the direction of Vehedi said: "My village is on this side."
13. Recognition of Srimati Shyamo as "aunt."	Rajkali Jaganath Prasad Sukla Paltu Singh		Jasbir used the familiar term "Tai" (father's brother's wife) instead of "Phoopi" (father's sister). The expression "Tai" would be appropriate for the relationship of Sobha Ram to Srimati Shyamo in Vehedi, since Srimati Shyamo

Item	Informants	Verification	Comments
13. (continued)			had married an older "brother" (the term is used loosely in India) of Sobha Ram's father. But since Srimati Shyamo came from Rasulpur she was a "sister" (again roughly) of Girdhari Lal Jat, Jasbir's father. Therefore, he ought to have called her "Phoopi." (See also footnote 13). All informants were secondhand witnesses of this item. Srimati Shyamo had died before my first visit in 1961.
14. Recognition of Sri Ravi Dutt Sukla.	Ravi Dutt Sukla		Jasbir gave the correct name in Vehedi, "Tau," for the relationship of Sobha Ram to Sri Ravi Dutt Sukla.
15. There was a tamarind tree in front of the courtyard.	Ravi Dutt Sukla	Tamarind tree seen by me in Vehedi.	The tamarind tree was on another man's property, but was in front of the Tyagi "quadrangle." Sri Ravi Dutt Sukla was a secondhand witness for this item and item 16. When he visited Rasulpur, the villagers asked him if he could verify these and other statements of Jasbir.
16. The Tyagi house had a well that was half in and half outside the house.	Ravi Dutt Sukla	This unusual well, the only one of its kind in Vehedi, was seen by me there.	
17. Recognition of Sri Shankar Lal Tyagi, giving name correctly.	Shankar Lal Tyagi Inder Pal, brother of Jasbir Bhim Sen, villager of Rasulpur		After seeing Sri Shankar Lal Tyagi at a distance, Jasbir met Inder Pal and told him: "My father has come. He is from Vehedi." Srimati Rajkali (not a witness of the actual recognition) said Jasbir came home after seeing Sri Tyagi and told her to have Brahmin meals prepared for his father who had come.

Item			
18. He had a son called Baleshwar.	Shankar Lal Tyagi	Shankar Lal Tyagi	Sri Shankar Lal Tyagi questioned Jasbir about family relationships when he first visited him in Rasulpur.
19. He had an aunt, Ram Kali.	Shankar Lal Tyagi	Shankar Lal Tyagi	
20. His mother was called Sona.	Shankar Lal Tyagi	Shankar Lal Tyagi	
21. He had a sister called Kela.	Shankar Lal Tyagi	Shankar Lal Tyagi	
22. His mother-in-law was called Kirpi.	Shankar Lal Tyagi	Shankar Lal Tyagi	
23. Recognition of Sri Santoshi Tyagi.	Santoshi Tyagi	Santoshi Tyagi	Jasbir was asked to tell the identity of Sri Santoshi Tyagi and he said: "He is my uncle."
24. Sobha Ram's wife was called Sumantra.	Shankar Lal Tyagi	Shankar Lal Tyagi	
25. When he died he had ten rupees in a black coat in a box.	Santoshi Tyagi, who heard from "someone" who had gone to Rasulpur to meet Jasbir that Jasbir had said this.		
26. Recognition of Surajmal, younger brother of Sobha Ram.	Surajmal Tyagi Girdhari Lal Jat		Surajmal's testimony on this item was that Jasbir recognized him as follows. Someone asked Jasbir: "Who is he?" and Jasbir said: "He is my brother," and gave the name Surajmal also. On one occasion Surajmal placed this recognition in Vehedi, but on another occasion in Rasulpur where Sri Girdhari Lal Jat also placed it in his testimony. (Possible error of transcription.) Jasbir's father also stated that Jasbir correctly described Surajmal as "younger brother."

Item	Informants	Verification	Comments
27. Recognition of neighbor of Tyagi family who had dealt unfairly in a dispute between the Tyagi family and some other neighbors.	Angan Pal Paltu Singh		This man had come to Rasulpur where Jasbir recognized him and described his behavior to Angan Pal. The latter told his father who talked with the man and he in turn acknowledged that he had engaged in a kind of double dealing with the two families in a dispute.
28. Sobha Ram had been bitten by a dog at a house to which he had gone in order to borrow a cot for a wedding party.	Angan Pal	Shankar Lal Tyagi	
29. Recognition of uncle Prithvi, maternal uncle of Sobha Ram, when he visited Rasulpur.	Hridaya Ram	Shankar Lal Tyagi	Uncle Prithvi came unannounced to Rasulpur. Jasbir saw him and spontaneously ran up to him saying, "Mama" (maternal uncle). Jasbir further said that he (as Sobha Ram) had received back from Prithvi some money which he had lent him. The family of Sobha Ram had not been able to confirm the repayment of the debt, but Jasbir also said where the money would be found and it was found in that place. This seems to have been the money described in item 25. There were discrepancies in the testimony about the actual amount of the debt and money found.
30. Recognition of the way in Vehedi from a point near the railway station to the Tyagi quadrangle.	Jaganath Prasad Sukla		Jasbir walked straight to the Tyagi quadrangle. The distance was about 200 yards. The Tyagi quadrangle was the third quadrangle on the road from the station. Although followed by a group of twenty people, these stayed behind Jasbir and did not guide him in any way.

Item	Persons recognized	Informant	Comments
31. Recognition of Baleshwar, son of Sobha Ram.	Baleshwar Tyagi, son of Sobha Ram Jaganath Prasad Sukla		A recognition through appropriate behavior only. Jasbir showed much affection for the boy, e.g., by clasping him and by giving him gifts, but Baleshwar Tyagi could not recall that Jasbir had recognized him by name.
32. Recognition of Sobha Ram's aunt.	Jaganath Prasad Sukla		Jasbir gave the correct relationship (Tai) of Sobha Ram to this person. Sri Jaganath Prasad Sukla was a secondhand witness of this item; he did not claim knowledge of the details of the recognition.
33. Remembrance of members of the village with whom the Tyagis were not on good terms.	Shankar Lal Tyagi	Shankar Lal Tyagi	Appropriate behavior of not speaking to these people with whom the Tyagis had quarreled.
34. Recognition of Sri Ram Swaroop Tyagi, brother-in-law of Sobha Ram.	Shankar Lal Tyagi		Sri Ram Swaroop Tyagi asked Jasbir: "Who am I?" and Jasbir replied: "I have not forgotten you. You are my brother-in-law."
35. Recognition of Sri Birbal Singh, younger cousin of Sobha Ram.	Shankar Lal Tyagi Birbal Singh Tyagi		Sri Birbal Singh came into a room where Jasbir was present. Jasbir saw him and said spontaneously: "Come in, Gandhiji." Someone present said: "This is Birbal." Jasbir replied: "We call him 'Gandhiji.'" Sri Birbal Singh was familiarly called Gandhiji because he had large ears and therefore some resemblance to Mahatma Gandhi. The testimony of Sri Birbal Singh Tyagi for this item and item 38 was obtained by Sri R. S. Lal in an interview at Meerut in January, 1965.
36. Recognition of Sri Mahendra Singh Tyagi, younger brother of Sobha Ram.	Mahendra Singh Tyagi		Someone asked Jasbir: "Who is he?" and Jasbir replied: "He is my younger brother."

Item	Informants	Verification	Comments
37. Recognition of the fields belonging to the Tyagi family in Vehedi.	Mahendra Singh Tyagi		Jasbir was taken out to the village fields and asked to say which fields belonged to his family. Family holdings in India are frequently divided up with units scattered around the village and each unit surrounded by land owned by other families.
38. Recognition of Sobha Ram's grandfather, Sri Raja Ram.	Birbal Singh Tyagi		Jasbir was asked to identify this man and said: "This is my grandfather Rai Sahib." Sri Raja Ram had been called Rai Sahib.
39. Sobha Ram's white ox had long horns, his black ox had short horns.	Shankar Lal Tyagi	Shankar Lal Tyagi	Sri Raghbir Singh Tyagi, Sobha Ram's uncle, offered discrepant testimony on this point, asserting that the white ox had the short horns and the black ox the long ones. This discrepancy may have arisen in confusion about whether curved horns are to be considered longer or shorter than straight horns. Differences in opinion could arise if "length" of horn was measured by one person taking the distance from root to tip and by another taking the over-all length of the horn.

tion of Jasbir's statements, his family accorded him more respect. In 1964 they seemed to cherish and exhibit the friendliest feelings for him, but his aloofness from them persisted quite clearly.

Although the Jat family and other villagers of Rasulpur received my party cordially, they did not show enthusiasm for Jasbir's visits to Vehedi. The Tyagis initiated such visits knowing that Jasbir longed for them. In 1964, Jasbir had not visited Vehedi for two years, but one of the Tyagi family, Sri Surajmal Tyagi, had visited him in Rasulpur two months before my second visit. When they parted, Jasbir wept. The Tyagis believed the Jats had some concern about losing Jasbir to the Tyagis and in 1961 the Jats would not give Jasbir permission to attend a wedding in Vehedi, apparently out of a fear that his ties with the Tyagis would become even stronger. Once, when Sri Shankar Lal Tyagi became ill, his family sent for Jasbir to visit him in Vehedi, but Jasbir's family refused. They also refused to allow Jasbir to meet the widow of Sobha Ram. Sri Jaganath Prasad Sukla also testified to the reluctance of the Jat family to let Jasbir visit Vehedi. He mentioned that he only persuaded Jasbir's father to permit the first visit after, in effect, bribing him with a concession (regarding some farming business) which he was in a position (as a government agent) to grant Sri Girdhari Lal Jat.

Readers may wish to know, as I did, what account Jasbir gave of events between the death of Sobha Ram and the revival of Jasbir with memories of Sobha Ram. To this question, Jasbir replied in 1961 that after death he (as Sobha Ram) met a sadhu (a holy man or saint) who advised him to "take cover" in the body of Jasbir, son of Girdhari Lal Jat. But by 1964, Jasbir's images of this period had become confused and he made several statements contradictory with other evidence. It seems likely that he was then trying to accommodate questioners who pressed him for details of this period. With regard to the memories of the life of Sobha Ram, however, he seemed to show little fading of clarity. His statements for this in general and in most details accorded with what others reported he had said earlier. I make this comment with regard to the condition of Jasbir in 1964, not as evidence of the worth of his testimony then. By that time what he then said could have been inextricably compounded of his own memories of the previous life (however derived originally) and what he had heard others say about his earlier expressions of these memories. I have not considered anything Jasbir himself said in 1961 or 1964 as evidence for the paranormal hypotheses of the case.

Although the apparent death of Jasbir occurred in the period April-May, 1954, close to the identified date of Sobha Ram's death, we do not know that the change in personality of Jasbir took place immediately on the night when his body seemed to die and then revive. In the following weeks Jasbir was still perilously ill with smallpox, barely able to take nourishment, and not able to express much of any personality. The change of personality may therefore have happened quickly or gradually during the weeks beginning immediately after the apparent death of Jasbir.

Comments on the Evidence of Paranormal Knowledge on the Part of Jasbir. That Jasbir had detailed knowledge of the life and death of Sobha Ram seems entirely clear from the list of the statements he made and recognitions he achieved. His recognitions of people included the saying of some names spontaneously, which diminishes the possibility of his having been guided by hints or leading questions. These can give rise to spurious apparent recognitions if improperly handled.

Although the two villages lie only twenty miles apart as the crow flies, they are quite remote when account is taken of their location in relation to main roads and of the conditions of transportation and caste which separate different groups in India. The isolation of Indian villages from each other cannot be adequately conveyed to Western readers by merely asking them to imagine towns separated by hundreds of miles in the West. There is far more traffic per capita between, say, New York and San Francisco than between two villages like Rasulpur and Vehedi, although they are much closer geographically. If the people interviewed were telling the truth, I see no way in which Jasbir could have learned normally the facts he knew about the life of Sobha Ram. And I have found no reason to doubt that the witnesses I spoke with did tell the truth. With occasional discrepancies, the statements of different informants stood up well against each other and in a repetition of the same testimony three years later.

As evidence of authenticity I would point to the strong behavioral features of the case, including the very strong identification of Jasbir with Sobha Ram. His personation of Sobha Ram, expressed in the pleasure of being with the Tyagis at Vehedi and the lonely isolation he experienced and showed in Rasulpur, provides some of the more impressive and more important features of the case. The reactions of the two families concerned matched this behavior on his part, their tears and other emotions responding to his.

Both Rasulpur and Vehedi are small villages where anyone's business can provide a public occasion. On my visits crowds of curious onlookers assembled and knew the purpose of the visits. Yet no one stepped forward to hint at fraud or sources of normally acquired information. Nor can I think of any motive for fraud even if such a grand display of assembled actors could have been arranged. Both families, particularly the Jat family, had their lives disarranged by Jasbir's claims of memories of Sobha Ram. If Jaspir, a boy of three and a half, recovering from a severe illness, thought this up, he gained some pleasant vacations in Vehedi, but at a cost of severe alienation among his own people in Rasulpur.

Careful inquiries in both villages failed to turn up anyone who could have acted as a normal means of communication of information from the family of Sobha Ram to Jasbir. I have mentioned earlier the few persons I found who had had some contact with both villages and both families. Only one man seems actually to have known personally both Sobha Ram and the family of Girdhari Lal Jat. But this man, Sri Niran Jan, did not seem to have had detailed information about Sobha Ram or his family or the opportunity of passing such information as he had on to Jasbir. He certainly did not think of himself as a repository of the information exhibited by Jasbir about the life of Sobha Ram, and I believe it extremely improbable that he could have communicated the relevant information to Jasbir normally. It remains possible that he, or some other villager of Rasulpur who perhaps came in touch with the Tyagi family in Nirmana, if not Vehedi, could have acted as a telepathic link whereby Jasbir might, if he had the requisite powers, have tapped the minds of the Tyagi family who did possess the relevant information. But such an hypothesis extends our concepts of telepathy almost beyond the limits of its occurrence in any instances for which we have independent evidence. And additionally, this hypothesis does not by itself adequately account for the strong personation of Sobha Ram by Jasbir. However, I shall leave a full discussion of this difficulty for a later section.

Finally, I should like to draw attention again to the fact that the transformation in Jasbir took place rather quickly when he was about three and a half years old. Prior to that age he had seemed a normal child, apart from some difficulty in speaking. It will be recalled that the period of transformation of personality in Jasbir coincided with the recovery of his body from an apparently mortal illness. During his early convalescence there was not much scope for any expression of personality and it is therefore impossible to state over what length of time the change of personality occurred. But the complete change took at most a few weeks and perhaps much less time. Moreover, we have to do here with a profound change of personality, including refusal to eat his family's food because of their alleged lower caste. The case therefore differs markedly from those of other children who seem to recall previous lives over a period of several years and in doing so more or less blend the previous personality with the presently developing one.

The Later Development of Jasbir. I did not meet Jasbir between August, 1964, and October, 1971. In the meantime, Dr. Jamuna Prasad and his team, studying correspondences in the behavioral patterns of subjects and previous personalities in six Indian cases of the reincarnation type, had met with Jasbir and his family and I had received some news of Jasbir from them.

In 1971 Jasbir and his family were living in the village of Kaval about three miles east of Muzaffarnagar. (Earlier they had moved from Rasulpur and lived at a village called Ghola, which is south of Muzaffarnagar. They had then moved again from Ghola to Kaval in 1968.) In Kaval I had a rather long talk with Jasbir and his parents, Girdhari Lal Singh and his wife Rajkali.

Jasbir, who was born at the end of 1950, had continued in school up to the tenth class. But he did not pass the work of that level and in 1969 he stopped school. In 1971 he was helping his father in his cultivation of lands. He was not altogether content with his peasant's life and hoped to obtain a clerical job, although this would be difficult for him without the leaving certificate from the secondary school.

Jasbir had continued visiting Vehedi. His parents said he went over there every three or four months and Jasbir himself said he had gone there just two months before my visit. On that visit he had remained in Vehedi two and a half months working in the Tyagi family's fields. Sobha Ram's father, Shankar Lal Tyagi, was still living then. The Tyagis regarded Jasbir as a full member of their family. They had consulted him about the marriage of Sobha Ram's son and he had attended the wedding ceremony. Jasbir had also been consulted about the marriage of one of Sobha Ram's daughters. When I asked Jasbir to whom, if anyone in particular, he was attached at Vehedi, he replied that his attachment was to Sobha Ram's father and his children. (Sobha Ram's mother had died many years earlier, even before Sobha Ram himself.)

Jasbir denied that his memories of the previous life had faded. He said he still remembered clearly falling off the chariot on his return from the wedding he attended (as Sobha Ram) at the village of Nirmana. He even mentioned the exact place where he fell off the chariot (Dabal Pathak), a detail I do not recall his having mentioned earlier. He still believed that he had been poisoned at the wedding ceremony by a man to whom Sobha Ram had loaned some money which the man did not wish to repay. This man, according to Jasbir, thought to avoid the debt by killing Sobha Ram. (I did not mention this man's name earlier and see no need to include it now.) The man in question later paid Jasbir (*not* Sobha Ram's family) 600 rupees. In 1971 Jasbir said this was the amount of the debt, although in 1961 he had mentioned the figure of 300–400 rupees to me. We should not consider the payment of this large sum to Jasbir as a confession of guilt on the part of the alleged poisoner, but we certainly can consider it as evidence of this man's conviction that Jasbir was in fact Sobha Ram reborn. For the legal heirs of Sobha Ram were certainly *his* children and not Jasbir.

Jasbir had retained a number of Brahmin habits and attitudes. He still believed Brahmins a superior group of persons compared to members of other castes. He still would not eat food cooked in earthen pots. To accommodate him, his family cooked food for him in metal vessels and allowed him to eat first.[16] Jasbir also wore around his neck the sacred thread which is a distinctive habit of upper caste Hindus. (Jats do not wear this thread.) Perhaps, however, he gave the most striking sign of his continuing attachment to the Brahmin caste when I asked him for his correct mailing address. Before he gave the address he first gave me his full name and said to send mail to him: Jasbir Singh Tyagi, son of Girdhari Lal Jat! Thus he acknowledged the reality of the paternity of his body, but at the same time also claimed membership in the caste of the previous life.

Jasbir's attachment to the Brahmin caste did not go so far as objection to marrying a Jat girl. Indeed, he said that he expected to marry in the near future and would marry a girl of the Jat group.

I asked Jasbir if he had any idea as to what happened to the mind or personality that had occupied the body of Jasbir before it apparently died of smallpox and before that body had seemingly been taken over by the mind of Sobha Ram. He did not know and nor do I. I have from time to time enquired in the area where he lives about the existence of a child who has claimed that in a previous life he was one Jasbir of village Rasulpur who died of smallpox at the age of about three; but I have never found any trace of such a child.

Jasbir said that in dreams he sometimes still saw the discarnate sadhu (holy man) whom he had said (when a child) he (as Sobha Ram) had met after the death of Sobha Ram. It will be recalled that Jasbir said this sadhu had advised the discarnate Sobha Ram to "take cover" in the body of Jasbir, who had ostensibly died. Jasbir spoke with some reluctance about these later contacts with the sadhu and gave the impression that he might be violating confidences in mentioning them. He said, however, that the sadhu gave him correct predictions of future events in his life. Once, I do not know exactly when, Jasbir's father had proposed and indeed forced a marriage on Jasbir which neither he nor the intended bride wished. At some point during the painful negotiations for this marriage the sadhu assured Jasbir (in a dream) that the bride would not follow through with the arrangement and in fact she did not, so the plans for it dissolved and Jasbir was saved. Inference based on normal information about the attitude of the girl and her family might well account for Jasbir's foreknowledge in this case; I cite it only as an example he offered of the sort of predictions he claimed to receive from the sadhu in dreams.[17]

---

[16] Brahmins insist on having their food cooked in metal vessels. Members of other castes, especially Jats, may cook food in earthen vessels. As a mark of deference, members of lower castes invite Brahmins to eat first when there is a mixed group at a meal and orthodox Brahmins expect such respect.

[17] Since I first studied the case of Jasbir in 1961 I have encountered other examples of claims by subjects to remember that during the discarnate state after death they met holy men (sadhus in India) who guided them toward the home for birth into the next incarnation. And in some of these instances, the subject has continued to experience contact with the holy

Since 1964 a remarkable change had taken place in Jasbir's demeanor. In the first edition of this book I mentioned that he was rather an outcast in his family. His snobbish attitude of superiority had led to retaliation on their part, including scolding, and a rift had developed between Jasbir and his family. I remarked in 1964 that he was noticeably depressed. But in 1971 he had developed into a smiling, self-confident young man. I think we should allow a large share of credit for this happy change to his parents who had done their best to adjust to a situation which must at times have been very difficult for them. And in the end they had helped Jasbir to make his adaptations to them. In 1971 Jasbir said that his older brother, who had formerly been particularly hostile to his pretensions of superiority, fully accepted him in the family. Notwithstanding this remarkable healing within the family of Girdhari Lal Jat, Jasbir felt that the Tyagi family showed him even more affection.

Jasbir's economic circumstances in 1971 were difficult, perhaps precarious. His family was less prosperous than the Tyagis and he regarded himself as having taken something of a "demotion" in socio-economic circumstances from one life to another. Hindus believe that such changes derive from sinful conduct in a former life, not necessarily the one immediately preceding that in which it occurs. Jasbir could not think of any offence by Sobha Ram which merited his "demotion," but he had regarded it as God's will and had tried his best to accept the circumstances in which he found himself. It seemed to me that he had succeeded rather well in this. Although the peasant life ahead for him would almost certainly be fraught with hard work and hazardous conditions, he was facing the future with cheerfulness.

The Case of Sukla [18]

Summary of the Case and its Investigation. Sukla, daughter of Sri K. N. Sen Gupta of the village of Kampa, West Bengal, was born in March, 1954. When she was about a year and a half old and barely able to talk, she was

---

man after his rebirth. Claims of memories of this type of experience occur rather commonly among cases in Thailand and Burma. The information I have obtained in studying cases in these countries prepared me for Jasbir's comment that he still "met" the sadhu of his case in dreams. But it did not stimulate him to tell me about this because he mentioned the fact spontaneously and without my having asked him a question concerning the sadhu.

[18] For another report of this case, see P. Pal. "A Case Suggestive of Reincarnation in West Bengal." *Indian Journal of Parapsychology*, Vol. 3, 1961–62, 5–21. In the present report of the case I have included some information derived from Professor Pal's report in the summary of the case and remarks about opportunities for contact between the two families. However, in the itemized list of statements and recognitions on the part of Sukla, I have included only testimony obtained by myself in the summer of 1961 unless an exception to this is noted. Readers may thus compare the two accounts of the case. Since each account includes details of the case or testimony of some witnesses omitted in the other account, readers can only obtain a complete view of the case by studying both Professor Pal's report and the present one.

often observed cradling a block of wood or a pillow and addressing it as "Minu." When asked who "Minu" was, Sukla said "My daughter." Over the next three years she gradually revealed additional information about Minu and "he," meaning her husband of the previous life.[19] She said "he," Minu, Khetu, and Karuna (the two latter being younger brothers of her "husband") were all at Rathtala in Bhatpara. The village of Bhatpara is eleven miles from Kampa on the road to Calcutta. The Gupta family knew Bhatpara slightly; however, they had never heard of a district called Rathtala in Bhatpara nor of people with the names given by Sukla.

Sukla developed a strong desire to go to Bhatpara and began to insist that she would go alone if not taken by her family. She claimed she could lead the way to her father-in-law's home. Sri Sen Gupta talked of the matter with some friends and mentioned it to a fellow employee of the railway where he worked. This man, Sri S. C. Pal, lived near Bhatpara and had relatives there. Through these relatives Sri Pal learned that a person called Khetu lived in a section of Bhatpara called Rathtala. It is a small area and so called because in it is housed a car (rath) for an image of a god. Sri Pal found further that the man called Khetu had had a sister-in-law, one Mana, who had died some years back (in January, 1948) leaving an infant girl called Minu. When Sri Pal reported these facts to Sukla's father he became more interested in a visit by Sukla to Bhatpara; this was then arranged with the consent of the other family, of which Sri Amritalal Chakravarty was the head.

In the summer of 1959, when she was a little more than five, Sukla and members of her family journeyed to Bhatpara where Sukla led the way to the house of her alleged former father-in-law, Sri Amritalal Chakravarty. There she recognized and correctly named a number of people and objects. Subsequently, members of the Chakravarty family visited Sukla and her family at Kampa. She was also visited by members of the family (Pathak) with which Mana had grown up. Srimati Pathak was the maternal aunt of the previous personality. Later Sukla made some additional visits to Bhatpara. The meeting of Sukla and her supposed former husband Sri Haridhan Chakravarty, and her supposed former daughter Minu, aroused great emotion in Sukla and further longings to be with them again. Unlike some other children of these cases, e.g., Prakash and Jasbir, she never expressed a wish to rejoin the other family permanently. But she did long for

[19] In India there exists a strong reluctance to use personal names in the family. Other persons are often referred to by relationships only. Indian girls and women especially will not refer to their husbands by their names. They refer to them only indirectly as "he" or "the father of Minu" (naming a daughter). Moreover, in the presence of their husbands and other senior male relatives, Indian women will often look away or down as a sign of respect. It is a rather definite gesture and since it usually includes a movement of the head as well as of the eyes, it can be quite easily observed by bystanders. This behavior also communicates the recognition of the husband or relative.

visits from Sri Haridhan Chakravarty and pined for him when he did not come.

Professor P. Pal visited both Kampa and Bhatpara repeatedly over a year during 1960 and investigated thoroughly the backgrounds and opportunities for contact between the two principal families concerned in the case. He also checked the testimony of each informant against that of the others. His detailed report resulted from these inquiries. In the summer of 1961, I spent two days in the area visiting both villages and interviewing many of Professor Pal's informants as well as a few new ones. In 1962 Professor Pal returned again to the area to learn of further developments in the case.

Relevant Facts of Geography and Possible Normal Means of Communication Between the Two Families. Bhatpara is a village about thirty miles north of Calcutta on the main highway going north. Kampa lies about eleven miles farther north a few miles off the main road. A rail line runs along the highway, which is also served by buses. Thus the two villages are quite accessible to each other. The members of the two principal families concerned in the case denied that they ever had any knowledge of the other family prior to the attempts to verify Sukla's statements.

The family of Sri Sen Gupta formerly lived about 150 miles away in East Bengal, but had moved to West Bengal after the partition of Bengal between India and Pakistan in 1947. After living in some other places, Sri Sen Gupta and his family settled in Kampa about 1951. Sri Sen Gupta worked on the railway and had passed through Bhatpara on the train. He was certain, however, that he had only once stopped there on an occasion when he gave a demonstration of magic at a school, he being an amateur magician.

The Chakravarty and Pathak families were long established in Bhatpara and some of their affairs would have been known to other residents of Bhatpara or could have been known upon inquiry by strangers. The case for paranormal cognition in the statements made by Sukla therefore depends considerably on her having expressed knowledge of intimate details of these families which would not be known outside the families and on her recognitions of some members of the families. The Chakravarty and Pathak families on their side firmly denied having had any previous acquaintance with the family of Sri Sen Gupta. Apart from living in different villages, the two families were separated by caste distinctions which would in India further diminish the likelihood of social intercourse between them.

Nevertheless, Professor Pal did learn of two persons who in fact had some acquaintance with both families. The first of these was Sri S. C. Pal, already mentioned. He was a fellow-employee of Sri Sen Gupta, who lived quite near Bhatpara and had relatives there. He himself had no initial acquaintance with the Chakravarty or Pathak families, but it was through his relatives that they were identified as the persons to whom Sukla was probably referring. Sri Pal had known Sri Sen Gupta only a month when the latter began to tell him about the claims to a previous life in Bhatpara of his daughter. Sri Pal had never visited the Gupta house. Sukla had talked of a previous life in Bhatpara for several years before her father met Sri Pal and it therefore seems quite safe to rule him out as a source of the information possessed by Sukla.

Sri Atul Dhar was another fellow-employee of Sri Sen Gupta and a friend of longer standing and much greater intimacy. Sri Atul Dhar had a friend who was a cousin of Sri Amritalal Chakravarty and he occasionally visited with his friend in the home of Sri Amritalal Chakravarty. On these visits he became slightly acquainted with Sri Haridhan Chakravarty and heard of his wife, Mana, but never met her. Of their personal affairs he knew only about some difficulties between Mana and her stepmother-in-law. Sri Atul Dhar never discussed the Chakravarty family with Sri Sen Gupta. When Sri Sen Gupta mentioned to him the statements of Sukla about a previous life in Bhatpara he was not at all certain that her statements referred to the Chakravarty family he knew; it "struck him casually" that the Khetu referred to by Sukla might be a member of the Chakravarty family whom he had met years before. Sri Atul Dhar encouraged Sri Sen Gupta to make inquiries, but did not participate himself in the initial exchanges of visits between the families. He did accompany the Gupta family, including Sukla, on their second visit to Bhatpara during which Sukla recognized various objects, including saris that had belonged to the deceased Mana. Of these intimate matters, however, Sri Atul Dhar had no knowledge whatever. Although Sri Atul Dhar definitely had more acquaintance with each of the two families than Sri Pal, I believe that he also can be excluded as a source of the information acquired by Sukla about the Chakravarty family.

Persons Interviewed During the Investigation. In Kampa I interviewed:

Sukla, daughter of Sri K. N. Sen Gupta
Sri K. N. Sen Gupta, father of Sukla
Srimati Shriti Kanna Sen Gupta, mother of Sukla
Srimati Nirod Bala Sen Gupta, paternal grandmother of Sukla
Sri Naraindra Nath Roy, brother of Srimati Shriti Kanna Sen Gupta. and maternal uncle of Sukla

In Bhatpara, I interviewed:

Sri Amritalal Chakravarty, father-in-law of Mana
Sri Amritalal Chakravarty's wife, stepmother-in-law of Mana
Sri Haridhan Chakravarty, eldest son of Sri Amritalal Chakravarty and husband of Mana
Sri Kshetranath Chakravarty (known as "Khetu"), second son of Sri Amritalal Chakravarty and brother-in-law of Mana

Sri Karuna Kumar Chakravarty (known as "Kuti"), third son of Sri
Amritalal Chakravarty and brother-in-law of Mana

Sri Rishikesh Chakravarty, fourth son of Sri Amritalal Chakravarty and
brother-in-law of Mana

Sri Dilip Kumar Pathak, cousin of Mana

Sri Gopal Pathak, younger brother of Mana

Srimati Reba Rani Pathak, wife of Sri Suresh Chandra Pathak and
maternal aunt (by marriage) of Mana who raised her

Sri Jatindranath Pathak, brother of Sri Suresh Chandra Pathak and
maternal uncle of Mana

Minu, daughter of Mana

Sri Gopal Chandra Ghosh, no relative, but friend of the Chakravarty
family

At Bali Station, West Bengal, I interviewed:

Sri S. C. Pal, friend of Sri K. N. Sen Gupta, whose inquiries led to
verification of Sukla's statements

After my visit in 1961, Professor P. Pal again sought out and interviewed
Sri Atul Dhar and I have drawn on the report of this interview which Professor Pal sent to me.

Statements and Recognitions made by Sukla. I give below in the tabulation
a summary of the statements and recognitions made by Sukla with regard
to her claim to be Mana reborn.

In this tabulation I have omitted two reported recognitions made by
Sukla on the grounds that these contributed little or nothing to the case
since they lacked the specificity for the life of Mana which can be claimed
for the items listed. On the other hand, at least one such recognition, that
of the sewing machine used by Mana, was accompanied by tears welling
into Sukla's eyes. Mana had worked much at this machine.

Items 1–6 occurred before (so far as I know) the two families had any
contact; items 6–16 occurred on the occasion of Sukla's first visit to
Bhatpara when the two families came in touch with each other directly;
items 17–22 occurred when Sri Haridhan Chakravarty, Srimati Pathak, and
Minu visited Sukla and her family at Kampa a week later; item 23 occurred
when Sri Rishikesh Chakravarty made an independent visit to Kampa for
the purpose of testing Sukla on his own, and items 24–29 occurred on the
occasion of another visit of Sukla and her father and mother to Bhatpara
two weeks after the first visit to Bhatpara.

*Relevant Reports and Observations of the Behavior of the People Con-
cerned.* The tabulation below records chiefly the cognitive aspects of Sukla's

behavior with regard to her claims to be the deceased Mana reborn. But the testimonies of the witnesses abounded in details of strong emotional expressions on the part of Sukla and other kinds of behavior completely appropriate to the relationships of Mana. Particularly impressive to witnesses were the tears with which Sukla greeted Minu and the attention and affection she afterwards lavished on her when they met subsequently. Their sizes were strangely disproportionate to the maternal role Sukla assumed in the relationship. Sukla herself commented on the fact that Minu had grown taller and said, "I am small." But within this limitation Sukla exactly acted the role of a mother towards a beloved daughter.

Professor Pal [20] witnessed an example of Sukla's emotional attachment to Minu when Sri Dilip Kumar Pathak told Sukla in Kampa (falsely to test her) that Minu was ill with high fever in Bhatpara. At this Sukla began to weep, and it took some time for her to be reassured that Minu was well. On another occasion, when Minu really was ill and news of this reached Sukla, she became extremely distressed, wept, and demanded to be taken to Bhatpara to see Minu. Her family could not quiet her until they actually took her the next day to see Minu, who was by then better. As already mentioned, Sukla also showed tears when she looked at the sewing machine with which Mana had worked so assiduously during her life.

Toward Mana's husband, Sri Haridhan Chakravarty, her behavior was that of a proper Hindu lady toward her husband. For example, she ate the remnants from his plate at a meal but would not finish anyone else's food. (In India a woman will finish food on her husband's plate after he has eaten, but will not eat from anyone else's plate.)

Sukla was somewhat aloof from the other children of her family and played alone. She did not like to eat with the other children. When she was about three (according to her father) she used to say, "Why should I eat with you? I am a Brahmin." (The Chakravartys are Brahmins, but the Guptas are of the Bania caste.) She was sensitive and withdrew from school when she received more attention than she wished. She later (1962) returned to school. Sukla showed a definite gravity beyond her years and also a tendency to stubbornness. Mana, according to those who knew her, also strongly exhibited the same qualities.

Such observations of rather general traits in both personalities contribute little to the evidence of paranormality in the informational aspects of the case, but Sukla's stubbornness does bear on this in another respect. With the exception of an indirect recognition of Mana's maternal aunt and a tendency to associate familiarly with the Pathak family, Sukla did not recognize the members of this family as she did that of Mana's in-laws. And Professor Pal has pointed out in his report that even after they were clearly

TABULATION
Summary of Statements and Recognitions Made by Sukla

Item	Informants	Verification	Comments
1. She had a daughter called Minu.	Shriti Kanna Sen Gupta, mother of Sukla Nirod Bala Sen Gupta, paternal grandmother of Sukla	Haridhan Chakravarty had a daughter, Minu, by his first wife, Mana, who had died.	The first communication of Sukla about a previous life was the behavior of caressing a block of wood representing the infant child left at her death by Mana.
2. Her brother-in-law was called Khetu.	Shriti Kanna Sen Gupta Nirod Bala Sen Gupta	I met and talked with Kshetranath Chakravarty, brother-in-law of the deceased Mana.	His familiar name was Khetu.
3. She had another brother-in-law called Karuna.	Shriti Kanna Sen Gupta Nirod Bala Sen Gupta	I met and talked with Karuna Chakravarty.	This item not included in the report of Professor P. Pal. Karuna was always known and called by his nickname Kuti; even neighbors did not know his real name of Karuna.
4. Her husband, Minu, and brothers-in-law lived at Rathtala in Bhatpara.	Shriti Kanna Sen Gupta Nirod Bala Sen Gupta	The housing for the "rath" of the god was about 100 feet from the house of Amrialal Chakravarty in Bhatpara, and close to the banks of the river. I saw these buildings.	Statement true of time when Mana lived. Sri Haridhan Chakravarty in 1961 lived a little distance from the Rathtala and Minu lived with her great-uncle, Sri Pathak, on the other side of Bhatpara. A "rath" is a large car or wagon on which the image of a god is placed during a religious parade.
5. Her husband and she had once gone to a movie and they afterwards had refreshments.	Haridhan Chakravarty, husband of Mana	Haridhan Chakravarty	P. Pal heard of this item with more detail from Sukla's family. The occasion was memorable because it was the only time Mana ever went to a movie in her life and she and her husband were afterwards reproached by her stepmother-in-law.
6. Recognition of route to home of Mana's father-in-law in Rathtala at Bhatpara.	Nirod Bala Sen Gupta K. N. Sen Gupta, father of Sukla		Although the route available was straight, not curved, there were many houses and lanes into which Sukla could have turned

58

Item	Informants		Comments
6. (continued)	S. C. Pal, friend of K. N. Sen Gupta All these informants accompanied Sukla along the route.		if ignorant of the correct way. There is one main crossroad also. Sukla was ahead of the others. Only Sri Pal knew the way and he was behind the girl.
7. Confusion of Sukla about entrance to the house of Mana's father-in-law.	K. N. Sen Gupta S. C. Pal	Amritalal Chakravarty, father-in-law of Mana	Since the death of Mana, a former entrance to the house had been closed and the main entrance moved to the side off the street and down an alley. Sukla's confusion was thus appropriate to the changes.
8. Recognition of Mana's father-in-law.	K. N. Sen Gupta S. C. Pal		As the party approached the house, Sri Amritalal Chakravarty came on to the street unexpectedly. When Sukla saw him she looked down, the usual respectful behavior of a young woman toward an older male relative. Sri Amritalal Chakravarty told us he did not notice anything unusual about Sukla's behavior on this first meeting. But he was out on the street looking for his son and perhaps did not notice Sukla carefully; he did say that she was leading the way ahead of the rest of the party.
9. Recognition of Mana's daughter Minu.	Nirod Bala Sen Gupta Amritalal Chakravarty		In the group at the house someone had announced the arrival of Minu by name, before Sukla saw her. The significant signs of recognition by Sukla were her tears when she saw Minu and her marked affection for her. See further notes on behavior in text.
10. Recognition of Mana's husband.	Haridhan Chakravarty Nirod Bala Sen Gupta		Sukla was asked, "Can you point out your husband?" There were twenty or thirty people in the room when Sukla indicated Sri Haridhan Chakravarty as "Minu's father," a correct style of address for a Hindu woman referring to her husband.

Item	*Informants*	*Verification*	*Comments*
11. Recognition of Mana's brother-in-law, Khetu.	Haridhan Chakravarty Kshetranath (Khetu) Chakravarty, brother-in-law of Mana		Made at the same time as recognition of Mana's husband. Khetu was not identified by name, but Sukla pointed him out as "uncle of Minu."
12. Recognition of Mana's brother-in-law, Karuna.	Karuna Kumar (Kuti) Chakravarty, brother-in-law of Mana		Karuna had just entered the house a few minutes before he asked Sukla: "Who am I?" She said: "Karuna" and also "Tumi," meaning younger brother-in-law. No one had called him by his name during the few minutes he was in the house. Moreover, he is always called by his nickname Kuti, even the neighbors not knowing his real name of Karuna. The conditions of this recognition were better than those for items 10 and 11, in which glances of the group might have given clues to Sukla. The recognition of Mana's brother-in-law, Karuna, was also appropriate to the closeness of Karuna with the deceased Mana. At the wedding of Mana and Sri Haridhan Chakravarty, Karuna had been best man.
13. Recognition of Mana's stepmother-in-law.	Amritalal Chakravarty		Sukla's grandmother asked her to point out "her" mother-in-law in a group of thirty people.

Item	Informants	Comments
14. Non-recognition of Mana's cousin, Dilip Pathak.	Dilip Pathak, cousin of Mana	Sukla behaved somewhat familiarly with Sri Dilip Pathak, but did not call him by his name. According to Professor Pal, Sukla had not called any of the Pathak family by name. Such familiar behavior constitutes a recognition of sorts, since it is virtually forbidden and unknown between children and adult strangers.
15. Non-recognition of Mana's brother, Sri Gopal Pathak.	Jatindranath Pathak, husband of Mana's maternal aunt	Another possible partial recognition, through behavior, since Sukla showed friendliness toward Sri Gopal Pathak.
16. Non-recognition of any feature of the home of the Pathak family.	Jatindranath Pathak	Mana lived in this house much more than she did in the Chakravarty home with which she seemed so completely familiar.
17. Recognition of Srimati Reba Rani Pathak, the maternal aunt of Mana.	Nirod Bala Sen Gupta / Reba Rani Pathak, maternal aunt of Mana	An indirect recognition. Sukla did not recognize her by name. When Srimati Pathak asked her "With whom did you leave Minu when you died?" Sukla replied: "With you." In fact, just before Mana died, her last words asked this aunt who would look after Minu, and the aunt had replied that she would do so.
18. Her husband's favorite food was prawns and buli.	Nirod Bala Sen Gupta	Sukla advised her family to prepare this food when Sri Haridhan Chakravarty visited. They did and found that she had selected correctly.
19. Dipu was still alive.	Reba Rani Pathak	When asked about Dipu, a child of the Pathak family, Sukla said Dipu was still alive, but in fact she had died after Mana died. So her statement was correct for the time of life of Mana.
20. In addition to Minu, she had had an infant son who had died.	Reba Rani Pathak	Sukla was asked if Minu was her only child. Mana had a son who died before Minu was born.

Item	Informants	Verification	Comments
21. Naming of three saris owned by Mana.	Reba Rani Pathak Haridhan Chakravarty	Haridhan Chakravarty	There are discrepancies in the statements about the colors of the saris, but the accounts agree that Sukla said correctly that Mana had three saris, two of them Benares saris, a specially fine type of sari. In fact, Sukla had more accurate information about the saris than Sri Haridhan Chakravarty, Mana's husband. The saris had been kept in a trunk after Mana's death.
22. She had lived at Kharagpur.	Minu, daughter of Mana Haridhan Chakravarty	Haridhan Chakravarty	Someone asked Sukla: "Have you lived anywhere else besides Bhatpara?" and she replied: "Yes, Kharagpur." Sri Haridhan Chakravarty and Mana had lived for fourteen months at Kharagpur. In Professor Pal's report the question is attributed to Minu, but the quoted question and reply were exactly the same in the statements given me and in Professor Pal's report.
23. Recognition of another brother-in-law of Mana, Sri Rishikesh Chakravarty.	Rishikesh Chakravarty, brother-in-law of Mana Nirod Bala Sen Gupta		Upon arriving at the house of the Guptas in Kampa, Sri Rishikesh Chakravarty announced a wish to see his brother's wife. Sukla may have overheard this remark. She nevertheless, when asked who he was, identified him as "Minu's uncle." She did not identify an accompanying male friend of Sri Rishikesh who had in fact never known Mana.
24. There were two cows in the Chakravarty family.	Shriti Kanna Sen Gupta Amritalal Chakravarty	Amritalal Chakravarty	Both the cows had died since the death of Mana. According to one witness, Sukla correctly gave the color of the cows.
25. The Chakravarty family had a parrot.	Shriti Kanna Sen Gupta	Amritalal Chakravarty	The parrot had flown away since the death of Mana.

26. She had a brass pitcher in a particular room of the Chakravarty house.	Shriti Kanna Sen Gupta	Shriti Kanna Sen Gupta	Sukla went to this room in the house and found the pitcher still there. She had not been to this room on her first visit. The room in question had been Mana's bedroom.
27. Location of places where Mana and her stepmother-in-law used to sit in the kitchen.	Shriti Kanna Sen Gupta	Shriti Kanna Sen Gupta	Not particularly significant. The information might be inferred.
28. Location of former position of Minu's cot in bedroom.	Shriti Kanna Sen Gupta	Shriti Kanna Sen Gupta	
29. Identification of three saris belonging to Mana in a trunk.	Shriti Kanna Sen Gupta Haridhan Chakravarty Gopal Chandra Ghosh, friend of Chakravarty family		Sukla identified Mana's saris among a considerable number of other clothes that had not belonged to Mana.

identified to her, she did not accord them the recognition she gave to Mana's in-laws. Nor could she recognize anything in the home of the Pathaks where Mana lived all her life with the exception of a few years. In short, Sukla did not allow anyone to tutor her on these points. This, in my opinion, speaks for the honesty of those concerned for if someone had taught her the information about the Chakravartys he might just as easily have taught her about the Pathaks. And it would make no sense to stage recognitions of the marital family and omit those of the family in which Mana grew up. Similarly, if Sukla herself was able and motivated to contrive her case, she would, I think, have included recognitions of the childhood family of Mana.

Sukla's father said she had some capacity for extrasensory perception and he told me of three episodes in which she seemed to show this. In each instance he himself was the "agent" when away from home and Sukla correctly stated either whom he was seeing or when he would (unexpectedly) return home.

Comments on the Evidence of Paranormal Knowledge on the Part of Sukla. In his report Professor Pal mentioned his extensive inquiries into the reputations for integrity of the people concerned in this case. He was unable to discover any evidence suggesting fraud or any motive for fraud. During my own inquiries in the area, the purpose of my visit became known to many other persons besides those I was interviewing and no one came forward to impute fraud to any of the persons concerned. On the contrary, I heard through my driver, who chatted with villagers, unsolicited testimony to the general authenticity of the case as I had learned about it.

In the present case, the possibility occurs of unconscious direction of Sukla in some of the recognitions she apparently accomplished. Items 9 certainly and 10, 11, 13 and 23 possibly incur this suspicion. But such objections can hardly be leveled, if we accept the accounts given, against other recognitions achieved by Sukla such as items 6, 7, 12, 17, 26, and 29. Although item 17 was an indirect recognition, it was most apposite and appropriate to the extraordinary attachment of Mana for Minu shown again by Sukla. In addition to the recognitions, however, Sukla unquestionably showed an impressively detailed knowledge of past events in the life of Mana. Although she expressed her knowledge of some of these matters only after the families came in contact with each other, she communicated substantial amounts of it to her family before that contact. Moreover, Sukla's knowledge was of these people or events as they had been during the life of Mana, not during more recent times. She knew that Mana's son had died, for example, but did not know that Dipu or the cows had died or that the parrot had flown away.

The Later Development of Sukla. I did not meet Sukla between August, 1961, and November, 1969, when I again visited her and her family at Kampa. During this long interval, however, Professor P. Pal followed the case through occasional meetings or correspondence with Sukla's father and other members of her family. The following information includes data furnished to me by Professor Pal as well as what I learned myself during my visit to Kampa in 1969. Subsequently I also received from Sukla herself a letter that she wrote me in August, 1970.

In 1969 Sukla, who was then fifteen years old, was in the eighth grade of school. Her mother said she was average in her work at school. At her age she should have been in the ninth class and so was a year behind her contemporaries.

Sukla's expression of memories of the previous life remained active between the ages of three and seven. Thereafter her spontaneous statements about the previous life diminished and at the same time her relationship with the previous family changed from strong attachment to indifference and even to a degree of antagonism. For about a year, after the two families had first met, Haridhan Chakravarty (Mana's husband) came to visit Sukla about once a week. Thereafter he diminished his visits mainly because of objections raised by his second wife to the attention he was giving to the girl he believed was his first wife reborn! He continued to visit Sukla, however, but less frequently. And she continued to welcome him up to about 1966 when she was twelve. In the meantime, after Sukla became about seven or eight, her parents began to discourage her from talking about the previous life and she ceased to do so. When someone later asked her about it, she would only smile.

Mana's daughter, Minu, married (in about 1967) and her family did not invite Sukla or her father to the wedding. Whatever the motives for this omission, it may have increased further the separation between Sukla and the previous family. It was at about this time, or possibly earlier, that Sukla began to become less friendly toward Haridhan Chakravarty. When Minu came with her new husband to visit Sukla in 1968, Sukla met them but showed, at least afterwards, discontent and complained of being "pestered by these people." It seems that Haridhan Chakravarty was still occasionally visiting Sukla up to 1969, but her mother said that Sukla would then remark: "Why has he come again?"

By 1969 Sukla no longer spoke spontaneously about the previous life and became annoyed if anyone asked her about it. In 1970 she wrote me: "I cannot remember anything about the life of Mana of Bhatpara."

Two questions arise. First, had Sukla really forgotten all the memories of the previous life? And secondly, if she had forgotten the memories, what factors contributed to this?

On the first question Sukla's own statement is certainly weighty. Her mother, however, in 1969 thought that Sukla still preserved some memories, but no longer wished to expose them publicly. In support of this belief she cited Sukla's rather petulant objection to visits by Haridhan Chakravarty. She thought Sukla's statement: "Why has he come again?" showed continuing recognition of his place in the previous life. Sukla's father, K. N. Sen Gupta, was unfortunately not at Kampa during my visit there in 1969. One of his cousins, K. C. Sen Gupta, said he had questioned Sukla about a year earlier concerning the previous life and that she had told him she had forgotten it. But he had asked her about it teasingly and I do not think that his attitude would have invited Sukla to confide in him if she had still been having memories of the previous life. I place more confidence in the statement of Sukla's paternal uncle, P. N. Sen Gupta, who was also present when I visited her in 1969. He said he thought Sukla had remembered the previous life up to the age of about ten and had thereafter forgotten. Taking all the available evidence together and weighing it as best I can, I have concluded that, by 1969–70 or thereabouts, Sukla had completely forgotten the previous life. This was almost certainly preceded by a period of keeping to herself whatever memories she had preserved up to that time.

As for the factors leading to her forgetting, I think repetition and expression of the memories an important factor in sustaining their freshness. (This is true of *any* memories, not just of those related to previous lives.) When Sukla's parents discouraged her from talking about the previous life and when Haridhan Chakravarty's second wife began restricting his visits to her she had fewer occasions to revive and freshen her memories. Sukla's mother described her as being "ashamed" of her memories and feeling conspicuous among her siblings and classmates, none of whom were claiming to remember previous lives. I took this allusion to mean that as Sukla reached puberty it became increasingly embarrassing for her to talk openly about having a husband, even if a previous one! So to the other two factors I have mentioned this third one of modesty became added and contributed to further forgetting. During this period a circular relationship probably developed between the fading of her memories and her attitude to the visits of Haridhan Chakravarty. The less she remembered of the (previous) relationship with him the less appropriate his visits became to her. And gradually they came to seem first unnecessary, then embarrassing, and finally, annoying.

In 1969 Sukla's mother said that she was still inclined to remain aloof from other children. She thought Sukla somewhat more religious than the other children of the family. But she said Sukla had never claimed superiority because she believed she had been a Brahmin. (Her family are members of the Bania caste, and the previous family were Brahmins.) Her father, however, had said (in 1961) that when Sukla was between three and three and a half she had objected to eating with other members of the family on the grounds that she was a Brahmin and they were not! Perhaps her mother had not heard such remarks or, more likely, had forgotten them in 1969. In any case I think she would have remembered if Sukla had shown anything like the degree of Brahmin caste consciousness that was shown by Jasbir, and by two other subjects (of whose cases I shall later publish reports) who remembered previous lives as Brahmins, although themselves of lower castes.

This case includes a detail of medical relevance that deserves mention. Mana Chakravarty, according to her husband, Haridhan Chakravarty, suffered from pimples on her nose. Sukla also suffered from pimples on her nose and was, according to her mother, the only member of the family, including parents and all other children, with this slight, but definite disease. In 1967 Sukla's father told P. Pal that, when she was a child, the pimples left her nose reddish and pockmarked, but that she had not then had any more pimples for several years. However, in 1969, her mother said that she still occasionally suffered from pimples on her nose.

The Case of Swarnlata

Summary of the Case and its Investigation. Swarnlata is the daughter of Sri M. L. Mishra. In 1961 he was assistant in the office of the district inspector of schools, Chhatarpur, Madhya Pradesh. She was born in Shahpur, District Tikamgarh, Madhya Pradesh, on March 2, 1948. When Swarnlata was between three and three and a half years old, her family lived in Panna, also in Madhya Pradesh. Her father took her with him on a trip to Jabalpur, one of the leading cities of the state which lies about 170 miles south of Panna. On the return journey, as they passed through the city of Katni (57 miles north of Jabalpur), Swarnlata unexpectedly asked the driver of the truck they were in to turn down a road toward "my house." A little later, when the group was taking tea in Katni, Swarnlata proposed that they could obtain much better tea at "her" house nearby. These statements puzzled Sri Mishra and the more so when he learned that Swarnlata later told other children of the family further details of a previous life in Katni as a member of a family named Pathak.

After two years of residence in Panna (during much of which time Swarnlata and her mother actually lived in Shahpur with Sri Mishra's parents), the family moved to another town, Nowgong, in the Chhatarpur District, also of Madhya Pradesh. After living approximately five years in Nowgong they moved to Chhatarpur itself. (Chhatarpur is forty miles west of Panna.) During their residence in Nowgong Swarnlata performed for her mother—and then in front of others—unusual dances and songs which she had had no opportunity to learn, so far as her parents knew. During the next few years, Swarnlata revealed fragments of her apparent memories, mostly to her brothers and sisters, but to some extent to her parents. In 1958, Swarnlata, whose family had by this time moved to Chhatarpur, met the wife of Professor R. Agnihotri, who came from the area of Katni and whom Swarnlata claimed to recognize from having known her during the previous life in that city. In this way, Sri Mishra first confirmed the accuracy of some of his daughter's numerous statements about her previous life in Katni. In September, 1958, Sri Mishra wrote down some of Swarnlata's statements. In March, 1959, Sri H. N. Banerjee spent two days in Chhatarpur investigating the case there; he then journeyed to Katni where he became acquainted with the Pathak family of which Swarnlata claimed to have been a member in her previous life. Sri Banerjee noted before going to Katni some nine statements Swarnlata had made about the Pathak residence and which he confirmed on arriving there. Before Sri Banerjee went to Katni the Mishra family did not know about which Pathak family Swarnlata was speaking. Sri Banerjee said he was guided by the statements of Swarnlata in finding the Pathak house. He found that the statements made by Swarnlata corresponded closely with the life of Biya, daughter of a family called Pathak in Katni and deceased wife of Sri Chintamini Pandey of Maihar. Maihar is a town north of Katni. Biya had died in 1939.

In the summer of 1959, members of the Pathak family and of Biya's marital family journeyed to Chhatarpur and were there recognized by Swarnlata under conditions I shall describe below. Shortly after these visits, Swarnlata and members of her family went first to Katni and subsequently to Maihar (and nearby towns) where the deceased Biya had lived much of her married life and where she died. In Maihar, Swarnlata recognized additional people and places and commented on various changes that had occurred since the death of Biya. Sri Mishra made some written records of these recognitions shortly after they occurred. In the summer of 1961, I spent four days in Madhya Pradesh and interviewed a number of people concerned in the case at Chhatarpur, Katni, Sihora, and Jabalpur. Swarnlata had continued to visit Biya's brothers and children, for whom she showed the warmest affection.

Swarnlata made statements of a much more fragmentary nature about another life she believed she had lived subsequent to the life as Biya in Katni. She stated that after she died (in the life as Biya) she was reborn as one Kamlesh in Sylhet, Assam (now in Bangladesh) and that in that life she died as a child of about nine and was then reborn in the Mishra family. Some of the statements made by Swarnlata with regard to this "intermediate life" accord with the geography and other facts of Sylhet. It has not yet been possible, however, to identify a child of this area whose life corresponds with the rather few details given by Swarnlata. (Investigation was hampered by the fact that Sylhet was included in East Pakistan and is now in Bangladesh.)

The songs and dances of Swarnlata apparently belong to the life in Sylhet. The language of the songs was identified as Bengali by Professor Pal, who transcribed some of them for further study. Sylhet is in a Bengali-speaking area whereas in Madhya Pradesh Swarnlata had lived entirely among Hindi-speaking people. I hope to issue a further report on these songs and their linguistic features at a later date.[21] Here I shall focus attention on the life Swarnlata said she lived as Biya in Katni and neighboring towns.

Relevant Facts of Geography and Possible Normal Means of Communication Between the Two Families. The Mishra family have never lived closer to Katni than Panna, which is about a hundred miles away. Katni, Jabalpur, and the towns of Maihar and Sihora, where members of the Pathak family lived, are located in a valley southeast of Panna. That city lies in hills while Chhatarpur is still farther west on the western side of these hills. The distance separating the Katni-Jabalpur and the Panna-Chhatarpur areas is sufficiently great for there to be a distinct difference in the dialect and accent of the two areas. Jabalpur and Katni lie on main line railroads, while railroads do not serve Panna and Chhatarpur. Buses, however, connect all these communities.

The Mishra and Pathak families firmly denied any acquaintance with each other prior to their meeting in connection with the verification of Swarnlata's statements. When Sri Banerjee visited Katni the Pathak family did not know of the Mishra family nor anything about Swarnlata's statements. Nor were they aware of having had any mutual friends with two exceptions.

First, as already noted, the wife of Professor Agnihotri had known Biya in the Maihar-Katni area. But neither Swarnlata nor her family had known the Agnihotri family prior to the time when Swarnlata made her initial statements about Katni. Both Sri M. L. Mishra and Sri Agnihotri stated that the families had never met until an occasion when Sri Agnihotri, having heard of Swarnlata's claims to remember a previous life, invited her and her father to his home to tell some friends of his about the previous life. At that time, Swarnlata learned that Srimati Agnihotri came from the Katni area and asked to see her. Swarnlata's recognition of Srimati Agnihotri then occurred. This happened in July, 1958, when Swarnlata was ten and had already been talking about the previous life for six years.

Secondly, Swarnlata's mother came from Jabalpur. Her maiden name was

[21] See the detailed report on these songs and dances beginning on p. 82.

Pathak, but her family was entirely unrelated to the Pathaks of Katni. These Pathaks (of Katni) do have business interests in Jabalpur and one of Biya's brothers, Sri Hari Prasad Pathak, had some acquaintance with a cousin of Swarnlata's mother, Srimati Mishra. The Mishra family did journey from Panna or Chhatarpur to Jabalpur, passing through Katni, from time to time and it is quite conceivable that Swarnlata picked up some knowledge of the city of Katni during such journeys. For example, the Pathak family was prominent in the area of Katni-Jabalpur and it may be supposed that the location of their house in Katni was widely known there. The same could not be said for the details of the interior of the house, e.g., trees and balconies within the compound. Knowledge of these would be restricted to a smaller group of friends of the Pathaks and knowledge of some details of their personal lives to an even smaller number of persons within the family. Also Swarnlata gave information about the structural details of the house as it was years before she began talking of the previous life. If she did somehow pick up knowledge of the Pathaks, such knowledge must somehow have evaded her parents for they knew nothing of the Pathak family when she first began to talk about the previous life. And as Swarnlata was never away from home except in the company of her parents, it is difficult to imagine how she could have learned about the Pathak family from some informed person if they (her parents) did not also acquire the same information at the same time. I shall return to the discussion of these matters after presenting the statements and recognitions of Swarnlata in detail.

Persons Interviewed During the Investigation. In Chhatarpur I interviewed:

> Swarnlata
> Sri M. L. Mishra, father of Swarnlata
> Sri Krishna Chandra Mishra, brother (three years older) of Swarnlata
> Sri R. P. Sukla, Principal, Maharaja College, Chhatarpur
> Sri B. M. Chaturvedi, Maharaja College, Chhatarpur
> Sri R. S. Mishra, older brother of Sri M. L. Mishra and uncle of Swarnlata

In Katni, I interviewed:

> Sri Hari Prasad Pathak, oldest brother of the deceased Biya, and his wife
> Sri Rajendra Prasad Pathak, second brother of Biya, and his wife
> Sri Brij Kishore Pathak, fourth brother of Biya
> Sri S. L. Koul

In Sihora I interviewed:

> Sri Murli Pandey, son of the deceased Biya
> Srimati Bindi, sister-in-law of Biya

In Jabalpur I interviewed:

> Sri Mahendra Kumar Pathak, son of Sri Rajendra Prasad Pathak and nephew of Biya

In addition, I have had access to extensive correspondence with a number of other persons familiar with the case, e.g., Sri R. Agnihotri. Their testimony, however, has for the most part concerned the *bona fides* of the chief witnesses and other persons connected with the case rather than particular details of the statements and recognitions of Swarnlata. Professor P. Pal made available to me extensive notes of his study of the case in 1963.

Statements and Recognitions Made by Swarnlata. I give next in the tabulation a summary of the statements and recognitions made by Swarnlata with regard to her claim to be Biya reborn.

The tabulation below omits a number of less important statements and recognitions as well as a few statements about which there were discrepancies or gaps in the testimony. Items 1–18 were statements made by Swarnlata in Chhatarpur before any contact between the Mishra and Pathak families had occurred and most of them were written down before verification was attempted; items 19–23 occurred in Chhatarpur when members of the Pathak family or the Pandey family visited the Mishra family; items 24–37 occurred on the occasion of Swarnlata's first visit to Katni in 1959; items 38–46 occurred on a visit by Swarnlata to Maihar and Tilora a few weeks later; items 47–48 occurred on a visit to Jabalpur in 1959; item 49 occurred on another visit to Maihar in 1960.

Relevant Reports and Observations of the Behavior of the People Concerned. The personation of Biya by Swarnlata was not so strong as the personation of other previous personalities by some other children of this type of case. Yet it remains remarkable enough. Her father noted that in Chhatarpur, among the members of her present family, Swarnlata behaved like a child, albeit one more serious and mature than the average child of her age. But at Katni, among the Pathaks, she behaved like an older sister of the house, and this with men forty or more years her senior, as the Pathak brothers were. They, moreover, completely accepted her as Biya reborn. She and the Pathak brothers engaged in the Hindu custom of Rakhi, in which sisters and brothers annually exchange gifts and renew their devotion to each other. When I visited Katni in 1961 I found Sri Brij Kishore Pathak distressed and even angry because Swarnlata had missed the Rakhi ceremony the previous year. He said she had lived in

TABULATION

Summary of Statements and Recognitions Made by Swarnlata

Item	Informants	Verification	Comments
1. She belonged to a family named Pathak in Katni.	M. L. Mishra, father of Swarnlata	Rajendra Prasad Pathak, brother of Biya	The Pathak family of Katni had a sister, Biya, who died in 1939.
2. She had two sons, Krishna Datta and Shiva Datta.	M. L. Mishra	Murli Pandey, son of Biya	Biya had two sons named Murli and Naresh. A near miss, possibly through association. Murli is another name for Krishna, rather as Peggy is another name for Margaret. Krishna Datta was the name of Biya's brother-in-law, who died less than a month after Murli was born. Biya's father-in-law was called Shankara Datta, which is another name for Shiva Datta. Swarnlata later recalled the names correctly. See notes about the recognition of these sons below.
3. Her name had been Kamlesh.	M. L. Mishra	Incorrect	Swarnlata seemed to be mixing different memories. Later these separated and she said she had been called Kamlesh in a life in Sylhet, Assam (now Bangladesh).
4. Her name had been Biya.	Krishna Chandra, brother of Swarnlata	Rajendra Prasad Pathak	
5. The head of the family was Sri Hira Lal Pathak.	M. L. Mishra	Incorrect	Biya's father was Sri Chhikori Lal Pathak; her oldest brother and the head of the family when she died was Sri Hari Prasad Pathak. The name Swarnlata gave seems to have derived from a fusion of the names of Biya's father and brother.
6. The Pathak house was white.	M. L. Mishra		The house and surroundings were examined by me. Items 6–14 also verified by Rajendra Prasad Pathak. Swarnlata was correct on all these items.

Item	Informants	Verification	Comments
7. The house had four stuccoed rooms, but other parts were less well finished.	M. L. Mishra	Same as item 6	Since the death of Biya the house had been considerably enlarged and improved. This statement was true of the house as it was when Biya was alive eighteen years earlier.
8. The doors were black.	M. L. Mishra	Same as item 6	
9. The doors were fitted with iron bars.	M. L. Mishra	Same as item 6	
10. The front floor of the house was of stone slabs.	M. L. Mishra	Same as item 6	
11. The family had a motor car.	M. L. Mishra	Same as item 6	A rare possession in India in the 1950's, and even more so in the 1930's.
12. There was a girls' school behind the house.	M. L. Mishra	Same as item 6	The school was located about one hundred yards from the back of the property. Not visible from the street on which the Pathak house is located.
13. A railway line could be seen from the house.	M. L. Mishra	Same as item 6	Across the road in front of the property.
14. Lime furnaces were visible from the house.	M. L. Mishra	Same as item 6	The lime furnaces were on the land adjoining the property. The description of the house and its location given by Swarnlata, i.e., items 6, 13, 14, enabled Sri H. N. Banerjee to find the house without help when he went to Katni in March, 1959.
15. Her family lived in Zhurkutia Mohalla.	M. L. Mishra	M. L. Mishra Murli Pandey	"Mohalla" means district of a city. The district where the Pathak house is located was formerly known as Zharratikuria. Thus Swarnlata had the name slightly off. Testimony of Sri Murli Pandey was obtained by Prof. P. Pal.

73

Item	Informants	Verification	Comments
16. She had had pain in her throat, and had died of throat disease.	M. L. Mishra	Incorrect	According to Sri Rajendra Prasad Pathak, Biya had had some trouble in her throat and had been treated for this. She died some months later of heart disease, and Swarnlata was therefore mistaken about this detail. The apparent memories of many cases of the reincarnation type include details of the last days or months of the life of the previous personality. The cases of Ravi Shankar, Parmod, and Sukla also illustrate this tendency.
17. Dr. S. C. Bhabrat of Napiertown, Jabalpur, had treated her.	M. L. Mishra	Murli Pandey gave the name of the doctor who treated Biya as S. E. Barat. He had accompanied his mother to the doctor in Jabalpur.	The discrepancy in the name of the physician may be due to an error in my transcription of the spoken names or to a deficiency of memory on the part of Swarnlata or Sri Mishra.
18. She had once gone to a wedding at Tilora village with Srimati Agnihotri and they had difficulty in finding a latrine.	M. L. Mishra Krishna Chandra	M. L. Mishra Krishna Chandra	Sri M. L. Mishra was a thirdhand witness of this item. Swarnlata reminded Srimati Agnihotri about this episode. Srimati Agnihotri told Srimati Mishra about this statement of Swarnlata and its accuracy. Srimati Mishra then told her husband. Swarnlata also told Krishna Chandra about the episode.
19. Recognition of Sri Hari Prasad Pathak, brother of Biya.	M. L. Mishra Hari Prasad Pathak, brother of Biya	M. L. Mishra Prasad Pathak, brother of Biya	Sri Hari Prasad Pathak arrived unannounced at the Mishra home in Chhatarpur. He did not introduce himself to Sri Mishra. Swarnlata at first called him Hira Lal Pathak, but recognized him as her younger brother. Then she called him correctly "Babu," the name by which Biya had known him.
20. Recognition of Sri Chintamini Pandey, husband of Biya.	Murli Pandey M. L. Mishra		Sri Chintamini Pandey and his son Murli arrived in Chhatarpur and concealed their identities from residents of that

20. (continued)

Item			Comments
			A meeting was arranged at which Swarnlata was asked to name the people present. The two anonymous visitors were present with nine other men from Chhatarpur, some known and some unknown to Swarnlata. When she came to Sri Chintamini Pandey, she said she knew him in Katni and Maihar and looked bashful as Hindu wives do in the presence of their husbands. She also recognized Sri Chintamini Pandey in a group photograph of nine people taken forty years earlier.
21. Recognition of Sri Murli Pandey, son of Biya.	Murli Pandey M. L. Mishra		Conditions as in item 20 except that Murli tried to mislead Swarnlata and for almost twenty-four hours insisted against her objections that he was not Murli, but someone else.
22. Non-recognition of stranger unknown to Biya.	Murli Pandey		Conditions as in items 20–21. Murli had brought along a friend of about the same age as his brother Naresh and tried unsuccessfully to persuade Swarnlata that this friend was Biya's son Naresh.
23. Sri Chintamini Pandey took 1200 rupees from a box in which she had kept money.	Murli Pandey	Murli Pandey	Mentioned by Swarnlata to Sri Chintamini Pandey who later told his son, and also stated that no one except Biya (his wife) and himself knew about his having taken this money. There was a discrepancy of 200 rupees between the amount remembered by Swarnlata as having been taken and the amount Biya's husband acknowledged taking. Sri Murli Pandey was a secondhand witness of this item.
24. Recognition of Sri Rajendra Prasad Pathak, brother of Biya.	Rajendra Prasad Pathak		Correctly assigned his place as second brother by Swarnlata.

75

Item	Informants	Verification	Comments
25. Recognition of Sri Vishwambar Prasad Pathak, brother of Biya.	Rajendra Prasad Pathak		Correctly placed by Swarnlata as the third brother.
26. Recognition of Sri Brij Kishore Pathak, brother of Biya.	Rajendra Prasad Pathak Brij Kishore Pathak, brother of Biya.		Correctly placed by Swarnlata as the youngest brother.
27. Recognition of the wife of Sri Rajendra Prasad Pathak.	Wife of Rajendra Prasad Pathak		Correctly placed by Swarnlata as the wife of younger brother.
28. Recognition of female servant of family.	Rajendra Prasad Pathak Krishna Chandra		The recognition was expressed when Swarnlata said: "She is my servant."
29. Recognition of family cowherd.	Brij Kishore Pathak Krishna Chandra		Presented to Swarnlata as a specially difficult test in recognition. Sri Brij Kishore Pathak also tried to persuade Swarnlata unsuccessfully that the cowherd had died.
30. Recognition of Sri B. N. Chaturvedi, friend of Pathak family.	M. L. Mishra Krishna Chandra		Swarnlata further commented on the fact that he was wearing spectacles, which he had not worn when Biya was alive.
31. Recognition of Sri Chaturvedi's wife.	Rajendra Prasad Pathak		Swarnlata called her by an appropriate familiar name, "Bhoujai."
32. Inquiring about neem tree formerly in the compound of the house.	Rajendra Prasad Pathak	Rajendra Prasad Pathak	There had been a neem tree in the compound, but a few months before Swarnlata's visit it had been blown down in a storm and removed.
33. Inquiring about a parapet at back of the house.	Rajendra Prasad Pathak	Rajendra Prasad Pathak	This parapet had been removed since Biya's death.
34. Non-acceptance of suggestion that Biya had lost her teeth, and statement	Rajendra Prasad Pathak M. L. Mishra	Rajendra Prasad Pathak M. L. Mishra	Sri M. L. Mishra said that Sri Brij Kishore Pathak tried to deceive Swarnlata by saying (falsely) that Biya had lost her

76

that she had had gold nails n her front teeth.		teeth. Swarnlata denied this and insisted she had had gold fillings in her front teeth. The Pathak brothers could not remember this and consulted their wives, who verified Swarnlata's statement as true of Biya. Sri M. L. Mishra was a second-hand witness of this item.
35. Recognition of a betelnut seller.	S. L. Koul, betelnut seller	This man was picked out of a crowd and identified by his occupation by Swarnlata.
36. Biya's father wore a turban.	M. L. Mishra	Sri Chhikori Lal Pathak had worn a turban, not a particularly common form of headdress in that part of India. Swarnlata was shown a cap and hat and asked which one her father wore. She replied that he wore neither, but a turban.
	M. L. Mishra (not independently verified by Pathak family)	
37. Recognition of bara as the favorite sweet of Biya.	Rajendra Prasad Pathak	This food was unknown to the Mishras. Swarnlata herself had never tasted it, but when given it at Katni said: "I used to eat this in my previous life."
	Rajendra Prasad Pathak	
38. Recognition of the sister of Biya's husband.	Murli Pandey Bindi, sister of Biya's husband	Sri Murli Pandey was a secondhand witness. Srimati Bindi stated that she was instantly recognized by Swarnlata. As Swarnlata entered the kitchen Srimati Bindi said: "Do you know me?" To this Swarnlata correctly replied: "You are my husband's sister."
39. Biya had another sister-in-law who had died before Biya.	Murli Pandey	Sri Murli Pandey was a secondhand witness of this statement.
40. Recognition of Biya's room in house in Maihar.	Murli Pandey	

Item	Informants	Verification	Comments
41. Recognition of a road to a river for bathing at Maihar.	Murli Pandey		
42. Recognition of Sri Kedarnath Pandey, cousin of Sri Chintamini Pandey.	Murli Pandey		Correctly identified as Sri Murli Pandey's uncle from a crowd of about forty persons. Items 42–44 occurred when Swarnlata was asked to go round a group of people seated in a room and recognize them one by one.
43. Recognition of another of Biya's sisters-in-law.	Murli Pandey		Recognized as "sister." The person recognized was the wife of Biya's brother-in-law.
44. Recognition of midwife.	Murli Pandey Krishna Chandra		Identified also as the mother of a man dead many years. Swarnlata gave his name. At this time the midwife was known by another name, but had formerly been known in connection with the deceased son as Swarnlata addressed her.
45. Recognition of rooms in house at Tilora.	Murli Pandey		Swarnlata identified the room where Biya had died.
46. Recognition of absence of verandah in house at Tilora.	Murli Pandey		The verandah had been removed since Biya had died.
47. Recognition of Sri M. K. Pathak, son of Sri Rajendra Prasad Pathak.	M. K. Pathak, son of Sri Rajendra Prasad Pathak		As they entered his house in Jabalpur, Sri R. P. Pathak pointed to his son and asked Swarnlata: "Who is that?" She immediately replied "Baboo," which was the pet name by which Sri M. K. Pathak was called in the family.

48. Recognition of wife of Sri Hari Prasad Pathak.	M. K. Pathak Wife of Sri Hari Prasad Pathak	Swarnlata recognized her as "brother's wife."
19. Recognition of Biya's other son, Naresh.	Murli Pandey	Sri Murli Pandey again tried to mislead Swarnlata by saying that Naresh was someone else called Bhola. Swarnlata insisted he was Naresh.

their family for forty years and with the Mishras only about ten, so he felt they had the greater claim on her! Such was the strength of the acceptance by the Pathaks of Swarnlata's claim to be Biya reborn. It is perhaps worth noting that the Pathaks are (among Indian families) rather "Westernized." Sri R. P. Pathak stated that he had had no convictions whatever about reincarnation prior to Swarnlata's visit, which had quite changed his mind.

Swarnlata modified her behavior with Biya's children according to those present. If parents or elders of her present family were around she was reserved. But Sri Murli Pandey reported that if Swarnlata was alone with him or his brother, she relaxed and treated them familiarly as a mother would. He was thirteen years old when Biya died and was thirty-five in 1961. Yet he did not find this behavior inappropriate because he too believed that his mother had been reborn. Sri Murli Pandey also had not believed in reincarnation until he met and observed Swarnlata.

Swarnlata exhibited strong emotion and wept when seeing or parting from members of the Pathak family. She even became sad and tearful when she thought about Katni, and when she talked with me in 1961 about the previous life her eyes brimmed with tears. When she sat alone she sometimes remembered the life in Katni. At times she wished she could return to stay there and this made her sad. In general, however, she felt devoted to the Mishra family and her loyalties seemed much less split than were those, for example, of Prakash and Jasbir. According to her older brother, Krishna Chandra, in 1961 Swarnlata talked less spontaneously about the previous life than she used to do. But her impressions of the life of Biya seemed not to be fading as do the similar images of most children of this type. A possible reason for this may lie in the complete tolerance and acceptance of her experiences by members of her present family. Swarnlata's parents at first delayed any attempt at verification and they did not find the publicity that had come their way of any help. But they felt blessed to have an intelligent, devout, and devoted daughter and, in contrast to the families of some of the other children, they did nothing to suppress Swarnlata's statements or her participation, when opportunity afforded, in friendships with the Pathak family.

Comments on the Evidence of Paranormal Knowledge on the Part of Swarnlata. As already mentioned, there is a slight possibility that Swarnlata and the Mishras may have known some few facts unconsciously absorbed about the Pathak family in Katni. The Pathak family of Katni (with members and a branch of their business in Jabalpur) was well known in the area and public items of information about them could easily have been picked up. There is no evidence that Swarnlata or her family did acquire any such knowledge, but we cannot exclude this possibility. The strength of paranormal explanations then seems to rest on (*a*) Swarnlata's knowledge of details of the family and the house which would not be in the public domain, e.g., the fact that Biya had gold fillings in her front teeth, a detail even Biya's brothers had forgotten; (*b*) her recognitions of members of the Pathak and Pandey families; and (*c*) her knowledge of the former (as opposed to the present) appearances of places and people. If we count her witnessed recognitions of people alone (not places), these amount to twenty in number. If we believe the witnesses who have been carefully questioned, most of these recognitions occurred in such a way that Swarnlata was obliged to give a name or state a relationship between Biya and the person in question. It was not a question of "Am I your son?" but of "Tell me who I am." And on several occasions serious attempts were made to mislead her or deny that she gave the correct answers. And her recognitions usually came quickly.

In judging various possibilities, we may consider first that of a rather widespread conspiracy among all the witnesses, especially the Mishras, Pathaks, and Pandeys. But a family of prominence, with extensive business interests such as the Pathaks have, is not going to participate in a hoax to which a large number of false witnesses would have to subscribe, any one of whom might later defect. If a hoax has occurred in this case, it must have come from the Chhatarpur side. Nothing I learned about the character of Sri M. L. Mishra among people who knew him in Chhatarpur gave grounds for any suspicion whatever that he had perpetrated a hoax. According to his own statement, he doubted for a long time the authenticity or veridicality of his daughter's statements, and he made no move to verify them for more than six years. When Sri Banerjee visited the area of the case in 1959, he indicated a wish to observe personally any recognitions of the Pathak family on the part of Swarnlata. He was therefore chagrined when the two families got together without notifying him so he could be present. In a letter to me of August 6, 1962, Sri Mishra stated that he did not want Sri Banerjee present because he feared Swarnlata would not accomplish the recognitions and that this would publicly embarrass him. We can suppose that if he had contemplated some gain to himself from fraud, he would have wished to involve independent witnesses to lend support and fame to the case.

But even supposing an attempt at fraud, we have next to ask ourselves whether someone could have tutored Swarnlata for such recognitions. We cannot say it could not have been done, but no one can imagine that it could be done easily or quickly. Then we have to ask ourselves who could take the time to do it. Sri M. L. Mishra, apart from Swarnlata, was the only member of the family who received some public attention, not always welcome by his account, from Swarnlata's case. If he got up a hoax he would have had to involve both his oldest son and Swarnlata and have risked their betrayal. We would also have to ask, for this theory, where Sri Mishra could have obtained some of the highly personal information possessed by Swarnlata about the private affairs of the Pathaks, e.g., the taking by Biya's husband of her 1200 rupees, or the incident at the wedding party with Srimati Agnihotri.

One may ask whether Swarnlata might have been tutored by some stranger who knew Katni and the Pathaks. But who could he have been and, even more important, how could he have obtained access to Swarnlata? Like all children in India, especially girls, Swarnlata's movements were controlled carefully by her family. She was never out on the street unaccompanied and she never saw strangers in the house alone. What would have been the venue of trysts for secret tutorials on the Pathaks? This suggestion also falls from its absurdity.

The Songs and Dances of Swarnlata. As already mentioned, Swarnlata performed unfamiliar dances and sang songs in a language incomprehensible to her parents. She was between five and six years old when she first demonstrated these and thus did not do so until more than a year after she had first talked about the previous life lived at Katni, which she had done when she was about three and a half.[22]

Swarnlata always performed the songs and dances together, never one without the other. It was as if she had learned them together and could not (or did not care to) separate them from each other. Professor P. Pal shared this impression because on a visit he made to Swarnlata and her family in 1963 he observed "she had difficulty in recollecting the words of the songs without performing the dances." She preserved the ability to perform these songs and dances up to 1971 when she graciously consented to perform for me. Although unable to understand the language of the songs, I was much impressed by her voice and the skill of her dancing. Her father, who observed this performance with me, said that it was invariably the same and that Swarnlata had forgotten nothing of what she had originally performed many years earlier. Professor Pal was a more important observer of these aspects of the performance and he wrote me that "the tunes appeared to be correct and the postures appropriate and attractive." Swarnlata repeated her performance for him three times so that he could transcribe the songs.

Professor Pal, who is a native of Bengal, identified the songs as Bengali and upon returning to his home in West Bengal he learned that two of them derived from poems by Rabindranath Tagore. The third song, also definitely Bengali, was by some minor poet whom Professor Pal could not identify.

[22] The estimates of Swarnlata's father, Sri M. L. Mishra, about her age when she first performed the songs and dances varied. In one statement written closer to the time of the event, that is about 1961, he said she was seven years old at the time. But this would still be within the period when the family lived at Nowgong and before they moved to Chhatarpur.

The poems by Tagore were "Pōush Tōder Dak Diyecche," and "Ōre Grihabāsi, Khōl Dūar Khōl." Professor Pal later visited the Visva-Bharati, an institution (in Santiniketan, West Bengal) founded by Tagore, where he attended a performance of one of the songs of Swarnlata's repertoire. This was a song of spring, the second of the two whose titles I have given. He noted that the music at this performance was "very much the same" as that of Swarnlata's rendition of the same song. Swarnlata's other identified song was a harvest song by Tagore.

The text of Swarnlata's songs, when compared to the original words of Tagore's two poems, showed a close similarity, but with some deviations. I will next give the transcription of the songs made by Professor Pal together with (for the two songs by Tagore) the original version of the poems and an English translation in prose furnished by Professor Pal.

A Harvest Song

Original Poem by Tagore	*As Sung by Swarnlata*
Pōush Tōder Dak Diyechhe, Āy Re Chale	Pōsheta Dāk Diyechhe Āyre Chute
Āy Āy Āy	Āy Āy Āy
Dālā Je Tār Bharechhe Āj Pākā Fasale,	Dālā Ji Āj Bharachhi Tāy Pākā Fasale
Mari Hāy Hāy Hāy	Ki Mari Hāy Hāy Hāy
Haowār Nesāy Uthla Mete Dik	Māthe Bānsi Shune Shune Ākās
Badhurā Dhāner Khete	Kesi Hōlō
Rōder Sōna Chhariye Pare Matir Ānchale,	Gharethe Mā Ke Elō Balō
Mari Hāy Hāy Hāy	Khōlō Khōlō Duār Khōlō
Māther Bānsi Shune Shune Ākās	Khōlō Duār Khōlō
Khusi Hōlō	Hāoyer Nishāy Uth Na Mithel
Gharete Āj Ke Rabe Gō, Khōlō	Dekhbo Mōrā Dhāner Shishe
Duār Khōlō	Rōda Sōna Chhariya Pare Ājio
Alōr Hānsi Uthlō Jege Dhāner	Chhale
Sishe Sisir Lege	Ki Mari Hāy Hāy Hāy
Dharār Khusi Dhare Na Gō, Ai Je Uthale	
Mari Hāy Hāy Hāy	

English Translation:
Poush [23] calls you. Come away, Come, Come, Come. Her basket is overflowing with ripe grains. Oh, Oh, Oh, The fairies are reveling in the paddy

---

[23] Poush is the tenth month of the Hindu Calendar. It comes approximately at the time of the month of December in the Western Calendar. This is the season for harvesting paddy in Bengal.

fields intoxicated with the wintry breeze. The golden sunbeams have spread over the skirt of the earth. Look how beautiful it is.

The sky is delighted hearing the notes of the field flutes. Who would stay indoors today? Unbolt your door. The smile of the sunbeams is kindled in the dew drops on the sheafs of paddy. The earth is overflowing with joy. Oh, Oh, Oh,

A Spring Song

Original Poem by Tagore	*As Sung by Swarnlata*
Ōre Grihabāsi Khōl Dūar Khōl,	Ōre Giōbāsi, Khōl Duār Khōl
Lāglō Je Dōl	Lāglō Je Dōlnā
Sthale Jale Banatale Lāglō	Thale Jale Banatale Lāglō
Je Dōl	Je Dōlnā
Dūar Khōl, Duār Khōl	Rāngā Hāsi Hāsi Rāsi Ansuki
Rāngā Hāsi Rāsi Rāsi Asoke	Palāshi
Palāshe	Rāngā Mengā Mengā Mesā Pōese
Rāngā Neshā Meghe Meshā	Ākāsi
Prōvat Ākāshey	Nabin Pātāy Lāgi Nabin Pātāy
Nabin Pātāy Lāge Rāngā	Lāgi Bande Bi Dullal
Hillōl	Khul Duār Khul Ōre Giōbāsi
Duār Khōl, Duār Khōl	Lāglō Je Dōlnā.
Benubōn Marmare Dōle Ghāse	
Ghāse	
Mōu Māchi Fire Yāchi Fuler	
Dakhinā	
Pākhāy Bājāy Tār Bhikhārir	
Bīnā,	
Mādhabi Bitāne Bāyu Gandhey	
Bivol	
Duār Khōl, Duār Khōl	

English Translation:

Oh you house dweller—open the doors of your houses. The spring breeze is rocking lands, waters, and the forests. Open out your doors! Open out your doors! Bunches of red flowers of Ashoka and Palash trees are like smiles on red lips. There is a red tinge of intoxication in the faces of clouds in the morning sky. There is a reddish wave of joy in the new foliage. Open out your doors! Open out your doors! The tall grasses are waving to the tune of the murmur of bamboo groves. The bees solicit favor from the flowers. The murmur of their wings is like the tune of the beggar's fiddle. In the Madhabi Creeper grove the breeze is overwhelmed with fragrance. Open your doors! Open your doors!

Another Spring Song (Source Not Identified)

As Sung by Swarnlata
Bhōmrā Āy Āyre Mahua Bōne
Jhumur Jhumur Neche Pākhā Pākhā Āy
Āpni Mōne Bhōmra Āy Āyre Mahuā Bōne,
Fuler Savāy Lāglō Pireet
Sudur Bōnā Benu Bāje Ki Reet
Bana Pari Hāy Nupur Bājāy
Apsu Makha Ai Ankher Kōne

English Translation:
Come thou black bee to the Mahua forest, thy dancing wings emitting a jingling sound. Come thou of thine own accord to the Mahua forest. There is love in the gathering of flowers. How sweet the bamboo whistles in the distant forest. The forest fairy jingles the bells tied to her feet with eyes moistened with tears.

Concerning Swarnlata's deviations from the original poems by Tagore, Professor Pal made the following comment in his report:

Some of the words are blurred, modified, or changed by Swarnlata, though the sound, meter, and tune are maintained fairly intact, just as would happen to someone who does not understand English, but learns an English song sung by an English singer from his singing. The original singer might also have deviated from the original song at places as is sometimes done by singers.

Professor Pal also observed that Swarnlata's dances accompanying the spring song were of the Santiniketan style which he had himself observed during his visit to the Visva-Bharati. This disposes of the possible objection that Swarnlata learned the songs by hearing them alone and then *ad hoc* applied to her singing of them dances which she made up but which did not in fact appropriately suit the songs.

Swarnlata said that she had learned the songs and dances from a friend, Madhu, during the previous life she remembered living as Kamlesh at Sylhet. I should remind readers here that none of her statements about the life in Sylhet have been verified. Her account of the life does, however, contain numerous plausible features, e.g., accurate details of geography. Her claim with regard to the opportunities for learning and speaking Bengali in Sylhet is quite reasonable. Although Sylhet is near Assam, the people of the area speak Bengali predominantly. (The names given by Swarnlata among the memories of that life, e.g., Kamlesh, are unusual for a Bengali family, but even if the previous family had been of another stock its members might well have had Bengali friends and been able to speak Bengali.) Moreover, Professor Pal learned that before the partition of India some of the children of well-to-do families in Sylhet had studied at the Visva-Bharati in Santiniketan, West Bengal. An annual Spring Festival is held there every year and on this occasion the Tagore spring song (one of those performed by Swarnlata) is invariably performed with dancing by a troupe of girls. It is, therefore, altogether reasonable to suppose that Kamlesh, the previous personality to whom Swarnlata referred, learned these Tagore songs in Bengali from a friend who had learned them at the Visva-Bharati itself or possibly elsewhere.

We come now to the question of whether Swarnlata could have learned these songs and dances normally before the age of (about) five when she first performed them. Through correspondence with members of the staff of Visva-Bharati, which held the copyright for the songs by Tagore, I learned something about their availability to the general public. This institution had given permission for the use of the songs in films, on the radio, and on phonograph records. From the Gramophone Company of India I learned that one of the songs had been released on a record in 1940 and the other in 1947, although this second record was cancelled in 1949. It would be well to assume that the songs could be available in films, on the radio, and on phonograph records in India during the period of Swarnlata's infancy and early childhood. She was born in March, 1948, and first performed the dances sometime before or around her sixth birthday say in March, 1954.

As I explained above, during the first several years of Swarnlata's life she and her family lived in Shahpur (District Tikamgarh) where she had been born. They then moved first to a town called Panna, where they remained about two years and then to another town called Nowgong, in the Chhatarpur District. All these places are in Madhya Pradesh, a Hindi-speaking state of central northern India. When M. L. Mishra was stationed in government service in Panna, Swarnlata lived with him there only a short time. The rest of the two years he was at Panna Swarnlata spent with her mother living at Shahpur with Sri Mishra's parents. The family was living in Nowgong when Swarnlata first performed the songs and dances. They remained in Nowgong for another five or so years and then moved to Chhatarpur when Swarnlata was approximately ten years old. (I met them, both in 1961 and in 1971, in Chhatarpur.) During all these years Swarnlata was with one or both of her parents except for one period of a few months when she lived with her maternal grandparents in Jabalpur, also in Madhya Pradesh. She was then about three and a half years old.

The Mishras owned no phonograph or radio until Swarnlata was about eight years old, that is, until about three years after her first performance of the songs and dances. (They then acquired a radio but still had no

phonograph.) She had never been to a moving picture theater so far as
Sri M. L. Mishra knew, until after she had first performed the dances. He
was quite positive that neither he nor his wife had taken her to one. (In
fact in those days there was no moving picture theater in Shahpur,
Nowgong, or Panna.) He could not assert with complete knowledge that
her maternal grandparents had not taken her to one during the few months
she spent with them in Jabalpur, although he thought this unlikely. This
would have occurred, if it did, about a year or more before Swarnlata
performed the songs and dances for the first time before her family. But
even if Swarnlata's grandparents had taken her to a moving picture theater
in Jabalpur, it is unlikely that they would have gone to see a Bengali
moving picture. These are only rarely shown in the Hindi-speaking areas of
India for the obvious reason that the mass of the Hindi-speaking people
could not follow the language of the films. And Bengali songs, such as
those of Tagore, would only be included in Bengali moving pictures.

There remains the possibility that Swarnlata might have learned the
Bengali songs and dances from some Bengali-speaking persons who were
perhaps friends of the family. There were a few Bengalis living in the areas
of Panna and Nowgong, but none were friends of the Mishra family before
the time of Swarnlata's first performance of her songs and dances. It is
unthinkable, given the circumstances of Indian life, that Swarnlata could
have somehow gone to the home of Bengali-speaking persons and learned
the songs and dances there without her visits being known to her parents.

That Swarnlata's parents themselves had a scanty knowledge of Bengali
is shown by the fact that as late as 1963 they still thought that her songs
were perhaps in Assamese, an inference they made from the fact that Sylhet,
where Swarnlata said she had learned the songs, is in northern Bangladesh,
and was in Assam. (There are Assamese-speaking people in the area, but
Assamese is a language distinct from Bengali, although related.) Earlier a
Bengali-speaking person whom they knew in Chhatarpur had said the
language of the songs was "impure Bengali." And a Bengali-speaking person in Nowgong had identified the language as Bengali. Yet they persisted
in thinking that the language of the songs Swarnlata was singing was
perhaps Assamese.

Additional factors make it improbable, if not impossible, that Swarnlata
learned the songs and dances normally. First, the discrepancies between
her songs and the original poems by Tagore would probably not have occurred if she had learned the songs directly from a person thoroughly
acquainted with them. The discrepancies ·make more sense if we accept
Swarnlata's account that Kamlesh, the previous personality whose life she
claimed she was remembering, had learned them from a friend (Madhu)
who had herself presumably been given proper instruction perhaps at the
Visva-Bharati. Distortions could thus have occurred either in the transmis-

sion from the friend to Kamlesh or in the transfer of the memories from Kamlesh to Swarnlata, however that may have occurred.

Secondly, the songs and dances are skills and skills can only be acquired by practice.[24] I do not believe that Swarnlata could have acquired her knowledge of these songs and dances by merely observing them passively as performed by others whether in moving pictures, or on radio broadcasts or phonograph records. (I am here assuming that despite all the evidence to the contrary, she somehow had managed to observe performances of the songs and dances before she herself performed them.) She must have herself practiced the songs and dances before she could have reached the skill in them she showed on the very first occasion when she revealed her ability to perform them to her family. In considering her performance as the expression of a skill, I am referring as much to the memories she showed of the songs and dances as to the fact that the songs were in Bengali. Hindi and Bengali are both Indo-European languages of Sanskritic origin. They are about as far apart as say Swedish and Norwegian and, at least to some extent, mutually intelligible to educated speakers. The important point of the songs being in Bengali therefore is that it seems improbable that Swarnlata could have heard them performed by living performers in the part of India where she lived since there were so few Bengali-speaking persons there and none on terms of friendship with her parents.

My own conclusion is that Swarnlata's songs and dances belong to the paranormal components of the case and are among its strongest features.

I should add that Swarnlata exhibited in these songs only a recitative xenoglossy. Professor Pal spoke Bengali to her in an effort to test her understanding of the language, but found that she could not understand it. She could not translate the songs she sang into Hindi for her family.

The Later Development of Swarnlata. I did not meet Swarnlata between August, 1961, and November, 1971. During this period, however, I exchanged letters with her and with her father from time to time. As I remained in touch with them through this means the elapse of ten years did not seem to interfere with our having a most friendly reunion when she and her family welcomed me to Chhatarpur in 1971. Swarnlata was then twenty-three years old. Subsequently Swarnlata wrote me a long letter (in August, 1972) clarifying certain points concerning her experiences and I have drawn on this in the following report.

She had done well in her studies. She graduated first with a B.Sc. degree

---

[24] For an exposition of my agreement with Polanyi that a skill can only be acquired with practice and my agreement with Ducasse that a skill cannot be transmitted by extrasensory perception between living persons, see I. Stevenson. "Xenoglossy: A Review and Report of a Case." *Proc.* A.S.P.R., Vol. 31, 1974, 1–268. (Also published by the University Press of Virginia, Charlottesville, 1974.)

in 1967 and then went on to obtain an M.Sc. in 1969, with distinction, in botany. In 1971 she held a position as Lecturer in Botany at the degree (community) college in Chhatarpur. She was ambitious to continue in graduate studies toward a Ph.D. degree, but was handicapped by the small number of fellowships available for the support of advanced studies in India.

In the ten years since I had seen her, Swarnlata had grown into a handsome woman of rather grave and perhaps slightly sad demeanor. She said very little spontaneously during the several hours I spent with the family, but I think this was due to the shyness many Indian women show toward men who are not members of their immediate family—and toward many who are. At her father's request she graciously demonstrated one of the Bengali songs and dances which she said she had learned in the life of Sylhet. Although I had not seen her perform these before, her father said that the performance was always the same and that she had forgotten nothing of what she first showed her mother many years ago when she was between five and six years old.

When I asked Swarnlata whether she had preserved the memories of the previous life which she had as a child, she said that she had forgotten nothing. In the above mentioned letter she wrote: "Letters or persons coming to me from Katni make me remember events of the previous life [there]. Sometimes when I sing the songs of life at Sylhet, I remember the environment of that place. . . . When I am absorbed in either of the past lives I forget the existence of the present life, but this is only for a short while and I again return to the present circumstances. . . . When I desire to have a particular thing that I do not have then in my mind the [related] event of the past life creeps in and thus I am satisfied that I did have this particular thing in my previous life. . . . In short, environment is the greatest factor to remember the past lives." [25] Swarnlata's attitude toward the memories of objects, e.g., of luxury, owned in the previous life is the opposite of that shown by many subjects who remember previous lives in better socio-economic circumstances than their own. They often grumble and scold or deride their parents for their poverty; Swarnlata, on the contrary, found the memories of the circumstances of the previous lives reassuring and that they assuaged any sense of current deprivation she might feel.

She continued to visit the Pathaks and met them about once a year. She still participated with the brothers of Biya in the annual Rakhi ceremony. In her letter (mentioned above) she wrote: "I share with them [the Pathaks at Katni] in their pleasure and pain. . . . I am sometimes a bit worried

---

[25] I have altered the order of parts of this quotation and slightly edited the letter, without changing the meaning, in order to make it easier for the reader to follow Swarnlata's statements.

when I do not receive any news . . . from their end." In the same letter Swarnlata also described an instance of extrasensory perception concerning a member of the Pathak family. She wrote: "Recently I had a dream that my [previous] brother Sri Hari Prasad Pathak (Biya's oldest brother) was leaving the house [at Katni] and was in an abnormal mood. After a week I heard that he was dead and I went to Katni to mourn his death. On this occasion all the events of the past life were fresh to me."

Swarnlata's father thought he might arrange a marriage for her in 1972 and that if he did so, he would consult the Pathak family about the marriage. Swarnlata had expressed herself as agreeable to marrying, but hoped also that she could continue her graduate studies. In 1973 I received a letter from Swarnlata's father announcing her marriage on May 27, 1973.

At my meeting with Swarnlata's family in 1971 her father told me that several other members of the family had also remembered previous lives. He said that in 1961 he had not mentioned these other cases to me because he knew I had come to Chhatarpur to study Swarnlata's case and he did not wish to distract attention from my planned work on her case. In 1971, however, he summarized for me some of the other cases in his family. He and his wife, Savitri Devi, had eight children. Of these, six had had some memories of previous lives, although none had remembered so much detail as Swarnlata. (In addition, at least three members of older generations of the family, including H. L. Mishra himself, had also had some memories of previous lives.) It seems that after listening to the recitals of several of his children about previous lives, H. L. Mishra had heard enough about these and so he suppressed one of his daughters, Snehlata, from saying what she wanted to tell the family about *her* previous life! Consequently little is known of it. Four of the other children, however, had memories of previous lives as persons related in one way or another to H. L. Mishra or his wife. (Swarnlata had also said she had been together in a previous life with one of her sisters, but she either did not specify which one or the detail had been forgotten.)

It became obvious to me that one could spend several days in Chhatarpur solely occupied in studying these other cases in the Mishra family. I hope that I and my colleagues in India can investigate them more fully in the future. It seems to me that they deserve mention here because I believe there are many more cases in India (and other countries) in which a child remembers some (or maybe many) details of a previous life, but because the case lacks sensational features such as a murder, or because the parents have no wish to pursue the matter or become involved in any publicity, the child's statements are ignored and he gradually forgets whatever he remembered. Investigations in India during recent years have shown several families with more than one child remembering a previous life and also with the previous personality being another member of the same family.

Although in the majority of the Indian cases presently known to me the subject is *not* a member of the family of the previous personality, we are still restricted to the study of cases reported to us more or less spontaneously. A more thorough investigation, perhaps a systematic search for cases in a predetermined sample—for example, in a whole village or small town—might well show a much higher incidence in India of cases in which the subject and previous personality are members of the same family than we find in the cases as presently obtained.

The Case of Ravi Shankar

Summary of the Case and its Investigation. On January 19, 1951, Ashok Kumar, familiarly called Munna, the six-year-old son of Sri Jageshwar Prasad, a barber of the Chhipatti District of Kanauj, a city of Uttar Pradesh near Kanpur, was enticed from his play and brutally murdered with a knife or razor by two neighbors. Munna was the only son of Sri Jageshwar Prasad and the motive for the crime seems to have been the wish to dispose of Sri Jageshwar Prasad's heir so that one of the murderers (a relative) might inherit his property. One of the alleged murderers (Jawahar) was a barber (like Sri Jageshwar Prasad) and the other (Chaturi) was a washerman. Someone of the area had seen Munna go off with these men and this led to their arrest and the unofficial confession of one of them (Chaturi). The mutilated and severed head of the boy and some of his clothes were subsequently found and clearly identified by his father. The alleged murderer who had confessed subsequently retracted his confession after being officially charged. There being no witnesses to the crime, the case against the alleged and confessed murderers collapsed and they were freed.

A few years later word reached Sri Jageshwar Prasad that a boy born in another district of Kanauj in July, 1951 (six months after the death of Munna), had described himself as the son of Jageshwar, a barber of Chhipatti District and had given details of "his" murder, naming the murderers, the place of the crime, and other circumstances of the life and death of Munna. The boy, named Ravi Shankar, son of Sri Babu Ram Gupta, kept asking his parents for various toys which he claimed he had in the house of his previous life. Ravi Shankar's mother and older sister subsequently testified that he had made such statements when he was between two and three years old. Later Ravi Shankar's schoolteacher listened to the boy's narrations about the murder when the boy was a little less than six years old.

When Sri Jageshwar Prasad heard about the statements of the boy he visited the home of Sri Babu Ram Gupta to obtain full information. Sri Babu Ram Gupta became annoyed at this intrusion and apparently feared that Ravi Shankar might be taken from him by Sri Jageshwar Prasad, especially since the boy talked much about "his" previous toys. Sri Babu Ram Gupta would not talk with Sri Jageshwar Prasad.

Subsequently, however, Sri Jageshwar Prasad arranged to meet Ravi Shankar's mother, who let him talk with Ravi Shankar himself. According to Sri Jageshwar Prasad, the boy after some time recognized him as his father of the previous life and also told him about events in the life of Munna. At this meeting, Ravi Shankar gave Sri Jageshwar Prasad an account of the murder (of Munna) which corresponded very closely with what he had been able to put together of the event from the retracted confession of one of the murderers, the inspection of the murder site by the river, and the mutilated body. This meeting occurred on July 30, 1955, when Ravi Shankar was just four years old. In the following March, 1956, Ravi Shankar's schoolteacher recorded in writing (in a letter to Professor B. L. Atreya) some of the statements of the boy about the previous life.

Ravi Shankar's father continued to oppose discussion of the case and beat the boy severely to make him stop talking about the previous life. Ravi Shankar's schoolteacher observed in 1956 the effects of the beatings Ravi Shankar's father had given the boy. He found Ravi Shankar afraid to talk about his statements regarding the previous life. Sri Babu Ram Gupta quarreled with his neighbors over his insistence that everyone forget the whole incident. (Some of them had confirmed to Sri Jageshwar Prasad the fact that Ravi Shankar had been talking about a previous life.) Sri Babu Ram Gupta went so far as to send Ravi Shankar away from the district for a year or more. Subsequently Sri Babu Ram Gupta died.

In addition to being afraid of his father, Ravi Shankar was also afraid of the murderers of Munna. Once when he happened to see one of them, he trembled with fear, and perhaps anger also, since he expressed his intention of revenging the murder. He also told his schoolteacher (in 1956) that he was generally afraid of all barbers and washermen and ran away when he saw any.

Ravi Shankar's mother testified that the boy had a linear mark resembling closely the scar of a long knife wound across the neck. She said she first noticed this mark when he was three to four months old. The mark was apparently congenital.

When Ravi Shankar talked about the murder of the previous life, he would say that the mark on his neck derived from the wounds of the murder. As Ravi Shankar grew, the mark gradually changed position until in 1964 it was high on his neck just below his chin. It had also faded somewhat by that time.

After Sri Jageshwar Prasad had satisfied himself regarding the accuracy of the knowledge of the murder of his son possessed by Ravi Shankar, he wanted to renew the legal charges against the alleged murderers who, for want of witnesses, had been released five years earlier. But this apparently was not feasible, although whether because of lapse of time or because the courts would not recognize the testimony of Ravi Shankar I do not know.

In 1956 Professor B. L. Atreya corresponded with Sri Jageshwar Prasad about the case and collected considerable written testimony from some other witnesses, e.g., Sri Shriram Mishra, Ravi Shankar's teacher at Kanauj. Professor Atreya did not personally interview any of the witnesses. The documents which he placed at my disposal seemed to justify a further investigation. Therefore in 1962, Dr. Jamuna Prasad with Sri R. S. Lal and Sri H. N. Banerjee visited the site of the case and interviewed a number of the witnesses. Sri Lal placed translations of his notes made at the time of my disposal.

As already mentioned, the father of Ravi Shankar had died in the meantime. Unfortunately also, Sri Jageshwar Prasad and his wife were both away from Kanauj at the time of this investigation in 1962, but some further corroborative testimony from neighbors of the family was obtained.

Subsequently (1963–65) I corresponded directly with Sri Jageshwar Prasad, who answered questions about certain details of the case.

In 1964, I visited the site of the case myself and interviewed many witnesses previously interviewed by Dr. Jamuna Prasad, as well as some new ones. Sri Jageshwar Prasad was again away from Kanauj, but his correspondence with Professor Atreya and myself mentioned above and the testimony of other witnesses, made this absence remediable, if regrettable.

Relevant Facts of Geography and Possible Normal Means of Communication Between the Two Families. From the testimony of the various witnesses it seems that the two families concerned in this case had only the slightest personal acquaintance with each other prior to the attempt at verification of the statements made by Ravi Shankar which Sri Jageshwar Prasad initiated in 1955. They apparently had only a "nodding acquaintance" with each other. Srimati Ramdulari Ram Gupta, Ravi Shankar's mother, stated that Sri Jageshwar Prasad had never visited her house prior to his visit for verification that year. The family of Ravi Shankar had heard of the murder of Munna four years earlier, as had indeed many and perhaps most people in the city of Kanauj. Srimati Ramdulari Ram Gupta had gone to the murdered boy's home to offer her condolences. She denied having known the family at all before the murder. Sri Jageshwar Prasad reacted with strong grief and anger to the murder of his son; his wife's mind became unhinged by the tragedy. Sri Jageshwar Prasad exerted himself strenuously to bring the culprits to justice. He apparently talked about the murder considerably around the city. But his behavior had the effect of deadening talk by other people who dreaded the possibility of being drawn into the courts as witnesses or perhaps of incurring the enmity of the murderers still at large. In 1962 Dr. Jamuna Prasad and his colleagues found the family of Ravi Shankar extremely reluctant to talk about the incident of Munna's murder and Ravi Shankar's claims to be Munna reborn. And their inhibitions had not diminished at the time of my visit in 1964. Their motives for this reticence consisted of the wish to avoid any legal embroilments and also the fear that Ravi Shankar might actually leave them to live with Sri Jageshwar Prasad, about whom he talked at length. For although Ravi Shankar's family talked little of Munna, Ravi Shankar dwelt upon the previous life a great deal when he was young.

In view of the above attitudes, I believe it unlikely that Ravi Shankar learned anything about Munna from members of his family who had heard of Munna's murder. Apart from this, however, we have to consider whether the family of Ravi Shankar would know any of the intimate details of Munna's life, e.g., his toys, even though they did know of the murder of a boy of that name. Some of the information known to Ravi Shankar was in the public domain; much of it almost certainly was not.

The possession by Ravi Shankar of information apparently quite unknown to his parents about the life of Munna raises the possibility that the boy might somehow have heard of this information from Sri Jageshwar Prasad or a person of his district unknown to his parents. This, however, seems unlikely when we recall that Ravi Shankar first began to speak of the previous life when he was less than three years old, and according to one witness, when barely two years old. A child of this age in India would stay closely confined within his house under the surveillance of his mother. The home of Sri Jageshwar Prasad lies about a half mile from that of Sri Babu Ram Gupta and both are approached through streets with many turns. It is unreasonable to suppose that such a child could have wandered so far from his home as to reach Sri Jageshwar Prasad's house without this fact being known to his mother. Nor could he have acquired normal knowledge of Munna's belongings (see the tabulation to follow) without the knowledge of Munna's parents, who had kept these belongings inside their house.

Persons Interviewed or Providing Written Testimony on the Case. Of the family and neighbors of Munna, murdered son of Sri Jageshwar Prasad of Chhipatti District of Kanauj, the following furnished testimony:

> Sri Jageshwar Prasad, father of Munna (Written statements in letters
>   to Professor B. L. Atreya. Additional statements in letters to me.)
> Srimati Mano Rama, mother of Munna
> Sri Asharfi Lal Rajput, neighbor of Sri Jageshwar Prasad
> Sri Swaroop Rajput, neighbor of Sri Jageshwar Prasad
> Sri Kishori Lal Verma, neighbor of Sri Jageshwar Prasad

Of the family and neighbors of Ravi Shankar, son of Sri Babu Ram Gupta of Haziganj District of Kanauj, the following furnished testimony:

Ravi Shankar

Srimati Ramdulari Ram Gupta, widow of Babu Ram Gupta, mother
of Ravi Shankar

Sri Uma Shankar, older brother of Ravi Shankar

Maheswari, older sister of Ravi Shankar, born in 1942 (interviewed
only in 1962)

Sri Raj Kumar Rathor, next door neighbor of Sri Babu Ram Gupta

Umkar, classmate of Ravi Shankar

Sri Shriram Mishra, schoolteacher of Ravi Shankar. (Ravi Shankar's
narrations to him were witnessed by another teacher and three other
persons and submitted in written form to Professor B. L. Atreya,
March 30, 1956.)

In addition I have used a written deposition furnished (March 31, 1956)
to Professor B. L. Atreya by Sri Kali Charan Tandon, a resident of
Kanauj. It describes his knowledge of the statements then being made by
Ravi Shankar.

Statements and Recognitions Made by Ravi Shankar. When in 1962 Dr.
Jamuna Prasad and Sri R. S. Lal talked with Ravi Shankar (then eleven
years old), he had largely forgotten the events of the previous life. In fact,
he could not remember either the statements about the previous life he
had earlier made or that he had made them. He did say, however, that
whenever he saw Chaturi or Jawahar, the alleged murderers of Munna, he
became filled with fear. Yet he said he was not acquainted with these two
men and apparently had no idea why they stimulated fear in him. In the
same way he described a sense of familiarity with the Chhipatti District of
Kanauj, but could not explain why it seemed familiar to him.

In the tabulation below I give a summary of the statements and recognitions of Ravi Shankar, together with the witnesses who testified to these,
and some comments. Of the various items, according to the witnesses at
least sixteen occurred before any members of the two families had met, the
rest at or after their first meeting.

I must mention one marked discrepancy in the testimony of this case
which I have not been able to resolve. Sri Asharfi Lal Rajput and Sri
Kishori Lal Verma (both neighbors of Sri Jageshwar Prasad) and Sri Raj
Kumar Rathor (a neighbor of Ravi Shankar) testified that Ravi Shankar
was once taken by his father to visit the home of Sri Jageshwar Prasad.
The testimony of these witnesses on this point was similar in 1962 and
1964, although there were discrepancies in statements as to who had ac-
companied Ravi Shankar on this visit. But such a visit was denied by
Ravi Shankar's mother and older brother and also by Munna's father (Sri
Jageshwar Prasad) and mother. (Ravi Shankar's father had died before the

TABULATION

Summary of Statements and Recognitions Made by Ravi Shankar

Item	Informants	Verification	Comments
1. He was the son of Jageshwar and was killed by having his throat slit.	Maheswari, older sister of Ravi Shankar Raj Kumar Rathor, neighbor of Ravi Shankar's family.	Jageshwar Prasad, father of Munna Kishori Lal Verma, neighbor of Jageshwar Prasad Confession of Chaturi, alleged murderer as reported by Jageshwar Prasad.	Sri Jageshwar Prasad had a son, Munna, six years old, who was murdered on January 19, 1951.
2. His father was a barber.	Raj Kumar Rathor	Jageshwar Prasad	
3. His father lived in the Chhipatti District of Kanauj.	Maheswari Raj Kumar Rathor Uma Shankar, older brother of Ravi Shankar	Jageshwar Prasad	
4. His murderers were named Chaturi and Jawahar.	Maheswari	Jageshwar Prasad Confession of Chaturi, alleged murderer as reported by Jageshwar Prasad.	In addition to the confession by Chaturi, some pieces of shoes owned by Jawahar were found near the clothing and body of the boy.
5. They were a washerman and a barber.	Shriram Mishra, Ravi Shankar's schoolteacher Raj Kumar Rathor	Jageshwar Prasad	The alleged murderers were a washerman (Chaturi) and a barber (Jawahar).
6. He had been eating guavas before he was murdered.	Maheswari	Mano Rama, mother of Munna	Munna had taken some guavas just before he left the house to play and it was while he was playing that the murderers had induced him to accompany them.
7. He had been enticed by the murderers with an invitation to play Geri.	Jageshwar Prasad Uma Shankar	Mano Rama	Sri Uma Shankar was a secondhand witness of this statement of Ravi Shankar. Geri is a game which Munna often played with Chaturi and Jawahar, so it is likely they would have invited him to play it in order to lead him away from the neighborhood. No one actually heard the alleged murderers invite Munna to play the game that day. This item is probably correct, but not verified.

8. He was taken by the murderers to the riverside.	Raj Kumar Rathor Kali Charan Tandon	Jageshwar Prasad Kishori Lal Verma	Munna's body and clothes were found near the river.
9. He was killed in an orchard.	Shriram Mishra	Swaroop Rajput, neighbor of Jageshwar Prasad	Probably not completely accurate; but the route from Munna's house to the site where the body was found traversed several orchards. The site where the body was found may not have been the exact place where the child was murdered, but presumably they would be in the same area.
10. He was murdered near Chintamini Temple.	Raj Kumar Rathor	Kishori Lal Verma	The head of the murdered boy was found about 250 yards from Chintamini Temple. It was thought that the murder was committed in this area.
11. The murderers cut his neck.	Raj Kumar Rathor Shriram Mishra Kali Charan Tandon	Asharfi Lal Rajput, neighbor of Jageshwar Prasad Kishori Lal Verma	The murdered child's head was found severed from his body. In his (retracted) confession, Chaturi had said they killed the boy with a razor.
12. The murderers buried him in the sand.	Raj Kumar Rathor	Kishori Lal Verma	At least part of the body was found buried.
13. He had a patti (wooden slate) at his home.	Ramdulari Ram Gupta, mother of Ravi Shankar Jageshwar Prasad	Mano Rama	According to Sri Jageshwar Prasad, Ravi Shankar also correctly stated that this slate was in the almirah (large closet) of their house. It is perhaps noteworthy that Ravi Shankar used to say that his slate and toys (see succeeding items) "had been kept." He seemed certain that they had been preserved so that he could have them again if only his parents would get them for him. In fact, his mother had carefully, almost reverentially, preserved many of Munna's belongings, including his toys.

97

Item	Informants	Verification	Comments
14. He had a bag for his books at his home.	Raj Kumar Rathor	Mano Rama	The school bag of Munna had been preserved by his family and was shown to me in 1964.
15. He had an ink pot.	Ramdulari Ram Gupta	Mano Rama	
16. He had a toy pistol at his home.	Maheswari Ramdulari Ram Gupta Raj Kumar Rathor Jageshwar Prasad	Jageshwar Prasad Mano Rama	Munna was particularly fond of toy pistols. Ravi Shankar had no toy pistol. Poor people cannot usually afford to purchase toys for their children, but as Sri Jageshwar Prasad had only one son, Munna, he could afford to buy him toys. The toy pistol had been kept and was shown to me in 1964.
17. He had a wooden elephant at his home.	Jageshwar Prasad	Jageshwar Prasad	The toy elephant of Munna had been kept and was shown to me in 1964.
18. He had a toy of Lord Krishna at his home.	Raj Kumar Rathor	Verified by me in 1964.	Munna's toy statuette of Lord Krishna had been preserved and was shown to me in 1964.
19. He had a ball attached to an elastic string at his home.	Raj Kumar Rathor	Verified by me in 1964.	This toy of Munna's had also been preserved and was shown to me in 1964.
20. He had a watch at his home.	Raj Kumar Rathor	Mano Rama Jageshwar Prasad	Munna's watch had been kept and was shown to me in 1964.
21. He had a ring given to him by his father which was in his desk.	Raj Kumar Rathor Jageshwar Prasad	Jageshwar Prasad	Ravi Shankar told Sri Jageshwar Prasad: "The ring which you got for me is in my desk. Have you not sold it?" Munna's father replied: "Your ring is safe. Would you recognize it?" To this, Ravi Shankar replied, "Yes." Srimati Mano Rama stated discrepantly that the ring was not in the desk at the time of Munna's death.

Item	Informants			Comments
22. Recognition of Chaturi, alleged murderer of Munna.	Ramdulari Ram Gupta	Ramdulari Ram Gupta		Chaturi was the alleged murderer who confessed to the crime. He was unknown to the family of Ravi Shankar when the boy noticed him in a group of people at a religious ceremony. Ravi Shankar told his host's son that he would revenge himself on Chaturi. Srimati Babu Ram Gupta lived in purdah and so cannot have known a man like Chaturi from outside her family and another district. When Ravi Shankar showed this reaction of fear on seeing Chaturi, his mother inquired as to the identity of the man her son pointed out and learned who he was.
23. Recognition of Sri Jageshwar Prasad.		Jageshwar Prasad		In a letter to me of July 9, 1963, Sri Jageshwar Prasad described the recognition as follows: "I sat down at the door [of Ravi Shankar's house]. Ten or fifteen women assembled. The boy, whose name is now Ravi Shankar, was called. He stood at a distance of about one and a half feet and looked at me quietly. First of all, I addressed him, 'Dear boy, come here, what is your name? Do you know me?' I repeated these words twice or thrice, but he did not speak and became shy, as if he were going to weep. I again said, 'Oh, dear boy! Do not be afraid. Did you forget that you used to take money from me?' After twenty to twenty-five minutes he drew close and sat in my lap. Then he said to me, 'Father, I used to read in Chhipatti school and my wooden slate is in the almirah. . . .'"
24. He had attended the primary school of Chhipatti District.	Kali Charan Tandon Jageshwar Prasad		Jageshwar Prasad	

Item	Informants	Verification	Comments
25. Recognition of watch owned by Munna.	Jageshwar Prasad	Jageshwar Prasad	Sri Jageshwar Prasad had put on Munna's wrist watch and was wearing it when he met Ravi Shankar. During their talk, Ravi Shankar said: "It is my watch." Munna's father had brought the watch for him from Bombay.
26. Recognition of Munna's maternal grandmother.	Jageshwar Prasad	Jageshwar Prasad	Sri Jageshwar Prasad was not himself present at this recognition. He wrote: "My mother-in-law went to some other person's house and a boy was sent to call him [Ravi Shankar]. He was chewing sugar cane. When he came the women asked him who had come there. For a while he looked downward and then said: 'Grandmother [mother's mother] has come. She has come from Kanpur.'" Ravi Shankar used the Hindi word "Nani," which means maternal grandmother. Munna's maternal grandmother did live in Kanpur.

investigation of 1962.) When I questioned Ravi Shankar himself on this point he at first could not recall any such visit, but later said that "he might have gone when he was young." I have considered the following two possibilities, among others, for this discrepancy. First, Ravi Shankar may have been taken to Munna's house secretly at a time when Sri Jageshwar Prasad was away. He often traveled out of Kanauj on business. Ravi Shankar's father (who was strongly opposed to any contact between the families) might have wished to conduct such a visit surreptitiously. And Munna's mother, rendered mentally ill by the loss of her son, was perhaps secluded in a back room and would not necessarily have seen the boy at the time of such a visit. Alternately, the neighbors may conceivably have mistaken the visit Ravi Shankar paid to another home, where he met and recognized Munna's grandmother (see item 26 of the tabulation), for a visit to the home of Sri Jageshwar Prasad.

Appearance of the Birthmark in 1964. When I saw him in 1964, Ravi Shankar was a well-developed boy who appeared in good health, although perhaps somewhat smaller than average for his age of thirteen years. He had a few faint marks on his face, but these had nothing unusual about them and suggested ordinary small scars of minor facial wounds.

Under the ridge of the chin, somewhat more to the right side than the left, I observed a linear mark crossing the neck in a transverse direction. It ran about two inches long and was about $\frac{1}{8}$ to $\frac{1}{4}$ inch wide. It was darker in pigment than the surrounding tissue and had the stippled quality of a scar. It looked much like an old scar of a healed knife wound. This, I was told, was what remained of a considerably longer mark which, during early childhood, had also lain lower in the neck about one-third the distance between the sternal notch and the chin.

Relevant Reports and Observations of the Behavior of the People Concerned. The testimony of several witnesses justifies our concluding that Ravi Shankar had fully identified himself with Munna. His family and neighbors testified to his repeated demands for Munna's toys which he said were in his other home, and to his wish to be taken to that home. He said he needed the toys. He complained that the house in which he lived was not "his house." At least once, when rebuked, he ran out of his house, saying he would go to his former home. He often spoke spontaneously about Munna's murder to members of his family. To neighbors and others he would often speak also, but after his father's beating more rarely and reluctantly.

He himself said (in 1962) he was afraid of the two men who had murdered him (Munna), even though he could not explain why he was afraid of them. His mother testified to his extreme fear when he first saw and recognized one of the murderers, Chaturi. In 1964, however, he said he no longer felt fear or anger when he saw Chaturi and he could not even recognize Jawahar. He remembered that he had been afraid of Chaturi when younger. Ravi Shankar's mother testified also to his showing marked fear whenever she took him to the Chintamini Temple, located in the area of the murder of Munna (see item 10 of the tabulation).

As mentioned earlier, Munna's mother became mentally ill after the loss of her son. Neighbors offered this opinion in 1962, and I confirmed it during my interviews in 1964. Srimati Mano Rama then showed a marked depression with agitation. The mention of her son troubled her greatly and several times during our interview she broke into painful weeping. She was trapped in the past memories of her son Munna, had preserved all his toys, books, and other belongings and attempted to deny the passage of later events. As a further sign of her imbalance I may note that one witness (a neighbor) testified that at times Srimati Mano Rama reproached her own husband with the murder of their son, an accusation which must certainly have added severely to his sufferings as well as to hers.

Srimati Mano Rama's attitude toward Ravi Shankar and his claims showed marked ambivalence. Part of her evidently wanted to believe that he was the reincarnation of her lost son; but another part evidently could not bear the thought that her son could live with another mother.

Comments on the Evidence of Paranormal Knowledge on the Part of Ravi Shankar. In the present case, the initiative for verification came entirely from the family of the deceased Munna. The family of Ravi Shankar took no steps toward verification of the boy's statements and his father actively opposed such steps, going so far as to beat Ravi Shankar to make him forget and later to send him away from Kanauj for a time. The boy nevertheless talked to neighbors and word of his statements spread back to Sri Jageshwar Prasad. In the opposition of the boy's family to verification, the case resembles that of Prakash and, to a lesser extent, that of Jasbir. Their resistance seems to have arisen partly from a fear that Ravi Shankar would leave them for the family of Sri Jageshwar Prasad. They had an additional reason to suppress the boy after he openly accused Chaturi of the murder for they might have feared reprisals on this account (see item 22 of the tabulation). Such opposition certainly makes it extremely unlikely that the case could have been worked up for fraudulent purposes by Ravi Shankar's family. I have already given reasons for thinking it unlikely that Sri Jageshwar Prasad ever had any contact with Ravi Shankar before he heard of the boy's statements. He himself and Ravi Shankar's mother both denied such acquaintance.

The distance between the homes of Munna and Ravi Shankar is about half a mile. Many turns occur in the intervening route and, as I have already mentioned, it seems most unlikely that a child as young as Ravi Shankar was when he first began to talk of a previous life could have wandered from one place to the other without this fact being known to his parents. On the other hand, the two homes are both in the same city, although in different districts, and persons going from the Chhipatti District to the center of the city for shopping would have to pass close to the house where Ravi Shankar lived. In 1964 I encountered a classmate (Umkar) of Ravi Shankar near the home of Sri Asharfi Lal Rajput, whose house in turn was in the Chhipatti District not far from Sri Jageshwar Prasad's home. Umkar was about twelve or thirteen years old and his presence in this district does not prove that much smaller children could wander into the district from other areas. But it does show that some traffic could have occurred between the different districts. In short, while I discovered no one who could have served as a link in the normal communication of information between the two families, I cannot deny that some persons going back and forth between the two districts might have acted somehow as telepathic links between the two families, and therefore on the telepathic hypothesis of this case, have played a part in its development. But I have deferred a full discussion of the strengths and weaknesses of this hypothesis to the last section of this monograph.

In this case, as with others which include birthmarks (see some further examples among the Alaskan cases, pp. 216–269 below), we cannot separate our evaluation of the informational and behavioral features of the case from our evaluation of the birthmark. The birthmark may lead to the child's story about a previous life through induction of this by the parents' efforts to explain the birthmark. But what creates the birthmark? According to Ravi Shankar's mother, he was born with the mark resembling the scar of a wound on his neck. The story of the previous life cannot alone explain the birthmark; this must have been caused by some influence anterior to the development of the story. But when the birthmarks are so specifically related to the details of the case as to suggest that they were caused by experiences in a previous life, cases of this particular type become of the greatest interest for our analysis of alternative explanations of cases suggestive of reincarnation. I shall revert to this significance in the section on Alaskan cases and in the General Discussion.

The Later Development of Ravi Shankar. I met Ravi Shankar again in 1969 in Kanpur. At that time he was studying Commerce at a college there. He was then eighteen years old. He said that he had completely forgotten the memories of the previous life, but he was evidently aware of the main features of what he had earlier remembered from hearing other people talk about his memories. He had seen Munna's father, Jageshwar Prasad, in June, 1969, and expressed pleasure at having met him.

In 1969 Ravi Shankar had lost all the phobias which he had shown when younger. He was not afraid of barbers or of knives and razors. His fear of the area around Chintamini Temple in Kanauj (near which Munna had been murdered) persisted to some extent until he was seventeen years old, but then receded. He no longer had any wish for revenge against the murderers of Munna.

In 1969 I also met (for the first time) Munna's father, Jageshwar Prasad, and had a long talk with him about the case. No important new details emerged, but we reviewed some events of the case, particularly the occasion of his first meeting with Ravi Shankar when the latter had spontaneously recognized Munna's watch which Jageshwar Prasad had worn to the meeting (item 25 of the tabulation.). This first meeting occurred in July, 1955, when Ravi Shankar was four years old. Ravi Shankar's father opposed further meetings between them. Nevertheless, they met on two later occasions, briefly in 1967, and (as mentioned above) in the summer of 1969. Jageshwar Prasad had the impression that Ravi Shankar was reluctant to meet him, probably because of the severe reprimands and beatings administered by his father. Jageshwar Prasad conjectured that after Babu Ram's death other persons supplemented his opposition to Ravi Shankar's meeting with Jageshwar Prasad.

Jageshwar Prasad said that his wife, Srimati Mano Ram, was still calling on him to "bring back my child." But at other times she expressed a wish to have "the whole thing forgotten." According to him, she was somewhat vexed at my visit to Kanauj in 1969 which she thought might endanger their lives since the murderers of Munna were still living in Kanauj.

I went to Jageshwar Prasad's house and met his wife again. She seemed much more rational than she had been at the time of our first meeting in 1964. She said she was feeling better, although not entirely well. She expressed some interest in meeting Ravi Shankar, but then added: "What is the use of seeing him if I cannot claim him." She believed that he was her dead son Munna reborn.

Jageshwar Prasad, who spoke no English, had had someone read to him in a Hindi translation the report of the case of Ravi Shankar given in the first edition of this book, of which I had sent him a copy. He said that all the details in the report were correct. As already mentioned, Jageshwar Prasad had wished to have the case against the murderers of Munna reopened on the basis of the statements Ravi Shankar had made about the murder. And he believed for a time that my investigation of the case and the evidence recorded in this book would have some influence in having the criminals prosecuted. He had not entirely abandoned this hope, unrealistic from the beginning, at the time of our meeting in 1969.[26]

[26] It seems unlikely to me that courts will accept the testimony of children who remember previous lives, and I myself do not believe that they should. The statements of such children may sometimes appropriately lead to renewed investigation of old criminal cases. But legal action should only follow if such investigation brings out new evidence independent of the child's statements.

I met Ravi Shankar again in November, 1971, this time once more in Kanauj. He was then twenty years old and in the final year of his college program expecting to obtain that year the degree of Bachelor of Commerce. He was doing satisfactorily in his college work. He had been held up one year (which he had to repeat) because of unjust accusations of cheating in an examination. But he had surmounted this difficulty and continued at his studies.

In 1969 and 1971 I again examined Ravi Shankar's birthmark. There had been a further alteration since 1964 in its position relative to his neck and chin. By this time the birthmark, which had been originally on his neck, then (in 1964) just below the chin, was under the chin and near its point. It was still clearly visible as a distinct line of darker pigmentation about 3 mm. wide running across the under surface of the chin near its point.

In August, 1972, Dr. L. P. Mehrotra met Ravi Shankar again in Kanauj. He learned that Ravi Shankar had graduated from college in Kanpur the previous June. He had then returned to Kanauj where he was working in the grain and salt shop of his brother, Uma Shankar. Since there was in 1972 a surfeit of college graduates in India in relation to the positions for employment available to them, Ravi Shankar had to content himself with working in his brother's shop instead of obtaining some clerical or other position for which his education seemed to quality him.

The Case of Mallika

Summary of the Case and its Investigation. In the present group of Indian cases suggestive of reincarnation I include the case of Mallika as an illustration of those cases with few verifiable details of information, but interesting behavioral features. In this respect the present case has similar features to some of the minor cases of Alaska and to that of Ranjith Makalanda of Ceylon (see below), in which the information permitted no verification whatever of his statements.

The case of Mallika was first reported by Mme Robert Gaebelé[27, 28] of Pondicherry. When I visited India in the summer of 1961, I obtained further information on the case from Mme Gaebelé and from interviews with Mallika's father, with the sister of the deceased woman with whom Mallika had identified herself, and with the sister's husband.

The deceased person in question was Kumari Devi Sabapathy, who had lived at Vellore, a city located some seventy miles northwest of Pondicherry. Devi had died unmarried of typhoid fever at the age of twenty-

27 Y. R. Gaebelé. "Un cas de réincarnation." *La Revue Spirite*, July–August, 1960, 126–127.
28 Y. R. Gaebelé. "Du nouveau sur Mallika." *La Revue Spirite*, May–June, 1961, 104–105.

eight in 1949. She had had a brother and two sisters who survived childhood. One sister after marriage lived in Pondicherry where her husband, Sri S. Mourougassigamany, was assistant librarian to Mme Gaebelé in the municipal library. In July, 1956, the Mourougassigamanys decided to rent the first floor of their house and did so to Sri K. Aroumougam and his wife who moved in with their infant daughter, Mallika, who was born in Madras on December 4, 1955. Her family moved from Madras to Pondicherry in July, 1956, and immediately occupied the apartment in the house of the Mourougassigamanys.

As Mallika grew up she became strongly attached to Srimati Mourougassigamany. When she was not quite four years old, Mallika visited the upstairs apartment of the Mourougassigamanys for the first time. There she noticed some embroidered cushions lying on some chairs in the apartment. She immediately pointed to them and said: "I made those." The cushions had in fact been made by Srimati Mourougassigamany's deceased sister Devi and when Srimati Mourougassigamany told Mallika that the cushions had been made by a woman who had died more than ten years earlier, Mallika shook her head and replied: "That was me!"

Mallika addressed Srimati Mourougassigamany as "sister" at first, but Srimati Mourougassigamany told her not to call her this. (She did not wish to be reminded of the death of her sister.) She instructed Mallika to call her "aunt" instead. This slight rebuff did not interfere with Mallika's developing an extremely strong attachment for Srimati Mourougassigamany, which persisted over the ensuing years. On every possible occasion Mallika would climb the stairs of the house to visit with Srimati Mourougassigamany and help in the housework. She stayed with her as much as she could. This attachment continued to 1962. When Mallika's parents took her to Madras for a vacation in 1962, and were there visited by the Mourougassigamanys, Mallika wished to return with them to Pondicherry.[29]

Srimati Mourougassigamany noted a number of similarities in behavior between Mallika and her deceased sister, such as a particular way of bathing, certain gestures, and a manner of walking rather independently in front of other people. She also showed considerable precocity in such accomplishments as cooking curries.

Some time after the initial statement and behavior of Mallika identifying herself with Devi, the Mourougassigamanys took her with them on a visit to Vellore. She was taken not to the house in which Devi and her family had lived, but to another house where Devi's brother then lived. There, in the living room, Mallika went up to two large photographs and said: "Here are my father and mother." These photographs were of Devi's parents. Indicating another photograph of a family group she said: "Here is

[29] Y. R. Gaebelé. Personal communication, July 27, 1962.

my brother" and then added: "But he is never at home." The brother of Devi (who appeared in the group photograph) was in fact often away attending to his property.

The Mourougassigamanys recalled only one other specific statement of Mallika relative to the life of Devi. During Devi's lifetime the Mourougas-sigamanys owned a cow of which Devi (when she visited them in Pondicherry) had become somewhat fond. Devi had even given the cow its name, "Coundavy," named after a Hindu princess. The cow had died many years before the birth of Mallika. One day in the presence of Mallika someone referred to the cow "Coundavy" and Mallika immediately said: "I remember Coundavy and the little puppy who would suckle the cow like a calf." This recalled to those present the fact that a dog owned by the Mourougas-sigamanys had suckled the cow Coundavy after the cow had a calf which was suckling. The Mourougassigamanys expressed certainty that no one had previously mentioned this incident to Mallika.

When Mallika later met Devi's brother she immediately addressed him as "brother." She became as attached to him as to Devi's sister, Srimati Mourougassigamany. When the former visited the Mourougassigamanys, Mallika attached herself to him and served him with great indulgence and affection, never leaving his side except to go to school. She continued to call him "brother" until 1962, a most unusual appellation for a small child addressing a man fifty-five years old and of a completely different family. Devi's brother was no longer living in the family home but some distance away. Mallika said to him one day, "Brother, why have you left the family home?"

Mallika's attachment to the Mourougassigamanys continued strong (up to the time of my visit in 1961) and, indeed, she seemed to have become more attached to them than to her own parents. Mallika's father himself testified to this. Unlike the parents of some of the other children concerned in these cases, e.g., Prakash and Ravi Shankar, Mallika's parents did not seem to have been made anxious or jealous by Mallika's attachment to her claimed previous family. In this respect they resembled the parents of Swarnlata, Sukla, and Parmod.

Mallika never said anything about the life of Devi upon request. Her few statements always came out spontaneously, apparently stimulated by some object, person, or comment occurring in her presence. She never talked about the previous life with her parents, but only with the Mourougassigamanys and other members of the family of Devi.

Comment. As already mentioned, the present case lacks much detail and for this reason the behavioral features of Mallika's strong attachment to the sister and brother of Devi provide its important aspects.

Since Mallika and her family moved into the lower floor of the home of the Mourougassigamanys when Mallika was less than a year old, she grew up near them, both families living in the same house. An attachment of some kind to a friendly neighbor is not surprising; it is rather the *degree* of this attachment in Mallika and its continuation which falls outside the normal range of such attachments of children for neighbors. It is possible that Srimati Mourougassigamany fostered Mallika's attachment, but unlikely that she promoted its particular form. She was childless and very much wanted a child of her own, but she did not wish to be reminded of her deceased sister. The memory of the latter's death remained painful for her years afterwards and this was why she forbade Mallika to call her "sister," telling her to call her "aunt" instead.

The attachment of Mallika for Devi's brother is even more difficult to understand since the opportunities for acquaintance between him and Mallika were slender and only possible on his occasional visits from Vellore to Pondicherry. Yet she showed a degree of familiarity and affection for him quite outside the proper behavior of an Indian child toward an older man, but entirely appropriate in the behavior of a sister for a brother, which is how she addressed him.

The case has additional interest because of its exemplification of the psychological "law" that recognition is stronger than recall. Mallika actually had no completely spontaneous recollections of the life of Devi when away from stimuli which could serve as associations for memories. She commented on the embroidered cushions after she saw them, on the parents and brother of Devi after noticing their photographs, and on the behavior of the dog which suckled the cow after someone had alluded to the cow by name. The imaged memories of the life of Devi lacked sufficient strength to penetrate into consciousness except when thus stimulated. The behavior of attachment to the family of Devi appeared much more frequently.

The case of Mallika presents the rather odd feature of her family just happening to move into a house also occupied by the sister of the previous personality. On the one hand, this seems like a most unusual coincidence and some readers may see in it support for the idea that Srimati Mourougassigamany seized on the idea of Mallika's being her deceased sister reborn and fostered the child's behavior. On the other hand, we should remember that on the reincarnation hypothesis, many persons may reincarnate with only dim memories of a previous life. The dormancy or arousal of these memories may then depend upon whether or not these persons happen to come into contact with persons or places which provide the stimulation necessary to bring the memories above the threshold of consciousness.[30]

---

[30] For some years after 1961 I received occasional news about Mallika from Mme Gaebelé. Subsequently Mallika's family left Pondicherry and my efforts to trace them were unsuccessful.

The Case of Parmod

Summary of the Case and its Investigation. Parmod Sharma, second son of Professor Bankeybehary Lal Sharma of Bisauli, Uttar Pradesh, was born in Bisauli on October 11, 1944. When he was about two and a half, he began to tell his mother not to cook because he had a wife in Moradabad who could cook. Later, between the age of three and four, he began to refer to a large soda and biscuit shop which he said he had in Moradabad. He asked to go to Moradabad. He said he was one of the "Mohan Brothers." He claimed to be well to do and to have had another shop in Saharanpur. He showed an extraordinary interest in biscuits and shops which I shall describe more fully later. He related how in the previous life he had become ill after eating too much curd and said he "had died in a bathtub."

Parmod's parents initially took no steps to verify the boy's statements. Word of them, however, reached members of a family called Mehra in Moradabad. The brothers of this family, who owned a soda and biscuit shop (called Mohan Brothers [31]) in Moradabad and another shop in Saharanpur, had had a brother, Parmanand Mehra, who had died on May 9, 1943, in Saharanpur. Parmanand Mehra had developed a chronic gastro-intestinal illness after gorging himself on curd. Eventually he seems to have had appendicitis and peritonitis from which he died. Parmanand had been an enterprising business man who shared a partnership with three brothers and a cousin. They had extensive interests in Moradabad and Saharanpur, including two hotels, two shops, and a cinema. Parmanand had himself started the family's biscuit and soda water manufacturing business and managed it himself for many years.

When Parmanand's family heard of Parmod's statements through the connections described below, they decided to visit the boy in Bisauli. In the summer of 1949, when Parmod was a little under five years old, several members of the Mehra family went to Bisauli, but found Parmod away. Shortly afterwards, however, Parmod journeyed with his father and maternal cousin to Moradabad. There he recognized several members of .he Mehra family and various places in the town. On a later occasion he visited Saharanpur and made further recognitions of people there.

Professor B. L. Atreya of Benares Hindu University investigated this case within a few weeks of the first visit by Parmod to Moradabad. He kindly made available for this report two letters written about the case in 1949 by Professor Sharma, Parmod's father, and one statement about veri-

---

[31] The oldest brother of the Mehra family partners was Mohan Mehra. His name, became attached to the family business which was called "Mohan and Brothers," shortened to "Mohan Brothers."

fications and recognitions written by Sri Mohan Lal Mehra, oldest brother of the deceased Parmanand Mehra. Professor Atreya published a report of the case in 1957.[32]

In 1961 I investigated the case with the help as interpreter of Sri Sudhir Mukherjee. In 1962, Sri Subash Mukherjee gathered some further testimony in interviews with witnesses. I returned to the area in 1964 and re-checked the case with Dr. Jamuna Prasad as interpreter. Most of the witnesses spoke Hindi only, but Parmod's father and older brother spoke English, as did Sri Raj K. Mehra (Parmanand Mehra's nephew) in Moradabad. Parmod himself spoke a little English only. In preparing this report I have relied chiefly on my interviews in 1964. I have, however, also availed myself of the earlier documents collected by Professor B. L. Atreya, of some interviews with informants recorded by Sri Subash Mukherjee, and of some earlier published reports of the case.[33, 34] All such previous reports have been based on correspondence with the principal witnesses and not on personal interviews. I have used these reports only when witnesses I interviewed read and endorsed them as accurate. The material collected by Professor Atreya and the earlier reports have the advantage of having been written soon after the main events of the case occurred.

The materials available for the study and authentication of the case thus include written statements made soon after the main events had occurred and the two families had met, and also data derived from two series of my own personal interviews in 1961 and 1964, together with some additional correspondence, notes of Sri Subash Mukherjee's interviews, and the earlier reports.

Relevant Facts of Geography and Possible Normal Means of Communication Between the Two Families. Bisauli is a small town some thirty miles southwest of the large city of Bareilly in the state of Uttar Pradesh. Moradabad is another large city of the state about sixty miles north of Bareilly. Saharanpur is still farther north by another hundred miles. Although Bisauli is somewhat "interior" and away from main line railways, frequent bus services connect Bisauli with Bareilly and from there one can go easily by bus or train to Moradabad.

The family of Professor Sharma had often been to Moradabad, although Parmod had not gone there prior to his first visit for recognitions in the summer of 1949, when he was just under five years old. Parmod's family had no knowledge of the family of "Mohan Brothers" and, as already

[32] B. L. Atreya. *Introduction to Parapsychology*. Benares: The International Standard Publications, 1957. (See Ch. 3, 116–121.)

[33] B. Samanera. "Five Year Old Boy Recalls Past Life." *Bosat.* Vol. 13, 1949, 27–32.

[34] B. L. Atreya. *Op. cit.*, n. 32.

mentioned, Parmod's family did not initiate a meeting between the two families.

The two families came into contact through Sri Lala Raghanand Prasad, who had relatives in Moradabad although he himself lived in Bisauli where he was a friend and colleague of Professor Sharma, Parmod's father. Sri L. R. Prasad mentioned Parmod's statements and behavior to one of his relatives from Moradabad and the latter, who knew the Mehra family, then mentioned the matter to them and this led to their first visit to Parmod in Bisauli.

In 1961 Parmod's mother stated that her brother, Sri Shiva Sharan Sharma, a railway employee, was for a time stationed in Moradabad. He also spoke with the Mehra brothers about Parmod's behavior after he learned of it. He and Sri L. R. Prasad may conceivably have served as telepathic links between the Mehra family and Parmod, a point to which I shall revert after presenting the main facts of the case.

Persons Interviewed During the Investigation. In Bisauli I interviewed:

Parmod Sharma
Srimati Bankeybehary Lal Sharma, mother of Parmod
Vinod Sharma, older brother of Parmod
Sri Madan Lal Sharma, cousin of Parmod's mother
Sri Lala Raghanand Prasad, friend of Parmod's father

In Chindausi I interviewed:

Sri Bankeybehary Lal Sharma, father of Parmod

In Moradabad I interviewed:

Sri Mohan Lal Mehra, oldest brother of Parmanand Mehra
Sri J. D. Mehra, second brother of Parmanand Mehra
Sri Raj Kumar Mehra, son of Mohan Lal Mehra, nephew of Parmanand Mehra
Srimati Nandrani Mehra, widow of Parmanand Mehra
Sri Nan Kumar Mehra, oldest son of Parmanand Mehra
Sri Pritan Kumar Mehra, second son of Parmanand Mehra
Sri Govardhan Das Mehra, fourth son of Parmanand Mehra
Kumari Premlata Mehra, daughter of Parmanand Mehra

Statements and Recognitions Made by Parmod. I give below in the tabulation a summary of the main statements and recognitions attributed to Parmod. The statements of the witnesses and the earlier reports indicate that the case was at one time much richer in details which might have been

Summary of Statements and Recognitions Made by Parmod

Item	Informants	Verification	Comments
1. He had a biscuit shop.	B. L. Sharma, father of Parmod M. L. Sharma, cousin of Parmod's mother	M. L. Mehra, oldest brother of Parmanand I visited the biscuit shop in Moradabad in 1961 and 1964	The family owned a large confectionary shop. The firm manufactured and sold biscuits.
2. The shop was also for soda water.	B. L. Sharma	M. L. Mehra Verified by me during visits to Moradabad in 1961 and 1964	The shop had a machine for manufacturing soda water. This rather complicated machine was shown to me in 1961 and 1964.
3. It was a big shop in Moradabad.	M. L. Sharma	Verified by me during visits to Moradabad in 1961 and 1964	The shop was relatively large and located in the center of Moradabad.
4. His shop belonged to Mohan Brothers.	B. L. Sharma	M. L. Mehra	Other witnesses of Parmod's statements, e.g., his mother and Sri M. L. Sharma, could not remember that Parmod had mentioned the name Mohan, and thought the correct shop and family was identified by Parmod's description. Although the family name is Mehra, the family business, shared by four brothers and a cousin, had the name of the oldest brother: "Mohan and Brothers," often contracted to "Mohan Brothers."
5. He had become ill after eating curd.	M. L. Sharma	M. L. Mehra N. K. Mehra, oldest son of Parmanand Nandrani Mehra, widow of Parmanand	Parmanand had been inordinately fond of curd, and at a wedding feast he gorged himself with it. After this he developed a chronic gastrointestinal illness followed later by appendicitis and then peritonitis from which he died. Two or three days before his death he insisted on taking some curd against advice.

112

5. (continued)			He said he might not have another chance to eat it. Parmanand blamed his illness and impending death on overeating of curd.
6. He "died in a bathtub."	M. L. Sharma	M. L. Mehra J. D. Mehra, second brother of Parmanand	According to Sri M. L. Sharma, Parmod said he "died in a bathtub." The witnesses of the Mehra family stated that Parmanand tried a series of naturopathic bath treatments when he had appendicitis. He had some of these treatments during the days just before his death but did not actually die in a bathtub. In a letter dated September 6, 1949, Sri B. L. Sharma stated that Parmod had said he died of being "wet with water" and that he (Sri B. L. Sharma) had learned (presumably from the Mehra family) that Parmanand had been given a bath immediately before his death.
7. He had four sons, a daughter, and a wife.	B. L. Sharma	N. K. Mehra	In Moradabad in 1964 I met Parmanand's widow, three of his sons, and his daughter. One of his sons was away at the time of my visit.
8. He also had a shop in Saharanpur.	B. L. Sharma	M. L. Mehra	The Mehra brothers owned shops in both Moradabad and Saharanpur. Parmod made the statements in items 8–10 *after* the two families had met; thus he might have learned these facts in Moradabad on his visits there.
9. He had a hotel at Saharanpur.	B. L. Sharma	M. L. Mehra	The Mehra family owned a hotel in Saharanpur.
10. He had a cinema at Saharanpur.	B. L. Sharma	M. L. Mehra	The family owned a cinema in Saharanpur.
11. His mother lived in Saharanpur.	B. L. Sharma	M. L. Mehra N. K. Mehra	Parmanand's mother lived in Saharanpur.

Item	Informants	Verification	Comments
12. Recognition of Sri Karam Chand Mehra, older cousin of Parmanand, at the railway station in Moradabad.	B. L. Sharma M. L. Sharma		Corroborated also by Sri M. L. Mehra, cousin of Sri Karam Chand Mehra, who was not, however, himself an eyewitness of the recognition. Parmod's father had already greeted Sri K. C. Mehra, but this would not account for Parmod's weeping and throwing his arms around Sri K. C. Mehra, nor for his saying that Sri Mehra was his "older brother." (An Indian can appropriately call a cousin his "brother" especially if there is a close relationship as in the case of Parmanand and his cousin.) Sri B. L. Sharma said Parmod also gave Sri K. C. Mehra's name when he greeted him.
13. His name was Parmanand.	B. L. Sharma	M. L. Mehra	Parmod had not used the name Parmanand until he greeted Sri Karam Chand Mehra at the railway station in Moradabad. Then he said, "Hello, Karam Chand. I am Parmanand."
14. Recognition of way from railway station at Moradabad to Mohan Brothers shop and recognition of shop.	B. L. Sharma M. L. Sharma M. L. Mehra	In 1964, when I visited Moradabad, I traversed this area between the railway station and the Mohan Brothers shop.	The shop was located some considerable distance (about a half mile) from the railway station on a road with a number of possible turnings. Parmod was taken from the railway station in a tonga, a two-wheeled horse-drawn vehicle commonly used in India. The driver was instructed to follow Parmod's directions in going from the station to the shop. There was nothing specially distinctive about the shop which made it easy to recognize. It did, however, have signs above it which advertised the biscuits and included the name of the business. Sri M. L. Mehra, not himself present during the

	Informants	Verification	Comments
14. (continued)			drive from the station, stated that the tonga driver was told to follow Parmod's directions, but that the people with him tried to mislead Parmod.
15. Recognition of the Town Hall in Moradabad.	B. L. Sharma	In going between the Mohan Brothers shop and the railway station I passed and examined the Town Hall.	Parmod used the words "Town Hall" (which he pronounced "Ton Hall") which Sri B. L. Sharma insisted no one had spoken in his presence. The Town Hall of Moradabad is a large building in the center of the city, but it has no sign or other indication of its function and resembles a mosque more than an official building.
16. The Mohan Brothers shop was near the Town Hall.	B. L. Sharma	Verified by me during a visit to Moradabad.	Statement made by Parmod after he reached the Town Hall in Moradabad on the way to the Mohan Brothers shop.
17. Complaint that "his" seat in the shop had been changed. Recognition of place in shop where "he" had sat.	M. L. Sharma B. L. Sharma Raj K. Mehra, cousin of Parmanand N. K. Mehra	Raj K. Mehra	Shops in India usually have an enclosed seat (gaddi) for the proprietor or manager at the front of the store. He sits there and receives the customers and directs the business. The seat and layout around the Mohan Brothers shop had been changed after Parmanand's death.
18. Explanation of how to work the soda water machine in the Mohan Brothers shop in Moradabad.	M. L. Mehra B. L. Sharma N. K. Mehra		When Parmod entered the shop one of his first remarks was: "Who is looking after the bakery and soda water factory?" (These had been the special province of Parmanand Mehra in the family business.) When taken to the soda water machine, Parmod knew exactly how it worked. The water had been disconnected to mislead him, but he understood without anyone telling him how this quite complicated machine ought to be arranged in order to work.

Item	Informants	Verification	Comments
19. Recognition of a room in Parmanand's home where he had slept. Comment on screen added to the room after his death.	M. L. Sharma J. D. Mehra	N. K. Mehra	After Parmanand's death, Sri J. D. Mehra installed a separating screen in the room where he had slept. When Parmod saw this screen, he asked Sri Mehra: "Did you do this?" The latter asked Parmod: "Was it not here?" and Parmod replied: "No."
20. Recognition of Parmanand's almirah (cupboard) in the house.	Nandrani Mehra		Indicating a particular almirah in the house, Parmod said he used to keep his things in this one.
21. Recognition of special low table (tipai) for eating which had belonged to Parmanand.	Nandrani Mehra		Parmanand had a special low eating table which he used. Parmod recognized this little table when he saw it in the kitchen and said: "This is the one I used to use for my meals." Sri M. L. Sharma and Sri B. L. Sharma were secondhand witnesses of this item.
22. Recognition of Parmanand's mother.	B. L. Sharma N. K. Mehra		When Parmanand's mother approached where Parmod was sitting, he immediately addressed her as "Mother" before anyone else present had made any comment about her.
23. Recognition of Parmanand's daughter.	B. L. Sharma M. L. Sharma Nandrani Mehra Premlata Mehra, daughter of Parmanand		Parmod called her "daughter," but did not give her name. See note 19, p. 53, concerning reluctance in India to use personal names in the family. I am uncertain whether Parmod's father and uncle were firsthand witnesses of this item.
24. Recognition of Parmanand's wife.	Nandrani Mehra B. L. Sharma M. L. Sharma		Unintentional suggestion might have entered into this recognition since Parmod was brought among a group of ladies and asked if he could recognize "his" wife.

24. (continued)

He showed an appropriate response of embarrassment and looked at Parmanand's widow. She then took him aside. Later she told others that Parmod had said: "I have come but you have not fixed bindi." This remark referred to the round mark of red pigment worn on the forehead by wives in India, but not by widows. The remark would be a most unusual one for a small boy to make to a strange older woman, but entirely appropriate in the relationship of husband and wife. It indicates how firmly Parmod believed the lady was "his" wife. He also reproached her for wearing a white sari, as Hindu widows commonly do, instead of a colored one as wives do.

25. Recognition of Parmanand's son, Sri N. K. Mehra.

N. K. Mehra
Raj K. Mehra
Nandrani Mehra

Sri N. K. Mehra said that Parmod addressed him by his familiar name "Bali." The other two informants did not hear or remember this detail, but said that Parmod stated the order of Parmanand's sons, e.g., "eldest son." Sri J. D. Mehra gave discrepant testimony about this item, on one occasion denying that Parmod had recognized Sri N. K. Mehra, and on another asserting that he had done so. Sri N. K. Mehra said that when he called Parmod by *his* name, Parmod objected, as would a father whose child called him by his name.

26. Recognition of Parmanand's son, Sri Govardhan Das Mehra.

Govardhan Das Mehra, fourth son of Parmanand
Nandrani Mehra

Govardhan Das Mehra, still a child, returned from school when Parmod was visiting the Mehra family in Moradabad. Someone asked Parmod, "Who is that?" Parmod said: "My son," and was then asked his name. He then replied: "Gordhan." This was the correct shortened

Item	Informants	Verification	Comments
26. (continued)			form of "Govardhan" used in the family. Srimati Nandrani Mehra said Parmod gave the correct relationships of Parmanand's children, e.g., oldest, youngest, etc., but did not state any names. Sri Govardhan Das said that Parmod told him to address him (Parmod) as "father" and not by his name.
27. Recognition of Sri M. L. Mehra, brother of Parmanand.	M. L. Mehra		Parmod identified Sri M. L. Mehra as "older brother," but did not give his name. The recognition took place when Parmod reached the Mohan Brothers shop. One witness, Sri B. L. Sharma, recalled it in 1964 as having taken place at the railway station in Moradabad, but Sri M. L. Mehra said he did not go to the station to meet Parmod.
28. Recognition of Sri Raj K. Mehra, nephew of Parmanand.	Raj K. Mehra		In 1961 Sri Raj K. Mehra said Parmod had called him "Raj" when he recognized him. In 1964 he did not remember this, and thought Parmod had recognized him only as "nephew."
29. Comment on new sheds having been added to Victory Hotel.	M. L. Mehra J. D. Mehra		Some new sheds had been built at the hotel since Parmanand's death.
30. Recognition of almirahs (cupboards) brought from previous hotel to Victory Hotel.	J. D. Mehra		The family had owned another hotel (Churchill House) before buying the Victory Hotel. They moved some almirahs which Parmanand had had constructed from the first hotel to the Victory Hotel. Parmod saw these almirahs as he was going around the Victory Hotel and said: "These are the almirahs I had constructed in Churchill House."

118

Item	Informants		Comments and Verification
31. Recognition of a doctor known to Parmanand in Saharanpur.	Raj K. Mehra		During his visit to Saharanpur, Parmod spontaneously pointed out this man and said: "He is a doctor and an old friend of mine."
32. Recognition of Yasmin, a Muslim debtor of Parmanand. Parmod said to him: "I have to get some money back from you."	B. L. Sharma Raj K. Mehra		Yasmin was at first reluctant to admit the debt, but when a member of the Mehra family present assured him they had no intention of reclaiming the money he said Parmod was quite right about the debt. Witnesses disagreed on the actual amount owed.
33. Recognition of a driver of a lorry in Hardwar.	B. L. Sharma		Sri B. L. Sharma, in a letter written Nov. 18, 1949, placed this recognition in Hardwar, but in 1964 he remembered it as occurring in Saharanpur. He additionally stated that Parmod had spontaneously noticed the driver and had called out to him, "Hello, Tauji."
34. Recognition in Hardwar of family doctor (Sri Nawal Bahari Mathur) of Parmanand.	B. L. Sharma J. D. Mehra		Sri J. D. Mehra did not witness this episode himself, but stated that he had been told of it by Sri Karam Chand Mehra, his cousin, who did witness it and stated that Parmod had correctly given the doctor's name.
35. Recognition of the rest house Parmanand used to stay in at Hardwar and of room in it where Parmanand slept.	B. L. Sharma		Not independently verified, Sri B. L. Sharma verified these facts from persons at the rest house who remembered Parmanand.
36. He had been to Delhi on business.	B. L. Sharma	M. L. Mehra	Parmanand had been to Delhi. Parmod had been to Delhi and stated that he had there found various places, e.g., Chandni Chowk and the Red Fort "familiar." But he did not claim any special knowledge of these or other places in Delhi.

corroborated and verified earlier. I have, however, confined myself in this report to the smaller number of details in which I felt confident of the authentication by the witnesses.

Of the items in the tabulation, items 1 to 7 were mentioned by Parmod in Bisauli and before he had visited Moradabad. The statements of items 8 to 10 were made after Parmod's first visit to Moradabad and so (probably) was the statement of item 11. Items 12–29 consist chiefly of recognitions or statements made during Parmod's first visits to Moradabad. Items 30–32 occurred on Parmod's visit to Saharanpur in the autumn of 1949. Items 33–35 occurred during a visit, also made during this period, to Hardwar, a mountain town near Saharanpur. I do not know when Parmod made the statement of item 36.

Relevant Reports and Observations of the Behavior of the People Concerned. For about four years, from age three to age seven, Parmod showed behavior indicating a strong identification with the previous personality, Parmanand Mehra. His first recorded remark related to the previous life occurred when, at the age of about two and a half, he told his mother not to bother cooking any more since he had a wife in Moradabad who would do the cooking. Fuller manifestations of his identification with Parmanand Mehra developed when he was between three and four years old.

At about that time he began to show in his play a strong interest in building models of shops with electrical wires running around them. His play with mud included the making of mud biscuits. He would offer these to others, served with water which represented the tea. (He did not eat any of his mud biscuits.) He showed a fondness for biscuits and tea quite unusual in his family. Through the association of biscuits he began to talk of soda water. He also liked to drink soda water, and disliked milk. Then he began to give additional items of information about the size of the shop in Moradabad, what was sold there, his prosperity, and his activities connected with the shop such as his journeys to Delhi.

During this period he tended to remain by himself and avoided play with other children; he seemed preoccupied with the life in Moradabad and frequently importuned his parents to take him there, sometimes crying in his desire for this. Reluctantly he began to attend school on the promise of his mother that he could go to Moradabad when he could read. But he protested that he would work at his own shop and not read. Parmod complained of the financial status of his family, which he compared unfavorably to "his" former prosperity.

In addition to behavior already mentioned, Parmod exhibited other cravings, habits, and dislikes that I found corresponded with related traits or experiences of Parmanand. He had, for example, a strong aversion to eating curd, which, as already mentioned, was said to have been an important contributory cause of the illness and death of Parmanand. He advised his father against eating curd, saying that it was dangerous. As he grew older, he began to take curd when mixed with other food, but did not eat pure curd until he was about seventeen years old. At nineteen, in 1964, he ate curd, but still without relish, although most Indians enjoy it very much.

Parmod showed also a strong dislike of being submerged in water. He had no objection to water running over him from a pipe, for example, but became anxious if it was proposed to swim or even bathe in a river where his whole body would be immersed. This fear related to the tub baths Parmanand had before he died. It also had faded away at the time of my second visit when Parmod was nineteen years old.

In early childhood Parmod showed an unusual devoutness which corresponded to a similar trait of religiousness in Parmanand. Parmod said he could recall a few fragments of a life preceding that of Parmanand when he was a sannyasi or holy man. In 1964 he had a persisting interest in palmistry which I learned had been a hobby of Parmanand. Parmod said that in his life as Parmanand he had once read the palm of his sister-in-law. Parmanand's widow confirmed that her husband had in fact read his sister-in-law's palm and correctly predicted the age at which she died.

Parmod used several English words and phrases which his father said he could not have heard in the family, but which were appropriate for Parmanand, who could speak English. So could Sri B. L. Sharma, but his wife could not and English was not spoken in their family. Among the English words noted were: "bakery," "tub bath," and "town hall." Parmod also mentioned the names of Tata, Birla, and Dolmia, large companies of India. The last is a manufacturer of biscuits.

When a small child, Parmod seemed to his father to have superior intelligence. Nevertheless, Parmod had not done well in his studies on the whole, and although he had gone into an intermediate college he had continued to have academic difficulties. His mother believed that the recall of the previous life had interfered with his learning. Considering the fact that Parmod seemed much preoccupied with the previous personality during some of the critical years of learning, i.e., from four to seven, this explanation has much merit. In one sector of his behavior, Parmod showed superior skill. A relative who owned a small shop left someone in it to handle business when he had to be away. Parmod showed great aptitude for managing the shop and this man preferred him above all other persons as his substitute in the shop. Notwithstanding this capacity for business affairs, Parmod stated he preferred not to go into business, although his family thought this most appropriate for his future career. Parmod had decided that times in India remained unsuitable for business and in 1964 he was trying to train himself for a career as a chemical engineer.

Upon first meeting members of Parmanand's family, Parmod showed strong emotions, including tears and demonstrations of affection. Sri M. L. Mehra said that Parmod in Moradabad showed a preference for being with him rather than with his father. His attitude toward the members of Parmanand's family corresponded to the relationships Parmanand had with them. Thus he behaved toward Parmanand's wife as a husband would, and toward his children as a father would. He showed familiarity with Parmanand's sons, but not with his nephew. He would not allow Parmanand's sons to call him by name, but said they should call him "father." He said, "I have only become small."

Parmod asked the wife of Parmanand if she would give him trouble again. On another occasion he said, referring to Parmanand's wife, "This is my wife with whom I always quarreled." One informant stated that Parmanand had been bothered by his wife and that he had moved to Saharanpur to get away from her.

Parmod made several visits to Parmanand's family when he was between five and six years old, and some members of this family visited him in Bisauli. On these occasions he showed the greatest fondness for the members of the other family. On one of these occasions he indicated great reluctance to return to Bisauli and wept upon being taken from Moradabad. After his first visit to Moradabad, he ran away from home one day and got as far as the railway station in Bisauli. When brought back, he said he wanted to go to Saharanpur to run the family business there.

After his first visits, his desire to go to Moradabad and his strong interest in the Mehra family gradually diminished, along with spontaneous statements about the previous life. Yet even then he preserved a considerable interest in the family. He expressed annoyance once when he learned that he had not been invited to the wedding of one of Parmanand's sons. During the years 1961–63, Parmanand's daughter, Kumari Premlata Mehra, worked in Budaun, a city much closer to Bisauli than Moradabad. From there she used to visit Parmod from time to time. On these occasions he showed great affection for her and also annoyance when she neglected to visit. He showed toward her at first the attitude of a father toward his daughter until she eventually suggested that, the past being over, they should act toward each other as brother and sister; whereupon Parmod modified his behavior toward her. In 1961 Parmod said that his memories had definitely faded somewhat, but he still retained some. He showed no sign whatever of having elaborated the accounts further. For example, he then denied that earlier he had recalled the name "Mohan Brothers," although his father had so testified.

In 1962 Professor Sharma reported (in testimony recorded by Sri Subash Mukherjee) that Parmod had "totally forgotten" about the previous life. But this statement seems to have referred to what members of Parmod's family noted about his spontaneous expression of statements or behavior related to the previous personality and not to a capacity of Parmod to recall voluntarily what he earlier seemed to remember; for in 1964, Parmod stated that he could still recall what he had previously remembered. He no longer thought much about the previous life unless he happened to visit some place like Delhi and had a sense of familiarity with some area or building. Then he would try to place the area and its seeming recollection in the life of Parmanand. And he spoke even less of the previous life to others unless, as on my visit, someone would specially ask him about it.

Comments on the Evidence of Paranormal Knowledge on the Part of Parmod. In contrast to some other cases in India, the present case occurred among persons of education and responsibility in their communities. Parmod's father, for example, was a Sanskrit scholar and professor at an intermediate college. With regard to the educational level of the witnesses, the case stands on a par with that of Swarnlata among the other Indian cases of this monograph. Nor could I find any evidence that the details had been elaborated on by witnesses. The evidence of paranormality in the case rests chiefly, but by no means entirely, on the statements Parmod made as a child of three to seven years about the previous life, and on the observations of his behavioral identification with the deceased Parmanand Mehra at the same period. On these matters the testimony of different witnesses shows clarity and concordance.

We have no grounds for rejecting the firm statements of the two families that they knew nothing of each other before the first meeting for recognitions in Moradabad when Parmod was just under five years old. But then we are almost forced to suppose some kind of paranormal communication in order to account for the possession by Parmod of information of a quite personal and specific nature relevant to the life of Parmanand and for his exhibition of behavior appropriately matching that expected to follow the experiences of this deceased personality.

Earlier I mentioned that the maternal uncle of Parmod, Sri Shiva Sharan Sharma, was a railway employee stationed for about three years at Moradabad during the time when Parmod was a small child and talking of his interest in biscuits and soda water. Because of this expressed interest in biscuits, his uncle used to bring him biscuits from Moradabad when he visited his family and sister living in Bisauli. And he purchased and brought to Parmod biscuits from the Mohan Brothers shop in Moradabad. These biscuits, I further learned, had "Mohan Brothers" embossed on them, but were not put up in labeled boxes. (Mohan Brothers sold biscuits only to their retail customers, not for shipment elsewhere.) Parmod, according to his mother, did not recognize the Mohan Brothers biscuits. I was unable to interview Sri Shiva Sharan Sharma, but gathered as much information as I could from other witnesses about his movements and acquaintance with the Mehra brothers. It seems that Sri Shiva Sharan Sharma was not stationed in Moradabad during the life of Parmanand and had no personal acquaintance with any of the Mehra brothers, although he bought biscuits at their shop. He was not the first person to make contact between Parmod's family and the Mehra brothers for the purpose of verifying Parmod's statements. The initiative for this was taken by Sri Lala Raghanand Prasad. Then afterwards Sri Shiva Sharan Sharma spoke with the Mehra brothers about Parmod's statements. In short, it seems unlikely, if not impossible, that Sri Shiva Sharan Sharma knew Parmanand, and improbable that he had any knowledge whatever of the personal affairs of the Mehra family. But he was a customer of their shop, and going back and forth between Moradabad and Parmod's family during the period of Parmod's most active personation of Parmanand, he could conceivably have acted as a telepathic link between the Mehra family and Parmod.[35]

Comment on Long-Term Observations in this Case. The present case provides some information on an aspect of cases of this type which calls for much more intensive study in the future; namely, how the identification with another personality gradually diminishes with the passage of years so that eventually only traces remain on the surface, or perhaps nothing at all. In Parmod's case we have much testimony about his behavior as a small child between three and seven years of age, when the identification with the previous personality was strongest. And we also have considerable information about his later development, at least into manhood at the age of twenty. In most respects Parmod's development proceeded entirely normally. He certainly provides no support for the belief sometimes expressed that persons who seem to remember a previous life have or will develop some serious fragmentation of personality. On the other hand, his case belongs to a group in which we find some evidence of a residual effect on the adult personality of the strong identification with another personality which the subject showed in childhood. As already mentioned, Parmod's mother believed that this identification during his early school years distracted him from the ordinary tasks of learning in school and home and set him behind his contemporaries. In some other cases of the reincarnation type I have found evidence that the intrusion, if I may call it such, of memories and behavior related to a previous personality interferes with the development of the present personality. I hope that from careful

[35] I have learned of persons who might furnish such telepathic links in other cases, e.g., those of Sukla and Jasbir, in the present group and also in the case of Marta in Brazil and Imad in Lebanon, to be described later. I shall revert to this important subject of possible telepathic links in the General Discussion.

follow-up observations of Parmod and other cases we can learn more about these effects.

The Later Development of Parmod. I did not meet Parmod between August, 1964, and November, 1971. During these years, however, I heard some news of him through Dr. Jamuna Prasad, who had included Parmod's case among those in which a team led by himself had been studying correspondences in behavioral traits between subjects and related previous personalities of reincarnation type cases. During these years I also received occasional letters from Parmod or his father with news of his current activities.

In November, 1971, I was able to have a fairly long talk with Parmod in Pilibhit, U.P. We met at the office of the Soil Conservation Service in which he was currently employed. Parmod was then just over twenty-seven years old.

As I mentioned earlier, Parmod had difficulty in the later years of his education, something his mother attributed to his absorption with the previous life when a child and his consequent neglect of school work. Parmod failed the examinations of the twelfth class of school and then finally passed them in 1966. At this time he was more than twenty-one years old and so some years behind his contemporaries. He then entered a civil aviation training school with the intention of becoming a pilot. But the fees were beyond his means and he left the school at the end of 1968. Early in 1969 he joined the Soil Conservation Service of Uttar Pradesh and was assigned as a clerk to the office of the Service in Pilibhit where I met him in 1971. His position was what is called "temporary" in India which means that although it may last for years, it may also be discontinued on almost no notice at any time. Parmod was well aware of the precariousness of his employment and was trying to continue his education privately in order to improve his qualifications for a better position. He had not succeeded in one attempt to pass an examination at the university level, but was studying for another try at the time of our meeting. He was then thinking that he would, after all, prefer to be in business as Parmanand had been.

Parmod's father had retired in the meantime and was living in Bisauli. Parmod himself had not married and was living alone in Pilibhit.

In answer to my question about preservation of his memories of the previous life, Parmod said that there had been considerable fading of these after the age of seven, but he thought that he had retained all the memories which he had not lost at about that age. He still thought about the previous life, but could at first mention no special stimulus for doing so. Asked about what features of the previous life he thought about most, he mentioned Parmanand's children and the factory (for soda water) that he had owned. He then went on to say that situations similar to those of the previous life might remind him of it. Thus if he saw children he might think of the business Parmanand had owned. He said he did not think often of Parmanand's wife with whom Parmanand had not been happy.

Parmod still maintained friendships with members of Parmanand's family and saw them rather often. He sometimes stayed with them in Moradabad, although he had not lived with them at a period when he had been working (I am not sure just when) in Moradabad. In line with Parmanand's preferences, Parmod saw more of Parmanand's sons than of his wife in Moradabad.

Parmod also said that he still occasionally thought of the life as a sannyasi or holy man (anterior to that of Parmanand) which he had earlier remembered. He was reminded of this life at times when he found himself with persons of philosophical interests. But of the three lives of which he had memories—that of the sannyasi, that of Parmanand, and that of Parmod —he said that he preferred that of Parmanand. He could not explain this preference.

I asked Parmod about residues of the phobias he had shown earlier for immersion in water and the eating of curd. He had completely lost the fear of immersion in water and could take baths without difficulty. (Parmod had actually lost this fear by the time of my meeting with him in 1964 when he was nineteen years old.) He said that he could eat curd, but added that he still did not like it.

We then discussed his opinion of the value to him of having remembered a previous life. He first replied that the experience had seemed neither helpful nor harmful, but then immediately qualified his answer by giving examples suggesting that it had been both. On the one hand, he agreed with his mother that his earlier preoccupation with memories of the previous life had interfered with his studies; and if this were so, he had not fully recovered from the handicap since his future advancement depended very much on his completing higher education and earning a degree. On the other hand, he believed that his memories of a previous life had also given him advantages. At the practical level he thought his acumen in business derived from what he had learned of that vocation as Parmanand. And in a more general way the assurance of a continuity of life after death which his memories conveyed to him gave him a poise and balance which greatly aided his personal relationships.

Parmod then asked me whether anyone whose case I had studied had benefited from my investigations. I had to admit frankly that none had done so to the best of my knowledge. I said that the benefit from these researches, if any comes, will be spread more generally by whatever contribution they may make to our understanding of human personality and to the evidence that at least a part of us survives death.

Parmod seems to me a person of average or superior intelligence; his talents will be underemployed if he remains a clerk, but he can do little else in government service unless he obtains a university degree. He can advance much more rapidly in financial gain by entering business, and I am inclined to predict that he will eventually choose this course in life. I consider his case to be among the rare few in which remembering a previous life has interfered with development in childhood and has therefore hampered the subject in later life.

Three Cases
Suggestive of Reincarnation
in Ceylon

Introduction

THE majority of the inhabitants of Ceylon[1] are descended from people of the Indo-European linguistic group and are therefore related to the northern Indians. These are called Sinhalese. An important minority of the Ceylonese are Tamil-speaking persons related to the southern Indians of Dravidian origin. Buddhism arose in India in the sixth century B.C. as a reform movement within ancient Brahmanism. Its founder was Siddhartha Gotama, who was probably born in 563 B.C. He lived a life of extraordinary goodness and, according to Buddhists, attained enlightenment about the true nature of man and his relationship to terrestrial life and the rest of the universe. He thus became a Buddha or enlightened one, and spent the remainder of his long life imparting (and practicing) his teachings about life, suffering, and the means of liberation from suffering. Although today Buddhism has few followers in India, the Buddha occupies a place in the Hindu pantheon as an Avatar or Incarnation of God along with other Hindu incarnations such as Rama and Krishna. Buddhism flourished and spread widely in India during the reign of the great Emperor Asoka in the third century B.C. Asoka sent missionaries to Ceylon and they converted the Sinhalese who have remained Buddhist, for the most part, ever since. Most Tamils are Hindus.

Buddhism itself split into a number of branches. The Sinhalese belong to the Theravada (sometimes called Hinayana) branch whose adherents derive their beliefs and practices from the Pali Canon, a record of the Buddha's teachings made in the first century B.C. This branch of Buddhism differs from the northern or Mahayana branch in certain points of doctrine which do not need exposition here. I shall, however, mention briefly some important features of Buddhism which bear on the study of cases suggestive of reincarnation in which Buddhists believe as much as do Hindus. Both believe also that terrestrial life inevitably includes some suffering, that such suffering results from our desiring the sensuous pleasures found in

---

[1] After the publication of the first edition of this book Ceylon changed its name (in 1972) to the Republic of Sri Lanka.

terrestrial life, that such desires pull us back again and again to successive lives, and that final liberation from the "wheel of rebirth" comes only with the abandonment of such desires and the attainment of detachment from corporeal pleasures. This goal can be reached by various techniques, including right conduct and the assiduous practice of meditation, which gradually lead to the extinction (Nirvana) of the craving which promotes reincarnation.[2]

Hindus believe in the persistence after physical death of an essential element or Atman in each person, which idea corresponds roughly to the Western idea of a soul. The Atman (after a varying interval) associates itself with a new physical organism and comes into terrestrial existence again, thus continuing the growth (or decline) of the personality that lived before. These ideas call for the postulation of a continuing and presumably permanent entity. In contrast, most Buddhists, especially of the Theravada branch, do not believe in the persistence of a permanent entity or soul. There is a constant flux of desire, action, effect, and reaction, but no persisting soul. When a person dies, the accumulated effects of his actions set in motion a further train of events which leads to other consequences, one of which may be the terrestrial birth of another personality. If the first personality has achieved detachment from sensuous desires, a birth into another "plane" may occur instead of a new terrestrial birth. But this newly born personality will relate to the first one only as the flame of a candle (before it finally extinguishes) can light another candle's flame. Buddhists often prefer the term "rebirth" to "reincarnation" to emphasize this distinction. Different schools of Buddhists subscribe to somewhat different concepts of what may persist after physical death. But they agree among themselves (and also with Hindus) in believing that the conduct of one personality can affect the behavior, physical organism, and life events of another later personality that is related to the first one through the process of rebirth.

[2] Further information and bibliographies about Buddhism will be found in the following: W. Rahula. *What the Buddha Taught.* London: Gordon Fraser, 1959; C. Humphreys. *Buddhism.* Harmondsworth: Penguin Books, 1951; A. Coomaraswamy. *Hinduism and Buddhism.* New York: Philosophical Library, n.d.; Nyanatiloka Mahathera. *The Word of the Buddha.* Kandy, Ceylon: Buddhist Pub. Soc., 1959; De la Vallée Poussin. "Buddhism," in *The Legacy of India.* (Ed. G. T. Garratt.) Oxford: Oxford University Press, 1937; *The Tibetan Book of the Dead.* (Ed. W. Y. Evans-Wentz.) London: Oxford University Press, 3rd ed., 1957; N. P. Jacobson. *Buddhism: The Religion of Analysis.* Carbondale: Southern Illinois University Press, 1966; Piyadassi Thera. *The Buddha's Ancient Path.* London: Rider and Company, 1964. The foregoing are selected from a vast literature on Buddhism.

For the observations and opinions on Sinhalese Buddhism of some modern anthropologists and social psychologists see: M. Ames. "Magical-animism and Buddhism: A Structural Analysis of the Sinhalese Religious System," in *Religion in South Asia* (Ed. E. B. Harper). Seattle: University of Washington Press, 1964; G. Obeyesekere. "The Great Tradition and the Little in the Perspective of Sinhalese Buddhism." *Journal of Asian Studies,* Vol. 22, 1963, 139–153; R. F. Gombrich. *Precept and Practice: Traditional Buddhism in the Rural Highlands of Ceylon.* London: Oxford University Press, 1971.

Buddhism completely discarded the Hindu ideas and practices concerning caste. Hindus have preserved the idea of caste for centuries (although it is now weakening), thinking that it expresses and regulates important differences in people. But they also believe that a person can change his caste from one life to another for better or worse through merit or wickedness. The case of Jasbir in the section on Indian cases of this monograph is one of numerous Indian cases I have studied in which the two personalities belonged to different castes. Some of the subjects of these cases had considerable difficulty in adjusting to conditions in the "strange" castes in which they found themselves.[3] Buddhists can use such cases to point out that, on the empirical evidence they afford, caste distinctions do not always govern the next rebirth. A man's caste may be valid for only one life and a tenacious fondness for caste distinctions is just another form of sensuous attachment which delays final liberation from the wheel of rebirth.

The Buddhist traditions attribute to Gotama the Buddha the capacity to recall previous lives he had lived and even that he offered some instructions for others who wished to do this. Numerous cases of persons who claim to remember previous lives occur in the Buddhist countries, e.g., Ceylon, Thailand, Burma, and Tibet. As with Hinduism, such cases have provided some continuing empirical support for the beliefs of Buddhism which, although largely disappearing from India, has continued to flourish throughout much of the rest of southern and eastern Asia.

In 1961 I spent a week in Ceylon in the investigation of several cases suggestive of reincarnation, including the three reported here. The methods of investigation used did not differ from those described in the introduction to this series of cases and need little further description here.

In the case of Gnanatilleka, I interviewed members of the child's present family and of the family in which she claimed to have lived before. I gathered additional evidence from eyewitnesses of Gnanatilleka's recognitions of the members of the latter family. In the case of Wijeratne, this boy claimed to have been reborn into his own family as "his" previous brother's son. It may be thought that in these circumstances we cannot altogether exclude the possibility that Wijeratne acquired what information he had about the deceased personality he claimed to have been from his father, who knew the facts about the deceased person very well. Certainly we cannot positively rule this out as an explanation of some features of the case, but I shall present later my reasons for thinking it equally or more probable that Wijeratne did not in fact hear about the other life he

---

[3] Other subjects of this book, e.g., Sukla, remembered a previous life in a different caste. Sukla and some other subjects had much less difficulty than Jasbir in adjusting to the awareness of being born in a different caste. But still other subjects (of cases to be published) experienced difficulties almost as severe as those of Jasbir in making this adaptation.

described from members of his family, at least before he himself began to talk about details of that life.

The case of Ranjith Makalanda differs from all the other Asian cases of this series in the lack of information sufficiently detailed to permit identification of a previous person corresponding to the personality he claimed to have been. Nevertheless, I present this case because, relatively minor though it is, it demonstrates certain features of such minor cases suggestive of reincarnation that I have found repeatedly all over the world. I have investigated a large number of such minor cases and will, as I have said above, later publish summaries of the common features that occur repeatedly in the minor and also the major cases suggestive of reincarnation.[4] The case of Ranjith Makalanda provides a fairly typical example of a minor case of this type.

As I have mentioned in the Introduction, Mr. Francis Story accompanied me in the study of these cases. Mr. E. C. Raddalgoda, of Kotte, Ceylon, was the chief interpreter from Sinhalese into English. For the case of Wijeratne I had the additional assistance of the Venerable Ananda Maitreya, who acted as a second interpreter during the interviews. Further, the interviews in Ceylon were all witnessed by Dr. William A. Coates, then Fulbright Professor of English at the University of Ceylon, Peradeniya, and later at the Department of Modern Languages and Linguistics, University of Rochester. Dr. Coates spent two years in Ceylon teaching English and studying Sinhalese. Although at the time of my interviews, he could not speak or understand Sinhalese fluently, he could understand some of what was said and stated afterwards that he never had any reason to doubt the accuracy of Mr. Raddalgoda's translations. Mr. D. V. Sumithapala acted as interpreter for one interview. A few of the witnesses spoke English and so required no interpreters.

Case Reports

The Case of Gnanatilleka

Summary of the Case and its Investigation. Gnanatilleka Baddewithana was born near Hedunawewa in central Ceylon on February 14, 1956. When she was one year old she began talking about another mother and father, but she was two before she made her first clear references to a previous life. She

---

[4] Up to 1973 I had published three such summaries. These are: "Cultural Patterns in Cases Suggestive of Reincarnation Among the Tlingit Indians of Southeastern Alaska." *Journal A.S.P.R.*, Vol. 60, July, 1966, 229–243; "Characteristics of Cases of the Reincarnation Type in Turkey and their Comparison with Cases in Two Other Cultures. *International Journal of Comparative Sociology*, Vol. 11, March, 1970, 1–17; "Characteristics of Cases of the Reincarnation Type in Ceylon." *Contributions to Asian Studies*, Vol. 3, 1973, 26–39.

then said she had a mother and father in another place, and also two brothers and many sisters. At first she did not give the place of her previous life a specific location, but did so after a visit to her home by some villagers who had been to a town called Talawakele. Hearing about this visit, Gnanatilleka stated that her mother and father were at Talawakele. She then said she wanted to visit her former parents, and gave further details of the location of her former home and names of members of her family. News of her declarations reached the Venerable Piyadassi Thera and Mr. H. S. S. Nissanka in Kandy, and they were able from the details furnished by Gnanatilleka to identify a particular family in Talawakele which corresponded accurately with the statements she had made. On November 9, 1954, this family had lost a son called Tillekeratne. He had been born at Talawakele on January 20, 1941.

Shortly afterwards (in 1960) Gnanatilleka's family took her to Talawakele where she correctly recognized a number of buildings in the town. However, the house at the place to which she directed them had been torn down and the family had moved. The family of Tillekeratne, the deceased boy she claimed to have been in her previous life, had lived in this particular place, but had moved from it not long after the death of Tillekeratne at the age of (approximately) thirteen years and nine months. At the time of Gnanatilleka's first visit to Talawakele, the two families did not meet.

Tillekeratne had attended a school, Sri Pada College in Hatton, twelve miles from Talawakele. Three of the schoolteachers from this college visited Gnanatilleka at Hedunawewa and she recognized them appropriately and described in detail certain aspects and events of the school. Then, early in 1961, Gnanatilleka was again brought to Talawakele where, in the presence of the Venerable Piyadassi Thera, Mr. Nissanka, and Mr. D. V. Sumithapala, various relatives and acquaintances of Tillekeratne were brought into her presence one by one and she was asked: "Do you know this person?" Gnanatilleka identified accurately seven members of Tillekeratne's family and two other persons of the community.

In the summer of 1961, I visited Talawakele, Hatton, and Hedunawewa for the purpose of conducting an independent investigation of the case.

Relevant Facts of Geography and Possible Normal Means of Communication Between the Two Families. Talawakele and Hedunawewa are both located in central Ceylon about sixteen miles from each other. Talawakele is in the highlands, whereas Hedunawewa lies in a deep valley and for this reason the climate and vegetation of the two areas differ considerably. Communication between them is much more difficult than the comparatively short distance which separates them would suggest. A hard-surfaced road runs from Talawakele to Kotmale about twelve miles to the north and buses travel along this route. But from Kotmale to Hedunawewa the road is poor and for much of the distance unpaved. Talawakele is the nearest town to Hedunawewa, since Kotmale (and Hedunawewa itself) is a mere village. There is some visiting by persons of Hedunawewa to Talawakele, although almost none in the other direction.

Members of Tillekeratne's family asserted that they had absolutely no acquaintance with the family of Gnanatilleka prior to the investigation of the case and that none of them had ever visited Hedunawewa. Gnanatilleka's family had only a slight acquaintance with Talawakele and her mother and father denied any acquaintance with the family of Tillekeratne prior to the development of the case. Her father had been to Talawakele to stop there only once, twenty years earlier; since then he had passed through the town only on the train. Her mother had never visited Talawakele. Her older brother had gone there for an exhibition of dancing.

After the case came to general knowledge in the village, Gnanatilleka's family learned that a person who had lived in Hedunawewa, but who originally came from Talawakele and later returned there, knew the family of Tillekeratne and had gone to his funeral. However, this man had never visited Gnanatilleka's home until after the case became known, when he called on her. And as mentioned earlier, a family from Hedunawewa had moved for a month to Talawakele and then returned to Hedunawewa. During a visit by this family to that of Gnanatilleka they mentioned in her presence that they were from Talawakele, and this remark stimulated Gnanatilleka's first reference to Talawakele as her home in the previous life. However, this family had not known Tillekeratne's family during their stay in Talawakele.

Gnanatilleka's home lay in the jungle, reached only by a tortuous footpath some half mile distant from the village of Hedunawewa, which, as I have mentioned, was itself rather difficult to reach from the main road between Talawakele and Kotmale. Nobody would reach the house of Gnanatilleka's family unless they were intent on visiting them. For inaccessibility, it would be difficult to plan or achieve a better location. I am confident therefore that no one from outside the village of Hedunawewa itself (and probably no one in the village) could have reached the home and talked with Gnanatilleka without her family knowing of the visit. And if we accept her parents' statement that they had no visitor from Talawakele prior to the verifications, then Gnanatilleka must have acquired through some paranormal means the detailed information she had about Tillekeratne and his family and life.

Persons Interviewed During the Investigation. In Talawakele I interviewed:

> Mrs. Beliwatte Liyanage Alice Nona, mother of Tillekeratne (Tillekeratne's father was not in Talawakele during my visit.)
> Salinawathie, older sister of Tillekeratne

In Hatton I interviewed:

Mr. D. V. Sumithapala, teacher of Sri Pada College and former teacher of Tillekeratne

In Hedunawewa I interviewed:

Gnanatilleka
Mr. D. A. Baddewithana, father of Gnanatilleka
Mrs. D. P. Baddewithana, mother of Gnanatilleka
Mr. Ariyapala Baddewithana, brother of Gnanatilleka
Mr. K. G. Ratnayaka, Principal, Government Central College, Hedunawewa

In addition, I have corresponded with the Venerable Piyadassi Thera about his investigation of the case and about certain details in the statements of witnesses.

Statements and Recognitions Made by Gnanatilleka. The tabulation below lists the main statements and recognitions made by Gnanatilleka which have been verified. It does not do justice to the numerous observations of Gnanatilleka's behavior appropriate to the events in Tillekeratne's life. Some of these will be summarized below.

Items 1 to 15 inclusive are statements made by Gnanatilleka before there had been any contact between the two families or any attempts made at verification.

Items 16 and 17 occurred on the occasion of Gnanatilleka's first visit to Talawakele with her family.

Items 18 to 21 occurred on the occasion of the visit by Mr. D. V. Sumithapala and his colleagues to Gnanatilleka at Hedunawewa.

Items 22 to 34 occurred during Gnanatilleka's second visit to Talawakele. Of these items, 22 to 32 occurred when Gnanatilleka was in a room with the observers, who introduced the persons she was to recognize, usually singly, although twice in groups of three. For each person they asked Gnanatilleka: "Do you know this person?" Present in the room were: Gnanatilleka and her parents, the three observers chaired by Venerable Piyadassi Thera, all of whom had been strangers to both families concerned, Mr. D. V. Sumithapala, former teacher of Tillekeratne, and the person or persons who were to be recognized by Gnanatilleka. A crowd of curious people assembled in the street outside the rest house (local inn) where these proceedings took place. But although this throng may have enhanced the excitement of the occasion, they could not possibly have influenced the details of the recognitions by Gnanatilleka, which took place on the second floor of the rest house under the conditions mentioned.

Gnanatilleka made the last two recognitions (items 33 and 34) spontaneously when she picked the persons concerned out of groups of other people. No one had asked her to recognize these persons.

Relevant Reports and Observations of the Behavior of the People Concerned. When angry with her parents, Gnanatilleka threatened to return to her "Talawakele mother," as she called Mrs. Alice Nona. When she recognized Mrs. Alice Nona at the meeting in Hedunawewa she showed great affection for her as well as for Tillekeratne's father. She showed a markedly greater affection for Tillekeratne's older sister Salinawathie than for his other three sisters and a distinct coolness toward his brother Buddhadasa. These responses were entirely appropriate to the relationships of Tillekeratne because Salinawathie had been his favorite sister and Buddhadasa had been an unfriendly and sometimes hostile brother.

Yet Gnanatilleka did not seriously wish to live with the Talawakele family. She gave and received much love in her family. This, too, matched the probable attitudes of Tillekeratne. He had not found life easy in his home before he died. His father stayed away much of the time, as did an older brother toward whom he felt friendly; the younger brother who remained at home, Buddhadasa, was unfriendly toward him. And although Tillekeratne seems to have been his mother's favorite son, his relations even with her became strained and unhappy at times. An episode recounted by the parents of Gnanatilleka may illustrate both the intensity and the ambivalence of Gnanatilleka's attitude toward the Talawakele mother. When Gnanatilleka was about four and a half a woman of Talawakele drowned and her body floated down the river toward Kotmale where it was found. When the family talked about this Gnanatilleka became extremely upset and cried, saying: "It could be my Talawakele mother." According to Mr. Sumithapala, this possibility affected her for a week.

Gnanatilleka's behavior toward Mr. D. V. Sumithapala seemed impressively appropriate to the part played in the life of Tillekeratne by this much loved schoolteacher. Mr. Sumithapala seems to have taken a special interest in Tillekeratne. He appeared to be a gentle person who prided himself on his ability to manage children without harsh punishment. Once Tillekeratne had asked Mr. Sumithapala: "Is it true that after we die, we are reborn?" The attachment between Tillekeratne and his teacher became duplicated in the fondness which Gnanatilleka and Mr. Sumithapala showed for each other. Gnanatilleka manifested an affection and indeed veneration for Mr. Sumithapala which she did not offer anyone else except her parents, and at times her affection for him even surpassed that for her parents. For example, she allowed Mr. Sumithapala to use her cup, although she would not permit her parents to use it under threat of her leaving the house. She eagerly awaited his visits and specially asked him to accompany

Summary of Statements and Recognitions Made by Gnanatilleka

Item	Informants	Verification	Comments
1. She had a mother and father, two brothers and many sisters living in Talawakele.[1]	D. A. Baddewithana, father of Gnanatilleka D. P. Baddewithana, mother of Gnanatilleka	Alice Nona, mother of Tillekeratne	Tillekeratne was one of ten children, including two other sons.
2. Her father was a postman.	D. A. Baddewithana D. P. Baddewithana	Salinawathie, sister of Tillekeratne	
3. Her brother was once bitten by a dog.	D. A. Baddewithana D. P. Baddewithana	Not independently confirmed. Mr. and Mrs. Baddewithana said they confirmed this episode.	
4. She had seen the Queen pass in a train.	D. A. Baddewithana D. P. Baddewithana K. G. Ratnayaka, principal of Gnanatilleka's school	Queen Elizabeth visited Ceylon in 1954. Her train passed through Talawakele, where it was easily visible to the townsfolk, on April 15, 1954. Mr. D. V. Sumithapala saw the Queen's special train at Hatton so it is very likely that the children of the school also saw it.	The Queen's train passed through Talawakele where it would have been easily visible to children. Her visit was an important event of that year. Mr. and Mrs. Baddewithana stated they had not spoken of the Queen's visit to Gnanatilleka, whose remark about it was stimulated by seeing a photograph of the Queen.
5. There were no coconut trees at Talawakele.	D. A. Baddewithana D. P. Baddewithana	Verified by me from informants about the local flora.	Coconut trees are abundant in the low jungle where Gnanatilleka lived. They are rare or absent in the highlands near Talawakele.
6. Her Talawakele mother used to have to buy firewood.	D. A. Baddewithana D. P. Baddewithana	Verified by me from informants about the loca flora.	In the low jungles near Gnanatilleka's home, wood can be easily gathered free. In the highland towns it is scarce and must be purchased.
7. She used to go to school from Talawakele in a train that passed through a tunnel.	D. A. Baddewithana D. P. Baddewithana	D. V. Sumithapala	The longest tunnel in Ceylon is on the line between Talawakele and Hatton. Tillekeratne went through this tunnel

Statement	Informants	Verification	Comments
8. Her Talawakele father did not have a knot of hair on the back of his head.	D. A. Baddewithana D. P. Baddewithana		Correct, but not independently confirmed. The hair styles of the two fathers differed, according to the Baddewithanas.
9. Her Talawakele mother was stout.	D. A. Baddewithana D. P. Baddewithana		Correct, as determined by me. Alice Nona is considerably heavier than Gnanatilleka's mother.
10. She went to school with one sister.	Alice Nona Salinawathie	Alice Nona	Tillekeratne also went to school with an older brother, Buddhadasa, whom he did not like.
11. One sister, Sudu Akka, went to school in Nawalapitiya.	D. A. Baddewithana D. P. Baddewithana		Correct, but not independently confirmed by me.
12. She had a brother called Dharmadasa.	D. A. Baddewithana D. P. Baddewithana		Correct, but not independently confirmed. It happens that a much older brother of Gnanatilleka was also called Dharmadasa.
13. Her house was located between the bus stand and post office in Talawakele.	Ariyapala Baddewithana, brother of Gnanatilleka	Ariyapala Baddewithana	The house she located was the house of Tillekeratne's family until some months after his death. It was not their house when Gnanatilleka went to Talawakele.
14. Narration of a Jataka story taught to Tillekeratne by Mr. D. V. Sumithapala.	D. V. Sumithapala, teacher of Tillekeratne. D. A. Baddewithana D. P. Baddewithana	D. V. Sumithapala	Mr. Sumithapala had in fact taught this mythological tale to Tillekeratne. Gnanatilleka told the story in great detail and with dramatic gestures. She had never heard the story in her family. Jataka stories are supposedly based on the previous lives of the Buddha.

¹ Although I have used the pronouns "she" and "her" in reference to Gnanatilleka's statements, readers should remember that she (Gnanatilleka) referred in her statements to Tillekeratne and to places and events in his life.

Item	Informants	Verification	Comments
15. She had climbed Adam's Peak with some monks.	Venerable Piyadassi Thera D. A. Baddewithana D. P. Baddewithana	Venerable Piyadassi Thera verified this with Alice Nona. Tillekeratne had climbed Adam's Peak twice, once with monks and once with his mother.	Adam's Peak, the tallest mountain in Ceylon, is considered sacred and often climbed by Ceylonese people, so this was not an unusual event in the life of Tillekeratne.
16. Recognition of place where family house of Tillekeratne used to stand.	Ariyapala Baddewithana	Ariyapala Baddewithana	When taken to the site of the house in Talawakele, Gnanatilleka said: "The house is not here, but it was." This occurred on the first visit of Gnanatilleka to Talawakele. The families did not meet then; verification of this and item 17 occurred later.
17. Recognition of house where laundryman lived.	Ariyapala Baddewithana	Ariyapala Baddewithana	This occurred on the first visit of Gnanatilleka to Talawakele.
18. Recognition of Mr. D. V. Sumithapala as a teacher who had never punished her.	D. V. Sumithapala	D. V. Sumithapala	This occurred when Mr. Sumithapala (with two other men) visited Gnanatilleka at Hedunawewa. He was certain no one introduced him and his companions. They simply asked her in turn, "Do you know me?" It appears that Mr. Sumithapala was an unusually gentle teacher. He said he had never punished Tillekeratne.
19. Failure to recognize Mr. Asoka Gautamadasa, principal of Sri Pada College.	D. V. Sumithapala	D. V. Sumithapala	Entirely appropriate since Mr. Gautamadasa was not at Sri Pada College when Tillekeratne had attended it. Conditions the same as for recognition of Mr. Sumithapala.
20. Failure to recognize Mr. Tilak Samarsinghe, a teacher of Anrudha College, Nawalapitiya, and a friend of Mr. Gautamadasa.	D. V. Sumithapala	D. V. Sumithapala	Conditions the same as for the recognition of Mr. Sumithapala. Entirely appropriate as Mr. Samarsinghe had never known Tillekeratne.

Item	Witnesses	Comments
21. Description of area between school at Hatton and the railway station near the school, including a bridge and steps between the station and school.	D. V. Sumithapala	She supplemented her description of a complex area with an accurate chalk drawing of the relationships.
22. Recognition of Tillekeratne's mother.	Venerable Piyadassi Thera D. V. Sumithapala Alice Nona	When Mrs. Alice Nona was brought into the room, Gnanatilleka was asked: "Do you know her?" All the following recognitions were conducted in the same manner. Gnanatilleka would not openly recognize Mrs. Alice Nona until her mother had left the room. Then Gnanatilleka said: "That is my Talawakele mother," and embraced her warmly. This took place at Talawakele on the second visit.
23. Recognition of Tillekeratne's father.	Venerable Piyadassi Thera D. V. Sumithapala	Conditions same as for recognition of mother of Tillekeratne.
24. Recognition of Tillekeratne's sister, Gunalatha.	D. V. Sumithapala Alice Nona Salinawathie	Conditions as for recognitions of other members of the family at Talawakele. Mr. Sumithapala recalled that Gnanatilleka recognized Gunalatha as "sister from Talawakele." The other witnesses of this episode said Gnanatilleka had further stated that Gunalatha was "The sister I used to go to school with." They were not present in the room during this recognition as was Mr. Sumithapala, and presumably heard this from Gunalatha, whom I did not interview. It is true that Gunalatha went to Hatton with Tillekeratne on the train every school day.
25. Recognition of Tillekeratne's sister, Leelawathie.	Alice Nona Salinawathie D. V. Sumithapala	Gnanatilleka placed this sister by mentioning where she lived. Salinawathie

Item	Informants	Verification	Comments
25. (continued)			was a firsthand witness of this recognition (as was Mr. Sumithapala) since the three older sisters went into the room together.
26. Recognition of Tillekeratne's sister, Somawathie.	Alice Nona Salinawathie D. V. Sumithapala		Recognition occurred in the same way and at the same time as that of Leelawathie.
27. Recognition of Tillekeratne's sister, Salinawathie.	Alice Nona Salinawathie D. V. Sumithapala		Correctly recognized as "Sudu Akka" (fair sister). Gnanatilleka showed more affection for Salinawathie than for the other sisters; Tillekeratne had been closer to her than to the other sisters. She was unmarried.
28. Requested Salinawathie to bring her pears.	Salinawathie		In the former house of the family, where Tillekeratne had lived, the family had had a pear tree. Pears would be associated with this sister, but are not common where Gnanatilleka lived.
29. Recognition of Mr. U. K. D. Silva.	D. V. Sumithapala		Conditions as for other recognitions of persons at Talawakele given above. Gnanatilleka recognized him as a "Talawakele uncle. He taught me at Sunday school."
30. Recognition of Mr. N. A. Nayakkara.	D. V. Sumithapala		Conditions as for previous recognitions at Talawakele. Gnanatilleka said Mr. Nayakkara "had taught me in the Talawakele school." He had taught Tillekeratne in the Sunday school at Talawakele.
31. Failure to recognize stranger unknown to Tillekeratne.	D. V. Sumithapala		Appropriate as this person had not known Tillekeratne. Conditions as for above recognitions. This stranger was brought in to see if Gnanatilleka would make any false recognitions.

Item	Informant(s)	Verification	Comments
32. Recognition of Buddhadasa, Tillekeratne's brother.	Alice Nona Salinawathie D. V. Sumithapala		Recognized as "my brother." She took a long time to acknowledge Buddhadasa, turned away from him, and generally received him very coolly. Tillekeratne and Buddhadasa had not been good friends. Buddhadasa often teased Tillekeratne about model shrines which Tillekeratne built and valued highly.
33. Recognition of Upasakamma, a female devotee of the temple.	D. V. Sumithapala	D. V. Sumithapala said the woman in question confirmed the previous association with Tillekeratne	A woman devotee of the temple, picked out of a crowd of people spontaneously by Gnanatilleka. Gnanatilleka said "She came to the Talawakele temple with me."
34. Recognition of a neighbor who had quarreled with her Talawakele mother.	D. V. Sumithapala		This neighbor formerly had quarreled with Mrs. Alice Nona, but they had composed their differences since.

her on her first day of school when she began in the kindergarten class. Mr. Sumithapala returned her affection warmly. He said that he became tearful when she first recognized him at the time of his first visit to her at Hedunawewa in 1960. He was a witness of her recognitions of the family and friends of Tillekeratne in Talawakele and when she became excited there he comforted her. He had continued to visit her regularly since then. Mr. Sumithapala accompanied me to the home of Gnanatilleka in Heduna- wewa and I had an opportunity to observe the great friendliness the child and schoolteacher had for each other. Considering that in Gnanatilleka's life they had only met eight or ten times, the friendship seemed remarkably strong. Each of them fully believed that Tillekeratne had returned as Gnanatilleka. On three occasions Gnanatilleka had precognitions of Mr. Sumithapala's visits to her.

Mrs. Alice Nona, the mother of Tillekeratne, showed great emotion and cried, as did her husband, when Gnanatilleka recognized them in Heduna- wewa. When I interviewed Mrs. Alice Nona in Talawakele, some eight months after this reunion, her emotions on the subject still remained lively. As she talked with me about Tillekeratne and Gnanatilleka, she became overcome with grief and was unable to speak easily. The emotion I saw may have expressed only grief for Tillekeratne without indicating any special attachment for Gnanatilleka on her part. However, the display of emotion which I witnessed certainly suggested strongly to me that she was acting quite spontaneously and was not a party to any contrived drama. And her remarks at the time of her first meeting with Gnanatilleka, and later to me, made it clear that she too believed her son had been reborn. Gnanatilleka's parents also believed this to the point of fearing sometimes that she might carry out the threat she had made in moments of petulance to return to her Talawakele mother.

By 1962 Gnanatilleka had stopped talking spontaneously of the previous life and seemed to remember little of it.[5]

Comparison of Behavioral Characteristics of Tillekeratne and Gnanatilleka. In the entire series of cases now under survey in the international census of cases suggestive of reincarnation, instances of differences in the sexes of the subjects and related previous personalities occur rarely. In a total of some 600 such cases, differences of sex between the two personalities have occurred in only about five per cent. Whenever possible I have investigated the behavioral characteristics of both personalities with a view to studying differences and similarities between them. In cases of sex difference be- tween the two personalities, my scrutinies have naturally focused on the

---

[5] Letter to me from Mr. D. V. Sumithapala, November 12, 1962.

sexual behavior of the personalities. In the present case I have obtained some information which deserves attention at this time.

As already mentioned, Tillekeratne had no close male person in his family with whom he could identify. An older friendly brother and his father were away from home much of the time. The brother a little older than Tillekeratne was unfriendly and hardly a subject for identification by the serious Tillekeratne. Mr. Sumithapala came nearest to fulfilling the function of providing a male model for Tillekeratne, but obviously could not provide all that he needed. Tillekeratne was his mother's favorite son, but this probably alienated him further from his brother and possibly from his father also. It certainly did nothing to guide him toward masculinity. Perhaps as a result of these influences, Tillekeratne had developed at the time of his death a definite tendency toward effeminacy. His mother and his schoolteacher both testified to this. The evidence consisted of a marked preference for the society of girls over boys (he would prefer to sit with them), an interest in sewing, a fondness for silk shirts and, on occasion, painting his fingernails.[6] He had once asked his teacher, Mr. D. V. Sumithapala, if it was possible to change sex from one life to another.

Gnanatilleka showed, according to her parents, some tendency toward masculinity. She was still young and her development had not proceeded far. But her parents considered her more masculine than her older sister with whom they compared her. They cited as evidence of her boyishness her greater fearlessness than the average girl of her community (with the exception of two fears to be noted shortly). They also asserted that Gnanatilleka was more mature than other girls of her age and used much longer words than most children of her age employ. Some of these words were not current in her family, yet she spoke them before she had started school in 1961. The principal of Gnanatilleka's school had not noticed any tendency to masculinity or precocity in Gnanatilleka. This contradictory testimony will receive different credit accordingly as readers believe that a schoolteacher is more objective in his observations than the parents or that parents have better opportunities to observe their children than principals of schools.

Gnanatilleka said to her parents quite simply: "I was a boy. Now I am a girl." On the day of my visit to Hedunawewa she said that when she had been a boy, she had wished to be a girl. When asked whether she was happier as a boy or as a girl, Gnanatilleka replied that she was happier as a girl. I did not learn of any explicit statement by Tillekeratne to this effect, although his behavior permits this inference.

---

[6] Painting the fingernails by a boy is considered effeminate in Ceylon, although not as extreme a sign of effeminacy as it is in the West. Nevertheless, Tillekeratne was the only boy Mr. Sumithapala had ever observed who painted his fingernails.

Gnanatilleka preferred blue dresses and had said (according to her parents) that she preferred blue in her previous life. Mr. Sumithapala recalled that Tillekeratne always liked blue and wore blue shirts.

Tillekeratne was more religious than the average Sinhalese boy and he used to make small Buddha shrines for his own worship. Gnanatilleka also showed a strong interest in religion.

The exact circumstances of Tillekeratne's death at the age of nearly fourteen remain obscure. He seems perhaps to have had some visceral disease, but it appears that injuries suffered when he fell off a chair contributed to his terminal illness and indeed led immediately to his admission to the hospital in which he died some one or two weeks later. In view of this history of Tillekeratne, I think it worth noting that Gnanatilleka's parents testify to her having a noticeable fear of doctors and hospitals and a very marked reluctance to climb on anything from which she might fall down.

Comments on the Evidence of Paranormal Knowledge on the Part of Gnanatilleka. Under this heading I will mention first my strong general impression of the complete integrity of all the witnesses with whom I talked. Gnanatilleka herself seemed far too young to get up a case like the present one on her own. I could find no motive for working up a fraud on the part of Gnanatilleka's family. There were no financial gains to be obtained and such publicity as occurred would likely prove more vexatious than welcome to them. In any case, a fraud on the part of Gnanatilleka's family would hardly have sufficed alone. Any conspiracy must surely have included the family of Tillekeratne and his teacher, all of whom were then supposedly drilled before the presentation of their play in the simulation of tears and other expressions of strong emotion which were witnessed by outside observers such as the Venerable Piyadassi Thera and Mr. Nissanka, not to mentioned my own observations of the expression of emotions in some of the participants. The probability of all this seems to be remote enough to justify setting aside fraud in favor of more promising hypotheses.

Cryptomnesia may provide an explanation of the information acquired by Gnanatilleka about the affairs of Tillekeratne if we can find any reason to believe that she could have had access to someone (it would have to be someone quite intimate with the family of Tillekeratne) who knew the facts she revealed about Tillekeratne. I have already mentioned my reasons for believing that in the remote home of Gnanatilleka's family in the isolated village of Hedunawewa, no stranger could have had access to her without her parents being aware of his presence. They deny knowledge of any such person. This brings us back to the possibility of a fraud, which I have already considered most unlikely. But supposing that somehow a person from Talawakele had reached Gnanatilleka before the age of three and filled her with the necessary information, could he also have inculcated in her the appropriate behavioral responses which she showed so powerfully to the family and teacher of Tillekeratne and which evoked equally powerful emotional responses in them? This seems to me also unlikely.

Beyond the normal explanations of the case, i.e., fraud and cryptomnesia, lie explanations which require some kind of paranormal communication and I shall reserve my consideration of these possibilities for the General Discussion which follows the presentation of all these case reports. At this point, however, I should like to draw the attention of readers to the recognitions achieved by Gnanatilleka of persons who figured in the life of Tillekeratne.

Sometimes the families of children claiming memories of previous lives conduct recognition tests which leave open the possibility that suggestions are communicated, covertly perhaps, to the child about the person whom he is asked to recognize. This occurs when a child is asked such questions as: "Do you see your previous mother here?" The glances of the crowd toward the right person may quickly lead the child to "recognize" the previous mother. In the present case, Gnanatilleka achieved twelve recognitions. Ten of these occurred under circumstances in which she was asked only: "Do you know this person?" or "Do you know me?" In nine of these instances, Gnanatilleka stated unequivocally the correct relationship of Tillekeratne to the person concerned. In the tenth instance, the witnesses disagreed as to whether she recognized Gunalatha, Tillekeratne's youngest sister, as "the sister I used to go to school with," or only as "sister from Talawakele." The latter statement would be correct for Tillekeratne and is a recognition of a kind, but does not differentiate this sister from the other three sisters who were present, as does the former statement. In all other instances, Gnanatilleka gave the relationship so specifically that no doubt could occur about the identity of the person intended. Gnanatilleka also failed to recognize three "blank" persons introduced to her as tests to see whether she would claim acquaintance with persons whom Tillekeratne had not known. In the other two recognitions, Gnanatilleka spontaneously picked two women out of the crowd of people and correctly stated their relationship to Tillekeratne or his family.

Recognitions of the two kinds achieved by Gnanatilleka, i.e., spontaneously picking persons out of a crowd and correctly placing persons when asked "Do you know this person?" cannot be easily accomplished without prior acquaintance with the persons recognized. Information about a deceased personality picked up casually from a stranger would hardly suffice. One cannot imagine the feat accomplished without prior acquaintanceship except by careful and very extensive tutoring on the part of a parent. And could such tutoring extend to the appropriate emotional responses such as Gnanatilleka showed toward members of Tillekeratne's family? I doubt this. In my opinion the achievement by Gnanatilleka of these recognitions on any reasonable view eliminates fraud and cryptomnesia as explanations of the case.

The Later Development of Gnanatilleka. I was able to visit Gnanatilleka and her family again in July, 1966, just after the publication of the first edition of this book. At that time Gnanatilleka (who was then ten years old) said that she still remembered the previous life and, judging by her responses to questions concerning it, I think this probably correct. She said that sometimes when she was idle her thoughts went back to the previous life; she did not think any special circumstances reminded her of it. She had continued to exchange visits with Tillekeratne's family. Tillekeratne's family had come for a visit to Hedunawewa and spent the night there about two months before my visit that year; and Gnanatilleka had also visited Talawakele at about the same time. On her visits to Talawakele she continued to behave in an unfriendly manner toward Buddhadasa, Tillekeratne's older brother, who had been unkind to him and who had knocked down one of his model shrines just two weeks before his death. And Buddhadasa at that period did not come to visit Gnanatilleka at Hedunawewa.

Gnanatilleka was then in the fifth grade at school and said she was first in her class. Her mother said that she had lost the masculine traits (never extremely prominent) which she had shown when younger and was developing normally as a girl. She continued to have a preference for blue among other colors. And she was still much interested in religion and kept her own Buddha shrine in the house where she worshipped.

Gnanatilleka told me that she preferred being a girl, and also that she preferred her family to that of Tillekeratne. (I did not ask her to elaborate on this last statement, but did not find it surprising in view of the somewhat unhappy circumstances of Tillekeratne's life.)

This visit afforded an opportunity to inquire further about Gnanatilleka's manifestations of extrasensory perception with living people to which I alluded above. On the basis (mainly) of her predictions of the unexpected visits of Mr. D. V. Sumithapala to Hedunawewa, Gnanatilleka had acquired some reputation in her family for paranormal faculties. They sometimes consulted her about the outcome of a journey before undertaking it. But in 1966 the evidence of Gnanatilleka's having above average abilities at extrasensory perception did not seem strong. Sometimes Gnanatilleka's predictions turned out to be correct and sometimes not. She had continued to predict correctly sometimes that Mr. Sumithapala would visit, but sometimes he had come when she had not announced his arrival in advance to her family. Gnanatilleka herself denied that she could tell in advance when Tillekeratne's mother was coming to visit from Talawakele.

I visited Gnanatilleka and her family again in November, 1970. At this time Gnanatilleke was nearly fifteen years old. She was in the ninth grade at school and was still doing well there, being placed sixth among 37 students.

Gnanatilleka said that her memories of the previous life were fading. Evidently she preserved some memories, however, and she said she still thought about the previous life. She remembered particularly Tillekeratne's experiences at school. She remembered also that Buddhadasa, Tillekeratne's older brother, had damaged one of his Buddha shrines. Gnanatilleka also said that she still dreamed about her Talawakele mother. She dreamed of her visiting Hedunawewa and also of her cooking! Her mother said that Gnanatilleka still considered that she had two mothers.

Gnanatilleka's mother said she was developing normally along feminine lines. She had begun menstruating just a few days before my visit. Her hair style, physical form, blue dress, and manner all indicated a typical Sinhalese girl.

Gnanatilleka and her family continued to have some contact with Tillekeratne's family although it seemed less than it had formerly been. Gnanatilleka's older sister, Karunawathie, married in 1970 not long before my visit to Hedunawewa. Tillekeratne's mother and older sister had attended the wedding and so had Buddhadasa, his older brother, with whom both Tillekeratne and Gnanatilleka had not been on good terms. Mr. D. V. Sumithapala also came to the wedding. Prior to this occasion he had not visited for two years.

Gnanatilleka continued to be strongly interested in religion. She was a vegetarian (on religious grounds, although Buddhism as such does not require vegetarianism of its adherents) and had influenced her mother also to become one. Her family still credited her with some ability at extrasensory perception. As evidence this time they cited instances when she had said that her father, who was away from Hedunawewa working elsewhere, would return and he did return unexpectedly.

In recent years I have become increasingly interested in the question of why, if a case is best interpreted by reincarnation, a particular previous personality is reborn in one family rather than in another. This is not the place to offer even an outline of the data beginning to emerge from inquiries directed toward this question. But in the course of recent investigations I have often asked the informants of cases for their opinions on the matter with respect to the case they know about. When I discussed this question in 1970 with Gnanatilleka and her family, I learned that Gnanatilleka herself had told her family (when she was about five) that as

Tillekeratne she had seen her older brother, D. A. Baddewithana, dancing in Talawakela and had developed "a fascination for him." I mentioned above that Gnanatilleka's older brother had once gone to Talawakele for an exhibition of dancing. This occurred in April, 1954, at the time of the Queen's visit. This was the only occasion of his having gone there before the development of the case. He was about fifteen at the time. D. A. Baddewithana, who was present during my visit to the family in 1970, could not recall meeting Tillekeratne at this occasion, although he did not deny that he might have done so without remembering the fact or the name. The visiting dancers probably met a large number of people during the course of their one night stay in Talawakele and Tillekeratne could have been one of them. I do not, however, have any independent confirmation of Tillekeratne's having attended the exhibition of dancing in which D. A. Baddewithana participated at Talawakele. Gnanatilleka's mother mentioned that when Gnanatilleka was young she showed particular affection for D. A. Baddewithana, but she added with appropriate caution that in those days he was the only other of her children at home. Gnanatilleka was born seventeen years after the birth of her next older sibling. The older children had already largely scattered by the time Gnanatilleka began talking about the previous life.

In 1966 I learned that when Gnanatilleka had been talking most actively about the previous life she had mentioned a sister Sudu (really a nickname which means "fair"; see item 11 of the tabulation) and also a sister Dora, whom she sometimes referred to as Lora. When Gnanatilleka was young she used to write scribbles on pieces of paper and would say these were letters to be given to Lora who would, she said, either be at a boarding school or at home. (This item does not figure in the tabulation because I did not learn about it until 1966.) The person Gnanatilleka was referring to was identified as Lora Almeda, who had been a schoolmate of Tillekeratne. Since she had never seen Gnanatilleka up to 1970, I met her at her home not far from Talawakele and invited her to accompany us on our unannounced visit to Hedunawewa. She brought along a friend who had not known Tillekeratne. At Hedunawewa we did not introduce these two strangers, but asked Gnanatilleka if she could recognize them. She replied that one was called "Dora" and when asked where she had known her she said "Talawakele," but could not specify further where she had known the visitor. I regard this as a definite recognition even though Gnanatilleka got the name slightly wrong. It is evidence, I think, that her memories of the previous life had not completely faded even at the age of nearly fifteen. It remains a little surprising, however, that Gnanatilleka remembered Lora Almeda. For upon inquiring about her friendship with Tillekeratne, I learned that Lora and he had been classmates for several years when they were about seven to nine years old. But afterwards they did not have much contact, although Lora thought that they might have seen each other sometimes at various school functions.

The Case of Wijeratne

Summary of the Case and its Investigation. H. A. Wijeratne was born in the village of Uggalkaltota, Ceylon, on January 17, 1947, the son of H. A. Tileratne Hami. At his birth his parents noticed a marked deformity of his right breast and arm, which they attributed in a general way to some karma [7] from a previous incarnation. Wijeratne's father also noted certain resemblances to his deceased brother, Ratran Hami. Wijeratne, for example, was dark in complexion (like Ratran Hami), while the other children in the family were rather fair. And his father noted other resemblances of facial features between Wijeratne and Ratran Hami. He said to his wife: "This is my brother come back," but she seems not to have paid much attention to this remark, and neither of them related the deformity of the boy's right side to Ratran Hami.

When Wijeratne was between two and two and a half years old he began to walk around his house in a solitary way talking to himself. His behavior attracted the attention of his mother, who listened to his talk. She overheard him saying that his arm was deformed because he had murdered his wife in his previous life. He mentioned a number of details connected with a crime of which she, until that time, had heard nothing. She asked her husband about the boy's statements and he confirmed the accuracy of what the boy was saying for in fact his younger brother, Ratran Hami, had been executed in 1928 for the murder of his wife.

Wijeratne's father attempted to dissuade him from talking about the previous life, but he persisted in doing so, often in a brooding solitary way to himself and at other times to persons who asked him about his arm. He narrated the details of the crime, arrest, and execution of Ratran Hami with a vividness and abundance of detail which I shall describe below. According to Wijeratne's mother, he told what he remembered in pieces, telling

[7] For the benefit of Western readers who may be unfamiliar with the idea of karma, I may mention here that this word refers to the effects in the present life of causes in an earlier life which become carried into the succeeding personality in the next life. The word can apply to both "good" and "bad" residues and to aspects of behavior or of the physical organism. In Hinduism and Buddhism the explanation of karma is often applied to congenital deformities as it is indeed to any misfortune, or good fortune, for which no adequate explanation can be found in the circumstances or behavior of a person in the present life. The reader who wishes a longer, but still brief summary of the doctrine of karma as developed in Buddhism may consult *Karma and Rebirth* by Nyanatiloka Mahathera, Kandy, Ceylon: Buddhist Pub. Soc., n.d. It will be noted that in the case of Wijeratne, the birthmark (a deformity actually) is associated with the presumed previous personality of a *murderer*. In contrast, in the cases of Ravi Shankar (pp. 91–105) and some of the Alaskan cases of this monograph, the birthmarks are associated with the previous personalities of the *murdered* persons.

them one thing one day and then a little later speaking about some other episode or detail. She did not note any circumstances which seemed specially to stimulate his narrations of the life of Ratran Hami.

When Wijeratne was between four and five years old his statements came to the attention of the Venerable Ananda Maitreya, Professor of Buddhist Philosophy, Vidyalankara Pirivena, Colombo, who interrogated the boy at that time. Shortly after this, that is, when Wijeratne was about five and a half years old, he stopped speaking spontaneously about the previous life, but continued to speak about it when asked to do so.

In June 1961, Mr. Francis Story interviewed Wijeratne (without his father), the teachers of the college where Wijeratne studied, and the monks of the area to whom Wijeratne's family had told the details of what he had said several years before. In August, 1961, I interviewed Wijeratne with Mr. Story and also his father, mother, and older brother. The Venerable Ananda Maitreya, who had enquired about the case some years earlier, accompanied us and also kindly put his information on the case at my disposal. I have procured a certified transcript of the trial for murder of Ratran Hami and this has enabled me to ascertain certain dates and established facts as well as to discover certain discrepancies between the testimony offered at the trial of Ratran Hami (by himself and others) and the statements of Wijeratne about the same events made between twenty and thirty years later.

Relevant Facts of Family Relationships and Geography with Regard to Possible Normal Communication of the Information Obtained by Wijeratne. Tileratne Hami, the father of Wijeratne, was the older brother, by about fifteen years, of Ratran Hami. They were farmers in the village of Uggalkaltota at the time Ratran Hami murdered his wife [8] because she refused to leave her parents' home and accompany him to his village. The murder occurred on October 14, 1927, and Ratran Hami was tried in June, 1928, and executed in July, 1928. The crime took place in the village of Nawaneliya, which is some five miles distant from Uggalkaltota.

At the time of the murder, Mr. Tileratne Hami was not married, but about 1936 he met and married his wife, Mrs. E. A. Huratal Hami. She came from another village, Alakola-ella, in the district of Morahala, near Balangoda. This village lies about twenty-six miles to the west of Uggalkaltota. Mrs. E. A. Huratal Hami declared that she knew nothing about the

---

[8] In Ceylon some marriages take place in two steps. After a marriage is arranged (usually agreed upon by the families of the bride and groom), a legal contract is drawn. A delay may then occur before a wedding feast and the domestic union and consummation of the marriage. During the interval between legal marriage and wedding feast it is not uncommon for the bride to continue to live at her parents' home, but in readiness to depart with her husband when he calls for her. In the case of Ratran Hami and Podi Menike, the legal ceremony had taken place, but the final ones had not. However, at that point she could be considered his "wife."

crime of Ratran Hami until she heard her son Wijeratne talking to himself about it. She asserted that her husband never mentioned this episode in his family's history to her until she questioned him about their son's strange declarations. She could not remember her husband telling her (after the birth of Wijeratne) that his brother had returned. She had heard that villagers in Uggalkaltota said Wijeratne resembled Ratran Hami. But she did not hear from them anything about the crime of Ratran Hami, which she first learned about from Wijeratne's remarks.[9] On the question of whether others in the family knew about the crime of Ratran Hami before Wijeratne talked about it, the testimony of Wijeratne's older brother, Ariyaratne, entirely confirms that of their mother. Ariyaratne was seven years old when Wijeratne was born. He stated that although comments were made about the possible karmic origin of the deformed arm noted at Wijeratne's birth, they did not relate this deformity to the crime of Ratran Hami since they (members of the family other than Wijeratne's father) had never heard about it (from the parents or anyone else) until Wijeratne began talking about it when he was about two and a half years old. I shall discuss all these statements later.

Persons Interviewed During the Investigation. In 1961 I interviewed the following persons in Uggalkaltota:

H. A. Wijeratne

Mr. H. A. Tileratne Hami, brother of the deceased Ratran Hami and father of Wijeratne

Mrs. E. A. Huratal Hami, wife of H. A. Tileratne Hami and mother of Wijeratne

H. A. Ariyaratne Hami, older brother of Wijeratne

Venerable Ananda Maitreya, Professor of Buddhist Philosophy, Vidyalankara Pirivena, Colombo

Mr. Wattegama, Principal of Central College (school of Wijeratne), Pelmadulla, was interviewed on June 29, 1961, by Mr. Francis Story.

Physical Examination of Wijeratne. In the summer of 1961, Wijeratne was a boy of fourteen years who appeared well developed and normal in physique except for his right upper chest and right arm.

[9] Readers will note that Mrs. E. A. Huratal Hami did not recall her husband saying to her what he distinctly remembered saying, i.e., that Wijeratne was his brother come back. I cannot easily resolve this discrepancy. Possibly, Mr. Tileratne Hami only *thought* that his son resembled his brother and did not actually say so to his wife. Mr. Tileratne Hami may understandably have preferred to keep his brother's crime in the background of his life. But it is also possible that he did make this remark and his wife subsequently forgot he had made it. Since parents in Ceylon and other Buddhist countries often make such speculations regarding the previous lives of their newborn children, it is quite possible that Wijeratne's mother paid no particular attention to the remark. At that time she had no special reason to do so.

In the right upper chest below the clavicle there was a hollow area about two inches in diameter. The skin was intact in this area, but the muscle tissue of pectoralis major seemed markedly deficient. On palpation of this area, an impression was given that an underlying rib, approximately number six, on this side was deficient or missing, but this was not definite.

The entire right arm was small in comparison with the rest of the body. It was several inches shorter than the left arm and only about half as thick. The fingers of the right hand were developed only in a rudimentary way. Each was no longer than one phalanx of the normal left hand and had only one joint, i.e., the metacarpophalangeal joint. The first, second, third, and little fingers were (partially or completely) webbed together with skin, the thumb being detached from this group. With this hand Wijeratne could grasp a pen or pencil, but could not hold anything heavier; it was in fact almost useless for grasping or holding objects.

Statements Made by Wijeratne About the Crime and Punishment of Ratran Hami. Before listing the various statements made by Wijeratne concerning his claim to remember a previous life, I wish to clarify several points. First, there was in this case little to verify by consulting persons outside the family since both personalities occurred in the same family and almost everything (there are a few important exceptions) Wijeratne stated was known to his father, the brother of Ratran Hami. Secondly, I reached this case twelve years after Wijeratne first began talking about his past life. During this time, he and his parents and other members of the family had undoubtedly talked among themselves a great deal both about the statements of Wijeratne and the crime and execution of Ratran Hami. It is possible that Wijeratne, who still claimed to recall the main events he had narrated in detail, had acquired some and perhaps much information about Ratran Hami from his father. I can say, however, that if he did so acquire information, he must have done so extremely early because his mother testified that at the age of about two and a half he narrated the story in great detail; and Venerable Ananda Maitreya, who interrogated Wijeratne when he was between four and five years old, said that at that time he told the story in detail. Thirdly, although I shall point out certain discrepancies between the statements of Wijeratne and the testimony of witnesses at the trial of Ratran Hami, I am not necessarily committed to a belief in the accuracy of the court witnesses as against Wijeratne. We may consider an independent observer the medical officer who performed the post-mortem examination of the body of Podi Menike, the girl killed by Ratran Hami. But the other witnesses at the trial of Ratran Hami were all deeply concerned either with sending him to the gallows or preserving him from it. At his trial, Ratran Hami gave a spirited defense of his actions, alleging that he had not intended to kill Podi Menike. He asserted that in a scuffle started by her family, a friend of Podi Menike beat him while she held him and prevented his escape. In his efforts to escape, he said, he happened to stab her, but not with fatal intent. The other witnesses asserted that he began a deliberate assault with a kris (Malay knife) on Podi Menike and that only then did they attempt to beat him. The jury accepted their evidence and found Ratran Hami guilty. Wijeratne seems to have reached the same conclusion himself since he stated quite openly that he, as Ratran Hami, killed Podi Menike. In my opinion, this strongly supports the supposition that the account of the murder given by Wijeratne in 1961 is the true version, as against the case made up for the defense of Ratran Hami at his trial.

The tabulation below summarizes the statements and recognitions made by Wijeratne about the life of Ratran Hami and their verifications.

Comparison of the Personalities and Attitudes of Ratran Hami and Wijeratne. The transcript of the trial of Ratran Hami gives a quite imperfect view of his attitude toward the murder of Podi Menike since at that time he publicly denied that he had in fact intended to kill her and pleaded "Not Guilty." Nor can we rely any more on the opposing testimony of witnesses who wished to see him hanged.

But the brother of Ratran Hami and father of Wijeratne recalled some of the closing scenes of Ratran Hami's life. After the judge passed sentence of execution on Ratran Hami, his older brother went to him and asked him how he felt. He recalled that Ratran Hami said: "I am not afraid. I know that I will have to die. I am only worried about you." And later Ratran Hami told his brother that he "would return."

Of the character of Ratran Hami, his brother mentioned to me only that he was "very obedient," a trait he noted in Wijeratne also. At the trial of Ratran Hami, witnesses testified that he had maltreated his first wife, but I have already expressed my doubts about their assessment of his behavior.

At the time of my interviews with him in the summer of 1961, Wijeratne still said that "he" (as Ratran Hami) had murdered Podi Menike, but expressed no contrition for it. Indeed, he told me that confronted with a similar situation in the present life, of a legally wedded wife refusing to come to his home, he would again probably murder her. However, of his own previous character as Ratran Hami, Wijeratne said: "I had an unbearable temper at the time. I did not think of the punishment I would get." But he stated that his temper in his present life was milder than in his life as Ratran Hami. In 1961 Wijeratne had no concern about the deformity of his hand. And although he regarded the deformity as a just punishment for his behavior and fully as much so as his being hanged, on balance he evidently thought that he had behaved correctly as an injured husband should.[10]

---

[10] Western readers will find these views of such a crime strange. But they are not unusual in Ceylon. The homicide rate of Ceylon is high. Many offenses arouse a Sinhalese person to an

TABULATION

Summary of Statements and Recognitions Made by Wijeratne

Item	Informants	Verification	Comments
1. In his previous life he was Ratran Hami, brother of his present father, a farmer who lived in Uggalkaltota.	Wijeratne H. A. Tileratne Hami, Wijeratne's father	H. A. Tileratne Hami	Ratran Hami's first wife had died. The court testimony also included reference to the fact that the accused was a widower.
2. He had been married before his courtship and second marriage, but did not remember his first wife.	Wijeratne H. A. Tileratne Hami	H. A. Tileratne Hami	Mrs. E. A. Huratal Hami stated that Wijeratne first connected the deformity of his hand (and arm) with the karmic debt of Ratran Hami. At the time of the murder Ratran Hami and Podi Menike had not completed the ceremonies of marriage but it would not be inaccurate to describe Podi Menike as "wife" at the time of the murder. (See footnote 8.)
3. He had stabbed his second wife with a knife and that is why his hand and chest were deformed.	Wijeratne H. A. Tileratne Hami, E. A. Huratal Hami, Wijeratne's mother	All the witnesses at the trial of Ratran Hami agreed he stabbed Podi Menike. They disagreed about who started the altercation and whether Ratran Hami intended to kill his wife.	Wijeratne attributed the deformity of his right hand to the fact that "he" (Ratran Hami) had "killed my wife by using my hand." One may compare this to Archbishop Cranmer's behavior when being burned at the stake in 1556. Cranmer steadfastly held out his right hand to the flames because this hand had signed the recantations he withdrew.
4. His wife was the eldest sister of Punchimahataya.	E. A. Huratal Hami	E. A. Huratal Hami	The court testimony referred to Punchimahataya as a witness, but he was not called and I have not ascertained his relationship to Podi Menike. On another occasion, Wijeratne himself said that

154

4. (continued)			Podi Menike was the daughter of Punchimahataya. It is therefore only certain that a man of this name had some connection with the crime of Ratran Hami.
5. His wife lived at the village of Nawaneliya.	E. A. Huratal Hami Wijeratne	All the witnesses at the trial agreed that the murder occurred at the home of Podi Menike in Nawaneliya.	
6. He believed his wife had fallen under the influence of another man, Mohottihamy, who had persuaded her not to go on with her marriage to Ratran Hami.	Wijeratne	No confirmation of this assertion in the court testimony. A man called Mohottihamy was living with Podi Menike's family and was a witness of the murder.	Mohottihamy stated at the trial that he was a cousin of Podi Menike's mother and had been living with the family at the time of the murder.
7. When the time came for the final steps of marriage, he went to his wife's home and pleaded with her to accompany him to his home, but she refused.	Wijeratne	At the trial, Podi Menike's mother testified that Ratran Hami came to their home in the morning and tried unsuccessfully to persuade Podi Menike to leave with him.	Other witnesses at the trial agreed that Podi Menike had refused to accompany Ratran Hami home when he had asked her to do so in the morning.
8. Meat was hanging and some was being boiled at the home of Podi Menike.	E. A. Huratal Hami	H. A. Tileratne Hami Not independently corroborated. Not mentioned in the court testimony.	Wijeratne commented to his mother on the possibility that the meat was being prepared for the wedding feast which was expected to occur up to the time of Podi Menike's adamant refusal to go through with the marriage.
9. After Podi Menike had refused to return with him, he walked back to his village five miles away.	Wijeratne	H. A. Tileratne Hami	The court testimony of two witnesses stated that Ratran Hami came once in the late morning to Podi Menike's home, then went away and returned again in the evening. This would give time for Ratran Hami to return to his village for his knife.

Item	Informants	Verification	Comments
10. At his home he sharpened a kris (Malay knife) on a plank under an orange tree.	Wijeratne H. A. Tileratne Hami E. A. Huratal Hami	H. A. Tileratne Hami	Mrs. E. A. Huratal Hami recalled that Wijeratne said he sharpened his knife under an orange tree. She did not mention an orange tree. Wijeratne pointed out to his family the orange tree and plank which were in the same place as they had been twenty years earlier.
11. He borrowed fifty rupees from his brother to pay his debts to laborers who had built his house. He paid them and returned to Podi Menike's home in Nawaneliya.	Wijeratne	H. A. Tileratne Hami as to the borrowing of fifty rupees.	There is no verification of whether Ratran Hami actually paid the laborers.
12. Being unable to persuade Podi Menike to return with him and seeing at the house the man he thought his rival, Mohottihamy, he stabbed Podi Menike.	Wijeratne	Ratran Hami at his trial alleged that he was set upon and beaten by Mohottihamy before he stabbed Podi Menike.	Ratran Hami was fighting for his life at the trial. Wijeratne said what the jury in 1928 believed, that Ratran Hami deliberately murdered Podi Menike when she did not come home with him.
13. He stabbed Podi Menike in the right breast.	Wijeratne	The post-mortem examination reported at the trial indicated that Podi Menike had received severe and fatal stab wounds in the back and especially under the left axilla, but not in the right breast. Three wounds penetrated the chest wall.	At his trial Ratran Hami alleged that he stabbed Podi Menike once in the back. He said he could not recall having stabbed her more than once. As the family and friends of Podi Menike beat him up after the murder, this may have impaired his memory for what had happened in the fracas. Wijeratne appeared to believe that the concave deformity of his own right chest was at the site of the fatal wound "he" "gave his wife. But none of the actual wounds of Ratran

13. (continued)

		Hami's wife were at this site according to the physician who conducted the post-mortem examination.
14. After the murder he was beaten up by Mohottihamy.	Wijeratne	Acknowledged by Mohattihamy in his court testimony.
15. He was taken to Balangoda after the murder.	Wijeratne E. A. Huratal Hami	This detail was not brought out in the court testimony.
16. The trial dragged on for two years.	Wijeratne	An exaggeration. The murder occurred on October 14, 1927, and the trial on June 12, 1928.
17. He was sentenced to hang.	Wijeratne	Official transcript of the trial of Ratran Hami
18. Five days before his execution his brother (H. A. Tileratne Hami) arranged an almsgiving on his behalf at the prison.	Wijeratne	H. A. Tileratne Hami. Ven. Ananda Maitreya said that when Wijeratne was younger, i.e., five years old, he recounted the almsgiving ceremony in great detail, mentioning ten monks and their leader who conducted the ceremony.
19. He tried to pin the crime on Mohottihamy, but was prevented by a servant who saw that he had murdered Podi Menike.	Wijeratne	In fact Ratran Hami did not at the trial attempt to pin the crime on Mohottihamy and no servant testified at the trial. Wijeratne may conceivably have been referring to an explanation of the murder offered by Ratran Hami before the actual trial, but abandoned by him when the trial came. It seems quite clear that Ratran Hami's defense was concocted along classical lines by his counsel. His lawyer would naturally not want to incriminate an innocent man, and probably rejected a story which Ratran Hami may have thought up quickly and offered to the police in his first statements.

Item	Informants	Verification	Comments
20. At the almsgiving he told his brother he would return (meaning he would be born again).	Wijeratne H. A. Tileratne Hami	H. A. Tileratne Hami	Wijeratne told me only that as Ratran Hami he said he would come back again. His father added that Ratran Hami said he would come back as his son.
21. The day before his execution, a bag of sand was weighed on the gallows.	Wijeratne	Account of executions in Ceylon written by a hangman. *Ceylon Observer*, Colombo, October 15, 1961.	I have ascertained that it was customary in Ceylon to test the rope and trap of a gallows by "hanging" a heavy bag of sand the day before an actual execution. (See footnote 12 below.)
22. At the execution a Buddhist priest offered last rites for him just before he was hanged.	Wijeratne	Not verified	Probably correct.
23. A black cloth was placed over his head before the trap was sprung.	E. A. Huratal Hami	Correct as to the hood.	Hoods were commonly placed over the heads of criminals executed in Ceylon. Ratran Hami's brother (father of Wijeratne) was not present for these last episodes in the life of Ratran Hami.
24. When the trap was sprung, he was thinking only of his brother. He felt his neck tightening and then had the sensation of dropping into a pit of fire.	Wijeratne		The belief in a pit of fire as a punishment for sins is as widespread among Buddhists as it is among Christians.
25. He did not remember anything that happened afterwards until he realized his father was his brother when he was two years old.	Wijeratne		Witnesses said that when he was younger, Wijeratne spoke about experiences after his death as Ratran Hami and before his birth as Wijeratne.
26. At the time of his execution, he was about twenty-three or twenty-four and his brother about thirty.	Wijeratne	Correct for Ratran Hami, who was born in 1904 and so was twenty-four years old when executed.	

| 27. Recognition by Wijeratne of a belt left by Ratran Hami with his aunt. | H. A. Tileratne Hami | H. A. Tileratne Hami | Ratran Hami left the belt in question with his aunt shortly before the murder. The aunt gave it to her son, who pre-empted it and wore it. Wijeratne was about six or seven years old when he identified the belt of Ratran Hami on his cousin. Due to a family quarrel there had been no contact between the family of Wijeratne and the man who had had the belt for many years before Wijeratne met him and recognized it. This recogni-tion was not independently corroborated. Mr. H. A. Tileratne Hami and his wife were not present when Wijeratne recognized the belt which he told them about later. |

Wijeratne stated that his memories of the previous life were becoming somewhat dimmer. I have already mentioned the report of his mother that he stopped talking to himself when he was about five. His mother did not think that Wijeratne when talking of these things did so sorrowfully, but his father depicted him as "brooding" in his solitary soliloquies. In his narration to me of the almsgiving ceremony provided by his father (brother of Ratran Hami), Wijeratne recalled few details. But the Venerable Ananda Maitreya said that when Wijeratne described this scene to him at the age of five, he included many details of the event.

Although some details seemed to be fading from his memory, Wijeratne at the age of fourteen said that he recalled the main events of the last year of Ratran Hami's life (which had occurred more than thirty years earlier) more clearly than events of the early years of his present life which had occurred less than ten years before. He still regarded his father as his older brother.

Comments on the Evidence of Paranormal Knowledge on the Part of Wijeratne. Since the brother of Ratran Hami expected him to be reborn as his son and apparently recognized certain aspects of face and complexion of the baby Wijeratne as those of Ratran Hami, we can easily believe that he might then have influenced Wijeratne, albeit unconsciously, toward an identification with his dead brother. We then have to ask how he could have done this without his wife and Wijeratne's older brother knowing anything about the story of Ratran Hami until Wijeratne began to talk about the previous life at the age of two and a half. Children are so closely cared for by their mothers in Ceylon that we cannot imagine the father having much access to them in the absence of the mother. In some cultures this may occur, but for Ceylon the suggestion does not make sense.

We should also consider the evidence supporting the statement by Wijeratne's mother (and the similar statement by his older brother) that she had never heard of the crime and execution of Ratran Hami until Wijeratne told her about it and she asked her husband if it were true. This at first may seem unlikely, but in Ceylon such ignorance of the murder may well have existed. The crime and execution of Ratran Hami took place in 1927–28, some seven years before Wijeratne's parents married. Although newspapers in Colombo, seventy-five miles away, where the trial took place,

---

anger of murderous intent and accomplishment which in the West would call for other solutions. Yet the Sinhalese are essentially a peace-loving, gentle people and they are deeply imbued with the Buddhist doctrines of rebirth and karma. Thus a crime such as murder, although not approved, is more often considered "natural" or "forgivable" than it is in the West; but it is also considered to carry with it penalties of retribution in the next life. For Buddhists such moral or psychological forces, so to speak, become as important to count in the reckoning as the punishments of courts and sheriffs.

would have reported it, news of it through either newspaper or radio probably never reached the village of Morahala near Balangoda where Mrs. E. A. Huratal Hami, Wijeratne's mother, grew up. There remains the possibility that news of the crime traveled from Nawaneliya by word of mouth to Morahala. This may have happened, but need not necessarily have happened. Murder, as I have mentioned, occurs quite often in Ceylon; it is indeed almost a commonplace circumstance. A murder in one village would have little news value in another one twenty-six miles away.

We can also believe that Mr. H. A. Tileratne Hami may not have told his wife before or after his marriage about his brother's history. The crimes and punishments of relatives are not usually reviewed during courtship in any culture.

In my opinion, further evidence of the plausibility and authenticity of the story narrated by Wijeratne and his family comes from the fact that Wijeratne's father at least, and probably other members of his family, attempted sternly to suppress his remembering or telling the story of Ratran Hami. The Venerable Ananda Maitreya himself witnessed efforts of Wijeratne's father to stop the boy from talking when he was telling the story to the Venerable Ananda Maitreya at the age of five. At that time the father gave as his reason for wishing to suppress the story a fear of retaliation by the surviving and angry relatives of Podi Menike, the girl killed by Ratran Hami. The details were told first to Venerable Ananda Maitreya because he was a monk well known to the family. The other monks were only told later. Mr. H. A. Tileratne Hami was so anxious to suppress the story that for a time he sent Wijeratne away from the home and village where they lived. In my interviews with the family some nine years after the monks had heard the story, the danger of retaliation seemed to have passed, but the family's wish to avoid publicity continued and was justified by a fear of derision on the part of neighbors. The family at no time sought any publicity for the case of Wijeratne in newspapers or otherwise and I only happened to hear of it through Mr. Story's friendship with some of the monks of the area who conducted the school which Wijeratne attended.

And I would add, finally, that the telling of the story to these monks provides evidence of the honesty of the family in their narration of the case. For the village people of Ceylon hold the monks in the highest respect. The villagers would not trump up a false story to deceive them, nor would they dwell on the occurrence of a murderer and executed criminal in a family if they did not believe wholeheartedly in the evidence they presented. The family of Wijeratne and Ratran Hami would not have casually revived and rehearsed before these much-venerated monks the story of the twenty-five-year-old crime of Ratran Hami unless profoundly convinced themselves of the authenticity of Wijeratne's claim to be Ratran Hami reborn.

In supposing some paranormal source for the information about Ratran Hami exhibited by Wijeratne, I cannot do much more than point to the various factors in the total situation which make me believe that Wijeratne somehow obtained his knowledge of Ratran Hami by paranormal means. But clearly, since nearly everything he knew his father also knew, the possibility remains that Wijeratne acquired his information directly from his father either in verbal communications or perhaps partly or entirely by extrasensory perception.

Several fragments of the information declared by Wijeratne, however, seem to fall completely outside this explanation. Wijeratne spoke of three details (items 21–23 in the tabulation) of the last day of the life of Ratran Hami which seem to have been unknown to his father until mentioned by Wijeratne. I refer to the preliminary "hanging" of a sandbag to test the gallows, to the wearing of a black hood at the time of being hanged, and to the administration of last rites by a Buddhist priest before the execution itself.[11] The last two are common enough details of many hangings in Ceylon, but the first detail is not and was in fact quite new to me; I thought it doubtful until I was able to verify it from an account by a prison executioner of the conduct of executions in Ceylon.[12] We must ask ourselves whether it is probable that Mr. H. A. Tileratne Hami would know of this detail, or that, if he did, he would have told it to his son. His brother having been executed, perhaps his mind lingered on the details or he specially studied them whenever he could, and if he told anything to his son about Ratran Hami before the boy spoke of his recollections of a previous life (which he denied) he would perhaps have spoken about this item as much as any other. But in view of his strong wish to suppress the whole story at first, for which I have already cited evidence, it seems unlikely that he ever said anything to Wijeratne about the murder, trial, and execution of his brother before Wijeratne himself told the details.

The episode of Wijeratne's recognition of the belt Ratran Hami had given his aunt deserves brief comment. When Wijeratne recognized and pointed out to his father the plank on which "he" had sharpened the kris with which Ratran Hami stabbed Podi Menike and the orange tree under which the plank stood, he showed his father objects which the latter knew already, together with their part in the murder. The boy might then have acquired this information from his father either through normal means or

[11] Ratran Hami's brother (Wijeratne's father) was not present during these last episodes in the life of Ratran Hami, although he might perhaps have known or inferred what went on before and at the execution.

[12] *Ceylon Observer*, Colombo, October 15, 1961. Wijeratne could not have obtained his information from this source since he spoke about details of the hanging of Ratran Hami years before this account appeared. The practice of stretching the rope of execution with a sandbag on the day before a hanging is mentioned in J. Laurence. *A History of Capital Punishment.* New York: The Citadel Press, 1960.

telepathy. But when Wijeratne recognized the belt of Ratran Hami then being worn illicitly by his cousin, his parents were not present and only heard of this later. Wijeratne's father could not so easily have been the source of information for this recognition; and indeed, if the facts have been stated correctly by the parents of Wijeratne, we can only account for Wijeratne's recognition of the belt either through some form of survival or by a complex form of telepathy between Wijeratne and either Ratran Hami's cousin or Wijeratne's father.

We cannot plausibly suppose that Wijeratne derived all his information from a clairvoyant reading of the court testimony because (*a*) this did not contain some verified details, e.g., the episodes at Uggalkaltota between Ratran Hami's two journeys to Podi Menike's home and (*b*) because at the trial Ratran Hami denied any intention to murder, whereas Wijeratne acknowledged such an intention. On the other hand, both Wijeratne and Ratran Hami (at the trial) stated that Ratran Hami stabbed Podi Menike only once, although the pathologist testified to several wounds, three penetrating the chest. Wijeratne's location of the fatal wound in the right upper chest supposedly matching his own concave deformity in that location also disagrees with the location of wounds on Podi Menike's body. This suggests a distortion of information by Wijeratne, who may have wished to explain the deformity in his own chest, as well as the shrunken arm, along karmic lines. Other explanations may apply also.[13] Since Mr. H. A. Tileratne Hami was presumably familiar with the testimony at his brother's trial, it is unlikely that Wijeratne derived this erroneous detail from the mind of his father.

As I have already mentioned, Wijeratne stated that as Ratran Hami he had killed Podi Menike. Moreover, he said that in similar circumstances he would act in a similar fashion. Ratran Hami, however, pleaded "Not Guilty" at his trial. I am inclined to think that this difference somewhat supports the reincarnation hypothesis as opposed to the view that Wijeratne acquired his information either normally or (wholly or partly) through extrasensory perception from his parents or (conceivably) from the court

---

[13] I venture to offer one of these possible explanations on the understanding with the reader that it is quite speculative. Uneducated Ceylonese people frequently confuse left and right, often referring to the "right" side of the person they are talking to as the "left" because it is left for them. It is therefore quite possible that Ratran Hami remembered stabbing Podi Menike on the "right" side for him, which was actually the left for her and where the pathologist found the wounds. Then, supposing that mental images, rather than physical changes, govern changes in the physical organism of the person holding the images, and supposing an influence on the body of Wijeratne by the mind of Ratran Hami, we could account for a deformity on the right chest of Wijeratne. On this last point, I wish to remind readers of the observations of Father Thurston that when stigmata appear on the bodies of religious persons worshiping before a crucifix, the stigmata on the mystic appear in the same places as the wounds in the image of Christ before which the mystic has meditated and worshiped. (H. Thurston. *The Physical Phenomena of Mysticism*. London: Burns Oates, 1952. See p. 123.)

records. If these had been the source of his information, would he not then have adhered to the position of being "Not Guilty?"

The Later Development of Wijeratne. From 1961 until the time of publication of the first edition of this book (1966) I did not meet Wijeratne. In July, 1966, I met him again in Colombo where he was then staying. Subsequently I met him in March, 1968, near Colombo, in November, 1970, at Uggalkaltota, in April, 1973, at Kandy, and in October, 1973, at Angoda. On the occasion of visiting Wijeratne in Uggalkaltota, I was also able to talk at some length with his older brother, H. A. Ariyaratne Hami. On this visit Mr. Francis Story, Mr. V. F. Guneratne, Mr. E. C. Raddalgoda, and Mr. Godwin Samararatne accompanied me. All of them were well acquainted with Wijeratne and the first three in particular had been active in the investigation of the case during previous years. Additional to these personal meetings with Wijeratne, I have obtained further information about his later development from several other sources. Wijeratne himself has written to me from time to time. Also, Mr. V. F. Guneratne has followed his development closely and shared information about him with me. Mr. Guneratne has taken a kindly interest in Wijeratne and has met him in Uggalkaltota or elsewhere on several occasions since 1966. I also have a report obtained by Mr. E. C. Raddalgoda from Mr. B. A. Francis, the vice-principal of the school Wijeratne attended between 1966 and 1969.

I shall first mention that in the summer of 1966 Mr. Guneratne arranged for an X-ray examination of Wijeratne's chest. In the first edition of this book I mentioned that he had a deep concavity of the muscular tissues overlying the ribs of the upper right chest. I had the impression that an underlying rib, which I thought the sixth, was somewhat deficient. The report of the X-ray examination (by Dr. Q. Peiris dated June 26, 1966) of Wijeratne's chest stated that "the right third rib is shorter than its fellow of the opposite side. Apart from this there is no bony characteristic noted in the chest."

In 1966 and 1968 Wijeratne told me that the memories of the previous life had faded considerably, although some persisted. He remembered only vaguely how Podi Menike had looked before the marriage ceremony. The single new memory he mentioned, additional to those noted at the time of my first interview of 1961, was of the judge who passed sentence on Ratran Hami at his trial for murder in June, 1928. He recalled his black robe and thin figure. (I think this memory was newly mentioned rather than newly recalled.) In 1970 he said he no longer thought spontaneously about the previous life, but only when someone reminded him of it. Nevertheless, certain memories of the previous life, when brought into his consciousness, were still clearer to him than memories of his childhood. This was true of the memories of the events of the last year of the life of Ratran

Hami, such as the murder of Podi Menike in October, 1927, and the subsequent trial and execution of Ratran Hami in the summer of 1928.[14]

In the first edition of this book I mentioned that during my interview with Wijeratne in 1961 he had expressed no remorse for the murder of Podi Menike and said that, under similar circumstances, he would feel justified in murdering a woman who cancelled a marriage contract as she had done. In subsequent years he came to modify this stand. He first told me in 1966 that he then thought that he would *not* murder a wife who thus provoked him. In 1968 he still expressed the same opinion. I formed the impression that his altered attitude arose not from any sense of guilt with regard to the death of Podi Menike, but rather from an assessment that, all things considered, the penalties of murder did not justify the transient satisfaction of revenge or of removing an enemy which it provided. He still considered that the malformed arm with which he was born was a punishment for the murder of Podi Menike. Wijeratne said he would send me a statement recording his modified position on murder for inclusion in a new edition of this book. This he did and I quote the following (with a few minor changes in the English) from a letter he wrote me, dated January 26, 1969.

I carefully considered the assertion of what one should do if a wife behaved in an unseemly manner. I thought it is wise that as a primary step she should be made aware of her weakness and advised accordingly. These are common occurrences in society. [Wijeratne here means misconduct by wives!] If, however, a wife disregards her husband's advice it is wise to divorce her. Or else the sudden anger that can arise in a person can lead to the destruction of many lives. Thus according to Buddha's teaching if one's actions are guided by patience and wisdom it can lead to a happy life.

Wijeratne's reference to the destruction of many lives, not just the single life of the murdered person, refers, I think, principally to his own life which he regarded as substantially altered, if not ruined, by the murder Ratran Hami had committed.

In 1969 Wijeratne became rather seriously mentally ill and was admitted to a psychiatric hospital at Ratnapura for almost a month in November–December, 1969. A discharge card given to him, presumably for attendance at a psychiatric clinic, and which I examined, stated that he had been diagnosed as having hebrephrenic schizophrenia. In 1970 I obtained a con-

---

[14] The case of Bishen Chand (I. Stevenson. *Journal* A.S.P.R., Vol. 66, October, 1972, 375–400) provides a somewhat similar example of the selective fading of memories. In 1971 Bishen Chand had forgotten all of a large number of details about a previous life, except one—that of the murder of a man by the previous personality whose life he remembered.

siderable amount of information about Wijeratne's mental illness from Wijeratne himself, his older brother, and the vice-principal of the school he had been attending. In 1973 I was also able to discuss the illness with Dr. N. B. Hettiaratchy, the psychiatrist who had treated Wijeratne at the psychiatric hospital in Ratnapura. Dr. Hettiaratchy gave me a copy of his notes of Wijeratne's admission to the hospital and confirmed that he had had a schizophrenic illness. He had not, however, gone extensively into Wijeratne's early life history and knew none of the details of his memories of a previous life, although he was aware that Wijeratne had had such memories. He also did not learn about the immediate circumstances and stresses which emerged from the information furnished by Wijeratne and the other persons mentioned above as important in the causation of his illness.

The precipitating factor in the illness was, almost certainly, an infatuation Wijeratne had with a girl in his class at school. Wijeratne talked with this girl in class, but seems never to have had any social relations with her even to the point of sharing a meal with her. The girl responded to him in a kindly way that increased her attractiveness to him, but she does not seem to have otherwise encouraged Wijeratne. And she seems later (according to thirdhand testimony) to have shunned him. Nevertheless, Wijeratne evidently elaborated fantasies about her and then at some point began to imagine that she had rejected him. He said that he had "broken away" from the girl because he believed that thinking about her would interfere with his studies. So far as I could learn, the relationship had never progressed to the point where either could really have rejected the other; it was largely if not entirely constructed in his own mind. But his classmates knew of his infatuation and, according to H. A. Ariyaratne (who heard about this from his and Wijeratne's older brother), they were teasing Wijeratne about the girl.

In this situation Wijeratne began to have difficulty sleeping, his thoughts became confused, and he developed delusions. One of these was that he was a bird. He broke branches off trees and when his brother asked him why he was doing this, he replied: "I am now a bird." The delusion of being a bird persisted for about a week. Later (when I talked with him in the autumn of 1970) he remembered the experience and said that he had felt light (in weight) at the time. The delusion was not developed with further details such as having the appearance of a bird with feathers, wings, etc.

In the hospital Wijeratne was treated with tranquilizers on which he continued for a time afterwards. He was moderately or severely ill altogether for about five months. He had stopped taking medication by the autumn of 1970. When I saw him in November of that year he impressed me as being substantially well, but there was a trace of abstractedness in his manner as if his contact with his environment was still slightly impaired. I also thought his affect somewhat inappropriate and his plans for studying for the college entrance examination by himself without the help of school, or at least of a tutor, seemed rather unrealistic. The difficulty of assessing these signs became greater because his entire family was at that time under threat of a suit brought against them as a consequence of a quarrel with the headman of the village about land usage; they were all much concerned over the outcome of the impending trial which was subsequently called off on the plaintiff's withdrawal of his complaint against Wijeratne's family.

Both the presumptive precipitating factor of Wijeratne's psychosis and the delusion of being a bird during it *may* have some connection with his memories of a previous life.

In a written report about Wijeratne's conduct at school and the circumstances at the time of his illness, B. A. Francis, the vice-principal of his school, wrote that Wijeratne had told some of his classmates that the girl to whom he was attracted had reminded him of the wife of the previous life, Podi Menike.[15] This had presumably stimulated his desire to be friendly with her. When I later asked Wijeratne directly whether the girl in question had reminded him of Podi Menike, he said that she had not. But he showed considerable reluctance even to admit the part played by his attraction to the girl in the emotional disturbance which preceded his psychosis. He initially tried to say that he became ill because of worry over impending examinations, but when drawn out further he admitted that he had been worried about a girl in his class. It might have been even more difficult for him to admit to someone like myself that the girl had in fact reminded him of Podi Menike.

Be that as it may, I think we can safely suggest at least some resemblance between the situation of Ratran Hami when his fiancée rejected him and the fantasied (or real) rejection of Wijeratne by a girl who may or may not have resembled Podi Menike. I think we may fairly say that this girl could have stood for Podi Menike in the mind of Wijeratne, even if she did not resemble her. Wijeratne had resolved not to resort to violence in such cases, a resolution which, incidentally, he reaffirmed at our interview in 1970. Psychiatrists who believe that strong unexpressed emotions generate psychoses may debate with philosophers of ethics whether Wijeratne's illness, if it was precipitated by the frustration brought on by an unresponsive woman, as seems likely, was an advance over Ratran

---

15 Wijeratne's classmates would be quite familiar with the story of the previous life he remembered. Thus, they may have conjectured that the girl reminded him of Podi Menike and passed this interpretation on to the vice-principal as what Wijeratne told them. The vice-principal did not say he had heard Wijeratne himself state that the girl he was attracted to resembled Podi Menike. But he evidently thought Wijeratne's classmates were telling him truthfully what Wijeratne had told them.

Hami's solution to such a situation. Let no one think that I am an advocate of murder in such circumstances!

When Wijeratne and his brother mentioned that during his psychosis he had had the delusion of being a bird, Mr. V. F. Guneratne, Mr. Francis Story, and Mr. E. C. Raddalgoda all said they remembered that Wijeratne had earlier, going back as far as 1961, made remarks implying that, during the long interval between the death of Ratran Hami in 1928 and the birth of Wijeratne in 1947 (eighteen and a half years), he had passed at least some of his time reincarnated as a bird. According to them, he had never specifically said that he had been a bird, but had said that after dropping into the pit of fire (p. 158, item 24) following the execution of Ratran Hami (here I quote from my notes of 1970), "he had flitted through the air and perched on tree tops." These three observers all had assumed that Wijeratne was referring to an "intermediate" life as a bird. I could not remember Wijeratne having mentioned such an experience during the interview of 1961 (or later) and could find no trace of this in my notes.[16]

It is not necessary to believe that Wijeratne, after Ratran Hami's death, actually had an intermediate life as a bird in order to consider that there may have been some connection between Wijeratne's memories of the life perched on treetops (assuming now that my colleagues' memories are better

---

[16] Nor could any written record of it be found in the notes of the three observers who said they remembered that Wijeratne had made remarks implying he had had a life as a bird. I asked for a search of their notes to be made. Mr. Raddalgoda, who acted as interpreter in 1961, had destroyed his notes. A tape recording of Wijeratne's statements made by Mr. Guneratne showed no reference to a life as a bird. And Mr. Story said he had omitted the detail from a report of the case he had sent me (in the summer of 1961 before my first visit to Ceylon) because he thought I would find a bird life too incredible! There was thus no document to support the memories of my three colleagues and their concordance naturally made me think that perhaps I had not heard or remembered anything about the bird life, if Wijeratne had mentioned it in 1961, because I had indeed found such a concept too incredible.

I have generally adopted the policy of not including references to lives as subhuman animals that have occasionally come into some of the cases of the reincarnation type that I have investigated. I have thought that it was inappropriate to allude to these without taking space for a thorough discussion of the concept of rebirth in the bodies of subhuman animals, often referred to as metempsychosis. I hope for an opportunity of discussing the subject at length in some future work. Here I shall only add that although the belief in subhuman animal rebirth is an integral part of both Hinduism and Buddhism, I have heard very little about it during all my investigations in south Asia. Only very rarely has any informant offered to tell me about an actual case illustrative of this belief. In the nature of things evidence bearing on subhuman animal rebirth would be very difficult to come by, but even so, I cannot help being surprised by the paucity of material presented to me under this heading, as compared to the mass of evidence relating to claims of reincarnation in human bodies. Readers interested in the subject of rebirth in subhuman animal bodies are referred to articles by W. Roos ("Is Rebirth in a Subhuman Kingdom Possible?" *The Maha Bodhi*, Vol. 75, 1967, 238–242.) and F. Story ("The Buddhist Doctrine of Rebirth in Subhuman Realms." *The Maha Bodhi*, Vol. 76, 1968, 28–39, and Vol. 76, 1968, 58–70) where the concept (not the evidence for it) is discussed very thoroughly with regard to Buddhism.

than mine) and the later delusion he had of being a bird. The content of memory and delusion resemble each other closely. But the memory itself could also have been a delusion based on Ratran Hami's expectation that his crime deserved punishment in the body of a subhuman animal. Wijeratne denied (during my interview with him in 1968) that as Ratran Hami he had been afraid before the execution that he would undergo a life as a subhuman animal. It is true also that Ratran Hami told his brother, H. A. Tileratne Hami (Wijeratne's father), that he "would return," presumably meaning into his brother's family. But the belief that serious crimes are followed by rebirth as a subhuman animal is so widespread among Buddhists that I find it difficult to think that this possibility did not enter into the conjectures of a future life considered by Ratran Hami as he awaited execution. Such strong expectations of an experience in an animal body might have become converted later into pseudo-memories of a delusional type in the mind of Wijeratne.[17]

As I have already mentioned, Wijeratne was still at school at the time of onset of his mental illness in 1969. He was then nearly twenty-three years old and readers may wonder why he remained in school when most young men of his age would have left it some years earlier or passed on to college or university. At that time he was already about four or five years behind his peers. This came about at least in part because he would prepare for the college entrance examination and then not take it. He wrote me about one occasion in December, 1969, when physical illness prevented him from taking the examination, but he also missed it on at least two other occasions when, as far as I know, nothing interfered with his taking it. On a fourth occasion (in 1970) his mental illness prevented his sitting for the examination. However, his family could still afford for him to remain in school. His father was a small trader and cultivator who, though far from wealthy, had sufficient means to allow Wijeratne to continue his studies. Wijeratne himself wanted to pursue his education and at least up to 1973 he expressed a wish to study medicine. At the time of his mental illness in 1969–70 he left school and he had not returned when I met him

[17] If I am correct in this line of thought, the case then resembles in this feature that of Gopal Gupta (I. Stevenson. *Cases of the Reincarnation Type*. In preparation). Gopal said that after the death of Shaktipal Sharma (the previous personality of this case) he had an "intermediate life" as a boy in London. Although Gopal gave some details about this claimed life in London, these included almost nothing that was verifiable, in contrast to the abundance of statements he made of verified details concerning the life of Shaktipal Sharma. I am strongly inclined to think Gopal's "intermediate life" in London a fantasy, but it could have been one that first arose in the mind of Shaktipal Sharma. For it is a matter of record that Shaktipal Sharma had an intense longing to go to London and study there for the bar, a craving which the opposition of his father had frustrated. For a fuller exposition of the idea that our premortem thoughts influence our post-mortem experiences, see *The Tibetan Book of the Dead* (Ed. W. Y. Evans-Wentz). 3rd ed. London: Oxford University Press, 1957.

in Uggalkaltota in the autumn of 1970. But at that time, as I mentioned earlier, he felt sufficiently recovered to start studying again and was preparing himself at home for the college entrance examination. Later he arranged for assistance from a private tutor. And in December, 1970, and May, 1971, he finally passed the entrance examination and thus qualified to enter a university in Ceylon.

When I next met Wijeratne in April, 1973, he was studying at the University of Ceylon, Peradeniya (near Kandy), and staying with Mr. Godwin Samararatne (one of my interpreters) in Kandy. By this time Wijeratne had learned to speak English quite well and we communicated without an interpreter. He was studying scientific subjects at the University with the hope of qualifying himself to enter the medical school. He was in good spirits and his affect seemed quite appropriate. He seemed to me to have recovered fully from the mental illness of 1969–70 and this was also the opinion of Dr. N. B. Hettiaratchy, who had followed him as an outpatient for a time and then discharged him as recovered.

Although Wijeratne's right hand was both small and badly deformed to the point where he had greatly shortened fingers, several of which were webbed together, the deformity did not seem to have been a severe disability to him either physically or psychologically. It had no doubt been a constant reminder of the previous life, but his family and friends apparently had not made much of the deformity and Wijeratne said that other people had not drawn attention to it. In December, 1971, he entered a hospital and successfully underwent surgery to separate the fingers of the right hand that were webbed together. His hand healed well and he was able to make better use of it after the operation.

In April, 1973, he showed me with pleasure the results of the operation on his right hand. His index finger and little finger had been separated by the operation and it was easy to observe that he had much more use of his hand than formerly. A further operation to separate the two middle fingers was planned for a later occasion.

In the late summer of 1973 Wijeratne relapsed into another psychosis. In October, 1973, I was back in Ceylon and went out to the psychiatric hospital at Angoda to see him. (After a short stay at the hospital in Ratnapura, he had been transferred to Angoda, so that Dr. N. B. Hettiaratchy could again supervise his treatment.) By the time of my visit Wijeratne was much improved, although still not recovered. Subsequently I learned that after I left Ceylon he had become well enough to return home.

The precipitating factor in this psychotic episode, as in the previous one, had been a rejection of Wijeratne by a girl to whom he had become attached. I hope to obtain more information about what went wrong. It could bear not only on the relationship between Wijeratne's illness and his memories of the previous life, but on the proper management of his susceptibility to recurrences of the illness.

It would naturally have interested me greatly to find a girl in Ceylon who had memories of the Podi Menike murdered in 1927 by Ratran Hami. I initiated inquiries that I hoped might lead to the discovery of such a girl and Mr. Godwin Samararatne conducted this search diligently. It turned out then that a girl had been born in Podi Menike's family on December 25, 1928, that is, about fourteen months after the death of Podi Menike. She had no birthmarks, but some real or imagined resemblance to the first Podi Menike impelled her family to give this girl the same name. Later she had no memories whatever of the life of the murdered Podi Menike, or of any other previous life. Nor could we find in the locality where Podi Menike had lived any other hints, or stronger evidence, of a girl who had claimed to have been the first Podi Menike.[18]

The Case of Ranjith Makalanda

Introductory Remarks. In the following case, the scanty details of information and behavior demonstrated by the child did not permit even an attempt at verification of the facts allegedly remembered. Thus, unlike many of the others in this entire group of twenty cases, it does not provide any direct evidence for reincarnation, although it does *suggest* it. But it seems worth presenting at this time because it provides an excellent example of a type of case which occurs even more commonly than do the cases with rich detail susceptible of verification. Cases with insufficient detail for verification, but with prominent behavioral features and claims by the child to recall a previous life, occur not uncommonly in Europe and also in the United States, which has, compared to other countries I have surveyed, provided fewer of the more detailed cases than nearly every other country, and many fewer when relative sizes of populations are taken into

[18] As I now think of Sinhalese cases, after analyzing the characteristics of more than forty of them, a search for a child claiming to have been Podi Menike reborn in the area where she lived was quite wasteful of time and effort. The two personalities in Tlingit cases nearly always belong to the same family (I. Stevenson. "Cultural Patterns in Cases Suggestive of Reincarnation Among The Tlingit Indians of Southeastern Alaska." *Journal A.S.P.R.,* Vol. 60, July, 1966, 229–243). The two personalities in Turkish cases nearly always come from neighboring villages (I. Stevenson. "Characteristics of Cases of the Reincarnation Type in Turkey and their Comparison with Cases in Two other Cultures." *International Journal of Comparative Sociology,* Vol. 11, March, 1970, 1–17). But in Sinhalese cases the two personalities rarely belong to the same family or to the same or nearby villages. (I. Stevenson. "Characteristics of Cases of the Reincarnation Type in Ceylon." *Contributions to Asian Studies,* Vol. 3, 1973, 26–39). In the majority of Sinhalese cases the subject remembered a previous life in another part of the island a considerable distance, often 50 or 100 miles, away from where he had been born. So although we had no good leads about where to look for a child claiming to have been Podi Menike, we would now know, I think, *not* to bother looking in her own neighborhood.

account. These minor cases, although not adding anything to the evidence for reincarnation, are nevertheless compatible with it. They call for *some* explanation and it seems to me that there are only two hypotheses—the reincarnation hypothesis and what I call the "imposed identification" hypothesis—which can account for the facts if we believe they have been accurately reported.

The case came to my attention in 1961, at which time Mr. Francis Story interviewed the father of the boy Ranjith, who was then nineteen years old. Later that year, I interviewed Ranjith's father and made detailed notes of his statements about the boy and replies to my questions. At that time Ranjith was in England where he remained two years. Later he returned to Ceylon where Mr. Story interviewed him apart from his parents on three separate occasions. I have drawn on Mr. Story's notes for my report.

The Statements and Behavior of Ranjith Makalanda Suggestive of Reincarnation. Ranjith Makalanda was born in Kotte, Ceylon, in 1942,[19] the seventh child of a pure Sinhalese family. His father was Mr. Makalamadage Sam de Silva. The sixth child of the family was three years older than Ranjith. The eighth child of the family, a girl, was born five years after Ranjith. When Ranjith was less than two years old, his father began to notice signs in him of an unusually strong memory, but he did not give any details of this evidence. At about the same time, Ranjith's father also began to notice certain traits of behavior in the boy which appeared to him far more characteristic of English people than of Sinhalese children. These traits, or a certain attitude which underlay them, made the boy an outsider in the family. He regarded them with coolness and showed less affection for his parents than the other children. The parents on their side regarded him as a "freak" who had somehow strayed into their midst. This did not prevent a flow of affection from them to the boy, however, although the strong independence and refractoriness to parental guidance which Ranjith showed perplexed and often sorely troubled them.

In the home the family spoke both Sinhalese and English and the children had an opportunity to learn both. But Ranjith learned English earlier and better than any of the other children. It may be thought that he had the advantage of hearing English spoken by his older siblings and no doubt he did. However, his younger sister had this advantage as much or more and yet she learned English more slowly and less well than Ranjith.

When Ranjith was about two years old, his father noticed that if he became nauseated and wished to make himself vomit, he would put fingers

[19] There have been discrepancies in the dates given me at different times for Ranjith's birthdate.

down his throat to induce vomiting. His father recognized this as an English method of inducing vomiting, and the habit is unfamiliar among the Sinhalese people. Ranjith cared little for rice, and did not eat it in the Sinhalese style, but threw the grains into his mouth. On the other hand, he enjoyed eating bread spread more liberally with butter than is customary in Ceylon and he handled it in the English style with his fingers. When he ate in a hotel, he used a knife and fork skillfully, again in contrast to the ineptitude, through lack of experience, of the other children in the family. He insisted on calling his mother and father "Thatha" and "Amma," not "Mummy" and "Daddy" as did all the older children. "Thatha" and "Amma" in Sinhalese refer to the biological parents, but become replaced in many homes (including that of the de Silvas) by the terms "Mummy" and "Daddy," which denote affectionate relationships. This form of address was thus the boy's way of asserting his conviction that although he lived with his biological parents, he had elsewhere other parents for whom he reserved his full affection. Ranjith's younger sister also called the parents "Thatha" and "Amma," which habit Mr. de Silva thinks she picked up from Ranjith. As a small child Ranjith addressed older people familiarly and often by their first names without any addition of "Mr." or "Sir," either of which most Sinhalese children would include in talking to an older person.

Ranjith had a pronounced dislike for being photographed and shied away from cameras, but this phobia was never related to the events of the previous life—or at least he never expressed any such relationship.

When Ranjith was between three and a half and four years old, his father heard him telling his mother, brothers, and sisters: "You are not my mother, brothers, and sisters. My mother, father, and others are in England." As Ranjith continued to behave as if this were a fact, failing to show any filial attachment to him and his wife, Mr. de Silva sometime later decided to question Ranjith directly about his "other family."

He took Ranjith aside and first asked him where he was from. Ranjith replied that he was from England. When asked the names of his parents, he could not remember, but he gave the names of two brothers as Tom and Jim and one sister as Margaret. He could not remember his own name. But when Mr. de Silva asked about his father's occupation, Ranjith seemed to have additional memories. He said his father worked on big steamers. He brought home pineapples. (It is not clear whether Ranjith meant the other father brought the pineapples from the steamers or from a trip he (the other father) took to foreign ports.) He worked in the ship and Ranjith took his lunches to him at work where there was a place to keep the lunch. His house was on a top of a hill without other houses close by, but with another at the bottom of the hill. Ranjith then added spontaneously that at times he put on a jersey and an overcoat and moved near a fire in the morning because there was ice in the garden and on the roads. Wagons came to pick up the ice on the roads. When Mr. de Silva asked Ranjith whether the wagons were motor wagons, he said they were horse wagons. Ranjith further stated quite spontaneously that he was not a Buddhist, but a Christian. He said he took his brothers and sister to church every Sunday on the pillion of his motorcycle. He then added, again spontaneously, that he himself and his mother were very fair and when asked how fair, he said much fairer than a Burgher [20] lady who was a neighbor of the de Silvas. When asked by his father what his other mother wore, Ranjith said she wore a skirt and jacket. This contrasted with the saris worn by most Sinhalese women. When asked about fruits he ate in England, Ranjith said "grapes and apples."

With regard to the declarations of Ranjith cited in the preceding paragraph, Mr. de Silva expressed confidence that the subjects touched on by Ranjith had not been discussed in their family. Nor is it likely that they ever would be. Natural ice is completely unknown in the tropical lowlands of Ceylon. There are very few horse-drawn vehicles in Ceylon and Mr. de Silva was sure Ranjith had never seen a horse carriage or wagon. Nor could Ranjith have learned about these things at school since this conversation took place when he was under four years of age and not yet at school. It is possible that he might have heard something of these topics from his older brothers and sisters, but not very probable since these are not normal subjects of conversation among children in south Asia.

At the time of Ranjith's fourth birthday, his father arranged for this event to be announced over the radio which a local radio station would do on payment of a fee. Ranjith's older sisters then told him that at 5 P.M. on his birthday his "mother" would speak to him from England. As the time approached, the family gathered around the radio, Ranjith closest of all to the instrument. When a female voice speaking with a definite English accent announced Ranjith's birthday, he cupped his hands around his mouth and said into the radio, "Mother, I am staying in a Sinhalese family's house. Take me there." (Meaning back to his old home.) The radio then provided a rendition of the song "Happy Birthday" which includes the word "darling" in the verses. After the song, Ranjith said, "That is my mother. My mother calls me 'darling' and sometimes she calls me 'sweetheart.'" Ranjith's uncle who was present then asked him how he recognized his mother's voice. To this he replied that his mother "speaks softly like that." This usage of the word "softly" was new to Ranjith's

---

[20] Holland controlled Ceylon from 1640 to 1796. Many descendants of Dutch soldiers and colonists live in Ceylon today, especially in and around Colombo. They are known as "Burghers." Although many, perhaps most, have intermarried with the Sinhalese, they are noticeably more fair in hair and complexion than the Sinhalese and are often as fair as other Europeans living in tropical countries.

father for, although correctly used by Ranjith, it happens that in Sinhalese-English the word "slowly" is used to refer to the quality meant by "softly" in the English of Great Britain and the United States. Mr. de Silva said he first learned of this other meaning of the word "softly" from his son.

Immediately after the above episode, Mr. de Silva noted his young son alone in the yard of the home and looking sad. He advised his other children not to talk of the episode and to try to make Ranjith forget his memories.

In the following years, Mr. de Silva thought that Ranjith had forgotten the previous life. However, when Ranjith was in his early teens he came to his father and expressed a wish to leave school and go to work for his own living. He said he wanted to work in a garage and was willing to wash cars if he had to do so. This request astonished and pained his father, for although boys in Great Britain and the United States may work when they are young, a sensible student in Ceylon strives to complete his education and certainly would not take a job washing cars if he could possibly do anything else, which Ranjith could since his father wanted him to stay in school. Moreover, most Ceylonese boys would consider washing cars quite undignified. Nevertheless, Mr. de Silva reluctantly agreed and Ranjith went to work in garages. There, and perhaps earlier at school, Ranjith learned with astonishing rapidity about automobile mechanics and how to drive automobiles and motorcycles. When Ranjith was eighteen, his father decided to discipline this aptitude further by sending him to England for training in automotive engineering. He mentioned this idea to Ranjith without any definite proposal of when he should go to England. But Ranjith, whose desire to go to England had not abated in the years since he had first expressed this wish, promptly booked passage for himself on a ship going to England without consulting his father again. His father then reluctantly assented to his leaving almost immediately. At a farewell party given for Ranjith by his father, Ranjith told assembled friends that he still believed he had lived before in England.

On the ship and in England, Ranjith reported himself completely comfortable with the English people. He found his way around London with ease and pleasure. I have no evidence that Ranjith had any paranormal knowledge of London and England and I emphasize as impressive here not that he said he knew London, but that it seemed familiar to him and he felt comfortable there, and with the English people everywhere. Not all Sinhalese youths could write their parents of such mutual acceptance among the English.[21] The report of Ranjith's ease in London does not depend on

---

[21] Mr. de Silva may have exaggerated the adjustment of his son in London as compared to other Ceylonese boys who had the opportunity of a trip to England. But there is no doubt that Ranjith, in his later interview with Mr. Story, showed much pleasure in his accounts of

his statement to his father alone, for Mr. de Silva's daughter (Ranjith's sister) who was living in London when Ranjith arrived there, also reported to her father how easily Ranjith moved around in London.

Ranjith had some expectations that in England further memories of his old home might arise and enable him to identify a particular town or house as formerly his. But this did not happen. He did, however, continue to show further evidence of a precocious mastery of automobiles. Against advice, he entered an automobile race in Scotland and came in first among twenty-two contestants. He was the only entrant from Asia in the contest.

The Attitude of Ranjith's Father Toward the English. Mr. de Silva described to me an intense dislike on his part for the English. He shared this dislike with most of the Sinhalese during the British occupation of the country from 1796 to 1948. In his case, however, dislike of the English seems to have run stronger than in most other Sinhalese people. When members of the British royal family visited Ceylon, Mr. de Silva stayed away from the welcoming parades. He seems to have been horrified at the presence in his family of an English enclave in the form of his son Ranjith, who exhibited many of the behavioral traits of the hated English. Mr. de Silva described his attitude toward the English as contributing evidence that he, at any rate, had done nothing consciously to promote the creation within his family of the strange "English boy."

However, Mr. de Silva's attitude toward England was in fact more complex than his avowals of conscious thoughts suggest. He told me of a remarkable series of dreams he had experienced between about 1932 and 1950. He related five of these dreams in considerable detail. In each he found himself in friendly discourse with the reigning British monarch, George V, Edward VIII, or George VI. Indeed, "friendly" seems too mild a word, for in these dreams Mr. de Silva enjoyed intimacy with the kings, introducing one at a meeting, holding hands with another, preparing food for a third, etc. Mr. de Silva's dreams puzzled him for they did not fit into his conscious ideas of antagonism toward everything English. But they showed another side of his character and attitude toward the English; namely, identification with their wealth, ceremonies, power, and dignity as symbolized by the British monarchs.

Comments. I have no reason to believe that Mr. de Silva would go out of the way to narrate a story of this kind which he had invented for some purpose of his own. Moreover, the story of an "outsider" in his own family,

---

how the English had loved him! And he certainly does seem to have felt at ease in London. When a toothache bothered him, he simply walked into a hospital he saw (immediately upon arrival in London) and had the tooth extracted.

who flagrantly violated the customs of behavior among Sinhalese children and claimed to belong elsewhere, could hardly be a matter for self-congratulation to Mr. de Silva as a parent. I therefore believe that he reported what he observed, not what he invented.

In view of Mr. de Silva's strongly ambivalent attitude toward the English, it is possible that his attitudes distorted his observations. He might, for example, have seen his son as more English in his ways than did other people who noticed less of the unusual in Ranjith's behavior. We may think of Mr. de Silva as being too vigilant, too suspicious, we might almost say, with regard to English traits. If his son seemed to learn English quickly, Mr. de Silva might have made more of this than a more objective observer. We might imagine, perhaps, that Mr. de Silva derived some unconscious gratification from the idea of having an "Englishman" in his family. His dreams suggest this. But it is unlikely that the entire family (who, he reported, shared some of his observations of Ranjith) shared his ambivalence toward the English. And it seems unlikely that bias on the part of Mr. de Silva could account for the whole case and particularly for the detailed statements which Mr. de Silva said Ranjith made about a previous life in England. Either the boy made these statements or he did not, and I have no grounds for thinking Mr. de Silva did not hear his boy say what he reported him to have said.

As I have already mentioned, the case might be accounted for on the hypothesis of "imposed identification." According to this hypothesis, an older person, usually a parent (in this case, Mr. de Silva himself), unconsciously imposes a certain personality on a child who gradually assumes the characteristics desired by the parent. The process is subtle and consists in slight rewards for conformity to the desired type or slight withdrawals or punishment when other behavior is presented. It is well known that parents who strongly desire a child of one sex, say a girl, may thus guide an unwanted boy along lines of feminine development until he becomes almost irresistibly channeled toward homosexuality. Sometimes such reinforcing of behavior desired by the parent occurs openly and crudely, but it can also go on underground, so to speak, with the parent quite unaware that he is promoting the behavior he (unconsciously) wishes in his child. For the purposes of the present case and similar ones, the question is not whether parents influence the personalities of children (which we know they do), but whether such influence has limits. Can it alone account for such an alteration of personality that the child has imposed on him the awareness of a completely different identity? For nothing less than this occurs in many of the cases suggestive of reincarnation, including the present one. In order to be able to include the benefit of data from other cases of the present series, I shall defer a fuller review of this hypothesis until the General Discussion at the end of this monograph.

The Later Development of Ranjith Makalanda. In July, 1966, I had another interview with Ranjith's father, Mr. de Silva. (At that time Ranjith was in another town, Polonnaruwa (in central Ceylon), and I did not meet him.) Ranjith was then about twenty-three years old. He was working for a tractor company. He had married, but unhappily, and was divorcing his wife.

Mr. de Silva described Ranjith as still somewhat alienated from the rest of the family. He was still "not like a Sinhalese boy." He enjoyed the company of English people and when he could do so, he would drive English visitors around Ceylon without charging them simply because he enjoyed their company. On the other hand, according to Mr. de Silva, Ranjith had not been completely satisfied with life in England during his two years there.

In March, 1968, I finally met Ranjith Makalanda himself and had a long talk with him as well as another interview with his father. At that time Ranjith was about twenty-six years old. He was working in Colombo for a taxi and car rental company. He had retained his interest in motor vehicles. He said that he had also preserved his love of England and would go there immediately but for his conviction that he should not leave his parents who were, by this time, becoming somewhat elderly. He said the two years he had spent in England were "the happiest of his life." (This remark obviously did not accord with his father's statement mentioned above.) He continued to like Western food and, for example, preferred bread and butter to rice. Whenever he could afford to do so, he went to one of the large hotels in Colombo used by Western visitors and enjoyed a Western meal. If he could not eat at these hotels he would prefer eating noodles in a Chinese restaurant to the Sinhalese food, which is ordinarily extremely hot with chilis and spices. Mr. de Silva confirmed the persistence of Ranjith's food preferences.

Ranjith said that he expressed himself more comfortably in English than in Sinhalese and that his English grammar was better than his Sinhalese grammar. He remembered that he had learned English very readily as a child. I noticed myself that his English accent had much less of the characteristic accent and rhythm used by most Sinhalese when they speak English. It must be remembered that his parents spoke English to each other when he was a child, that English was spoken very widely in Colombo (of which Kotte is a suburb), and that (before I met him) Ranjith had spent two years in England. Therefore, I do not wish to emphasize any aspect of Ranjith's speaking English except his preference for it; and even this he may have derived from his family.

Ranjith said that all his life he had had a strong urge to kill animals. He remembered having such desires when a small child, and he still liked to hunt and kill animals in the jungles of Ceylon. He was aware that this tendency violated the precepts of Buddhism and he struggled against it, but sometimes could not control it. One interpretation of this trait is that it may have been a residue of a previous life as a Christian (whose religion would not have condemned the killing of animals) and as an Englishman, many of whose countrymen are well known for hunting and killing animals with enthusiasm.

Ranjith said that he still remembered the things he had said and done (related to the previous life) when he was a small child. In particular, he thought that the episode of his fourth birthday (when he spoke to the English voice announcing his birthday on the radio) remained quite clear in his memory.

In November, 1970, I met Mr. de Silva again (in Kotte) and also had another interview separately with Ranjith in Kandy where he was then working.

Mr. de Silva said that Ranjith had still not really fitted into Sinhalese society, but persisted in "English ways." He had received a letter from Ranjith expressing contentment over the availability at the place where he worked of Western food. As another example of Ranjith's "English ways," Mr. de Silva mentioned that he never went out of the house in a sarong, a popular dress in Ceylon. To evaluate this comment we should emphasize "never" since many educated Sinhalese wear trousers much of the time; but most of them would also sometimes, even if only rarely, wear sarongs when going out of their houses.

In 1970 Ranjith was employed in Kandy as an instructor in automobile mechanics at a training institute supported by a Christian church. He was thus still engaged in work having to do with motor vehicles.

Ranjith said he still preferred Western food to Sinhalese food, but that he could manage to eat Sinhalese food when he could obtain nothing else. (He was boarding then with one of the European members of the mission supporting the training institute and was thus able to enjoy their English cooking.)

Ranjith recalled a period at the age of about nine years when he had a longing to give up being a Buddhist and become a Christian. He thought he could eat more freely if he was a Christian and also that Christian worship (which, for example, does not require taking off shoes before entering a church) was simpler than Buddhist worship. But we cannot attribute these ideas exclusively to residues of a previous life as a Christian Englishman, since they became prominent when Ranjith was attending a Christian school in Nugegoda where most of the students were Christian. Ranjith himself thought that his attraction to the Christian religion at this period derived from the influence of his friends at the school.

Because a number of Asian subjects of these cases who have remembered previous lives as Europeans or Americans have complained of the heat in the tropical countries in which they live, I asked Ranjith about his preference for climates. (His father had previously stated that Ranjith had never complained of the climate in Ceylon.) In reply Ranjith said that the climate of Kandy appealed to him. (Kandy, in the highlands of central Ceylon, has a generally cool climate.) He considered the climate of Kotte (on the lowlands near the coast) too hot. On the other hand, he thought the climate of such places as Nuruwa Eliya too cold. (Although Nuruwa Eliya is not far from the equator, it is six thousand feet above sea level and I myself spent there one of the coldest nights I have ever experienced anywhere!)

Since Ranjith had remembered a previous life as a Christian, I asked why he thought he had been reborn in a Buddhist family. He then offered the speculation that he had been a British airplane pilot who had been killed in an airplane crash near Kotte. The (British) Royal Air Force had had a base about a mile and a half from Kotte and some pilots had been killed in crashes at and near this base during World War II. Ranjith's conjecture harmonized with his fondness for vehicles and his intense love of flying. He said that he had always wanted to be a pilot, but had not been able to afford the cost of the training program. He said his interest in airplanes went back as far as he could remember. He had managed to fly in airplanes many times and had not experienced any fear when doing so.[22]

---

[22] Ranjith's conjecture about being a British pilot in the previous life, which was quite unprompted by me (as to its details) and indeed surprising to me, resembles the statements made by a number of subjects whose cases I have studied in Burma. These are children who remember previous lives as British or American pilots (or other airmen) shot down over Burma during World War II. (Detailed reports of these cases will be published later.) The Burmese subjects reporting such memories are all fair in complexion and hair. Ranjith, on the other hand, although remembering a previous life as a fair person, had the usual black hair and heavily pigmented skin of the Sinhalese people. It must be remembered that whereas the Burmese subjects have had imaged memories (although often only scanty and fragmented ones) of having been British or American airmen, Ranjith did not claim to *remember* that he had been a British pilot who had crashed near Kotte in the previous life. He presented this idea simply as a possible explanation why, if he had been a Christian Englishman in a previous life, he had come to be reborn in Kotte in a Buddhist family if rebirth is the best interpretation of his case. Ranjith's conjecture offered an answer to the question why, if he had been an Englishman in a previous life, he had been reborn in Ceylon, but it did not, strictly speaking, explain why he had been reborn in a Buddhist family. There are many Christian families in Ceylon, especially in and around Colombo where Kotte is.

IV

Two Cases
Suggestive of Reincarnation
in Brazil

Introduction

THE idea that some portion of human personality survives physical death has persisted more strongly in Brazil perhaps than in any other country of the West. No less than five per cent of the population of Brazil list themselves formally as spiritualists, but there exists strong evidence that another twenty-five per cent of the population are spiritualists, although the census taker has recorded them as Roman Catholic. Two cultural streams from Africa and France have united to diffuse the belief in survival throughout all classes of Brazilian people. The Brazilians have integrated and assimilated their African citizens to a far greater extent than has any other country in America, North or South. And from the African elements in the culture are derived a powerful belief in a spirit world and in associated practices designed to draw its participation into our affairs. The African heritage of belief in a spirit world chiefly influences the poorer and less well-educated people of Brazil. The better educated persons are likely to derive their interest in survival from the French branch of spiritualism founded by Kardec [1] which spread to Brazil in the nineteenth century when Brazilians looked more to Europe for cultural enrichment than they do today.[2] Kardecian spiritism (its adherents prefer this term to "spiritualism") includes reincarnation as one of its primary tenets, thus differing from most other forms of spiritualism of the West.

The widespread belief in survival (with reincarnation) in Brazil has created a cultural climate favorable to the narration of claimed memories of a previous life. Children who make such assertions have the respect of their parents in unfolding their stories.[3] Moreover, the children may be

---

[1] A. Kardec. *Le livre des médiums.* Paris: Librairie des Sciences Psychiques, 1922. For an exposition of Kardec's views on reincarnation see his *Heaven and Hell.* (Trans. by Alma Blackwell.) London: Trubner and Co. 1878.

[2] Readers interested in the history of the mingling of African and European spiritualism in Brazil will find this outlined in L. J. Rodriguez. *God Bless the Devil.* New York: Bookman Associates, Inc., 1961.

[3] But the mother of one child who had told of a previous life paid no attention to the details of the child's claims. Firmly convinced of reincarnation herself, she did not think it important for her child, or anyone else, that he should remember details of a previous life. This attitude

able more often to tell their stories to educated persons capable of evaluating what they say. Such a person was Mr. Francisco V. Lorenz, a schoolteacher of Rio Grande do Sul, in whose family occurred the two cases here reported. Mr. Lorenz made extensive notes of the first of these cases and apparently observed both of them from their inception with a sympathetic, but by no means uncritical eye. Mr. Lorenz died in 1957 and his wife in 1944; but their son, Mr. Waldomiro Lorenz, continued an active interest in the cases that had occurred in his family and in others. Mr. Waldomiro Lorenz had discussed the cases of Marta and Paulo Lorenz with his father after he, Waldomiro Lorenz, grew up. He became familiar then with his father's observations and interpretations of the cases. After correspondence with Mr. Waldomiro Lorenz, I visited Brazil in the summer of 1962 and there investigated seven cases suggestive of reincarnation. Only two of these merit presentation at this time. Three of the remaining cases lack sufficient detail to permit verification of the child's statements, but the investigation of another two continues.

Methods of Investigation

The methods of investigation I followed in studying the present cases resemble those described in the Introduction to this monograph. I spent two weeks in Brazil, of which five days were devoted to the investigation of these two cases. Two of the witnesses spoke English, the remainder Portuguese. Mr. Waldomiro Lorenz acted as an interpreter for all but one of these interviews. Mrs. Cordelia Anuda interpreted for one interview. However, I can understand considerably more Portuguese than I can speak and could follow in most instances the conversation between the witness and the interpreter.

In one of the cases reported here the two families concerned knew each other before the occurrence of the case, and in the other case both personalities were members of the same family, that of Mr. F. V. Lorenz. These circumstances certainly make possible the transmission of information from one personality to another through normal means although, as will be seen, we may doubt whether this accounts for all the apparent recollections and behavior of the children concerned. And in other respects the cases differ importantly from many of those I have studied in other parts of the world. In the first place, Mr. F. V. Lorenz kept detailed contemporaneous notes of the case of his daughter Marta. Unfortunately these notes were subsequently lost, but Mr. Lorenz published a moderately full account of

___

contrasts with that in India in which also most people accept reincarnation, but many persons there believe that a child who remembers a past life will die young. They often try to stop him from talking, not because of indifference, but because of concern for his welfare.

the case of Marta.[4] And secondly, although both cases originally occurred almost forty years ago, I was able to interview, usually independently, a number of older sisters and brothers of the persons who claimed to have lived before. These persons were older children or young adults when the principals were children. They were thus contemporary witnesses of the main events of the cases.

Case Reports

The Case of Marta Lorenz

Summary of the Case and its Investigation. Maria Januaria de Oliveiro (known familiarly as Sinhá or Sinházinha) was born about 1890, the daughter of a prosperous fazendeiro (rancher) of Rio Grande do Sul, the southernmost state of Brazil. Her father's estate lay some twelve miles west of the small village of Dom Feliciano, which itself is about one hundred miles southwest of Porto Alegre, the state's largest city and port. Sinhá, to use the name by which she was most often referred, loved the rural life of her father's land on which she grew up. Nevertheless, she seems to have suffered from loneliness in her somewhat isolated location. She often visited the village of Dom Feliciano and enjoyed there the friendship of Ida Lorenz, wife of F. V. Lorenz, the schoolteacher of the district. Twice Sinhá fell in love with men of whom her father disapproved. One of these men committed suicide. On the second occasion of such frustration, Sinhá herself fell into a state of melancholy. Her father arranged a trip of consolation for her to the coastal city of Pelotas where she attended a carnival, but with little interest. She neglected herself, and tried to catch cold by exposing herself in cold, damp weather without adequate covering; she also tried to exhaust herself and even drank cold water to damage her health. Her voice thereafter became hoarse and she was then found to have an infection of the larynx which spread to the lungs. Her illness was diagnosed as tuberculosis, and after a few months she died. On her deathbed she acknowledged to Ida Lorenz that she wanted to die and had tried to become infected. Then she promised her good friend that she would return again and be born as her daughter. Sinhá further predicted that "when reborn and at an age when I can speak on the mystery of rebirth in the body of the little girl who will be your daughter, I shall relate many things of my present life, and thus you will recognize the truth."[5] Sinhá died in October, 1917,

---

[4] F. V. Lorenz. *A Voz de Antigo Egito.* Rio de Janeiro: Federação Espirita Brasileira, 1946. (This volume summarizes for Portuguese readers the Rosemary case of apparent Egyptian xenoglossy described by F. H. Wood in *This Egyptian Miracle.* London: John M. Watkins, 1955.) *Inter alia,* Lorenz includes in the book an account of the case of his daughter, Marta.

[5] F. V. Lorenz. *Op. cit.,* n. 4. (My translation.)

the day after she had made this remarkable declaration. She was about twenty-eight years old.

Ten months later, on August 14, 1918, Ida Lorenz gave birth to a daughter, Marta. When Marta was two and a half years old, she began to speak about events in the life of Sinhá. She made her first remark on this subject to her older sister Lola.

I quote here F. V. Lorenz' account of the first statements made by Marta to Lola and himself:

One day, when Marta was two and a half years old, as she was returning from the stream near our house with Lola, after they had been washing clothes, she asked her sister: "Lola, carry me on your back."

Her sister who (like all our children and neighbors) knew nothing of the deceased girl's promise [to return], replied: "You can walk well enough. I don't need to carry you."

To this Marta replied: "When I was big and you were small, I used to carry you often."

"When were you big?" asked Lola, laughing.

Then the little girl replied: "At that time I did not live here; I lived far from here where there were many cows, oxen, and oranges and where also there were animals like goats, but they were not goats." (In this last remark she referred to sheep.)

These words described the farm of the dead Sinhá's parents in the country.

Thus conversing, Lola and Marta walked on and reached the house. Then Lola told us about the strange ideas of her little sister, and I said to the latter: "My little daughter, I have never lived there where you say you have lived."

To this she replied: "Yes, but in those days I had other parents."

Another one of Marta's sisters then jokingly said: "And did you then have a little Negro servant girl such as we now have?" (She was referring to a little Negro orphan girl whom my wife and I had sheltered.)

The girl was not embarrassed and replied: "No. Our Negro servant there was already big and so was the cook; but we did have a small Negro boy and one day he forgot to fetch water and my father beat him."

On hearing this, I said: "I have never beaten any Negro boy, my little girl."

She replied: "But it was my other father who beat him. And the Negro boy cried out to me: 'Sinházinha, help me!' and I asked my father not to beat him and the little Negro boy ran off to fetch water."

Then I inquired: "Did he bring the water from the stream?"

"No, father," Marta explained, "there was no stream there. He brought the water from a well." (This was correct for the house of Sinhá.)

"Who was this Sinhá or Sinházinha?" I asked.

"That was myself. But I then had another name. My name was Maria and I had one other name which I cannot remember now." [6]

---

[6] F. V. Lorenz, *Op. cit.*, n. 4. (My translation.)

F. V. Lorenz stated in his report that at the time Marta began her declarations neither Lola nor any of the other older brothers and sisters of Marta knew anything of the prediction by Sinhá that she would return in the Lorenz family. F. V. Lorenz and his wife had, it appears, carefully withheld this information from the children with a view to observing what would develop in Marta spontaneously. After her initial remarks to Lola and their father, Marta went on to make at various times no less than 120 separate declarations about the life of Sinhá or recognitions of persons known to Sinhá. F. V. Lorenz kept detailed notes of these declarations. Unfortunately he wrote them in a German shorthand incomprehensible to another member of the family who, not recognizing their importance, discarded them. Sometime after this misfortune F. V. Lorenz wrote from memory his recollections of the case which he published in 1946. In doing this, however, he omitted considerable information known to other members of his family who still remembered the declarations of Marta. Marta's older brother, W. Lorenz, collected some of these additional items and a few more were recorded at the time of my visit to Brazil in 1962. In the tabular summary of the declarations, I have omitted all discrepant or unverified testimony or commented on such deficiencies if I have chosen to retain an item about which doubts occurred.

If it had been possible to publish the 120 items contemporaneously recorded by F. V. Lorenz, the case of Marta would perhaps have become the best witnessed and most thoroughly documented case suggestive of rebirth ever observed in a child. Readers now have before them a portion only of the previously available material. Much of that material consists of statements by Marta about details of the life of Sinhá already known to members of the Lorenz family. But a small portion of the verified statements of Marta concerned matters entirely unknown to F. V. Lorenz, his wife, or the other children of the family.

Marta apparently talked much of Sinhá's home and often asked to go there. Her father did not actually grant this wish, however, until she was twelve, at which time she had ceased to talk much of the life of Sinhá. Ema Bieszczad (one of Marta's older sisters) stated that C. J. de Oliveiro only learned of the supposed rebirth of his daughter at the time of this visit and that his wife never was told. It seems likely that for some reason F. V. Lorenz did not think it appropriate to tell C. J. de Oliveiro earlier about his daughter's (Marta's) statements.

Between the ages of seven and ten, Marta gradually ceased to talk much spontaneously about the life of Sinhá. She grew up, married and had children of her own. In 1962 she was living in Porto Alegre, where I spent some hours with her. She had forgotten much of the life of Sinhá, but by no means all and said she still retained certain vivid memories of events which happened to Sinhá, most particularly the last scenes of Sinhá's life and her death from tuberculosis.

Relevant Facts of Geography and Possible Normal Means of Communication Between the Two Families. As already mentioned, the families of F. V. Lorenz and C. J. de Oliveiro, Sinhá's father, lived twelve miles apart and knew each other well. F. V. Lorenz and his wife were in a position to know at the time they were made whether or not most of Marta's assertions about Sinhá's life were correct. Their children, however, did not have much of the relevant information, so that Marta sometimes told them about events in the life of Sinhá of which they had no knowledge. And some of the declarations or recognitions made by Marta concerned matters unknown to her parents, or occurred in their absence.

Persons Interviewed During the Investigation. In addition to using the written account of the case by F. V. Lorenz, I interviewed the following nine other witnesses.

In Porto Alegre, Rio Grande do Sul, I interviewed:

> Mrs. Marta Ines Lorenz Huber, born August 14, 1918
> Mr. Waldomiro Lorenz, older brother of Marta, born May 10, 1913
> Mr. Paulo Lorenz, younger brother of Marta, born February 3, 1923
> Mrs. Florzinha Santos Menezes, older foster sister of Marta, born in 1905

In Taquara, Rio Grande do Sul, I interviewed:

> Mrs. Ema Estelita Lorenz Bieszczad, older sister of Marta, born February 12, 1907

In Dom Feliciano, Rio Grande do Sul, I interviewed:

> Mrs. Luisa Carolina (Lola) Moreira, older sister of Marta, born August 29, 1908
> Mrs. Ana Luiza Lorenz Arginiro, older sister of Marta, born April 28, 1912
> Mrs. Dona Moça Antonietta de Oliveiro Costa, surviving sister of Sinhá, born in 1893

In São João Novo, São Paulo, I interviewed:

> Mrs. Ema Bolze Moreira, older foster sister of Marta, born in 1900

In addition, readers should remember the names of the following persons, deceased at the time of my interviews, but important participants or witnesses of the events of the case:

Mr. F. V. Lorenz, schoolteacher of Dom Feliciano, father of Marta Lorenz

Mrs. Ida Lorenz, his wife, good friend of Sinhá, and mother of Marta Lorenz

Mr. C. J. de Oliveiro, fazendeiro of the Dom Feliciano area, father of Sinhá

Statements and Recognitions Made by Marta. The tabulation below presents in summary form some of the statements and recognitions attributed to Marta with regard to her claim to be Sinhá reborn.

Relevant Reports and Observations of the Behavior of the People Concerned. As with other cases suggestive of reincarnation, the behavior of the subject of the present case provides much additional material which we must take account of in its final evaluation.

The tabulation of the information communicated by Marta about the life of Sinhá tells us very little about the *meaning* for Marta of her memories of Sinhá. For Marta identified herself with Sinhá completely. (She did this, however, along a line of continuous development, not as a substitution for her identity as Marta.) Thus it was especially appropriate for Marta to have reproached others for maltreating Carlos, her brother, if she thought they had. Florzinha Santos Menezes stated, for example, that she heard Marta on two different occasions express annoyance at others who were, she thought, mistreating Carlos. When asked why she protested thus, Marta replied: "Because when I was Sinhá I liked Carlos very much." (Carlos had been Sinhá's godson and, as mentioned below, Sinhá had given him two cows.) F. V. Lorenz in his report of the case stated that when Marta recounted episodes in the life of Sinhá, she would usually begin: "When I was Sinhá." Another common opening phrase of her utterances about Sinhá (when she was a child) was: "When I was big."

Marta's conviction of the continuity of her own life after death led her as quite a small child to offer comfort to bereaved adults. On one occasion a lady who was visiting the Lorenz family complained of the recent death of her father and said: "Oh, dear. The dead never return." At this Marta said: "Don't say that. I died also and look, I am living again." [7] On another occasion, during a rainstorm, when one of her sisters expressed concern that the deceased sister Emilia of the family would get wet in her grave, Marta said: "Don't say that. Emilia is not in the cemetery. She is in

[7] F. V. Lorenz. *Op. cit.*, n. 4. (My translation.)

TABULATION

Summary of Statements and Recognitions Made by Marta

Item	Informants	Verification	Comments
1. Sinhá used to carry Lola when Lola was a child.	F. V. Lorenz,[1] father of Marta Lorenz Huber Lola Moreira, older sister of Marta Lorenz Huber	Apparently known to F. V. Lorenz as correct.	According to W. Lorenz, Sinhá had wanted to be godmother to Lola, but instead was asked to be godmother to Carlos, another child of the Lorenz family. In 1962, at the age of sixty-four, Lola could not remember being carried by Sinhá, but did remember Sinhá's affection for her.
2. In Sinhá's home there were cows, oxen, oranges, and "goats that were not goats."	F. V. Lorenz Lola Moreira	F. V. Lorenz Dona Moça Costa, sister of Sinhá.	The two and a half year old girl did not know the word for sheep. At the fazenda of C. J. de Oliveiro there were sheep, cattle, and horses, but no goats. At the Lorenz home there were goats, but no sheep and Marta had not then seen sheep.
3. Her names were Sinhá, Maria and one other.	F. V. Lorenz Ema Bieszczad, older sister of Marta Lorenz Huber Marta Lorenz Huber	F. V. Lorenz	Sinhá was the familiar name or nickname for Dona Maria Januaria de Oliveiro. Marta said she remembered that when she could not recall the other name her father said: "Was it Januaria?" to which she replied, "Yes, it was."
4. Sinhá's father was older than her father; he had a great beard and talked gruffly.	F. V. Lorenz	F. V. Lorenz	Items true of Sinhá's father, C. J. de Oliveiro, but not of Marta's father, F. V. Lorenz. Marta gave an impressive imitation of the manner of speaking of Sinhá's father.
5. Sinhá's father had a Negro female cook and a Negro servant boy he beat.	F. V. Lorenz W. Lorenz, brother of Marta Lorenz Huber	F. V. Lorenz	
6. Once Sinhá's father beat the Negro boy for not	F. V. Lorenz W. Lorenz	F. V. Lorenz Ema Bieszczad	This episode not known to F. V. Lorenz at the time Marta made this statement.

188

Item	Informants	Verification	Comments
fetching water and Sinhá intervened when he cried for help.	Ema Bieszczad		According to W. Lorenz, his father verified the episode from C. J. de Oliveiro. Dona Moça Costa recalled in 1962 that Sinhá had once intervened when her father was beating the Negro servant boy, but she did not remember what his offense had been. Ema Bieszczad believed her mother, Ida Lorenz, probably also verified this episode, because she had seen C. J. de Oliveiro beat this boy on other occasions.
7. They obtained water from a well, not a stream.	F. V. Lorenz	F. V. Lorenz	True of the home of Sinhá; at the Lorenz home they obtained water from a stream behind the house, not from a well.
8. Recognition of Florinda de Almeida as former sweetheart of Sinhá.	F. V. Lorenz	F. V. Lorenz W. Lorenz	Another statement whose accuracy was unknown to F. V. Lorenz when Marta made it. When he questioned the man Marta recognized, the latter acknowledged the truth of what she had said. He had been one of the two men with whom Sinhá had been in love, but whom her father had prevented her marrying.
9. Sinhá and F. V. Lorenz were related as godparents.	F. V. Lorenz	F. V. Lorenz	Sinhá had been godmother to F. V. Lorenz' son, Carlos.
10. When Ida Lorenz came to visit Sinhá, Sinhá would prepare coffee and wait in front of the house playing a phonograph she placed on a stone.	F. V. Lorenz Lola Moreira	F. V. Lorenz Dona Moça Costa	Marta made this statement when her mother asked her if she could say how Sinhá used to receive her (Ida) when she visited Sinhá. Dona Moça Costa recalled Sinhá's playing the phonograph on the stone before the visits of Ida Lorenz. She did not mention the coffee. Ida Lorenz naturally knew about this way of greeting her, but no one else in the Lorenz family knew about it.

[1] In citing F. V. Lorenz I refer to either his written account of the case in *A Voz de Antigo Egito* (*op. cit.*, n. 4) or his somewhat fuller notes on the case placed at my disposal by his son, Waldomiro Lorenz.

Item	Informants	Verification	Comments
11. Description of the manner of Sinhá's speaking at the time of her death; Sinhá had much pain in her throat.	F. V. Lorenz W. Lorenz Ema Bieszczad Ana Arginiro, older sister of Marta Lorenz Huber	Ida Lorenz, as described by F. V. Lorenz	Ida Lorenz asked Marta how Sinhá had spoken to her the last time. Marta approached her mother, whispered in her mother's ear and pointed to her throat, saying that she could not speak, that her voice had gone. In fact, Sinhá died of tuberculosis and with tuberculous laryngitis which hoarsened and weakened her voice in her last days. Marta's imitation of Sinhá's way of speaking was witnessed by several members of the family. Only Ida Lorenz actually knew how Sinhá had talked just before she died.
12. Sinhá had acquired her last illness on a trip to a city where there were many masqueraders.	F. V. Lorenz	F. V. Lorenz Dona Moça Costa	After refusing to allow his daughter to marry the man she loved, C. J. de Oliveiro took her on a trip to Pelotas at carnival time to help her forget her lover. But on this trip and the return journey, Sinhá began her ultimately fatal illness. These facts were almost certainly known to F. V. Lorenz and were definitely known to his wife Ida, before Sinhá's death.
13. On the return journey from the trip (to Pelotas, mentioned in Item 12), they were caught in a heavy rain and had to spend the night in an old house.	F. V. Lorenz Ema Bolze Moreira, older foster sister of Marta	F. V. Lorenz Ema Bolze Moreira	Apparently F. V. Lorenz did not know this detail until he checked it with C. J. de Oliveiro after Marta made this statement. Ema had heard Sinhá describe the trip in detail before her death and about five years later heard Marta give an identical account of the same journey. Ema's account included two details omitted in F. V. Lorenz' account and his account included one detail not found in Ema's version.

14. Recognition of relationship of Sinhá with Francisca de Oliveira, cousin and godchild of Sinhá.	F. V. Lorenz Ema Bieszczad W. Lorenz	F. V. Lorenz Ema Bieszczad W. Lorenz Dona Moça Costa	F. V. Lorenz was not a primary witness of this episode, but the other two informants were. Francisca de Oliveira was a complete stranger in Dom Feliciano when this episode occurred. None of the Lorenz family knew of her relationship with Sinhá. As she had heard of Marta's declarations, she said to her: "If you were really Sinhá, tell me what our relationship was." Marta replied accurately and without hesitation.
15. Sinhá had given Carlos Lorenz, her godson, two cows before she died.	F. V. Lorenz	F. V. Lorenz Dona Moça Costa Lola Moreira	This fact known to F. V. Lorenz before Sinhá's death. Dona Moça Costa knew of only one cow given to Carlos by Sinhá. But she had married and left her father's house in 1914. She may well not have heard of the gift of the second cow which, according to Lola Moreira, took place shortly before Sinhá died.
16. The two cows given to Carlos by Sinhá had had calves in the meantime.	F. V. Lorenz Lola Moreira	F. V. Lorenz Lola Moreira Marta Lorenz Huber	The cows had stayed on at the fazenda of C. J. de Oliveiro. When Marta made this statement F. V. Lorenz did not know that one of the cows had had a calf, and confirmed this from C. J. de Oliveiro. F. V. Lorenz wrote in his notes that only one of the cows had had a calf; Lola Moreira stated that both had had calves. Marta Lorenz also stated (1962) that both had had calves. According to the witnesses of this episode, Marta had knowledge of events occurring after the death of Sinhá at Sinhá's fazenda.
17. Sinhá had a white horse; however, it was not called thus, but "barroso" (English: clay colored).	F. V. Lorenz	F. V. Lorenz Dona Moça Costa	Fact probably known to F. V. Lorenz before the death of Sinhá. According to Dona Moça Costa, the horse actually belonged to Sinhá's father, but Sinhá pre-

Item	Informants	Verification	Comments
17. (continued)			ferred riding the white horse instead of her own, which was red.
18. Sinhá and Ida Lorenz had once on the same day bought identical saddles.	F. V. Lorenz W. Lorenz heard of this statement soon after Marta made it. Florzinha Menezes, foster sister of Marta Lorenz Huber	F. V. Lorenz Dona Moça Costa	Marta stated (1962) that she still remembered this episode. She recalled that as a child she used to play with her mother's saddle and said she then remembered that it was like the one she had had as Sinhá. But she did not speak of this resemblance for some time. She was stimulated to make the statements of items 17 and 18 one day when she was watching a horse being saddled with Ida's saddle, which resembled Sinhá's.
19. Preference for C. J. de Oliveiro and rejection of other visitor, Mr. Valentin.	F. V. Lorenz Ana Arginiro	F. V. Lorenz Ana Arginiro	The two men visited the Lorenz house at the same time. Mr. Valentin showed every sign of friendliness, but the little girl Marta went toward the other man, Sinhá's father, and caressed his beard in friendly fashion even though he did not welcome her, apparently not liking children. Ana Arginiro recalled that Marta embraced Sinhá's father and said: "Hello, papa." This happened when Marta was less than a year old.
20. Sinhá used to sit next to her father at meals.	Lola Moreira	Lola Moreira Dona Moça Costa	When small, Marta refused to sit in the kitchen with the older children, asserting that she used to sit next to her other father at meals. Another fact not known to F. V. or Ida Lorenz.
21. Sinhá had a white cat.	Ema Bolze Moreira	Ema Bolze Moreira	Sinhá was particularly fond of cats, as was Marta. But other members of the family liked cats, although perhaps less so than Marta.

22. Sinhá was buried in white and with something on her head.	Ema Bolze Moreira	Unverified	
23. Sinhá's funeral was attended by many Negroes, but very few white women. Ida Lorenz attended the funeral.	Florzinha Menezes Lola Moreira Ema Bolze Moreira	Lola Moreira, quoting Ida Lorenz who atended Sinhá's funeral.	Many white women stayed away from Sinhá's funeral for fear of infection with tuberculosis. Ida Lorenz was one of only two or three white women who attended.
24. Marta's father attended Sinhá's funeral.	Ema Bolze Moreira	Ema Bolze Moreira	Ema Bolze Moreira asked Marta whether her father had attended Sinhá's funeral. Upon Marta replying that he had, Ema B. Moreira denied the fact, but when Marta insisted this was so, she asked F. V. Lorenz, who confirmed the fact that he had attended the funeral.
25. Sinhá used to bake roscas.	Lola Moreira	Lola Moreira Dona Moça Costa	Roscas are a twisted cake of the area. Sinhá's interest in baking cakes was generally known to the Lorenz family. Dona Moça Costa recalled Sinhá's baking cakes, but did not mention a special kind of cake.
26. Sinhá's father spoke harshly to the slaves.	Florzinha Menezes	Inferentially verified only.	One day when C. J. de Oliveiro was visiting the Lorenz family and speaking loudly, Marta said: "I never liked it when he spoke so loudly to the slaves. I wonder if he is angry with my present father." Slavery was abolished in Brazil in 1888, about two years before the birth of Sinhá. What is known of the character of C. J. de Oliveiro and the verified episode of his beating the Negro servant boy suggest that the formal emancipation of the slaves in Brazil would have influenced his behavior toward them very little.

Item	Informants	Verification	Comments

27. Description of road to the fazenda of C. J. de Oliveiro, including a turn around a large stone just before coming to the house.

Informants

Marta Lorenz Huber

Verification

Marta Lorenz Huber

Comments

When she was twelve (and long after the period of her most numerous declarations about the life of Sinhá) Marta's father took her on a visit to Sinhá's home. Unfortunately no other witnesses of this visit were available in 1962. Lola Moreira had accompanied the party, but was ill and paid little attention to what went on.

28. Recognition of a clock in the house of C. J. de Oliveiro which had belonged to Sinhá.

Marta Lorenz Huber
W. Lorenz, quoting F. V. Lorenz

Marta Lorenz Huber
W. Lorenz, quoting F. V. Lorenz

On the occasion of the visit referred to in item 27, Marta, inside the house, pointed to a clock on the wall and said it had belonged to Sinhá and that they would find her name on the back of the clock engraved in gold letters. The clock was taken down and on its back was written "Maria Januaria de Oliveiro." As with item 27, other witnesses of this episode were either dead or unavailable in 1962. W. Lorenz heard of the episode from his father who was a witness of Marta's recognition of the clock. C. J. de Oliveiro knew the clock had belonged to Sinhá and was at first reluctant to take it down and show the back, apparently fearing Marta Lorenz might claim it for herself. The clock was purchased by Sinhá who personally tended to it. When she was away the clock ran down and upon her return she would re-wind it and set it by the sunset. It was the only one of its kind in the district at that time. It was the only object in the home recognized by Marta on her visit when she went to Sinhá's home at the age of twelve. Unfortunately, efforts made in 1962 to verify independently the existence and

28. (continued)

details of the clock in the home of C. J. de Oliveiro were not successful.

Dona Moça Costa remembered nothing of a clock owned by Sinhá; however, as she married and moved out of her parents' house three years before Sinhá's death, she may not have known the clock if it was purchased after her marriage. After my visit in 1962, W. Lorenz enquired about this clock of Sinhá's younger brother and of a servant of the family of C. J. de Oliveiro, but neither could remember the clock, possibly because they were too young at the time Sinhá had the clock which may have been disposed of after her death. That the clock did exist seems clear enough from the corroboration of Marta's account of the episode by F. V. Lorenz' account of the episode by F. V. Lorenz' account of the episode by F. V. Lorenz' account of the episode by F. V. Lorenz' account to his son, W. Lorenz.

a safer and better place than this one where we are; her soul never can be wet." [8]

As she grew older, Marta's identification with Sinhá persisted, especially with regard to her own children. She became preoccupied with the idea that Florzinho, Sinhá's last sweetheart, might return as her own child. (Florzinho had committed suicide after Sinhá's father blocked his marriage with her.) Marta then, twenty-five years after the deaths of Sinhá and her sweetheart, hoped for a reunion between them just as Sinhá herself had predicted a reunion with Ida Lorenz whose daughter she said she would become. That Marta observed some evidence which satisfied her that Florzinho had in fact reincarnated as her own son is not of importance here; I am now concerned only with describing the strong sense of continuity between two lives which Marta experienced and still did in 1962.

Some observers who knew both Sinhá and Marta commented on resemblances between the handwriting of the two women although, so far as I know, independent authorities never made judgments on these supposed resemblances. Similar comments occurred with regard to resemblances of physical appearance between Sinhá and Marta. We can attach little importance to such observations on the part of members of Marta's family who knew about her claim to have lived before as Sinhá. One observation on this matter, however, stands somewhat apart and indeed offers us an example of a kind of observation which would be extremely helpful in the study of these cases if we could have it more often. When Marta was nineteen she was employed at a fazenda to teach children. While there an elderly Negro woman noticed her and said: "This girl [Marta] looks like Sinhá." The Negro woman turned out to be the former slave and servant of C. J. de Oliveiro mentioned in item 5 of the tabulation. Marta, who was the only witness for this episode, was quite certain that she told no one at the fazenda about her claim to remember the life of Sinhá. She remembered especially avoiding telling anyone at the fazenda about Sinhá because the owners were orthodox Roman Catholics likely to be unfriendly to the idea of reincarnation.

On one aspect of resemblance between Sinhá and Marta we have more detailed testimony. As mentioned earlier, Sinhá died of a severe pulmonary infection, probably tuberculosis. It particularly affected her larynx and in her final days Sinhá had a painful throat and a hoarse and weakened voice. Until the age of ten, Marta was especially vulnerable to upper respiratory infections during which her voice would become harsh. Several of her older brothers and sisters, e.g., Waldomiro Lorenz and Lola Moreira, re-

---

[8] Notes of F. V. Lorenz and of my interview with Ema Bolze Moreira. Their versions of exactly what Marta said on this occasion differ considerably in detail, although not in the idea conveyed by Marta that only the body lies in a grave. I have quoted the version recorded by F. V. Lorenz.

called her susceptibility to such infections. Marta's own recollection of her frequent attacks of laryngitis included other details. She recalled having hoarseness continuously until the age of nine. (Other witnesses thought her voice normal except during her respiratory infections.) She had, she said, such infections about once a month and then her voice would become particularly hoarse and she would have pain in her throat. At such times she also felt large in her body and thought that she was going to die.[9]

Several observers who knew both Sinhá and Marta commented on similarities in the personalities of the two women. Since most of these observers knew of the belief on the part of Marta that she had lived as Sinhá, this knowledge could have influenced their judgments. Moreover, several of the traits mentioned as strongly developed in the two women occur quite commonly and we cannot consider them in any way specific for them. Nevertheless, I consider these features not entirely worthless as evidence of similarity between the two personalities, although not contributing anything to the evidence of how the personalities came to resemble each other.

Sinhá was fond of cats and so was Marta. (Sinhá's white cat is mentioned in item 21 in the list of statements made by Marta about Sinhá.) When I inquired about a fondness for cats in other members of Marta's family, I learned that some of her brothers and sisters, notably Lola, also liked cats very much. Lola Moreira herself did not recall that Marta had a special partiality for cats. However, that Marta was in fact somewhat more attached to cats than other members of the family is suggested by the fact that when the family moved to another state to try coffee planting for a time, Marta was the only one to have cats in the home.

Sinhá lived a leisurely, although lonely, life as the daughter of a prosperous landowner. She enjoyed dancing. She did not sew and did not cook except for the little cakes (roscas) she baked. Sinhá wanted an education which she could not obtain at her remote inland home. When Marta was young, she liked fine clothes. but subsequently her tastes adapted to her means. She liked dancing particularly well. She wanted to be a teacher and did teach temporarily in a fazenda as mentioned above. But her family could not afford to train her completely as a teacher and so she trained as a seamstress, although she never liked sewing.

Sinhá was afraid of rain and Marta had a similar fear of rain. According

[9] This unusual experience resembles the perception of changes in the size of the body undergone by some subjects during hypnosis or intoxication with such drugs as lysergic acid diethylamide. It also resembles changes of body image experienced by some adult subjects during vivid apparent recall and reliving of a previous life either awake or when dreaming. In the present case, the laryngeal pain and hoarseness evidently led through associations to the full reproduction of the last scenes in the life of Sinhá. These are the scenes in the life of Sinhá which Marta at age forty-four still remembered most clearly. In this experience a somatic sensation seems to have stimulated further associations, just as in observing a horse being saddled, a visual stimulus did so (see comment to item 18 in the tabulation).

to Florzinha Menezes, when someone asked Marta why she was afraid of rain, she said: "When I was Sinhá I was afraid of rain." Both Sinhá and Marta had a fear, amounting to a phobia, of blood. A fear of blood seems to have affected other members of Sinhá's family, but Marta's phobia stood out in her family. W. Lorenz stated that blood phobia occurred uniquely in Marta in the Lorenz family. Lola Moreira stated that someone who had known Sinhá, but knew nothing of her supposed rebirth as Marta, once observed Marta react with panic when her finger bled. This woman spontaneously commented that Marta's reaction to blood was exactly like that of Sinhá.

Comments on the Evidence of Paranormal Knowledge on the Part of Marta.
As already mentioned, all but six of the items listed in the above tabulation were known to members of the Lorenz family, although sometimes to only one or two members rather than to the group as a whole. Items 6, 8, 14, 16, 20, and 28 had to be verified by asking persons outside the family who knew the facts. But because of the existing knowledge held by the Lorenz family about Sinhá and her family, we have to consider it possible and indeed likely that some information about Sinhá passed from them to Marta. The next question to be asked is whether this pathway lay sufficiently open to account for *all* the information Marta possessed about Sinhá.

W. Lorenz conversed at length with his father, F. V. Lorenz, about the development of the case. His father, he stated, was well aware of the possibilities for leakage of information through normal means to Marta. F. V. Lorenz had considerable acquaintance with the literature of psychical research. When his wife told him of Sinhá's proposal to return to their family, they resolved to tell no one of this until they themselves observed developments. Later they did tell one other person, the godfather of W. Lorenz, a good friend of F. V. Lorenz, but they told none of their children. The other children whom I interviewed testified to their own ignorance of Sinhá's prediction of her return until after the first episode of declarations by Marta (items 1 and 2 of the tabulation) and her different reaction as an infant to the two older men who came to visit the family (item 19). Soon after the first declarations of Marta about the previous life, Ida Lorenz seems to have told at least some of the other children about Sinhá's prediction. She apparently did this to try to make sense to the other children of Marta's behavior since one sister at least (Lola) initially thought Marta was talking complete nonsense in referring to a previous life. At the time of Marta's first declarations at the age of two and a half, her older siblings (those I interviewed) were aged seven (Waldomiro), eight (Ana), nine (Lola), thirteen (Ema Estelita), fifteen (Florzinha, foster sister), and twenty (Ema Moreira, foster sister). All these persons were probably old enough at the time to know then, and to remember later, whether they had heard about Sinhá's prediction of her return before Marta's first declarations. Waldomiro, Lola, and Ema Estelita insisted that they did not have such earlier knowledge; Ana and Ema Moreira did not recall when they first learned of Sinhá's prediction of her return. I did not question Florzinha Menezes on this point. The oldest of the group, Ema Moreira, herself a young adult of twenty at the time of Marta's statements, testified that the family had never talked about Sinhá in front of Marta and that Marta talked about Sinhá quite spontaneously.

We may find some internal evidence that F. V. Lorenz approached the declarations of Marta cautiously and with regard to the possibilities of suggesting answers to her from his own record of the first conversation about Sinhá. If we believe this to be a fairly accurate reproduction of his talk with the little girl, we must acknowledge that he did not give any leads to the child. According to Marta, when she hesitated over the name Januaria, after giving the names of Sinhá and Maria correctly, he offered it to her, but only then and not before. And otherwise he seems to have adopted a tone of inquiry, although we can surmise that he had expectations of some of Marta's answers in view of his awareness of Sinhá's promise to return.

In the above comments I have not mentioned the important behavioral features of the case, which indicate even more than the informational elements the identification of Marta with Sinhá. Some readers may decide that we can adequately account for the elements of personation on the basis of the information possessed by Marta about Sinhá (whether acquired normally or through extrasensory perception) and the promotion of such personation on the part of Marta's parents who wanted their dead friend to return and live with them as she had promised to do. This view of the elements of personation in the case has merit, but also important weaknesses. I shall defer full consideration of it until the General Discussion to follow all the case reports.

The Later Development of Marta. I did not meet Marta Lorenz between July, 1962, and February, 1972. At that time I went to Porto Alegre and met there first her older brother, Waldomiro Lorenz. After I heard his news we both went to Marta's house on the outskirts of Porto Alegre and had a long talk with her. Marta's husband, Fritz Huber, and her older sister, Ema Estelita Bieszczad, were also present during this meeting. In the ten years since I had seen Marta I had occasionally exchanged letters with Waldomiro Lorenz (especially concerning the suicide of his and Marta's brother, Paulo. (For details of this see the case report of Paulo Lorenz.)

When I visited Marta in 1972 she was fifty-four years old. Her marriage was a happy one. Her two children who survived infancy had grown up and both were married.

Marta said in 1972 that she had forgotten much of the life of Sinhá, but also remembered much. This was what she had said in 1962 and it seemed to me that her memories of the previous life had not undergone any additional fading in the ten years since our last meeting. On the contrary, I came away from this meeting in 1972 with the impression that I had perhaps overstated in the first edition of this book the amount of fading Marta's memories of the previous life had undergone and I now believe that she had carried more of them into adulthood than I then realized. This is not to deny that Marta had forgotten much that she remembered when younger, nor did she claim otherwise. But she obviously retained with vivid clarity many of the details of Sinhá's life. Particularly prominent in her memories seemed to be those associated with Florzinho, Sinhá's last sweetheart. Her marriage with him had been frustrated by the disapproval of their parents. Florzinho had then committed suicide and soon afterwards Sinhá herself indirectly committed suicide by exposing herself to cold and dampness. Marta was still thinking about Florzinho from time to time in 1972 and also about her belief that her first two sons (who had both died in infancy) had been reincarnations of him. (Her conviction about this was based largely on birthmarks on the heads of the babies which were said to have resembled corresponding marks on Florzinho.) Marta said that she still thought of herself as Sinhá. I do not think she meant by this that she did not also think of herself as Marta. There was no denial of her present life, only a sense of continuity with that of Sinhá. She said she sometimes spontaneously thought of Sinhá, especially at night when she was praying and preparing to go to sleep.

Marta had not returned to visit Sinhá's family since her childhood. Its members were all dead or dispersed so I could not say firmly that Marta's failure to keep in touch with them arose from a loss of her own interest, but I think that it did not. I believe that she would have visited them if they had been available and if, after her marriage, she had had the financial resources to travel the considerable distance from Porto Alegre to their place of residence beyond Dom Feliciano. Whatever the reason for Marta's not continuing to visit Sinhá's family, we can say that at least in her case the maintenance of the memories of the previous life was not assisted, as seems to have happened in some other cases, by visits between the families concerned. (For an example in which this does seem to have occurred, see the section on the follow-up interview in the case report of Prakash.)

Marta had been much affected by two deaths in her family which had occurred since my meeting with her in 1962. The first of these was the suicide of her younger brother Paulo in 1966, already mentioned. Paulo's death shocked and disturbed her so much that she required admission to a hospital where she remained for more than three weeks. She had not fully recovered from Paulo's death by 1972. Then, about 1969, her older brother Carlos died. Carlos had been Sinhá's godson and Marta's favorite brother. (I described earlier how Marta would defend Carlos when she thought him mistreated.) Carlos seems to have had a particularly miserable life characterized by too many children, too little money, and poor health. Marta tried to help him, but availed little. She wept as she remembered him in 1972.

Marta continued (in 1972) to suffer from the attacks of bronchitis which had troubled her when she was younger. She said that every time she caught a cold "it went to her chest and larynx." At such times she lost her voice. She was still having attacks of bronchitis about four times a year. In contrast, her brother Waldomiro and her sister Ema very rarely had colds and respiratory infections. In fact, Ema said that she had had a respiratory infection only once in her life and that was during an epidemic. Earlier, in 1967, Waldomiro Lorenz had written me (in response to a direct inquiry on this point) that none of Marta's ten siblings (who survived infancy) had suffered from laryngitis as she had. It will be remembered that after Sinhá deliberately exposed herself to cold and dampness she developed tuberculosis of the lungs and larynx from which she died. And before she died she could only speak in a faint whisper (see item 11 of the tabulation). I believe that we may reasonably consider Marta's vulnerability to bronchitis and laryngitis a kind of "internal birthmark" related to the previous life and death of Sinhá.

Marta also conserved up to 1972 several behavioral traits that had been prominent in Sinhá. She still had a fear of rain and of blood and she still liked cats. Her older sisters, Ema Estelita and Lola, also liked cats. So a fondness for cats was far from unique to Marta in her own family, but it was a prominent feature of her personality as it had been of Sinhá's.

Since Sinhá had indirectly committed suicide I have been interested in the occurrence of suicidal tendencies in Marta and discussed this with her in 1972. Her brother, Waldomiro, had never heard her say that she might commit suicide, but Marta herself rather frankly admitted to me that she had often wished to die. She had never actually attempted suicide, but thought that she might have killed herself at times if she had had a gun with which to do so.

I think I should have mentioned in the first edition of this book that both Sinhá and Marta were credited with more than average powers of extrasensory perception. Sinhá's most impressive demonstrations occurred when she would announce in advance that her friend Ida Lorenz (Marta's mother) was coming to visit her family's fazenda. Dom Feliciano, where Ida Lorenz lived, was about twelve miles from the fazenda owned by

Sinhá's family. Although Sinhá had no normal way of knowing when Ida Lorenz might choose to come out to visit the family at the fazenda, she would be so certain that Ida Lorenz was coming on certain days that she would arrange a phonograph ready to play music as a kind of welcoming gesture when she arrived. Sinhá's surviving sister, Dona Moça Antonietta de Oliveiro Costa, told me about Sinhá's accurate predictions of Ida Lorenz's visits in 1962. F. V. Lorenz, Marta's father, also testified to these predictions of his wife's visits made by Sinhá, in the notes he made about the case.

Two of Marta's siblings testified to her having an unusual capacity for extrasensory perception when she was young. Her brother Waldomiro told me that once her godmother gave her a book as a gift. Marta ignored it, leaving it in its wrappings. Her father asked her: "Are you not going to read it?" Marta replied: "No. The book is about a case similar to mine." She then correctly gave the title of the still wrapped book.

An even more impressive demonstration of apparent extrasensory perception occurred when Marta was between five and six years old. (Informants differed somewhat about her age at the time.) She awoke one night saying that she had had a vision of a girl called Celica who was (in the vision) calling her: "Sinhá, Sinhá." Her father, F. V. Lorenz (according to her sister, Ema Estelita Bieszczad), noted the time when Marta had this nocturnal vision of Celica. It was found to correspond exactly with the time of death of the girl Celica. This occurred at a place about fifteen miles away according to the statement made about it by F. V. Lorenz. No one in Marta's family had, or could have had, any normal knowledge of Celica's death at the time Marta had her vision and heard Celica calling her "Sinhá." A messenger came over from Celica's family the next morning to invite the Lorenz family to Celica's funeral. (Marta told me in 1972 that she still remembered very distinctly this vision she had had of Celica as a child.) Perhaps the most important point of the episode is that Celica was a close friend, and some informants said, a relative of Sinhá. Students of these cases who believe they are adequately interpreted by extrasensory perception may say that if Marta could know paranormally about the death of one of Sinhá's friends she might well have obtained *all* the correct information she showed about Sinhá and her family by the same means. I can only reply that in this case at least, we cannot exclude this possibility and the incident that I have described tends to increase the plausibility of the hypothesis.[10]

[10] Marta was credited with paranormal knowledge of at least one event happening in Sinhá's family after Sinhá's death as described under item 16 of the tabulation. Her information about this event might have derived from extrasensory communication with living members of Sinhá's family.

For other examples of evidence of extrasensory perception on the part of the subjects of

Since Marta had reached middle adulthood in 1972 it seemed appropriate and inoffensive to ask her to compare her life as it had passed to this point with that of Sinhá who had, however, died at the much younger age of about twenty-eight. Marta's judgment was that the two lives were about equal in allotment of happiness. She was less wealthy than Sinhá had been, for Sinhá's father was a moderately prosperous fazendeiro. But Marta did not think that wealth had much to do with happiness or that the life of Sinhá contained more of it than hers. A noticeable difference between the two—I am here giving my own comment, not Marta's—is that Sinhá's love affairs were frustrated and she never married. Marta had married and her husband had treated her well. The sorrowful loss of two of her brothers Paulo and Carlos, had been to some extent compensated by the affection she received from her husband, her son, and her brother, Waldomiro.

The Case of Paulo Lorenz

Summary of the Case and its Investigation. The case of Paulo Lorenz occurred in the same family as the case just described. In this case the alleged personality reincarnating as Paulo was that of his deceased sister, Emilia. Thus both present and previous personalities of the case were members of the same family. This fact certainly increases the possibility for normal (and for that matter paranormal) communication of information between the present personality and the older people who knew the previous personality. Despite this weakness, however, the case deserves presentation because it illustrates (a) a difference in sex between the two personalities, (b) a highly developed personation by the second personality of the first one, and (c) the expression in the second personality of a special talent for sewing which, although not unusual in itself, was in this family most highly, and indeed almost specifically, developed by these two children and no other child in a family of thirteen children.

Emilia Lorenz was the second child and eldest daughter of F. V. and Ida Lorenz. She was born on February 4, 1902, and given the name Emilia after the first child of the family, a boy called Emilio, who had died in infancy a few years earlier.

From all accounts Emilia was extremely unhappy throughout her entire short life. She felt constrained as a girl and some years before her death she told several of her brothers and sisters, but not her parents, that if there was such a thing as reincarnation she would return as a man. She also said she expected to die single. She had proposals of marriage, but rejected all suitors. She made several suicidal attempts. On one such occasion

these cases with members of the families or friends of the related previous personalities, see the case reports of Gnanatilleka, Swarnlata Mishra (in the section on the follow-up interview), and Shamlinie Prema (I. Stevenson. *Cases of the Reincarnation Type.* In preparation.) .

she took arsenic and was given large amounts of milk as an antidote. Finally, she took cyanide, from the effects of which she died very quickly on October 12, 1921.

Some time after the death of Emilia, Mrs. Ida Lorenz attended some spiritualistic meetings at which she received communications from a spirit purporting to be Emilia. These meetings comprised a group of amateurs among whom Ida Lorenz herself seems to have been one of the principal possessors of whatever psychical capacity was manifested. The communications from "Emilia" seem to have come directly to Ida Lorenz, a fact which we must remember in evaluating the inception of the idea that Emilia would return to terrestrial existence. "Emilia" expressed regrets at her suicide and said she wished to return in the family again, but as a boy. According to Lola Moreira (quoting her mother), Ida Lorenz doubted the wish of the "Emilia" communicator to return as a boy. But the same communication was given on three separate occasions, "Emilia" saying: "Mamma, take me as your son. I will come as your son." Among the children of the family only Ema Bieszczad heard about the prediction of "Emilia" at the séances that she would return as a boy; and she did not learn of this until Paulo was between two and three years old. The other children did not learn about this until much later. When Ida Lorenz reported this communication to her husband he expressed incredulity that Emilia should propose a change of sex. Whether or not the communications concerning this intention were from the discarnate spirit of Emilia is not important here; I mention them mainly for the bearing they and their reception by the Lorenz parents have on the possibility that Mr. and Mrs. Lorenz fostered a change of sexual orientation in their next child.

At the time of Emilia's death, Ida Lorenz had already borne twelve children, of whom the youngest was Marta Lorenz (born August 14, 1918, three years before), and did not expect to become pregnant again. She did nevertheless conceive once more and on February 3, 1923, a little less than a year and a half after Emilia's death, she gave birth to a boy. They gave him the name Paulo.

For the first four or five years of his life, Paulo resolutely refused to wear boys' clothes. He wore girls' clothes or none at all. He played with girls and with dolls. He made several remarks asserting his identity with Emilia. He exhibited an unusual skill for sewing and also had in common with Emilia a number of other traits or interests.

When Paulo was about four or five a pair of trousers was made for him out of a skirt formerly worn by Emilia. This seems to have appealed to him and he thereafter permitted himself to wear boys' clothes. Gradually his sexual orientation shifted toward the masculine side, but important elements of femininity were obvious into his teens, and a strong feminine identification (for a man) persisted to the time of my investigation of the case in 1962.

In the summer of 1962, I heard of this case from Waldomiro Lorenz, Paulo's older brother. Mr. Lorenz had himself witnessed some of the events of the case. I talked with Paulo and also with six of his older sisters, who said they remembered the events of Paulo's childhood. As I have already listed these informants in connection with the case of Marta Lorenz, I shall not identify them again here. Their ages at the time of the events in the case of Paulo may be derived from the information given on pp. 186, 198–199 above.[11]

Behavior and Statements of Emilia and Paulo Indicative of Paulo's Identification with Emilia. I give below in tabular form the details of the similarities between Emilia and Paulo and the behavior of Paulo which indicates his identification with Emilia. In this tabulation, I have listed relevant items of the behavior of Emilia or statements by her as well as those of Paulo. The informants for these items were themselves usually in a position to know and verify the relevance of the items to both personalities. In some instances, the informant testified only to the behavior of one of the personalities and another informant, mentioned in the Comments, furnished the information of a correspondence with the behavior of the other personality. I have not, therefore, included a separate column of verifications in this tabulation.

The Specificity of the Skill in Sewing Shown by Paulo. Emilia seems to have shown a genius for sewing. She enjoyed it and far excelled in competence all her younger sisters. Their mother, Ida Lorenz, cared little for sewing and never worked a sewing machine. But a sewing machine was bought for Emilia, and much used by her. After Emilia's death, an effort was made to teach Augusta, a younger sister, how to sew, but failed utterly. Then another younger sister learned to sew, but never became the expert Emilia had been. Marta and Lola also learned to sew, but did not show the skill of Emilia. As mentioned above, an attempt was made to train Marta as a seamstress (there being insufficient money to train her as a teacher), but she never liked this vocation or showed much competence at it.

---

[11] I think it worth mentioning again that I interviewed separately all the older sisters of Paulo who acted as informants in this case. However, Mr. Waldomiro Lorenz acted as interpreter in all the interviews except for the one with Mrs. Ema Moreira. It may be supposed that the presence, expectations, and interpretations of Mr. Lorenz diminished the independence of the different testimonies. This no doubt happened to a certain extent, but I could understand enough of the Portuguese spoken to know that the different accounts were unfolding on the whole quite spontaneously and with little guidance from the interpreter.

TABULATION
Summary of Behavior and Statements of Emilia and Paulo
Indicative of Paulo's Identification with Emilia

Item	Informants	Comments
1. Statements by Emilia before her death that she wanted to return as a man if she reincarnated.	Ema Bieszczad, older sister of Paulo Lola Moreira, older sister of Paulo Ana Arginiro, older sister of Paulo Ema Moreira, older foster sister of Paulo W. Lorenz, brother of Paulo	Not told to the parents by the children who heard Emilia make these statements. Lola Moreira stated that the children did not have sufficient familiarity with the parents to tell them something of this kind. W. Lorenz recalled that as an adult he told his father about Emilia's distaste for being a woman and his father showed surprise, not having heard this before. Emilia was better at making men's and boys' clothes than at making feminine clothes.
2. Interest of Emilia and Paulo in traveling.	Ana Arginiro	Apparently one reason why Emilia wanted to be a man. As a woman in Brazil in the early twentieth century she could not travel easily. Paulo, according to W. Lorenz, with whom he lived in 1962, was particularly fond of travel and occupied his vacations with it.
3. Unusual competence of Emilia and Paulo in sewing.	Ema Moreira Ana Arginiro Lola Moreira W. Lorenz Florzinha Santos Menezes, older foster sister of Paulo Marta Lorenz Huber, sister of Paulo Ema Bieszczad	Emilia had exhibited great skill in sewing and owned the only sewing machine in the family. Several witnesses testified to the precocious competence of Paulo in sewing. Lola Moreira recalled that when Paulo was "extremely small" and a servant of the family was trying clumsily to work the sewing machine, he pushed her aside, showed her how to work the machine, and made a small sack with it. W. Lorenz and Florzinha Menezes both recalled that once when Paulo was about four years old, she (Florzinha) was having difficulty in threading the machine and Paulo showed her how to do it. Marta Lorenz Huber and Lola Moreira recalled that once Marta left the sewing machine with some unfinished embroidery on it; in her absence Paulo finished the work she had left. All the above three episodes occurred before Paulo had any lessons in sewing. Ema Bieszczad recalled seeing Paulo working Emilia's sewing machine before he had had any lessons. She stated that once when someone asked Paulo about how he could sew without lessons, he replied: "I knew already how to sew." Ema

Item	*Informants*	*Comments*
3. (continued)		Moreira also recalled Paulo's ability to work the sewing machine when he was four and before he received any lessons. Ana Arginiro also recalled that Paulo could sew very well before he had instruction and resisted having instruction, saying he knew already. In addition to describing Paulo's *talent* for sewing, several informants mentioned his *liking* for it. He would frequently go to the sewing machine and work it by himself despite prohibitions from his older sisters.
4. Unsuccessful attempts of Emilia and Paulo to play the violin.	Ema Bieszczad	Both Emilia and Paulo wanted to play the violin, tried to do so, but lacked competence.
5. Preference of both Emilia and Paulo for Lola among the brothers and sisters of the family.	Marta Lorenz Huber	Lola was the favorite sister of Emilia and also of Paulo, who expressed a wish to move out of W. Lorenz' house and live with Lola, who was a widow in 1962.
6. Weak interest in cooking on the part of Emilia and Paulo.	Marta Lorenz Huber	Marta stated: "He [Paulo] was not much interested in cooking, and neither was Emilia."
7. The first words spoken by Paulo at the age of three and a half, on seeing another child put something in its mouth, were "Take care. Children should not put things in their mouths. It may be dangerous."	Ema Bieszczad	Paulo delayed speaking so long that doubts were entertained about his ability to do so or that he could hear. Some children (they are often younger children whose needs are met by others) do not speak until three or four years old and then begin in full sentences, and Paulo seems to have given an example of this behavior. After two suicidal attempts with swallowing poison, the second successful, a surviving Emilia might have become cautious about putting things in her mouth.
8. Emilia and Paulo each had a habit of breaking off corners of new loaves of bread.	Ema Bieszczad	This habit seems to have been uniquely possessed by Emilia and Paulo in the family.
9. Refusal of Paulo to wear boys' clothing before the age of four or five.	Marta Lorenz Huber Lola Moreira Ema Moreira	Florzinha Menezes and Ana Arginiro recalled that Paulo liked women's clothes. They did not mention any actual refusal on his part to wear boys' clothes.

Item	Informants	Comments
10. Statements of Paulo about being a girl.	Marta Lorenz Huber Ana Bieszczad Ema Moreira	To Marta, Paulo once said: "Am I not beautiful? I am going to walk like a girl." To Ema Bieszczad he used to say: "I am a girl." Ema Moreira also recalled that he said he was a girl.
11. Preference of Paulo for playing with girls and dolls.	Marta Lorenz Huber Lola Moreira Ema Moreira	
12. Claim by Paulo that he had been in the house of Dona Elena; accurate description of the house of Dona Elena.	Ema Bieszczad	W. Lorenz said that Emilia had taken sewing lessons from Dona Elena.
13. Statement by Paulo that he had taken sewing lessons from Dona Elena.	Marta Lorenz Huber as quoted by W. Lorenz, who did not himself hear this statement directly.	Emilia had taken sewing lessons from Dona Elena.
14. Dislike of Paulo for milk.	W. Lorenz Lola Moreira	Upon the occasion of her earlier unsuccessful suicidal attempt with arsenic, Emilia was forced to drink large quantities of milk. The phobia of Paulo for milk (his dislike was intense enough to justify this word) may have been related to this episode. W. Lorenz could not recall whether Emilia had such a dislike of milk during the interval between this unsuccessful suicidal attempt and her later successful one. He enquired of another older sister, Augusta Praxedes (born June 18, 1905, and not otherwise a witness for this case report) with regard to the occurrence of milk phobia in Emilia. She recalled that Emilia had taken milk with pleasure as a small girl and had developed a milk phobia in adulthood. It is therefore not known exactly when Emilia developed her phobia of milk, but it seems reasonable to infer that it came on after the use of milk in the treatment of one (and possibly another) suicidal attempt. At any rate a phobia for milk was observed in Emilia in adulthood and in Paulo at a very early age. W. Lorenz stated that Paulo had disliked milk "all his life."

Item	Informants	Comments
15. Recognition by Paulo of Emilia's sewing machine.	Marta Lorenz Huber Ema Moreira Lola Moreira	Upon the occasion of completing the embroidery of Marta Lorenz Huber which she had left unfinished on the sewing machine (item 3, *Comments*), Paulo said that the machine was his and he used to work it. On the occasion (see item 3, above) when Paulo pushed a servant aside in order to show her how to work the sewing machine, Lola Moreira asked Paulo: "How is it you know how to do this?" and Paulo replied: "This machine was mine and I have already sewed a lot with it." Ema Moreira also recalled that Paulo said that the sewing machine was his. He said: "This machine was mine. I am going to sew." The sewing machine had in fact belonged to Emilia.
16. Recognition by Paulo of Emilia's grave and concern for it on his part.	Marta Lorenz Huber Lola Moreira	Marta Lorenz Huber took Paulo to visit the cemetery. Instead of going around to see various graves, Paulo stood during the entire time of the visit on the grave of Emilia. He said: "I am looking after my tomb." Lola Moreira recalled that Paulo once stood a long time on Emilia's grave. Once he took a flower from another grave, put it on Emilia's grave and smiled. Florzinha Menezes recalled that when she visited the cemetery, Paulo gave her flowers to put on Emilia's grave.
17. Recognition by Paulo of a dress that had belonged to Emilia.	Marta Lorenz Huber	Material from a discarded skirt of Emilia was made into trousers for Paulo. He recognized the material and said: "Who would have said that after using this material in a skirt, I would later use it for trousers?" He was particularly fond of these trousers and preferred them to others. According to Lola Moreira, after having these trousers at age four or five he overcame his reluctance to wear boys' clothing.

In contrast, Paulo showed definite skill in sewing before he had received any instruction and when he was under five years of age. The witnesses agreed that Paulo showed not only interest and aptitude in sewing at an early age, but actual skill before he had received instruction. After his turn toward a more masculine development around the age of five, Paulo did not continue to develop his skill in sewing. As an adult his talent did not compare with that of his sisters who continued to sew. What we have to consider here is his exhibition of this skill at an early age and before receiving instruction.

Sexual Orientation of Paulo in Adulthood. As already mentioned, when he was about four or five, Paulo accepted boys' trousers, and when he was six he began to lose his intense feminine traits although these remained prominent until he reached his teens. Paulo in 1962, at age thirty-nine, retained a more feminine orientation than most men of his age. The evidence for this statement derives first from the fact that he had never married and had never shown any inclination to do so. Indeed, he had little to do with women except his sisters.

In 1962 I administered to Paulo the modified human figure drawing test.[12] In this test, the subject is asked to draw three human figures instead of the usual two. For the first figure, the choice of sex is open to the subject. For the second figure, the subject is asked to draw a person of the opposite sex. For the third figure, the choice is again left open to the subject. Inferences are drawn from the subject's choice on the "open" selections of sex as well as from the drawings themselves. Paulo chose to draw women on both occasions of his "open" selections. During this test he at first misunderstood the instructions for drawing "a person of either sex" (third drawing) and thought he was to draw a person of indeterminate or neuter sex. But the figure he then drew was also markedly feminine, with long hair on the head. From these evidences it seems safe to conclude that although Paulo was then much less oriented toward femininity than he had been as a child, a definitely greater degree of such orientation persisted in him than in most other men of his age.

Comments on the Evidence of Paranormal Knowledge and Behavior on the Part of Paulo. As in the case of Marta Lorenz, the parents of Paulo expected the return of Emilia. From the testimony already cited, however, it seems probable that the children and parents did not share the same information about the intentions of Emilia to return in the family.

Several of Emilia's brothers and sisters had heard her assert her wish to be a man and her hope that if she reincarnated she would return as a man. But there is reason to believe that the Lorenz parents did not know of these statements by Emilia (*a*) because Lola Moreira declared the children would not have reported such statements to the parents, and (*b*) because W. Lorenz recalled that his father was quite surprised when he (W. Lorenz) told him about Emilia's declarations on an occasion of discussing the case with his father after he was an adult.

For their part, the parents do not seem to have told the children any-

---

[12] L. Whitaker. "The Use of an Extended Draw-a-Person Test to Identify Homosexual and Effeminate Men." *Journal of Consulting Psychology*, Vol. 25, 1961, 482–485.

thing about the spiritualistic séances at which they believed Emilia had communicated her intention (for them surprising) to return as a boy. W. Lorenz stated that he only heard of these communications from his father in the conversation referred to in the preceding paragraph after he had grown up. Lola could not recall exactly when she heard about the communications of the séances, but thought that Paulo "had already become a large boy" at that time. Ema Bieszczad heard about the communications from "Emilia" at the séances when Paulo was between two and three years old and she herself eighteen. She stated that the matter did not interest her and she did not tell anyone else about it.

If we accept this testimony, we can suppose that the children of the family knew that Emilia had disliked being a woman and thought she might return as a male, but (with the exception of Ema Bieszczad) did not have any awareness of the intention of the communicating "Emilia" to return when they themselves were young. Conversely, the parents of Emilia knew nothing of her dislike for being a girl, but did know of the wish of the communicating "Emilia" to return as a boy.

These considerations become relevant in any assessment of the possibility that the family of Paulo might have influenced him toward femininity. If the children conceived the idea early that Paulo was in fact Emilia reborn, they might have responded so as to reinforce feminine behavior in Paulo. Yet their knowledge of Emilia's revolt against femininity might have equally guided them to influence Paulo toward the realization of Emilia's desire to be a man. Mr. and Mrs. Lorenz could have influenced Paulo toward femininity because they had reasons (they believed) for thinking that Emilia had been reborn as a son, and they had expressed some surprise at the communications of "Emilia" to the effect that she wanted to change sex and return as a boy.

W. Lorenz thought it most unlikely that the parents influenced Paulo in either direction. He did not think either of his parents favored either sex in their children. They had equal numbers of boys and girls. In a family of thirteen children, eleven survived to an age for marriage and of these all but Emilia and Paulo married. This record makes less likely any marked general thwarting of sexual development in the children on the part of the parents, although it remains possible that for unknown reasons Emilia and Paulo were selected by the parents for moulding in the direction of the opposite sex.[13]

---

[13] A. M. Johnson ("Factors in the Etiology of Fixations and Symptom Choice." *Psychoanalytic Quarterly*, Vol. 22, 1953, 475–496) reported a case of transvestism in a six-year-old boy with evidence (from therapeutic interviews with both child and mother) that the boy's mother fostered his transvestism. She hated males and favored the boy's two-year-old sister. In this case the boy "really wished to be the baby of the family rather than a girl. Strong remnants of his wish to be a girl remained, however, after the rivalry with his sister had been resolved by intensive therapy."

The possible influence of Paulo's parents on his sexual development is actually less important than the question of whether or not their influence on Paulo could have by itself resulted in the identification of Paulo with Emilia. The number of informational items expressing clear identification is far fewer than in the case of Marta Lorenz (items 12, 13, 15, 16, and 17 of the tabulation being the only items definitely in this group). But if we add to these items the observations of behavioral traits shared in common between Emilia and Paulo, e.g., love of traveling, strong interest in sewing, weak interest in cooking, dislike of milk, and habit of tearing off corners of bread loaves, we have altogether considerable evidence of an identification on the part of Paulo with Emilia. Paulo clearly considered his life a continuation of that of Emilia. Whether or not parental or other personal influences exerted on children can have the force to make a child assert a totally different identity is a question which I shall take up in the General Discussion to follow.

Even if we suppose that the influences on Paulo exerted by his family could account for his identification with Emilia, this would not account for his early skill in sewing.[14] Several witnesses testified to the exhibition of such skill by Paulo before he had received any instruction. An important and fundamental distinction exists between a skill on the one hand and an interest in a subject or the possession of information about it on the other hand. Paulo might have acquired his interest in sewing as part of his identification with the feminine sex who by occupation often become interested in sewing. (But he did not have much interest in cooking, and neither had Emilia.) And he might have acquired his information about the ownership of the sewing machine and the sewing lessons Emilia received from Dona Elena through information transmitted by members of the family either normally or by extrasensory perception. But these routes do not suffice to account for the exhibition by Paulo of a specific skill before instruction.

The present case seems less decisive than would be an authentic case of responsive xenoglossy since we do not know the limits of genetic transmission of skills. Most persons will think, I believe, that the idea of genetic transmission of the ability to speak a foreign language taxes credulity more than does survival itself. But genetic transmission of a skill such as that for sewing lies closer to what we are accustomed to acknowledge as possible through inheritance. In the present case, moreover, the two personalities exhibiting the skill were born into the same family. Perhaps inheritance

---

[14] Clear analysis of the possibilities involved in cases exhibiting skills requires careful discrimination between *interest* in an activity, *aptitude* for acquiring skill in that activity, and actual competence or *skill* in it. Unfortunately, these three qualities often occur together, perhaps necessarily so. Moreover, it is often exceedingly difficult to dissect aptitude and skill once some learning has occurred.

can account for the occurrence of a skill for sewing in two children of the same parents. But it is important not to settle the question by habits of thought. We are accustomed to attributing to inheritance the occurrence of skills in members of the same family (as a skill for music in the Bach family or a skill for science in the Darwin family). Yet such adult skills running in the same families do not *necessarily* mean that the skills were inherited. The person showing the skill may have inherited an *interest* in the subject of the skill and also been born in a family favorable to its development, or he may have inherited an *aptitude* for learning the skill. We may thus be noting examples of the rapid acquisition of a skill under favorable circumstances rather than examples of the inheritance of a skill.

Animal experiments on the inheritance of intelligence as judged by ability to run a maze illustrate the distinction I wish to emphasize. Tryon bred strains of rats which could learn to run a maze much more rapidly than strains bred from initially less intelligent rats.[15] These superior rats did not inherit the *skill* of running the maze; they inherited an *aptitude* for learning to run the maze in a smaller number of trials than the less well-endowed rats of the other strains.

Although we cannot decide between heredity and reincarnation as explanations of the skill in sewing shown by Paulo, in one respect reincarnation may appeal as a more complete explanation of the phenomenon. Genetic transmission may account for the recurrence in the same family of a particular skill; however, it does not by itself account for the occurrence of the skill in two particular members of the family, but not in any other of the thirteen children. In contrast, the theory of reincarnation as applied to the present case links the occurrence of the skill for sewing in Paulo with that of Emilia by supposing that the personality of Paulo was continuous with that of Emilia, but occupying a different body. In short, heredity may account for *resemblances* between members of the same family; reincarnation may account for some of the *differences*. I realize that the explanatory power of a theory does not make it necessarily superior over a competing one. But I mention this distinction between what heredity can explain and what reincarnation can explain because we need to remember the limitations in what genetics can at present tell us about human differences. We ought to continue trying other theories, including that of reincarnation, in attempting to close these gaps in our knowledge.

The Later Development of Paulo. After my meeting with Paulo Lorenz in 1962 I did not see him again. In 1967 his brother Waldomiro Lorenz wrote me that Paulo had committed suicide on September 5, 1966. He himself was still emotionally shattered by this event and unable to communicate

---

[15] R. C. Tryon. "Individual Differences," in *Comparative Psychology.* (Ed. F. A. Moss.) New York: Prentice-Hall, Inc., 1942.

many of the details of what had led to Paulo's suicide so I had to wait until February, 1972, before I could learn much about what had happened. At that time I was in Porto Alegre again and had a long talk with Waldomiro Lorenz as well as with his (and Paulo's) sisters, Marta Lorenz Huber and Ema Estelita Lorenz Bieszczad.

Paulo Lorenz spent some time in the Brazilian Army and retired early with the rank of sergeant because of ill health. He had pulmonary tuberculosis and spent some years recovering and convalescing from this illness. Afterwards (from 1952 on) he was employed in the Department of Highways. In later life he took some part in political activities on the side of the Trabhalista (Labor) Party. In 1963 the parliamentary President of Brazil, João Goulart, was deposed by a military insurrection and in the following years (1964–66) the military leaders tightened their control of the country and virtually suppressed all opposition, at least from officially permitted political parties. Paulo Lorenz had been a friend of one of the Trabhalista Party leaders who had fled to Uruguay. He became depressed and felt that the military government was watching him. This conviction became strengthened when he was actually picked up by the military authorities and beaten up during an "interrogation." After this he developed delusional ideas about being watched by agents of the military government. He believed that the military government was going to arrest him and lived in constant dread of this. Despite the rational basis for some concern on his part due to his actually having been beaten up by representatives of the military government, his family thought that his ideas of persecution exceeded what the facts justified and that he had become delusional on the subject. Nevertheless, and much to their regret later, they delayed taking steps to arrange for Paulo to have psychiatric treatment.

During the months before he killed himself Paulo made suicidal threats and at least one attempt to kill himself. He told Waldomiro Lorenz' cook that he was going to shoot himself. And once he tried to kill himself by injecting air into a vein, but was rescued from this attempt.[16]

The family had not ignored these warnings from Paulo, and Waldomiro had planned to take Paulo for medical treatment. But before he had done so and about two months after the above mentioned unsuccessful suicidal attempt, Paulo, who was then living with his sister, Lola Moreira, went into a bathroom, poured some inflammable liquid on himself and set his clothes and body on fire. He did this at about 7:00 A.M. and died about ten hours later without having expressed any regret for his action.

---

[16] Waldomiro Lorenz wrote me in 1967 that Emilia had also tried to kill herself in the same manner. I had not learned this in 1962. At that time informants told me that Emilia had made several unsuccessful suicidal attempts before she succeeded in killing herself. On one of these occasions she took poison and on another had tried to strangle herself. They had not then mentioned that Emilia had tried the method of injecting air into a vein.

Paulo's death shocked his family greatly. His older sister Marta became so disturbed that she had to be admitted and treated in a hospital for several weeks. And his brother Waldomiro was perhaps even more affected. Indeed, he himself became rather severely depressed and had not fully recovered by the time of my visit to the family in February, 1972.

Although my three informants about the suicide of Paulo concurred that Paulo's political troubles had been precipitating factors in his paranoid illness, depression, and suicide, they did not put forward the shallow interpretation that these political embroilments of Paulo were the sole, or even the most important, factors in his suicide.

In the first edition of this book I mentioned that Emilia before her suicide had expressed the wish to be reborn as a man. She gave as her reason for wishing to change sex the constraints on women that existed in Brazil in the first part of this century. In particular she wished freedom to travel, which was virtually impossible for a single woman then, and not often feasible for a married woman with children. Paulo, as a man, enjoyed freedom to move around as he wished and he used to spend his vacations in traveling, a habit he continued almost until his death. But he seems to have sought freedom at the price of loneliness. As I mentioned earlier, he was markedly feminine in his habits and attitudes as a child and retained some feminine tendencies into middle adulthood. It seems likely that a combination of his wish for freedom and his feminine identification prevented him from marrying, and he died a bachelor.

V

Seven Cases
Suggestive of Reincarnation
Among the Tlingit Indians
of Southeastern Alaska

Introduction

THE Tlingit [1] Indians who inhabit most of southeastern Alaska believe in reincarnation and this belief contributes an important feature to their religious and social behavior. Other native tribes in various parts of North and South America have had some belief in reincarnation, but those in the northwest corner of North America seem to have developed the belief more fully and to have retained it longer than other tribes. [2] The surrounding neighbors of the Tlingits, e.g., the Haidas who live to the south of the Tlingits in southeastern Alaska and in the Queen Charlotte Islands of British Columbia, the Tsimsyans [3] living on the coast of British Columbia east of the Haidas, the Athapaskans to the north, [4, 5] the Eskimos to the northwest, and the Aleuts to the west all believe in reincarnation. I will confine this report (almost entirely) to the Tlingit ideas of reincarnation and the cases suggestive of reincarnation which occur among them. With the Tlingits, as with other peoples, the ideas in the culture about re-

---

[1] Pronounced approximately "Klin-git," but the first consonant is closer to the "ch" in German (e.g., Achtung) or Scots (e.g., loch) than to the English "k." The natives of southeastern Alaska were called "Kolush" by the Russians (French: Koloche).

[2] The Incas of Peru believed in reincarnation, but into the same fleshly body, not into a new one. Their belief somewhat resembled that of the ancient Egyptians and similarly led to the practice of mummification of the physical body after death. In contrast, the Alaskan Tlingits who believed in reincarnation into a new body practiced cremation of dead bodies until missionaries suppressed this in the nineteenth century. However, some Eskimos of southeastern Alaska practiced mummification (into the nineteenth century) and also believed in rebirth into a new physical body.

[3] M. Barbeau. Personal communication, 1962. Dr. Barbeau stated that he had learned of the belief in reincarnation among the Tsimsyans during his investigations in British Columbia, but had not yet published his data. An allusion to rebirth occurs in one of the texts published by Dr. Barbeau (*Tsimsyan Myths*. Ottawa: National Museum of Canada Bulletin No. 174, Anthropological Series No. 51, 1961). In 1973 I investigated two cases of the reincarnation type among the Tsimsyans.

[4] Frederica de Laguna. Personal Communication, 1962. In 1965 I confirmed this by finding typical cases of the reincarnation type among the Athapaskans and Haidas in Alaska.

[5] C. Osgood. *Contributions to the Ethnography of the Kutchin*. Yale University Publications in Anthropology. New Haven: Yale University Press, 1936.

incarnation influence the attitude toward individuals who claim to remember a previous life, and may even prove relevant to the occurrence of such cases. I shall therefore precede the reports of cases with a review of the Tlingit ideas on reincarnation and certain other related topics.

Historical information about Alaska begins in 1741 with the visit to Alaska in Russian ships by the Danish mariner, Vitus Bering. After Bering came other explorers such as James Cook and after them many traders who valued the sea-otter pelts which the Indians caught and sold them. However, Western cultures had little impact on the area until the establishment of Russian forts and trading posts in the last decades of the eighteenth century.

The Tlingits fought fiercely with their neighbors and stoutly resisted their conquerors. The Russians, who governed Alaska from about 1780 to 1867, never fully subdued them, although they did establish satisfactory trading relationships with them. The Tlingits dominated surrounding tribes and obliged those of the hinterland to pay toll for their trade with the Russians. Under the Americans, the Tlingits continued sternly independent for many years and never allowed the government to herd them onto reservations. They showed an almost equally intransigent attitude toward attempts to influence their religious life. They cremated their dead and resisted for long the efforts of Christian missionaries to teach them how to bury corpses in graves. Nevertheless, their religion has gradually yielded so that today the Tlingits nearly all nominally profess Christianity. But many of them continue to believe in the world of spirits. Accusations of witchcraft have occurred even in recent years. Belief in reincarnation has persisted also and many Tlingits hold it more or less strongly.

Origins of the Tlingits

Anthropologists agree that the human species developed from its ancestors in the Eastern Hemisphere and that the ancestors of the pre-Columbian natives of America migrated from Asia. They generally agree also in believing that most of the migration from Asia occurred thousands of years ago across what is now the Bering Strait and at a time when Asia and America were joined by continuous land or separated by a much narrower passage of water than the present strait.[6]

Further agreement among ethnologists obtains with regard to the tribes which migrated from Asia last. For they generally (although by no means universally) believe that the ancestors of the Indians of the northwest coast of America, including the Tlingit Indians, were the last migrants from

---

[6] E. Antevs. "The Spread of Aboriginal Man to North America." *The Geographical Review*, Vol. 25, 1935, 302–309.

Asia. The evidence for this comes from the fact that the art, architecture, customs, and beliefs of the peoples of northeastern Siberia resemble much more closely those of the natives of northwest America than those of other American tribes.[7]

But although scholars concur that the ancestors of the Tlingits and their neighbors were the last migrants from Asia, they disagree on when these migrations occurred and when they stopped. As this question bears on the Tlingits' belief in reincarnation it deserves some further review here.

Most anthropologists believe that migrations from Asia and contact between the cultures of Asia and America ceased thousands of years before the Christian era. Some evidence suggests, however, that considerable contact between Asia and northwestern America persisted well into the Christian era and possibly until shortly before the beginning of the historical period in Alaska, in the eighteenth century.

The evidence for such late contacts derives from several sources:

(a) Funeral dirges sung by Indians of northwest America resemble closely funeral songs of China and Mongolia. One word, "Hayu," chanted repeatedly in a funeral song of a tribe of northwest Indians is also exclaimed repetitiously by dirge singers in China and means "Alas" in Chinese.[8, 9] Other expressions of grief among the northwest Indians, e.g., pounding the ground with the forehead, occur also in China. Drums covered with skin on one side only are used in songs of the northwest Indians and similar drums are used in Siberia only by the Buddhists.[10]

(b) Some similarities exist between the languages of Alaska and of Asia. I have mentioned one above. Another exists in the word "shaman," which denotes in many parts of Asia (and also in Finland) a priest or sorcerer and has exactly the same meaning in the Yakut language of Alaska. (However, the word for shaman in Tlingit is "ichta.") The word "shaman" is supposedly a corruption of "Sramana," which means Buddha and hence Buddhist priest in Sanskrit.[11]

(c) The Kurile Islands, the Kamchatka Peninsula, and the Aleutian Islands form a chain across the northern Pacific Ocean such that with one exception the distance between points of land is never more than one hundred miles; and in that exception, between Copper and Attu Islands, the distance is less than two hundred miles. In this area from Japan to

---

[7] F. Boas. "Relationships Between North-West America and North-East Asia," in *The American Aborigines: Their Origin and Antiquity.* (Ed., D. Jenness.) Toronto: University of Toronto Press, 1933.

[8] M. Barbeau. "The Aleutian Route of Migration Into America." *The Geographical Review,* Vol. 35, 1945, 424–443.

[9] M. Barbeau. *Alaska Beckons.* Toronto: The Macmillan Company, 1947.   [10] *Ibid.*

[11] E. P. Vining. *An Inglorious Columbus or, Evidence that Hwui Shan and a Party of Buddhist Monks from Afghanistan Discovered America in the Fifth Century, A.D.* New York: D. Appleton & Company, 1885.

Alaska and British Columbia flows the warm Japanese current which strongly favors navigation from west to east. In the mid-nineteenth century a disabled Japanese junk drifted to the shores of California along this current.[12] Japanese junks have more often drifted to the Aleutian Islands.[13]

(*d*) A Chinese manuscript of the fifth century A.D. reports the voyages of a Chinese Buddhist missionary, Hwui Shan, who described a voyage he had made to a country lying an immense distance to the east of China. This document came to the attention of Western scholars in the eighteenth century and received considerable study in the nineteenth century. The descriptions Hwui Shan gave of his voyage to the eastern land, which he called Fusang, have convinced some scholars that he traveled along the northern Pacific route via Kamchatka and Alaska and eventually came to what is now Mexico.[14, 15]

(*e*) Several objects of Oriental origin have been unearthed in situations which establish the strong probability of their having been brought from Asia in prehistoric times, yet not much earlier than the beginning of historic times in the eighteenth century. These objects include ancient Chinese coins and a pair of babirusa (wild boar) tusks from Celebes or neighboring islands of the South China Sea. Another such unearthed object was a Garuda bronze figurine of a type common in Bengal and Nepal. It is not unlikely that this figurine could have reached America before 1770, but it may not have come via the Kurile-Aleutian route; Spanish vessels crossing the Pacific from Manila in the sixteenth or seventeenth centuries could have brought it.[16, 17]

The Belief in Reincarnation Among the Tlingits

We know that the Tlingits did not acquire their belief in reincarnation from Europeans since travelers to Alaska in the early nineteenth century found the belief well established among them. Thus Veniaminov, a Russian priest and later bishop of Alaska, mentions the belief in reincarnation among the Tlingits.[18] Veniaminov observed the Tlingits after the start of trading between Europeans and the Alaska natives, but before any other substantial influences of Europeans on their culture such as began after American missionaries spread into Alaska in the late nineteenth century.

According to Veniaminov, "the Tlingits . . . believe that dead persons

---

[12] *Ibid.*

[13] C. G. Leland. *Fusang, or the Discovery of America by Chinese Buddhist Priests in the Fifth Century.* New York: J. W. Bouton, 1875.

[14] E. P. Vining. *Op. cit.,* n. 11.   [15] C. G. Leland. *Op. cit.,* n. 13.

[16] M. Barbeau. *Op. cit.,* n. 8.   [17] M. Barbeau. *Op. cit.,* n. 9.

[18] I. E. P. Veniaminov. *Reports About the Islands of the Unalaska Districts.* St. Petersburg: Imperial Academy of Sciences, 1840.

return to this world, but only among their relatives. . . . For this reason, if a pregnant woman sees often in her dreams a deceased relative, she believes that this man has entered into her; or perhaps if they discover on the body of the newborn some resemblance with a deceased person such as a birthmark or a defect which they knew had existed in the body of the deceased person, they begin to believe firmly that this same person has returned to earth, and for the same reason they give the newborn baby the name of the deceased person." [19]

A French anthropologist, Pinart, reported on the belief in reincarnation among the Tlingits (or Koloches) in 1872.[20] He drew attention to the fact that although the Tlingits chiefly expect a reincarnation into another human form, they also believe in transmigration from one animal species to another.[21] Pinart also wrote: "It happens often that if a pregnant woman sees in a dream some relative long deceased, she will declare that this same relative has returned in her body and that she will put this person back into the world." [22] Pinart also drew attention to the existence among the western Eskimos (of Alaska) of a much more elaborate religious system with five ascending strata of heaven each to be attained after a successive earthly incarnation with transformation, gradual purification, and eventual release from the cycle of rebirth. Pinart thought these beliefs very similar to those of South Asia.[23]

In the late nineteenth century (1885) the German ethnologist Krause wrote an extensive account of the customs and beliefs of the Tlingits.[24] He noted the belief in reincarnation among the Tlingits and Haidas, but seems not to have given the subject much attention and drew almost exclusively on Veniaminov for his references to it. Twenty years later (1904) Swanton, an American ethnologist, devoted considerable attention to the subject in his report on the Tlingits. Swanton related a story which in his time cir-

---

[19] *Ibid.* See p. 58. (Translation of Mrs. O. Podtiaguine.)

[20] A. Pinart. "Notes sur les Koloches." *Bulletins de la Société d'Anthropologie de Pa⁻is,* Vol. 7, 1872, 788–811.

[21] But Veniaminov, writing thirty-five years earlier, categorically denied that the Tlingits believed in transmigration of human souls into subhuman animal bodies. Nor have more recent anthropologists described this belief. The Tlingits do have many legends of transformations of humans into animals, e.g., man into bear, but these differ from the idea of rebirth into a new body whether animal or human. Only one of my numerous Tlingit informants interviewed during the study of cases of the reincarnation type among them said that the Tlingits believe in reincarnation in subhuman animal bodies. All other Tlingits whom I asked about this belief specifically denied that it was part of the Tlingit concept of reincarnation. I believe that Pinart confused this concept with that of transformation of humans into animals, which some Tlingits do believe can occur.

[22] A. Pinart. *Op. cit.,* n. 20. See p. 803. (My translation.)

[23] A. Pinart. "Esquimaux et Koloches: Idées religieuses et traditions des Kaniagmioutes." *La Revue d'Anthropologie,* Vol. 4, 1873, 674–680.

[24] A. Krause. *Die Tlingit Indianer.* Jena: Hermann Costenoble, 1885. American edition (Trans. by Erna Gunther), Seattle: University of Washington Press, 1956.

culated widely among the Tlingits and of which I heard a variant in 1961. I quote the account given by Swanton: "In a certain war a man was killed and went up to Kiwaa [a section of the Tlingit 'heaven'], and by and by a woman of his clan gave birth to a child. One time, when someone was talking about that war, the child cried persistently and they said to it, 'Keep quiet. What are you crying about? Why are you crying so much?' Then the infant spoke out saying, 'If you had done what I told you and let the tide go out first we could have destroyed all those people.' The child was the same man who had been killed. From him people knew that there was such a place and that people who died by violence went there. . . ." [25]

Swanton noted, as had Veniaminov, the attention given by the Tlingits to birthmarks as signs of reincarnation. One of his informants stated that "if a person with a cut or scar on his body died and was reborn the same mark could be seen on the infant."

De Laguna has summarized Tlingit ideas on reincarnation especially as these affect social relations and the complexities which occur when a family believes that a deceased member of one generation has returned in a later generation.[26]

The Tlingit belief in reincarnation is by no means as fully elaborated as the doctrines on this subject in Hinduism and Buddhism. But it does include concepts somewhat similar to that of karma with the expectation that misfortunes in one life may diminish in another.

On this topic Pinart wrote as follows: "It is common to hear a sick or a poor man say that he wants to be killed so that he can return to earth young and healthy. One reason for the extraordinary fierceness of the Koloches [Tlingits] is their lack of fear of death. On the contrary they often seek it out, fortified by the expectation of soon returning to this world and in a better position." [27]

Veniaminov reported that "The poor who see the better condition of the rich and also the difference between the children of the rich and their own, often say: 'When I am dead, I shall return surely in the family of so and so,' indicating the family they prefer. Others say, 'Oh, what good fortune it would be to be killed soon. Then I would return here again and much sooner.' " [28]

In one case to be described below (pp. 259-269) an elderly man expressed the wish that he would be less afflicted with stuttering in his next

[25] John R. Swanton. "Social Condition, Beliefs and Linguistic Relationship of the Tlingit Indians." In 26th *Annual Report of the Bureau of American Ethnology*. (1904–05.) Washington: Government Printing Office, 1908, 391–485. (See p. 463.)

[26] Frederica De Laguna. "Tlingit Ideas About the Individual." *Southwestern Journal of Anthropology*, Vol. 10, 1954, 172–191.

[27] A. Pinart, *Op. cit.*, n. 20. See p. 803. (My translation.)

[28] I. E. P. Veniaminov. *Op. cit.*, n. 18. See p. 59. (Translation of Mrs. O. Podtiaguine.)

life. And in another case (not here reported in detail), a simple fisherman who had felt himself much handicapped by being unable to speak English avowed before his death that he would develop linguistic skills in his next life. The person of the next generation with whom he was subsequently identified did in fact have much ability and interest in languages and learned not only English, but also Russian and Aleut, which he spoke as well as Tlingit.

In addition to the belief in reincarnation itself and in a concept somewhat similar to that of karma linking one life with another, the Tlingits have two other significant ideas with regard to reincarnation. First, they believe that children who remember their past lives are fated to die young and they endeavor to discourage a child who claims to remember a previous life from doing so. An identical belief exists in India, where families of such children frequently make strenuous efforts to suppress the apparent memories of a previous life told by a child. Secondly, the Tlingits also believe in rebirth as contrasted with reincarnation. According to the concept of rebirth, the old personality gives rise to the new as a candle burning low may light a new candle and so continue the series. In reincarnation, on the other hand, the same personality continues, although changed by the circumstances of the new life. Reincarnation as thus defined is a concept of Hinduism and rebirth a concept of Buddhism.

Buddhism, which began in India in the sixth century B.C., reached China in the first century A.D. and Korea in 372 A.D.[29, 30] It spread to Japan in the sixth century, and eventually reached Mongolia and Siberia as far as Kamchatka. Whether or not Buddhism actually reached Alaska we cannot say with certainty. But I find this possibility quite plausible to contemplate. I have already briefly reviewed above the external evidence of contact between Asia and northwest America after the founding of Buddhism and before historic times (i.e., 500 B.C.–1700 A.D.). This evidence compels attention although not conviction. The close similarities between the ideas on reincarnation among the Tlingits and Buddhists also suggest that the ancestors of the Tlingits imported rather than invented their ideas on reincarnation, an interpretation hinted at by Pinart in commenting on the similarity of the Eskimo ideas of heaven to those found in Asia.

The advent of missionaries and schools to Alaska in the late nineteenth century began the decline of the Tlingit culture. First spear fights, then cremation of the dead, and finally potlatches (ceremonial feasts) succumbed to religious persuasions and governmental control. One of the last of the old-time totem pole carvers and one of the few surviving craftsmen capable of expressing his people's legends in these wonderful monuments showed me his work in Alaska and deplored the fact that the younger generation

[29] E. P. Vining. *Op. cit.,* n. 11.

[30] C. Humphreys. *Buddhism.* Harmondsworth: Penguin Books, 1951.

(he was seventy-three) knew nothing of reincarnation and had ceased to pay attention to the birthmarks on a baby which would indicate, if noticed, who had been reborn. For the belief in reincarnation is now fading away among the Tlingits and one can discern a gradient of age for the belief. The generation of people now over sixty years of age believes completely in reincarnation and the doubts of younger people scandalize them. The next generation, of people between thirty and sixty, knows about the belief in reincarnation among the Tlingits and many (perhaps most) believe in its truth, though often acknowledging important doubts. Among the next younger generation, I found often either derision or ignorance with regard to reincarnation among the Tlingits. And I met one Tlingit high school student of seventeen who had heard of reincarnation in India, but not in Alaska among his own people!

Although most of my informants talked freely about their knowledge of the cases or of Tlingit beliefs, I encountered some persons who showed reticence in discussing these matters. Such reticence contrasted markedly with the almost universal ease with which informants and other persons in India discussed reincarnation during my similar investigations in that country. The difference may derive from the more rapid pace of Western acculturation in Alaska, where the pressure of Western religions and science has put those who still hold the ancient tribal religious beliefs on the defensive with regard to these. The Tlingit may fear that his ideas on reincarnation will arouse criticism or earn contempt at the hands of his critics. In contrast, Western religions have had only a slight impact in India and although India contains several million Christians, the belief in reincarnation probably remains as strong today in India as it was three thousand years ago. However, other reasons may account for the reticence of many Tlingits concerning reincarnation. Some of them still believe, as more of previous generations did, that misfortune comes to those Tlingits who talk about the religion of the Tlingits with outside persons. Finally, personal reasons undoubtedly account for some inhibitions in talking about particular cases. Many of the previous personalities connected with the subjects died violently or mysteriously or both, and the informants seemed reluctant to open up such topics or the subject of ancient clan feuds in which some of these deaths occurred.

Methods of Investigation

In 1961–65 I went to southeastern Alaska four times for the purpose of studying cases suggestive of reincarnation among the Tlingit Indians. During my trips to Alaska I visited ten communities inhabited by Tlingit Indians, namely, Juneau, Klukwan, Sitka, Hoonah, Wrangell, Petersburg, Angoon, Anchorage, Kake, and Ketchikan. Altogether I spent five weeks studying Tlingit cases at first hand. In 1972–73 I spent several more weeks in Alaska on follow-up interviews with subjects of cases already investigated and in a (successful) search for new cases.

Since I have already described the methods of investigation used in the Introduction to this monograph I shall not repeat these here.

During my study of these cases I interviewed altogether about one hundred persons; most of them were witnesses to the facts of the cases here reported, but some were informants on the culture of the Tlingits.

Nearly all the witnesses spoke English, but I needed interpreters with some elderly Tlingits who spoke only Tlingit. In most of these instances, a relative interpreted; in two instances, Miss Constance Naish, a missionary in Angoon, interpreted.

Incidence of Reported Cases Among the Tlingit People

In addition to the seven cases suggestive of reincarnation here reported, I learned during my first visits to Alaska of thirty-six other cases among the Tlingits and eight among the Haidas. I am still investigating some of these cases; some other cases, however, I cannot investigate further because the person having the experience and other relevant firsthand witnesses have died. However, I talked with at least one firsthand witness of each such case. From the accounts they gave me of these cases, I would judge them to be similar to the others on which I could obtain fuller testimony from witnesses. If we take all these cases together, we have forty-three reported cases among the Tlingits occurring among persons born during the period 1851 to 1965.[31] We can be confident that the incidence of *all* cases must be considerably higher than the incidence of *reported* cases, perhaps much higher. This becomes an obvious conclusion if one reflects on the fact that information on the above forty-three cases was elicited by one investigator during less than six weeks among the Tlingits. Moreover, I heard of still other cases which I did not have time to look into, but which seemed from the information given to resemble those I could study or learn more about. A more thorough survey would undoubtedly have brought to light many additional cases; but at present I shall consider further only the forty-three cases mentioned above. The earliest of these cases among the Tlingit peoples dates back to 1851 (the birthdate of the person having the experience of remembering a previous life). In 1883 Krause estimated the population of the Tlingits at not more than ten thousand persons. At the time of the 1960 census they numbered 7,887.[32] Between 1851 and 1965 we can estimate that

[31] For a review of characteristics of these forty-three cases see I. Stevenson. "Cultural Patterns in Cases Suggestive of Reincarnation among the Tlingit Indians of Southeastern Alaska." *Journal* A.S.P.R., Vol. 60, July, 1966, 229–243. Subsequent investigations in Alaska have increased the number of Tlingit cases under review to more than seventy.

some four generations of not more than 40,000 Tlingits have lived. This gives an incidence of reported cases among these people of forty-three in 40,000, or roughly one in 1,000. The figure thus arrived at (which, as mentioned above, must be a minimum figure) gives a much higher incidence for such cases than occurs in other cultural areas of the West. On a comparable basis, many thousands of cases suggestive of reincarnation ought to have occurred in the rest of the United States during the years 1851–1965. Even allowing for the fact that many cases suggestive of rebirth in the United States do not become known to investigators, the incidence in the continental United States of such cases cannot be anything like as high as it is in southeastern Alaska.[33]

Case Reports

The Case of Jimmy Svenson[34]

Summary of the Case and its Investigation. Jimmy Svenson's father, Olaf Svenson, was half Tlingit and half Norwegian. His mother, Millie Svenson, was a full-blooded Tlingit. Jimmy was born on November 22, 1952, in Sitka. When he was about two years old, he began to talk of a previous life, claiming that he had been his mother's brother and had lived in the village of Klukwan. Klukwan is a village one hundred miles away. He made a number of statements concerning matters that this uncle could have known about, but which it seemed unlikely that Jimmy could have learned by normal means. Often, and especially when angry, he would ask to go to the village of Klukwan to stay with his maternal grandmother. Jimmy talked considerably of his previous life for about two or three years and thereafter his references to it diminished.

By the time of my investigation of this case in the autumn of 1961, Jimmy (then not quite nine years old) no longer claimed to remember anything about a previous life. I therefore learned about what he had said and done earlier from interviews with his mother, father, a brother, two sisters, and members of his mother's family. Before recounting what these various informants told me, I shall first mention the relevant facts about the life of the deceased man, John Cisko (Jimmy's uncle), and suppositions about how he met his death.

---

[32] Data furnished by Bureau of Vital Statistics, Department of Health and Welfare, State of Alaska. The figure includes a number of Indians not Tlingits.

[33] Similar figures of reported cases will be derived for other areas, e.g., south central Turkey, Lebanon, India, and Ceylon, where the incidence of cases also seems high. Eventually it will be possible to study the relationships between various cultures and the incidence of reported cases and this may throw light on the reasons for the differing incidences in different cultures.

[34] As mentioned on p. 13, I have disguised the names of the persons having the experiences and testifying to the events narrated by using pseudonyms in this section of the monograph.

John Cisko was a full-blooded Tlingit Indian who, like so many of the tribe, enjoyed hunting and fishing. He showed much skill in these pursuits. He drank alcohol excessively, especially wine. At the time of his death in the summer of 1950, when he was about twenty-five, he was in the army and had returned to Alaska on furlough. He stayed at one of the numerous salmon fishing villages and canneries of the area. One day he went out in a small boat with two women, apparently on a pleasure trip. Several hours later the boat was found upright at the shore with its motor in place and the plug of the bilge hole missing. These features suggested that the boat had filled with water, perhaps rapidly and before its (presumably) in-ebriated occupants realized the danger. Searchers found the drowned bodies of the two women nearby, but never recovered the body of John Cisko. In the channels of southeastern Alaska tides run high and currents swift. An ebbing tide can carry a body rapidly and forever away. These circumstances make murder somewhat easy, often suspected, and extremely difficult to prove. Hans, John Cisko's brother, stated to me his conviction that a jealous lover of the two women companions of John had murdered him. Hans had heard that a witness had seen the murder but would not talk about it for fear of retaliation by the alleged murderer.

Another Tlingit who worked out of the same salmon cannery in the summer of 1950 as captain of a seine boat told me he thought murder an improbable explanation for the death of John Cisko. The captain thought it much more likely that John Cisko had drowned after clinging to the flooded boat as long as he could, and that the tide had carried away his body, although not the bodies of his companions.

John Cisko's sister, Millie, was very fond of him and mourned his death greatly. She wanted to name her next son, born two years later, after John, but was dissuaded from this because the name John already occurred fre-quently in her husband's family. She and her husband therefore gave the boy John as a middle name so that he became James John Svenson.

Jimmy had four round marks on his abdomen which I inspected in 1961. His mother stated that these marks were present at his birth. In 1961 they were about $\frac{1}{4}$ inch in diameter and clearly demarcated from the surround-ing skin. Three had less pigment than the surrounding skin, one had some-what more pigment. Three were along the line of the right lower ribs anteriorly, overlying the liver; the fourth was about two inches to the right of the umbilicus. The marks closely resembled healed bullet wounds of entry.

Statements made by Jimmy Svenson. Because the various informants with whom I talked remembered different statements made by Jimmy, I have listed all these attributed statements below in tabular form, with comments about their verification from the informants.

TABULATION
Summary of Statements, Recognitions, and Behavior of
Jimmy Svenson

Item	Informants	Comments
1. His name was John, not Jimmy.	Millie Svenson, mother of Jimmy	
2. He used to live in Klukwan (village where John Cisko had lived).	Olaf Svenson, father of Jimmy Elizabeth Kolov, older half-sister of Jimmy	Not mentioned by Millie Svenson who, however, emphasized Jimmy's repeated wishes to go to Klukwan.
3. He was shot to death.	Olaf Svenson Millie Svenson	Millie Svenson said Jimmy added: "By the skipper." Olaf Svenson said Jimmy added: "In the stomach," and pointed to his stomach as he said this. The latter statement accords with the birthmarks on Jimmy's abdomen, but the exact mode of death of John Cisko is unknown.
4. Talked much of Klukwan and often said he wanted to go there and visit his grandmother (John Cisko's mother).	Millie Svenson	Jimmy had seen his grandmother when a baby, but did not visit Klukwan until he was six and a half years old.
5. Gave an accurate description of one of the lakes near Klukwan.	Elizabeth Kolov	Details of the description not given.
6. Said he used to drink wine.	Olaf Svenson	John Cisko used to drink wine excessively. Olaf Svenson, a half-Norwegian, never had wine in the home, only beer. Jimmy's mother said Jimmy said he had drunk "whisky" (not wine) "a long time ago."
7. Said to his uncle: "I'm not your nephew, I'm your brother." (At age six.)	Hans Cisko, brother of John Cisko, uncle of Jimmy Svenson	Hans Cisko insisted that this remark was quite spontaneous and popped out when, as he was leaving (after his first visit to the Svenson family), he said to Jimmy, "Well, good-bye, nephew."
8. Familiarity with village of Klukwan and surrounding area, when taken there at the age of six and a half.	Millie Svenson	Jimmy recalled no details of specific knowledge. He merely seemed to be unusually familiar with people and places of the area.
9. Repeated entreaties to go fishing with George Young when he (Jimmy) visited Klukwan.	Millie Svenson George Young, cousin of Millie Svenson	George Young had been a close friend and fishing companion of John Cisko. Other relatives (except Jimmy's maternal grandmother) were out of the village when Jimmy visited Klukwan. George Young was the only relative available for possible recognition by Jimmy.

Secondhand witnesses reported additional items of information stated by Jimmy to his family. According to these informants, Jimmy had earlier told these relatives about specific details of life in Klukwan, e.g., the characteristics and habits of a family dog, and the details of the house in which John Cisko had lived in Klukwan. These were supposedly items of information known to John Cisko, but unlikely to be known through normal means to Jimmy Svenson. However, when I asked the primary informants about these additional items, they denied any recollection of them. I have therefore omitted them from the list above. Since two secondary witnesses agreed that they had heard of these items from a member of the family, this may be an example of the fading out of remembered details with the passage of time in the primary witnesses. Or the secondary witnesses may have embellished the story they heard originally.

Comments. The members of Jimmy's family parted with information about his statements most reluctantly. I gained the impression that the informants both held back information they then knew and had forgotten information they once had. I believe that the nine items I have listed represent a shrunken version of the original evidence rather than an expanded one. We must take the case as it is, however, and not as it might have been if better witnesses and earlier investigators had observed it. And taken as it is, the most we can say of it is that it is harmonious with reincarnation, but contains no strong evidence for it.

The case suffers from two very serious weaknesses which lower its evidential value with regard to reincarnation. In the first place, Jimmy made no statement that included information he definitely could not have acquired normally. Perhaps he came closest to this (in the evidence we have) when he claimed he used to drink wine. In the rest of the data we find hints of paranormal knowledge, e.g., in the description of the lake near Klukwan, but nothing that we can positively assert to be so. The case would become quite different if a reliable witness were to testify that he had seen John Cisko shot to death in the stomach. It would then seem that dead men can in fact tell tales. But John Cisko had not clearly accomplished this.[35]

A second and equally grave defect of this case with regard to its value as evidence for reincarnation arises from the fact that both John Cisko and Jimmy Svenson belonged to the same family and were related as brother and son to one woman. To be sure, Jimmy Svenson lived in a town a hundred miles from Klukwan, but he grew up with his mother who loved John Cisko as her favorite brother. She grieved much for him and named

---

[35] My collection of cases includes several other instances in which persons who claim to have lived before have shed new light on obscure deaths or murders. (See, for example, the case of Ravi Shankar, reported on pp. 91–105 above.)

her next son after him. And since she believed in reincarnation, she may well have talked about her brother to her son and thus communicated to him the information which the boy claimed to remember.

However, as in so many other cases suggestive of reincarnation, we must consider the behavioral as well as the purely informational features of the case.

For example, Jimmy not only claimed to know about Klukwan, but when angry with his parents he would ask to go there to stay with his maternal grandmother (John Cisko's mother). In short, Jimmy not only seemed to know about John Cisko; he acted as if he and John Cisko were the same person. Now since Jimmy's mother wanted her brother to return, she may have imposed on Jimmy an identification with her deceased brother. I propose to discuss this important theory of "imposed identification" in the General Discussion at the end of this monograph and I shall therefore mention it only briefly here. However, I must draw attention to one of the weaknesses of the theory of "imposed identification" in the present case. In my opinion, it fails to account satisfactorily for the fading of the personation of the deceased personality with the increasing age of the child. We commonly observe in cases suggestive of reincarnation that as the child grows older his memories of the previous life and the accompanying identification with the other personality diminish. (See tabulation on pp. 326–327.) In the case of Jimmy Svenson, apparent memories began to fade when he was four and had been entirely forgotten by the time I talked with him when he was nine. If we adopt the theory of imposed identification for this case, we must assume that when Jimmy was about four, it became acceptable to his mother for him to develop a personality other than that of her brother John Cisko. Then thereafter the personation of John Cisko and the pseudo-memories, which they would be on this hypothesis, receded over the next few years. Such a recession of pressure on the part of Jimmy's mother would be consonant with a diminution over the years of her grief for her brother. But in cases in which unconscious pressures on the part of a parent have fostered the development of a particular symptom or behavior in a child, the symptom has not receded with time alone; nor has the wish to have the behavior in the child diminished in the parent. This persistence in intensity of an imposed symptom may derive from the fact that the wish promoting it is both strong and unconscious in the parent.

I do not think we can reach any firm conclusions about this case at present. Reincarnation might explain the subject's behavior and so might the theory of "imposed identification." The evidence of paranormality in the case amounts to no more than hints; on the other hand, the theory of "imposed identification" applied to the case makes it an example beyond the previously demonstrated influence of parents on their children. The available facts do not permit us to choose between these possibilities.

The Later Development of Jimmy Svenson. I did not meet Jimmy Svenson between September, 1961, and May, 1972. At our first meeting he was not quite nine and at our second he was nineteen and a half years old. He only vaguely remembered our meeting in 1961.

In 1972 he said he had no imaged memories of the previous life. (These had actually all faded at the time of our first meeting in 1961.) He did remember an occasion of a *déjà vu* experience when he was about eight years old and visiting Haines. (Haines is a town about twenty miles from Klukwan, the village of the previous personality of this case, John Cisko.) In a particular shop of Haines he had an impression so that, as he said, "I could have sworn that I had been there before." [36] He thought that his uncle, John Cisko, had been in this shop, but could not say so from positive knowledge.

Jimmy told me that one of his aunts told him that John Cisko had remembered a previous life. I had not known of such a claim before. Jimmy's aunt said that John Cisko had at times the experience of thinking he had been in a particular place before when he had not. I did not learn whether John Cisko had specific imaged memories of a previous life. Jimmy's aunt seems not to have mentioned that John Cisko had imaged memories when she spoke to Jimmy about his seeming to remember a previous life. She apparently told Jimmy only that John Cisko had re-membered a previous life with *déjà vu* (my phrase) experiences.

As I mentioned earlier, the body of John Cisko was never recovered so that I do not know if he was drowned, as seems most likely, or shot, as Jimmy himself said he had been when he was younger. (He had some birth-marks on his abdomen to support this claim.) In either case Jimmy did not show in 1972 any specific phobia related to either of the presumptive causes of death of John Cisko, that is, drowning or shooting. Jimmy said he had no fear of water and enjoyed swimming. He did not like swimming by himself, but that is a matter of ordinary prudence. [37] As to firearms, he was somewhat uneasy with them, but this could be accounted for, I think, by the fact that when he was about twelve years old his left eye was hit (but not per-manently damaged) by a BB shot. Jimmy's caution with firearms did not pre-vent him from occasionally shooting a gun if a chance presented itself.

[36] This memory accords with what one of his half-sisters told me in 1961. She said that when Jimmy had visited Haines in (about) 1959 he had seemed to recognize a store there. Her recollection would have made him about seven years old at the time, while Jimmy (in 1972) thought he was then about eight years old. The store had belonged to the Cisko family and so would (almost certainly) have been known to John Cisko.

[37] In 1972 Jimmy said that when he was younger he had had a fear of drowning, but he learned to swim when his older half-brother threw him into the water off a dock. I had not heard before that he had any such phobia of water as a small child and indeed his half-sister had told me in 1961 that he liked swimming and went "swimming every chance he gets." This does not preclude a phobia of water earlier, but I do not think anyone mentioned it to me.

Jimmy had an unhappy and indeed turbulent adolescence. His parents separated when he was about ten or eleven, a year or two after my investigation of the case in 1961. Then on May 3, 1963, his mother drowned in Sitka harbor when a boat she was in hit a tug. She was inebriated at the time, but could not swim anyway. Jimmy's father had in the meantime become crippled and was unable to support him. So he signed papers which conveyed legal guardianship of Jimmy to his half-sister, Margaret, and her husband. His guardians changed residences at least twice, and Jimmy spent his teen years with them first in New Hampshire and then in the state of Washington. His father died of cancer in August, 1970. Jimmy continued his education and graduated from high school in Washington.

In the meantime, however, he had become involved with young persons who were taking drugs and he began taking them himself. (I presumed we were talking about heroin, but I did not ask specifically.) The use of drugs in turn led to involvement with the police and arrest. Jimmy finally decided to break away from the group of drug users and also from his half-sister and brother-in-law. So he left Washington and returned to Sitka where he was staying with his half-brother and looking for work when I met him in May, 1972.

Jimmy had not visited Haines and Klukwan (the village of the previous personality, his uncle, John Cisko) since 1962. He indicated that the branch of his family there would not welcome him because of his record of arrests by the police. However, his lack of interest in sustaining relations with that side of his family (his mother's) seems to have long antedated the later troubles of his adolescence.

Jimmy expressed ambition to go on to college and he impressed me as having the intelligence to enter and graduate from college if he had the motivation. His mother had left him a small amount of money which he had carefully saved and he was moreover eligible for a scholarship from the Bureau of Indian Affairs.

It will be recalled that John Cisko drank alcohol excessively. Jimmy told me that he took alcohol "now and again," but denied any craving for it and said he usually avoided distilled liquors. I think it perhaps premature to assert a connection between John Cisko's excessive consumption of alcohol and Jimmy's involvement with drugs. Jimmy is still young (but so was John Cisko when he drowned at the age of about twenty-five) and in 1972 he showed every sign of wishing to advance himself in life without resort to chemical alleviants.

The Case of William George, Jr.

Summary of the Case. This case includes a prediction of a rebirth prior to death and the apparent fulfillment of the tests proposed. It also conforms to the pattern of rebirth described by Veniaminov [38] in that the rebirth was heralded in a dream of the mother and indicated by physical markings resembling those of the deceased man apparently returning.

I shall first describe the case synoptically and then present in tabular form the statements of the three witnesses I interviewed.

William George, Sr. was a celebrated Alaskan fisherman of his day. Like other Tlingits, he believed in reincarnation. Toward the end of his life he evidently became assailed by doubts and also entertained a strong wish to return. On several occasions he told his favorite son (Reginald George) and daughter-in-law: "If there is anything to this rebirth business, I will come back and be your son." He expanded this statement several times by adding: "And you will recognize me because I will have birthmarks like the ones I now have." With this he would point to two prominent pigmented naevi, each about half an inch in diameter, one on the upper surface of his left shoulder and the other on the volar surface of the left forearm about two inches below the crease of the elbow. In the summer of 1949, William George, Sr., then about sixty years old, again expressed his intention of returning after death and on this occasion handed his favorite son a gold watch given him by his mother. As he did so he said, "I'll come back. Keep this watch for me. I am going to be your son. If there is anything like that [meaning rebirth], I'll do it." Reginald George went home for a weekend shortly after this and gave the gold watch to his wife, Susan George, telling her what his father had told him. She placed the watch in a jewel box where it remained for nearly five years.

Early in August, 1949, a few weeks after the above events, William George, Sr. disappeared from the seine boat of which he was captain. Members of his crew knew nothing of what had happened to him and searchers never recovered his body. Possibly he had fallen overboard and the tide had carried his body out to sea, as it can easily do in those waters.

Mrs. Reginald George, his daughter-in-law, shortly afterwards became pregnant and came to labor on May 5, 1950, barely nine months after her father-in-law's death. The baby was the ninth of her ten children. During her labor she dreamed that her father-in-law appeared to her and said that he was waiting to see his son. Apparently at this time Mrs. George did not connect this dream vision with the rebirth of her father-in-law because when she awoke from the anesthetic she was frightened and expected to see her father-in-law, presumably as an apparition in his previous adult form, as she had seen him in her dream. But what she did see was a full-term male baby who had pigmented naevi on the upper surface of his left shoulder

---

[38] I. E. P. Veniaminov. *Op. cit.*, n. 18. For further details and examples of both birthmarks and announcing dreams among the Tlingit cases of the reincarnation type, see I. Stevenson. "Cultural Patterns in Cases Suggestive of Reincarnation among the Tlingit Indians of Southeastern Alaska." *Journal A.S.P.R.*, Vol. 60, July, 1966.

and the volar surface of his left forearm at exactly the locations of the naevi mentioned by the boy's grandfather. The baby's birthmarks were about half the size of the grandfather's. The identification of these birthmarks justified the baby's parents in giving him his grandfather's name, so he became William George, Jr.

William George, Jr. had pneumonia severely when he was a year old. He did not speak until he was three or four years old and then spoke with a rather severe stutter which gradually left him over the following years, although his father, Reginald George, still showed much concern about the boy's impediment in 1961. William George, Jr. seemed to have average intelligence as judged by his performance at school, and my own conversation with him in Alaska.

As he grew up, William George, Jr.'s family observed behavior by him that strengthened their conviction that William George, Sr. had returned. This behavior was of several kinds. In the first group were traits of likes, dislikes, and aptitudes similar to those of his grandfather. For example, William George, Sr. had injured his right ankle severely when playing basketball as a young man. He afterwards walked with a limp and turned his right foot outwards so that he walked with a definitely characteristic gait. William George, Jr. had a similar gait and turned his right foot outwards as he walked. His parents testified to this and I also observed it in watching William George, Jr. walk. In the boy, however, the abnormality of the gait was not marked and I doubt whether I would have noticed it unless my attention had been drawn to it.

Members of the family also noted similarities of facial appearance and posture between William George, Jr. and his grandfather. William George, Jr. resembled his grandfather in a tendency to worry fretfully and to distribute cautionary advice to those around him. He showed a precocious knowledge of fishing and boats. He knew the best bays for fishing and when first put in a boat seemed to know already how to work the nets. He also showed greater than average fear of water for boys of his age. He was more grave and sensible than other children of his age.

A second group of observations of William George, Jr. consists of behavior indicating an almost complete identification of the boy with his grandfather. For example, he referred to his great-aunt as "sister," which was in fact her relationship with William George, Sr. Similarly, he referred to his uncles and aunts (brothers and sisters of Reginald George) as his sons and daughters. Moreover, he expressed concern appropriate to their behavior, for example, with regard to the excessive drinking of alcohol by two of his "sons" (uncles). The brothers and sisters of William George, Jr. entered into this personation and often called him "grandfather," to which he did not object. (The identification of William George, Jr. with his grandfather had diminished somewhat as he grew older.) His father believed that William, Jr. was becoming too concerned with the past. He noted that his mind "wandered." For this reason and because of warnings by "old folks" about the harmfulness of recalling past lives, William, Jr.'s parents discouraged him from talking about the life of William, Sr.

Thirdly, William George, Jr. exhibited a knowledge of people and places that, in the opinion of his family, transcended what he could have learned through normal means. I have listed these items in the tabulation below, but shall describe the most important item in more detail first.

When William George, Jr. was between four and five years old, his mother one day decided to go through the jewels in her jewelry box and spread these out in her bedroom. She also took the gold watch of William' George, Sr. out of the box. As she was examining the contents of the box, William George, Jr., who had been playing in another room, wandered into the bedroom. Noticing the watch, he picked it up and said: "That's my watch." He clung to it tenaciously, repeating his claim to it, and his mother could not persuade him to give it up for quite some time. Eventually he consented to have it returned to the box. Thereafter and up to 1961, William George, Jr. from time to time asked his parents for "his watch." Indeed, as he grew older, he claimed the watch somewhat more firmly, stating that he should now have it since he was older.

Both Mr. and Mrs. Reginald George asserted that the gold watch had remained in the jewelry box from the time Mrs. George put it there in July, 1949, until the time five years later when she took it out while looking over her jewels. They were equally certain that they never discussed the watch with William George, Jr., or in his presence. They recalled that they had mentioned to a number of people in the family the fact that William George, Sr. had given the watch to them before his death. (One of these, Mr. Walter Mays, testified to this.) They were confident, however, that none of these people could have mentioned the watch to William, Jr. The certainty they entertained on these points made William, Jr.'s parents much more impressed by the recognition of the watch than they had been by the occurrence of the moles in the same location as those of William George, Sr. In their opinion also, the recognition of the watch occurred quite accidentally. Mrs. Reginald George had not planned to show it to the boy. He simply happened to stray into the room where she had it lying out of the jewelry box, and he spotted it without the slightest prompting on her part.

By 1961 William George, Jr. had largely lost his previous identification with his grandfather, and apart from his occasional requests for "his watch" and a residue of his stutter, he behaved like a normal boy of his age. I talked with him in Alaska and hoped that he would have more to say about the watch which his mother brought out in my presence. He handled it fondly, but did not talk about it. I cannot say whether his reticence arose from shyness with me or from a fading of the images that originally led him to claim it as his own.

Statements Made by the Witnesses of the Case. I present below in tabular form a list of the various statements and other behavior of William George, Jr. The three principal informants were Mr. and Mrs. Reginald George and Mr. Walter Mays, cousin of Reginald George and nephew of William George, Sr. Mr. Mays had been a close companion on fishing trips and other occasions of William George, Sr. Circumstances arose which made it possible for me to interview all three informants separately, Mrs. George in Alaska and Mr. George and Mr. Mays in Seattle.

Readers who take seriously the hypothesis of reincarnation may wish to know about the attitude of Mr. and Mrs. Reginald George toward the wish expressed by Mr. William George, Sr. to return as their son. Mrs. George said she did not have any strong conscious wish for her father-in-law to return as her son. From the expression of pleasure on her face, however, as she told the story, I judge she found gratification that her father-in-law had chosen her from among a number of other female relatives to be his next mother. His selection of her apparently derived at least partly from affection for her in her own right, so to speak, and not only from the fact that she happened to be the wife of his favorite son. Mr. Reginald George was definitely his favorite son, the others having shown themselves irresponsible or careless of their father's welfare. Reginald George returned his father's affection. He did want his father to return as his son, and had some expectation that he would accomplish his intention.

Comments on Alternative Hypotheses. As in the previous case, the two principal hypotheses for explaining this case are reincarnation and an assumed or imposed identification with the previous personality. And also, as in the previous case, the occurrence of the two personalities in the same family makes much more likely the transference of information about the deceased personality to the boy by normal means than when the two personalities occur in two families entirely unknown to each other.

The grief of the parents over the sudden and mysterious death of the elderly fisherman may well have fostered their hopes and beliefs that he had returned. The common belief of Tlingits in reincarnation and the captain's expressed intention to return to them could certainly have encouraged them to think that he had returned as their child. According to this view, the dream of Mrs. Reginald George during her labor patently fulfilled her wish to have her father-in-law return, if not for herself, to please her husband. Then after the birth of the baby his parents could have, perhaps unconsciously, imposed on him the identification with his grandfather which they reported he showed.

TABULATION

Summary of Statements Made by Witnesses in the Case of William George, Jr.

Statements by Mrs. Reginald George	Statements by Mr. Reginald George	Statements by Mr. Walter Mays	Comments
1. William George, Sr. repeatedly said he was going to be reborn as her son.	Confirmed by Mr. George. His father talked like this for some years before he died.	Mr. Mays heard William George, Sr. make such a statement once in 1949.	
2. William George had prominent moles on his upper left shoulder and left forearm below the elbow. Moles about ½ inch in diameter. Did not recall whether the moles were raised.	Mr. George could recall only the mole on the left shoulder and said it was slightly raised. It was about ½ inch in diameter.	These two moles were clearly recalled by Mr. Mays.	The moles on William George, Jr. (examined by myself in 1961) were located at the sites mentioned. They were about ¼ inch in diameter. They were not raised.
3. William George, Sr. said they would recognize him when he returned by his moles.	Mr. George did not recall that his father drew attention to the moles as a sign of recognition.	Mr. Mays had not heard of this statement.	Whether or not William George, Sr. mentioned to others besides his daughter-in-law his belief that he would be recognized by the moles, the fact that William George, Jr. had moles at the same sites as his grandfather was the chief factor influencing his parents to give him the same name as his grandfather.
4. In the summer of 1949, her husband gave her a gold pocket watch, saying his father had given it to him and had said, "If there is such a thing as reincarnation, I will return in your family and claim this watch. Take good care of this watch."	In the summer of 1949, William George, Sr. gave Reginald George a gold pocket watch saying, "I'll come back. Keep this watch for me. I am going to be your son. If there is anything like that, I'll do it."	Mr. Mays had heard that William George, Sr. gave his son a watch by which he was to be recognized upon his return after death.	Mr. George said his father gave him the watch "one or two weeks" before his father died. Mrs. George recalled the interval as "several months."

Claim / Statement	Verification	Comments
5. She put the watch in a jewelry box where it remained five years until the day she removed it, on which occasion William George, Jr. recognized it and claimed it for his own.	Confirmed by Mr. Reginald George.	Mr. Reginald George was not present at the time of the recognition of the watch. Mrs. George was alone with her son at the time. Mr. Reginald George did testify from direct observation to his son's possessive behavior toward the watch in question.
6. During her labor at the birth of William George, Jr., she had a dream in which her deceased father-in-law appeared to her and said he was waiting to see his son.	Mr. Reginald George knew that his wife had dreamed during her labor that his father was returning.	I do not know whether Mrs. George told anyone about the dream before the delivery of her baby, but think this unlikely since she was anesthetized for the delivery shortly after having the dream. Upon awaking from the anesthetic after delivery, Mrs. George was frightened as she expected to see her father-in-law there.
7.	When William George, Jr. saw Mr. Mays, he said "I used to go fishing with him." He did not recognize Mr. Mays by name.	Quite correct as to fact that William George, Sr. and Mr. Mays frequently fished together.
8. William George, Sr. injured his leg when young and William George, Jr. walked with his right foot turned out in a manner similar to that of his grandfather.	His father had injured his right foot when young. This led to a deformity of gait. William George, Jr. had the same deformity in milder degree.	An abnormality of gait was present, but not marked in William George, Jr.
9.	When William George, Jr. was about four he ran into the house from the street where he had been playing and said excitedly that he	Mr. Reginald George believed that William George, Jr. had seen his great-aunt before. The important point is therefore his reference to her as "sister" (instead of great-aunt) and his excitement on

Statements by Mrs. Reginald George	Statements by Mr. Reginald George	Statements by Mr. Walter Mays	Comments
9. (continued)	had seen his "sister" pass by. His parents then found that William George, Sr.'s sister had in fact just passed the house.		seeing her. Such excitement would not be appropriate upon seeing a great-aunt whom the boy had perhaps seen only once or twice in the present life.
10. One day as Reginald George was about to go fishing in his boat, his son advised him to fish in a particular bay he named. William George, Jr. then added that he himself had once made an enormous catch in this bay. This was a fact of the career of William George, Sr.	Mr. Reginald George recalled that his son did advise him accurately about the fishing in a particular bay and was correct in this advice. He did not recall that the boy had at the same time claimed to have made a particularly impressive catch in this bay in his previous life.		William George, Sr. was a superb fisherman and detailed knowledge of the best fishing grounds was characteristic of him, but surprising in a boy who had just begun to get into boats

But an even greater difficulty than those mentioned in connection with the previous case arises from the need somehow to account for the occurrence of the moles in similar sites, for the occurrence of the abnormal gait in the boy, and for his recognition of the gold pocket watch which his grandfather had given to his father.

The Recognition of the Watch. The recognition of the gold watch may perhaps be disposed of by assuming that the Georges included some mention of it (although they deny this) in their training of the child to assume his grandfather's identity. We cannot say that this could not have happened. A more important point perhaps is whether such mention of the watch or even several mentions of it would have sufficed to enable the boy to identify it when he saw it. The recognition of the gold watch by William George, Jr. was not as difficult to accomplish perhaps as the recognition tests passed by the Dalai Lama (fourteenth incarnation), who successfully recognized the rosary, the drum, and the walking stick of the thirteenth incarnation when these objects were offered to him along with other similar objects once owned by the previous Dalai Lama.[39] Yet even in recognition tests of this kind, covert guidance may conceivably play a part since an audience is present who knows the object to be recognized and hopes the boy will recognize it. If we may believe Mrs. George's account of what happened in the present case, her son's recognition of his grandfather's gold watch was entirely spontaneous and unplanned on her part. Whatever we may think about the possibility that the boy had heard of the watch before, no one invited him to recognize the watch, or expected him to do so. He just happened to see it and immediately identified it. This fact diminishes the likelihood that cues from his mother influenced the recognition.

Even when we feel confident in excluding covert sensory cues leading to such recognitions, there remains the possibility of a transmission of information by extrasensory perception from those who know the identity of the object (or person) to the subject, who with paramnesia could then falsely recognize it (or him) as from his own memory. The important topic of recognition tests will receive further consideration in the General Discussion.

The Inheritance of Moles (Naevi). The use of moles by the deceased grandfather as a sign of his identity upon returning and their acceptance as such a sign by his son and daughter-in-law occurred without regard to the possibility of the inheritance of moles. This subject has occupied the

[39] H. Harrer. *Seven Years in Tibet.* (Trans. by R. Graves.) New York: E. P. Dutton & Co., 1954. For an independent and corroborating account (except for some discrepant details) of the tests given the fourteenth Dalai Lama, see also B. J. Gould. *The Jewel in the Lotus.* London: Chatto and Windus, 1957.

attention of a number of dermatologists and geneticists, chiefly in Europe. Several investigations in the 1920s established the fact that a tendency to have many or fewer moles is definitely inherited. Further investigations then showed that the location as well as the number of moles may be inherited. Unfortunately, not many cases have received careful study with regard to the presence or absence of a mole at the same location in different members of the family over three or more generations. Altogether I have been able to find only twelve such pedigrees published or cited in the literature on this subject in Europe and the United States.[40, 41, 42, 43, 44]

For the present case, the relevant question about the inheritance of moles is whether the tendency to inherit a mole (at a particular location) may be carried by a parent who does not himself manifest the mole on his skin. In genetic terms, is the inheritance fully dominant or is penetrance at times impaired? From a study of the twelve published pedigrees we can conclude that the inheritance is usually fully dominant, but with recorded exceptions. In two of the twelve families studied, a grandparent and one or more of his grandchildren had a mole or moles at exactly the same locations, but the parents of the intermediate generation did not, although these parents acted as carriers for the tendency to the mole in the grandchild.[45, 46] The occurrence of these rare exceptional cases in the inheritance of moles makes it impossible to attribute the occurrence of the moles on William George, Jr. firmly to reincarnation, but we can regard them as some evidence for it.

It would be a mistake to dismiss this question as if genetics alone can at present answer all aspects of it. Genetics can only point to the probability of inheritance of the moles by later generations. It does not contribute to our understanding of why in this case William George, Jr., alone out of all the ten children in his family, had moles at the sites of his grandfather's moles.[47] Reincarnation, for which other evidence is not particularly strong

[40] A. H. Estabrook. "A Family with Birthmarks (*Nevus Spilus*) for Five Generations." *Eugenical News*. Vol. 13, 1928, 90–92.

[41] S. J. Denaro. "The Inheritance of Nevi." *Journal of Heredity*, Vol. 35, 1944, 215–218.

[42] E. A. Cockayne. *Inherited Abnormalities of the Skin*. London: Oxford University Press, 1933.

[43] C. A. Maruri. "La Herencia de los Lunares." *Actas Dermo-Sifilográficas*, Vol. 40, 1949, 518–525.

[44] C. A. Maruri. *La Herencia en Dermatología*. Santander: Aldus, S. A. Artes Graficas, 1961.

[45] L. Leven. "Erblichkeit der Naevi." *Deutsche Med. Wochenschr.*, Vol. 55, 1929, 1544.

[46] A. Brauer. "Hereditärer symmetrischer systematisierter Naevus aplasticus bei 38 Personen." *Dermat. Wochenschr.*, Vol. 89, 1929, 1163–1168.

[47] In the interest of strict accuracy, I must mention that I have not personally examined the members of the George family other than William, Jr. with regard to the occurrence or absence of moles on them at the same sites. This omission was first due to my ignorance about the genetics of moles at the time of my first visit to Alaska. On the occasion of my second visit I was unable to persuade the family to cooperate in such an examination. Nevertheless, from the emphasis which the parents of William George, Jr. gave to the moles, including naming him after his grandfather on the basis of them, I think it safe to assume that they regarded these as a specific sign of the grandfather's return, which they would not have done if any other members of the family had moles at the same locations.

in this case, does offer an explanation of this. As already mentioned, genetics assists in understanding the similarities between members of the same family; reincarnation is a theory which may explain some of the differences between members of the same family.

The Inheritance of an Abnormality of Gait. As already mentioned, William George, Sr. injured his right ankle and became lame when he was quite a young man. William George, Jr. had a similar gait with a tendency, albeit a slighter one, to throw his right foot out as he walked. Both the parents of William George, Jr. independently and spontaneously commented to me upon the existence of the limp in their son and its resemblance to the faulty gait of his grandfather. Here we have to do with the inheritance of an acquired characteristic, something regarded as extremely improbable by all geneticists and as quite impossible by most. As it would seem difficult to include a specific abnormal gait in traits imposed on a child by his parents, the hypothesis of imposed identification will account for this feature of the case much less adequately than for its other features, such as the fatherly behavior of the boy toward his uncles. I believe that reincarnation accounts more satisfactorily for the occurrence of this limp than do other theories, if we believe that the gait of William George, Jr. specifically resembles the acquired limp of his grandfather.

The Case of Charles Porter

Summary of the Case. The principal informant for this case was the man who, as a boy, claimed to remember a previous life. At the time of telling me what he knew of his memories Mr. Charles Porter no longer claimed to recall a previous life. He could only remember what he heard his mother say when he was an older child. According to his recollection of her account, when he was a small boy he used to say that he had been killed by a spear in a clan fight of the Tlingit Indians. He named the man who had killed him, the place where he had been killed, and gave his own Tlingit name in the previous life. The man killed with a spear had been his mother's uncle. These facts were confirmed by the record of the killing in the history of the clan.

As the boy would tell the story of how he had been killed by a spear, he would point to his right side. According to Mr. Porter, when he first did this as a boy he did not know that he had, at the spot he pointed to, a birthmark somewhat in the shape of a spear wound on his right flank. Mr. Porter stated that he only came to know of this birthmark in his adulthood. I examined Mr. Porter's right flank and found there a large and unusually shaped pigmented area. It was located immediately under the lowest rib in the mid-line laterally. Because of its extreme lateral location, it might easily not have been noticed spontaneously by its owner. It was roughly diamond-shaped and measured about ½ inch wide and 1¼ inch long. It certainly bore a marked resemblance to the size and shape of an old scar that a spear might make. And a spear entering the body at this point would transfix the liver and probably important blood vessels so that it would kill almost instantly.

Although Mr. Porter was a full-blooded Tlingit, his family were among the first Tlingits to become educated in English. They spoke English in their home and he himself did not learn the Tlingit language until he was eleven or twelve years old. Mr. Porter therefore thought that his parents would not have told him about the clan fight or mentioned to him the name of the man who had killed the person he believed himself to have been in a previous life. He stated that the family never discussed Tlingit history when he was a child.

Mr. Porter said that his aunt commented to him that he liked a special kind of tobacco which she recalled was much desired by his great-uncle after whom he had been named, the man killed by the spear thrust.

Two other informants provided corroboration of the main facts of the case, but could not add to the details or remembered them somewhat differently.

Mrs. Elspeth Graham was an older sister of Mr. Porter by five years. She lived in another community where I interviewed her independently. She recalled that her brother had begun at the age of two to say that he had been killed in a previous life by a spear and to name the man who had killed him. This man, she said, was at that time an old man still living in the community where they grew up. According to Mrs. Graham, her brother stopped talking about the previous life when he was about eight years old. Prior to this he had talked much about the previous life and death, although their mother had tried to stop him from doing so. When I first interviewed Mrs. Graham in 1961 she did not remember that her brother had a birthmark on his side, but in a later interview in 1963 she stated that she did remember that he definitely had a birthmark on his side when born.

I also interviewed Mr. Porter's mother, Mrs. Gregory Hodgson (remarried), who lived in still another community. At the time of my interview she was an old lady of ninety who was just recovering from an infectious disease during which she had been temporarily psychotic. She acknowledged that her memory was poor and I considered this very likely from the account of her recent illness given me by her husband and from the fact that her mind wandered markedly during the interview.

She did recall that her son had said that he had been killed by a spear. She said that he would say this when he was asked where he got the unusual birthmark mentioned above. (This is not necessarily inconsistent with Mr. Porter's statement that he talked about being killed by a spear before he became aware of having a birthmark. It is, however, inconsistent with the combination of his statement that he did not know about the birthmark until he was an adult, and his sister's statement that he stopped talking about the spear wound when he was about eight.) Mrs. Hodgson seemed confused about what her son had said concerning the wounds received in the previous life and at one point in my interview with her she mentioned that he had said he had received a spear wound in his back and also one in his right knee.

Mrs. Hodgson stated that her son had identified the man who had killed the previous personality. At the time her son did this the person he named was still living.

A relative of Mr. Porter whom I interviewed in Sitka asserted that she had heard that as a child he greatly feared knives, bayonets, and spears and would go to great lengths to avoid even the sight of spears or long knives. Mr. Porter himself could remember no such fear as a child and his older sister, Mrs. Graham, could not remember his having had such a fear.

Comments. Mr. Porter was born in Sitka in 1907. According to his sister, Mrs. Graham, he was talking about being killed in a clan fight between approximately 1909 and 1915. The man who supposedly killed him was then an old man. Let us suppose that he was at least sixty-five in 1910, which means he was born in 1845. According to Krause, clan fights with spears had ceased by the time he visited the Tlingits in 1881–82; but Simpson had witnessed a clan fight with spears during his visit in 1841–42.[48] A notorious massacre with spears of the Wrangell tribe occurred in Sitka in the early 1850s. (This massacre will receive further discussion in connection with the case of Derek Pitnov.) This mode of warfare therefore died out sometime during the thirty years between 1852 and 1882. A man born in 1845 might easily have participated in a spear fight as a young man, so this part of the account has historical plausibility.

My informants had made no written record of Mr. Porter's statements as a boy and they did not recall any more details than I have given. I could not therefore trace the records of the particular clan fight and the names of its participants. And since there is such scanty information about the availability to a small boy of information about this fight, we cannot draw any firm conclusions about whether or not Mr. Porter derived his information paranormally. On the side of a paranormal explanation is his conviction that he told of being killed by a spear before he knew he had an appropriate birthmark, and his belief that his English-speaking parents would not have told him details of a Tlingit clan fight. On the other hand, the existence of such an unusual birthmark may have prompted the imagination of his

[48] G. Simpson. *An Overland Journey Round the World during the Years 1841 and 1842.* Philadelphia: Lea and Blanchard, 1847. (Part 2, 86–87.)

parents to compose a story harmonious with the diamond shape of the birthmark which they then imposed on the boy and he adopted. Somewhat against this view is Mrs. Graham's testimony that her mother discouraged her brother from talking about the spear wound, although it is possible that Mrs. Hodgson might have covertly promoted the story in her son while consciously attempting to suppress it. Any explanation of the case along normal lines would still leave the birthmark itself to be accounted for, but I shall defer discussion of this topic until later.

Charles Porter's Later Life. As already mentioned, Charles Porter was born in 1907 and so he was a mature adult when I met him in 1961. After that first meeting I saw him on subsequent visits to Alaska in 1962, 1963, 1965, and 1972. We also occasionally exchanged letters.

At our last meeting in May, 1972, he was 65 years old and looking forward to retirement from his position with the Alaska State Government which would occur a month later. His general health remained good, but he was melancholy because of the death of his wife, which had occurred a month before our meeting.

He said that he still occasionally thought of the previous life, a statement which seemed at variance with his earlier one (of 1961) according to which his memories of the previous life were then secondhand, that is, he only remembered what he had heard his mother tell other persons what he had said earlier about it. (Possibly, as with some other cases, the accessibility of the memories to consciousness fluctuated.) But his recollection of the previous life seemed quite vague and he could not recall the relationship to himself of the previous personality who had been identified in his childhood as his mother's uncle.

Because Charles Porter grew up in Alaska many years ago, I have been particularly interested in his adjustment to the opposite pulls of the competing cultures in Alaska. It seems to me that he has handled these very well.

He was one of the best educated Tlingits I have met. He was an ardent Presbyterian and had worked as a missionary before joining the Territorial Government. He was planning to resume some missionary work after his retirement. He had been active in one of the service clubs of Juneau of which he was one of the few Tlingit members. In general he would be considered one of the most "assimilated" Tlingits, at least of his age group. On the other hand, he remained proud of his Tlingit heritage and deplored the decline in the Tlingit culture. He complained that no one answered him if he spoke Tlingit any more. (Actually the Tlingit culture and language were undergoing a remarkable revival in Alaska in 1972.) And he felt considerable resentment at the Bureau of Indian Affairs which had refused to assist his wife before her death. He attributed this refusal to the

Bureau having kept in his dossier notations of his opposition many years earlier to reservations for the Tlingits. (The Tlingits, in contrast to the Indians of the southern forty-eight states, never allowed the government of the United States to place them on reservations.) For many years Mr. Porter was active in the affairs of the Alaska Native Brotherhood (a society founded to promote the welfare of the Alaskan natives) and was its secretary for several years between 1961 and 1967.

I found that some Tlingits who had become ministers or missionaries of the Christian Church adopted a hardened opposition to the traditional Tlingit beliefs. But Mr. Porter did not find Christianity and reincarnation incompatible. He not only cooperated patiently in my study of his own case, but helped me in various ways to learn about or investigate other cases. Perhaps our last two meetings in May, 1972, illustrated his ability to reconcile the two cultures to each of which he seemed to belong equally. One day we engaged in a rather long discussion of his own and some other cases of the reincarnation type and of the best translation into the English language of the Tlingit phrase which corresponds to "reincarnation." And then a day or two later I met him unexpectedly at the Juneau airport when he was leaving for another town where he was to engage in Christian missionary activity.

The Case of Norman Despers

Summary of the Case. This case, although slight in details, has certain features which recur in cases of *déjà vu* suggestive of reincarnation reported from many different parts of the world.

I obtained my information on this case from Mr. Henry Despers, Jr. in Hoonah, and his son, Norman Despers, a boy of eighteen whom I interviewed in Sitka where he was attending high school. Mrs. Henry Despers, the only other witness of Norman Despers' remarks suggesting a previous life, died some years before my investigation.

Norman Despers was born in Hoonah in 1944. When he was three or four years old his parents took him one day to a cove called Dundas Bay some thirty-five miles from Hoonah. While at the bay, Norman suddenly and quite spontaneously said: "I used to have a smokehouse on the strait here and I was later blind." He showed great excitement and indeed happiness as he made these statements. Mr. Despers could recall no other statements by the boy with regard to a previous life.

Norman had correctly stated two facts about the life of his grandfather, Henry Despers, Sr. He had been a fisherman who had in fact owned a smokehouse at Dundas Bay. He died at the age of eighty-five in 1937 after four years of blindness. Henry Despers, Jr. married his first wife in 1928 and had one child with her. She died and he remarried in 1942. Norman was the first child (of five) of this second marriage and he was the first child born to Henry Despers, Jr. since the death of Henry Despers, Sr.

Mr. Henry Despers, Jr. expressed absolute certainty that neither he nor his second wife had ever said anything to Norman about his grandfather's smokehouse or about his having been blind. He also felt certain that the boy could not have recognized the remnants of the smokehouse which still existed at the time of their visit to Dundas Bay. His father, the owner of the smokehouse, had abandoned it in 1930 and at the time of their visit to the scene in about 1947 nothing remained but a few pilings. Henry Despers, Jr. interpreted his son's remarks as evidence that his father (the boy's grandfather) had been reborn as his son. Although he had apparently been uncertain about it previously, the episode convinced him of the truth of reincarnation.

Norman Despers was named after a maternal uncle much beloved by his parents. His maternal grandmother and her surviving sons (brothers of the uncle after whom Norman had been named) used to talk much about the deceased uncle to Norman. The uncles used to say, when Norman became older, that he resembled his uncle. When I interviewed Norman, he recalled these facts himself. He also remembered that when he had first visited Dundas Bay it had seemed familiar to him. He had the same sense of familiarity when he first came to Sitka some four months before our interview. At the time of my interview, however, he did not remember the remarks attributed to him by his father. He thought he recalled a smokehouse and when I encouraged him to do so, drew a sketch of a smokehouse. But he could not say definitely that it was the smokehouse of Dundas Bay. Norman knew nothing of the belief in reincarnation among the Tlingits and had no knowledge of the impact of his own statements as a small child on his father. He was the youth mentioned above who had not heard of the belief in reincarnation among the Tlingits, but knew the Indians of Asia believed in reincarnation.

Norman himself had poor eyesight and began to wear glasses regularly at fourteen. Henry Despers, Jr., who was in his fifties in 1962, wore glasses, but for reading only.

Comments. If we accept the report of Norman's father about the sequence of events in this case, we may explain it by a combination of extrasensory perception and paramnesia. The two facts stated by the boy were certainly known to his father, who was present at the time. Norman Despers may have culled these facts from his father's mind and then mistakenly attributed them to himself as "memories" of a previous life. The boy's father could have been a passive agent for the information transmitted.

Yet before dismissing the case, we should ask ourselves why the boy made these statements only upon visiting the bay where the smokehouse had been. Why did he not derive and speak about these matters when he was at home with his parents? Perhaps the answer lies in a stimulation of Norman's father to think of *his* father when visiting this bay. So Norman might have picked up by extrasensory perception thoughts which rose to the consciousness of his father or perhaps lay just beneath its surface. Or he might have engaged in "object reading," the places of the neighborhood acting as vehicles for the transmission to him of accurate information about his grandfather. In either case, paramnesia would also have occurred if extrasensory perception is part of the correct explanation of the case.

At the same time, if reincarnation occurs we would expect that a visit to a scene of the previous life would stimulate real memories. This feature is therefore compatible with both extrasensory perception and reincarnation.

Déjà vu experiences, to the extent that they include definite evidence of paranormal cognition, often seem to illustrate the common observation that recognition is easier than recall, and they also often illustrate the stimulation of recall (presumably through associations) by visits to scenes connected with past events of the supposed previous life. In the present case, the visit to the area of the old smokehouse, itself in ruins, seems to have revived some "memory" of that smokehouse. Then almost instantaneously came the boy's statement about being blind. Norman Despers had no apparent recollection of a previous life or none recalled by either him or his father except when he visited the smokehouse of Henry Despers, Sr. for the first time.

Many cases suggestive of reincarnation show a marked preponderance among events apparently recalled of those in the closing years of life or surrounding the death of the previous personality. Norman Despers' apparent recollection of the fact of being blind in the last years of life illustrates this. Henry Despers, Sr. abandoned the smokehouse in about 1930 and became totally blind a few years later, in about 1933. Possibly he abandoned the smokehouse because his eyesight was already failing. This might account for the association in Norman's mind of the smokehouse and blindness.

I attach no significance to the drawing by Norman of a smokehouse. The drawing contained nothing specific that would identify it as a drawing of the smokehouse of Henry Despers, Sr. and no other smokehouse, since many other similar ones existed in southeastern Alaska.

As in the case of Jimmy Svenson, the child in this case received his name from a deceased uncle. Here we have also direct evidence from the boy himself that his relatives talked much with him about his uncle and drew attention to similarities of physical appearance between him and his uncle. These circumstances did not, however, influence him to an identification with his maternal uncle; he experienced the sense of identification instead with his paternal grandfather.

The Later Development of Norman Despers. I did not meet Norman Despers between September, 1962, and May, 1972. At that time I visited him in his home in Hoonah where he was then living with his wife and children. He was twenty-seven years old.

He had fully recovered from the tuberculosis which he had at the time of my first interview with him. I did not mention this illness earlier because it was not relevant to his memories of a previous life; but his having tuberculosis was the principal reason for his being in Sitka where he was a patient at the Alaska Native Hospital in Mt. Edgecumbe (really a part of Sitka) and where he was attending high school when I met him in 1962.

In 1972 Norman Despers' health was good in general, except for his eyesight, which was not. He had rather marked myopia (20/250) requiring correction with glasses. He had three siblings, two brothers, and a sister. Norman was the only one of the four children with any impairment of vision.[49] It will be recalled that his grandfather, of whose life Norman had two memories, suffered from poor eyesight and was blind for the last four years of his life.

Norman had had no additional memories of the previous life since our earlier interview.

He had continued in high school until his senior year, but when his father became ill he returned to Hoonah and stopped school. He married in 1964 and had three children. His father died in 1968. In 1972 he was working in a crab cannery at Hoonah.

The Case of Henry Elkin

Summary of the Case. The sole informant in this case was Mr. Henry Elkin himself. Mr. Elkin was born in 1899 at Angoon. He lived his early life there but moved later to Hoonah.

His mother told him that he was born with two birthmarks on the skin of his chest, one in front and one at the back on the left side. These marks were still prominent and I examined them carefully in 1962. On the skin of his left chest about midway between the nipple and clavicle, there was a round mark about ½ inch in diameter, slightly puckered and slightly pale compared to the neighboring skin. At the back of the left chest there was a larger, irregular mark somewhat triangular in shape, slightly depressed and not any different in color from the surrounding skin. This mark lay about six inches down the left back from the shoulder and about three inches

---

[49] In the first edition of this book I mentioned that Norman was one of five children of his father's second marriage. In 1972 Norman referred to only four children as living, so possibly one had died in the meantime. I did not ask a question about this because I did not notice the discrepancy at the time.

from the midline. On the right side of the back at about the same level and a little closer to the midline lay another similar, but smaller, irregular scar. Mr. Elkin stated that this latter mark resulted from a boil which he had after birth whereas the other two marks were, according to his mother, congenital.

The round, puckered mark on the front of Mr. Elkin's left chest looked exactly like the scar of a healed bullet wound at the point of entry. The mark on Mr. Elkin's left back had a much less specific appearance, but it could easily have been made by the exit wound of a bullet. The two marks on the left thorax lined up along the straight and nearly horizontal line which a bullet would make in traversing the chest from the front mark to the back one.

At the time of Mr. Elkin's birth, his parents did not identify him with any deceased relative (at least publicly) nor did they, so far as he knew, give him the name of a particular relative. Mr. Elkin did not claim to recall any death associated with the congenital marks suggestive of a bullet wound that would correspond with the congenital marks on his thorax. However, he did recall two other apparent memories of a previous life.

When Mr. Elkin was a child his mother took him to the old community house in Angoon. When looking around in it, he said he "saw his grand-mother there." His mother said that such an event had occurred before he was born, but would not discuss the matter further with him. When the Tlingits engaged in their tribal wars (which, as I have said, ceased between 1850 and 1880), their womenfolk would sit in the community houses until the surviving husbands returned from the battle. Henry Elkin's grand-mother had in fact waited in the community house at Angoon for her husband (and other male relatives) to return from their battles. He was therefore seemingly recalling events that had taken place twenty-five or more years earlier.

When Henry Elkin was eight, he suddenly "remembered" an occasion when his father with a companion out in a boat had saved the lives of two other men who, while cutting kelp, had encountered some misfortune and were about to drown. The details of his recollection of this episode were acknowledged as correct by his parents when he told them. However, once again they told him this had happened before he was born and would not permit him to talk about the subject any more. The memory of his father's rescue of these two men remained clear in Mr. Elkin's mind in 1962.

Comments. Since unfortunately Mr. Elkin was the only witness of his case, we must accept or reject his word that the two marks on his left chest were in fact congenital and not post-natal like the one on his right posterior chest. I find it difficult to imagine how he might have acquired them after birth. An actual bullet traveling between the sites of these two marks would quite likely have been fatal. It is barely conceivable that it would have missed all the great vessels in the thorax, the striking of any one of which would have led to almost instantaneous death from hemorrhage. But if such a wound were not immediately fatal it would surely be well remembered by some person. If it happened to Mr. Elkin after the age of five, say, he would have remembered it himself. If it happened when he was very young, say under the age of five, he might have forgotten such a wound himself, but his parents would have known about it and would presumably have had no reason to tell him they found the marks on him at birth. If they wanted to make him into a battle hero they might have done so, but they did not elaborate such a story and blocked him from remembering what little he could recall.

The same arguments seem to me to vitiate the idea, which occurred to me, that Mr. Elkin had inflicted such marks on himself for fraudulent purposes. Overlooking the pain he would experience, and the craft he would require to simulate bullet wounds so clearly, we would then confront the fact that he never seems to have elaborated his story in any way. So far from spinning a story of a heroic death in battle, Mr. Elkin seems to have parted with his account somewhat reluctantly. In short, I think its fragmentary character increases its authenticity.

As already mentioned, many Tlingits believe it a misfortune to recall a previous life, as do a good many Hindus. They therefore often discourage any child who claims to remember a previous life from talking. However, the insistence on the part of Mr. Elkin's parents that he not talk about his apparent recollections of a previous life seems to have run rather more strongly than the usual discouragement of children from talking about previous lives. This fact and the parents' acknowledgment of the correctness of his two statements suggests that perhaps his parents had in fact identified Mr. Elkin with a particular deceased person who did not die a natural death; and for sufficient reasons of their own they did not wish this identification developed in the child or announced around their village. We have no direct evidence for this speculation and I only emphasize it in connection with the theory of imposed identification. For in the congenital scars of Mr. Elkin materials lay at hand for a ready imposition on the child of a personality which his parents may have remembered as having had wounds of a similar kind. Anyone dying with such wounds would almost certainly either have been a hero of battle or murdered privately. Since the Tlingits honor heroes of battle, I conclude that Mr. Elkin also may fit into the category of dead men who do tell tales.

A Later Interview with Henry Elkin. I did not meet Henry Elkin between September, 1962 and May, 1972. In the latter month I was in Alaska, learned that he was still living in Hoonah, and went there to meet him.

He received me cordially, although he was extremely busy just then and preparing to go halibut fishing as I arrived. He was then seventy-three years old, but appeared somewhat younger. He seemed in good health, and said that he was, except for some residue of a heart disease that he had had many years earlier.

Henry Elkin told me that he still occasionally thought about the memories he had had of a previous life. This surprised me because I had expected him to say that he remembered nothing of it. Four of the other five Tlingit subjects with whom I have had follow-up interviews had said, at the time of the later interviews, that they had no persisting memories of the previous lives they had earlier remembered or been identified with. (Derek Pitnov actually never had *any* imaged memories of a previous life.)

When I asked Henry Elkin what he still recalled, he first gave me an account of the episode described above in which he had visited the community house at Angoon and had then had a memory, or vision perhaps, of his maternal grandmother sitting there. His description of this episode did not differ from the one he had given me in 1962 except that he said in 1972 that his sister (not his mother) had taken him to visit the community house in Angoon. He still said that it was his mother who told him that the event he remembered had occurred before he was born.

His account of the second memory of the previous life differed considerably from what he had told me earlier, or rather it put what he had told me in 1962 in a quite different light. I refer to his memory of being with his father in a boat when his father had saved the lives of two other men who were about to drown. In 1972 Henry Elkin did not change the details of what had happened when his father saved the lives of these men who nearly drowned. Indeed, he gave some additional ones such as the names of the men who were rescued from drowning. And he repeated that his mother told him that he was not yet born at the time of this episode. But in 1972 he added some information that he had not given before. He said that his parents had told him that his older sister was alive when this rescue took place and that she had been in the canoe with her (and Henry Elkin's) father.

The older sister in question died at the age of twelve or thirteen when Henry Elkin was himself a small boy. (From his description I have inferred that he was perhaps five or six years old when she died; he could not remember exactly how old he was and refused to give an estimate; a desire to confine himself strictly to what he can remember is one of his admirable traits.) Henry Elkin was born in 1899. Let us suppose that his sister died in about 1905. If she was then above twelve or thirteen years old we can place her birth year as being about 1892. But she would not have gone out with her father in a canoe much before the age of five or six. I conjecture therefore that the incident in question occurred some-

where around 1897–8, not long before 1899, but still definitely before
Henry Elkin's birth according to what his mother told him.

Henry Elkin's memory of the episode is that *he* was in the bow of the
canoe that his father was paddling. It includes no memory of his sister
being there. How then are we to understand this as a memory of his? I
confess to bafflement concerning the item. If we accept that Henry Elkin
had had a previous life, this particular memory may have derived from
his experiences as a discarnate spirit which had some awareness of events
in the family of the previous personality which was also to be the family
into which he would be reincarnated.[50] I have not encountered any other
Tlingit case in which the subject claimed a memory of events happening
in the previous family during the period between terrestrial lives. But
claims of memories of events occurring to the previous family during the
"intermission" period occur occasionally in cases of south Asia and in some
of these the subject states verified details of events that happened to the
previous family after the death of the previous personality and before the
subject's birth.

Alternatively, Henry Elkin's revised (or perhaps I should say in fairness
to him, amplified) version of the memory of the rescue of the drowned
men may have got into his mind by extrasensory perception from his
sister. His sister had been in her father's canoe at the time of the rescue
of the men. She must have had a memory of the episode and perhaps this
somehow became transferred to Henry Elkin and then subsequently became falsely remembered by him as an event that he had himself experienced. But we do not even need to invoke extrasensory perception because
it is also possible that Henry Elkin's sister simply told him her own
memories of the incident before she died and then he later—through an
illusion of memory—came to think that he, not she, had participated in the
rescue of the men their father had saved.

The Case of Derek Pitnov

Summary of the Case. Derek Pitnov was born in 1918 in Wrangell. At birth
he had a mark on his abdomen which, prominent in early life, had since

---

[50] In the majority (70%) of Tlingit cases of the reincarnation type subject and previous personality are related on the mother's side. (I. Stevenson. "Cultural Patterns in Cases Suggestive
of Reincarnation among the Tlingit Indians of Southeastern Alaska." *Journal* A.S.P.R., Vol. 60,
July, 1966, 229–243.) If the present case followed this pattern Henry Elkin's maternal grandmother whom (in his first memory) he saw sitting in the community house at Angoon was the
sister of the previous personality who participated in a tribal battle and died in it. According to
the pattern of Tlingit cases (and the expectations of the Tlingit culture) the deceased man would
then be reborn on his sister's side of the family. Thus the previous personality and the subject
would belong to the same family on the maternal side.

faded somewhat, but still remained quite distinct when I first met him. Mr. Pitnov permitted me to examine the mark in 1962.

This mark had a diamond-shaped form. It was about one inch long and half an inch wide. It lay about one inch to the left and slightly below the navel. The mark seemed skin deep only and the tissue of the skin in the area of the mark was not attached to the underlying muscle. There was a slight depression in the center of the mark. In 1962 the mark was rather darker in color than the surrounding skin in the center and somewhat paler than the surrounding skin at its borders. Mr. Pitnov stated that when he was younger the mark was an inch longer and much deeper in color, especially after he became cold as when bathing in cold water. Mr. Pitnov said that formerly it gave the appearance of a recently inflicted wound. Mr. Pitnov had no mark on his back. A spear entering the abdomen at a right angle at the site of the mark on Mr. Pitnov's abdomen would bring almost instantaneous death by severing the descending aorta.

Mr. Pitnov knew of the birthmark on his abdomen as a child, but had only recently learned of its supposed relationship to an actual wound on an ancestor. He learned in about 1955 that at his birth the mark on his abdomen was related by some elderly ladies of Wrangell to the fatal wound of a celebrated native of Wrangell, Chah-nik-kooh. The latter, although not a chief, had led a large party of men from Wrangell to a potlatch (ceremonial feast) in Sitka which took place in 1852 or 1853. The Sitkas and their chief, Yakwan, had announced this potlatch as an amicable occasion for a peaceful settlement of a long-standing feud between the Wrangell and Sitka tribes. The party of Wrangells received and ignored some warnings of forthcoming treachery in Sitka. When they reached Sitka a friendly reception opened the ceremonies. The Wrangells had no arms and did not expect to use any. But in the middle of the festivities, Yakwan and a few of his men fell upon the Wrangells and treacherously murdered about forty of them with spears. A few survivors escaped to Wrangell with tales of this massacre. Ill-feeling between the tribes ran high until another (and effective) peace-making in 1918, but some mutual animosity and fear persists to this day.

The massacre at Sitka receives some attention in the written histories of Alaska,[51,52] but the oral traditions of the Wrangells include more details. Among these we find an account of how Chah-nik-kooh met his death. For it is said that when Yakwan first showed his spear and his intention to slaughter the Wrangells, Chah-nik-kooh said: "If you want to kill someone, kill me!" This remark indicates a mixture of resignation to inevitable death and defiant courage in facing it. He was thus the first to be speared.

[51] H. H. Bancroft. *History of Alaska.* San Franciso: A. L. Bancroft & Co., 1886.
[52] C. L. Andrews. *The Story of Alaska.* Caldwell, Idaho: Caxton Printers, 1938.

Yakwan actually spitted several bodies on one spear, although it is not reported that Chah-nik-kooh was one of those thus treated. The bodies of the slain men remained in Sitka.

As already mentioned, a few survivors reached Wrangell with the story of the massacre and their escape. From them the Wrangells derived the details of the murders and passed these along to their descendants. Some details about the wounds of each man killed would thus become known or surmised in the community at Wrangell.

In 1918 (some sixty-six years after the massacre) some elderly inhabitants of Wrangell claimed that the birthmark on the abdomen of Derek Pitnov was identical in location with the site of the fatal wound of Chah-nik-kooh, who was also Mr. Pitnov's great-great-granduncle.

We may entertain serious doubts about the evidence of uniqueness of the birthmark on Mr. Pitnov which enabled the elders of Wrangell to connect it so confidently with the wound of Chah-nik-kooh. In the slaughter of forty Wrangells how could anyone later know positively just where each victim received his wound? The inability of the Wrangells to inspect the bodies of their kin afterwards must have enhanced the difficulty and the story of the massacre and of how Chah-nik-kooh met his death depended upon the reports of the eyewitnesses who escaped. As I say, we may question the reliability of the elders' memories when they asserted that Mr. Pitnov was in fact the reincarnation of Chah-nik-kooh. But we ought not to doubt the inherent plausibility of the story, for the narration of such minute details as the exact manner of death and the location of the spear wound are entirely characteristic of the tribal stories of the Tlingits handed down from one generation to another.[53]

[53] Many Tlingits believe that their oral traditions are more accurate than written records. They rehearse a child in the reproduction of a story until he can repeat it perfectly. This assures them of accurate reproduction from one generation to another. They claim that written accounts may carelessly include and perpetuate errors avoided in oral tradition. Nor do all modern historians reject oral tradition as worthless. Some even incline to agree with the complaints about written records of peoples who depend on oral tradition. (R. M. Dorson. "Oral Tradition and Written History: The Case for the United States." *Journal of the Folklore Institute,* Vol. 1, December, 1964, 220–234.) P. Drucker (*Indians of the Northwest Coast.* New York: McGraw-Hill Book Company, Inc., 1955) shares this confidence and states "In connection with these traditions, it must be pointed out that while the Indians had no written records, and had to rely on oral transmission of their clan and family histories, the traditions of all the groups from Vancouver Island northward are so specific and consistent—and insofar as they can be checked, so correct—that there is little doubt that for the most part they are historically accurate. . . ."

An incident during my second visit to Alaska illustrates the confidence of the Tlingit storyteller in oral tradition and his contempt for written records. At the request of Mr. George Hall, an elderly Tlingit and authority on the tribal legends and stories, began to narrate a Tlingit legend to us. Wishing to preserve this for later study, I took out my pen and began to write down what he said. Seeing this, the narrator became incensed and complained to Mr. Hall that this sort of thing (writing the stories down) was the way errors got into the stories and distorted them.

Mr. Pitnov himself gave all the foregoing information about the occurrence of the congenital mark on his abdomen and its connection with the fate of Chah-nik-kooh. He recalled having the mark when he was a child, but had only heard of the connection with Chah-nik-kooh when an adult. The question arose, as it has in other similar cases, whether the mark was found on Mr. Pitnov at birth or acquired later.

In Wrangell, where Mr. Pitnov was born, I enquired of several members of his family about the existence of this mark on him at birth. And I interviewed one of Mr. Pitnov's sisters in Anchorage. Mr. Pitnov's mother, father, and two older sisters did not know anything about the existence of a birthmark on Mr. Pitnov. We can disregard the testimony of one older sister since she was only two years older than her brother and unlikely to have comprehended the significance of a birthmark when he was born or to have heard of it later. And his other sister, although four years old when he was born, went away from the family to a school a few years later and grew up in a different environment from that of Mr. Pitnov. So she would have been unlikely to have heard of his birthmark. The testimony of Mr. Pitnov's father also counts for little, since he, eighty-nine years old in the autumn of 1962, had an obviously failing memory. Moreover, he seems never to have been close to his wife or attentive to her or their children; the marriage ended in separation and divorce about a year after Mr. Pitnov's birth. But it is strange that Mr. Pitnov's mother did not recall any birthmark on her son's abdomen. She seemed to have an alert mind and although seventy years old in 1962, showed no obvious signs of its decay. She recalled that her son had a birthmark on his knee, but knew nothing of one on his abdomen. (Mr. Pitnov himself said nothing of a mark on his knee.) Her failure to recall this becomes all the more inexplicable in view of the fact that another lady of Wrangell, Mrs. Robertshaw, did recall that Mr. Pitnov had been born with a mark "below his left lung." This informant, ninety-four years old in 1962, had shown some signs of confusion according to other informants. She spoke only Tlingit and no English; her great-nephew interpreted for her. Her location of the mark, while not as accurate as could be, was in general correct and it would seem that she did have some knowledge of the particular mark in question.

Mr. Pitnov did not claim to remember the life and death of Chah-nik-kooh or, for that matter, of anyone else. He did, however, exhibit two interesting and relevant behavioral traits. First, he recalled having had, since childhood, a marked fear of knives, bayonets, and spears. As a boy he was afraid of knives and did not play with them like other boys. He had an intense dislike of bayonet drill when he was in the army during World War II. He would not let his own children play with knives. This phobia did not extend to other dangerous weapons such as firearms, but was restricted to dangerous bladed weapons.

Mr. Pitnov did not know of any events earlier in his life which could account for his phobia of knives and spears. Once in a fight a man pulled a knife on him. But Mr. Pitnov was certain that his fear of knives antedated this episode and that his intense reaction of anger toward the man who threatened him was a result, not a cause, of his fear of knives.

Mr. Pitnov's wife stated that she had noticed his marked fear of knives and that he definitely was more restrictive of their children's use of knives than other fathers of the community.

Pictures of spears did not arouse marked emotion in Mr. Pitnov, because when I showed him a photograph of a Tlingit battle spear he showed no visible signs of anxiety as he studied the photograph. In 1965 Mr. Pitnov told me that he thought his fear of bladed weapons had largely abated.

Secondly, Mr. Pitnov, although born in Wrangell, had a strong interest in improving relations between the people of Wrangell and the people of Sitka. He has made his home in Sitka where some people still showed marked reserve toward Tlingits from Wrangell. He would undoubtedly have chosen an easier course if he had stayed in Wrangell or if, living in Sitka, he had remained obscure and out of local organizations. But instead he entered fully into these and even held high office in the organizations of the Tlingits in Sitka. Mr. Pitnov told me that he felt a strong desire to bring harmony to the two clans and to be of service to the people of Sitka. Mr. George Hall, who knew both Mr. Pitnov and the circumstances well, testified to the compulsion he had to immerse himself in the affairs of the Sitka Tlingits, which he continued despite frustration and disappointment.

In Mr. Pitnov's behavior towards the Sitka Tlingits we can recognize resemblances to the behavior of Chah-nik-kooh, who led a peacemaking expedition of Wrangells to Sitka and lost his life. Mr. Pitnov stated that he did not know of any attributed connection between himself and Chah-nik-kooh until 1955 and if this is so, then his compulsion to heal the wounds between the Wrangells and the Sitkas antedated any idea he may have had that he had played the same role in a previous life.

In my studies of cases suggestive of reincarnation, I have found a number of persons who report some illness topically related to an event of a previous life.[54] Mr. Pitnov stated that he had a tendency to abdominal pain when tense. He did not think he had such pain more than other persons when they are tense. But since many people when tense do not have abdominal pain, but symptoms in other organs, it is of some interest that Mr. Pitnov's physical symptoms of tension localized chiefly in his abdomen.

---

[54] In the present series of cases, Sukla (pp. 52–67), Marta (pp. 183–203), and Norman Despers (pp. 245–248) provide other illustrations of such correlations between an illness of the previous personality and one of the subject. Other still unpublished cases give additional examples.

Comments. The failure of Mr. Pitnov's mother to remember the mark on his abdomen asserted to have been there at birth by Mrs. Robertshaw poses a perplexing problem in this case. But it may have the following explanation. Mrs. Robertshaw was generally regarded in Wrangell as one of the last of the older people thoroughly informed on the tribal history and on such matters as the relationship between rebirth and birthmarks. When Mr. Pitnov was born in 1918 it is quite likely that Mrs. Robertshaw heard about the mark and paid attention to it, whereas his mother showed little interest in the matter and in the ensuing years forgot all about it. In a later conversation with Mr. Pitnov, he attributed his mother's failure to confirm the fact of his having had a birthmark to deliberate suppression of the topic rather than to real loss of memory. He believed that she wished to avoid any reference to the previous clan feuds of the Tlingits which, as I have already mentioned, persisted to some extent even to recent times.

If the mark on Mr. Pitnov's abdomen is *not* a birthmark we will have to account for its existence in some other way. As in the case of Henry Elkin, it is difficult to imagine how a mark of this size could have occurred on Mr. Pitnov's body post-natally without either he or his mother knowing about it. However, this could have happened, and in Mr. Pitnov's case a comparatively superficial wound or burn might have led to a residual mark. As already mentioned, the mark on Mr. Pitnov's abdomen had no associated mark on his back where a hypothetical spear would have emerged. Nevertheless, the problem of the special shape of the mark remains. The mark had a very distinct and symmetrical diamond shape. In general outline it resembled closely the diamond-shaped pigmented mark on the right flank of Mr. Porter. Mr. Porter's mark was somewhat less regular in shape, at least on one side where its line was quite jagged. But both had in general a diamond-shaped form.

It happens that the Tlingit battle spear has a flattish blade which at its base becomes diamond shaped and fitted into a diamond-shaped haft. The haft joins a long, round handle. The round portion of the spear has no greater diameter than the diamond-shaped haft.[55] When this spear enters a body the blade would slit the tissue and the following haft would make a diamond-shaped wound. The round handle would not modify the wound made by the blade and haft. The Tlingit battle spear had a rather narrow blade and haft not more than 1-½ inches wide. In short, its size and shape indicate that it would make a wound closely corresponding in size and

[55] Mr. George Hall kindly made available to me a photograph of a Tlingit battle spear together with some other Tlingit battle gear which permitted an estimation of the size of the spear. The photograph also permitted inferences about the shape of the blade, haft, and handle of the spear. The spear itself was not available when I visited Alaska, but my conclusions about the size and shape of the spear were confirmed in a conversation with the former owner of the spear.

shape to the marks on the flank of Mr. Porter and the abdomen of Mr. Pitnov. That two persons should be born with diamond-shaped marks corresponding closely with the wounds that would be inflicted by the spears used in Alaska calls for some kind of explanation.[56]

The Later Life of Derek Pitnov. I did not meet Derek Pitnov between August, 1965, and May, 1972. But on May 24, 1972, I had a long talk with him in Sitka, Alaska, and also met his (second) wife.

In the first edition of this book I mentioned Derek Pitnov's interest in trying to improve the relations between the formerly hostile and feuding Tlingit people of Wrangell and Sitka. He had continued to be somewhat interested in this matter but less so than formerly, possibly because the former ill-feeling had abated, although he did not himself mention this to me as his reason for lessened interest. He had also been less active than formerly in the affairs of the Alaska Native Brotherhood in which he had previously participated with enthusiasm. He had, however, served four years as member of the Sitka City Council from 1966 to 1970 and only lost this office after an amalgamation of the city and surrounding borough which led to the abolition of some of the councillors' offices.

Mr. Pitnov had had unsatisfactory experiences with employment since our last meeting. He had worked for three years at a pulp mill outside Sitka and then gave this up to rejoin the Federal Park Service. (The Department of the Interior maintains an historical park in Sitka.) But about 1971 he resigned from this position and with his (first) wife borrowed a great deal of money and tried a business venture. This failed at least partly because his wife divorced him at this time and withdrew her equity from the jointly owned company. After this disaster, he spent a winter in Anchorage unemployed. Then his fortunes mended again when he was offered a rather well-paying job in construction work back in Sitka. And at about this time he met his second wife.

Although he was receiving comparatively high wages for his work in construction, Mr. Pitnov certainly was capable of more skilled and more intellectual employment. He had an excellent vocabulary and a profound, if not scholarly, knowledge of the Tlingit people. These attainments should have qualified him for a position with the Bureau of Indian Affairs, but for reasons that I do not understand, he had not been able to obtain employment in this branch of the federal government.

[56] Yet I would not want to leave the impression that I consider the diamond shape of the birthmarks decisive by itself with regard to the possibility of some paranormal explanation for them. Dr. R. M. J. Harper has published a photograph of a diamond-shaped pigmented birthmark rather similar to that of Mr. Porter. (R. M. J. Harper. _Evolution and Illness._ London: E. and S. Livingstone, Ltd., 1962.) In Harper's case, the birthmark appears on the left lower chest, in the milkline, of a child of seven. Harper relates such marks to supernumerary nipples, but this is only one possible explanation.

In 1972 his general health was good, although he was still susceptible to pain in the abdomen when under stress. As I listened again to his account of this symptom, it seemed to me that he was suffering, at these times, from gastric hyperacidity; he said that his abdominal pains were relieved by antacids.

He denied at this time any conscious aversion for knives such as he had had when younger and even into earlier adulthood. His wife, however, remarked that he never used a knife in eating. She had read the first edition of this book (of which I had given him a copy) and when she came to the passage in which I described his phobia for knives, she had spontaneously remarked on his failure to use a knife in eating. If anything on his plate of food required cutting he severed it with the edge of his fork, as I observed myself when we had a meal together. He was not aware of deliberately avoiding the use of a knife, but this habit may conceivably be the last trace of his former rather severe phobia of knives.

I examined again the birthmark on his abdomen. I found that it had become somewhat less prominent and paler than when I had seen it seven years before. (Even then, it had already faded, according to Mr. Pitnov, from its prominent appearance in his childhood.) It had, however, retained the diamond shape that I had observed before. Since he had put on some weight in the seven years between our last meeting and this one, I think this accounted for some distortion, as it now appeared to me, in the diamond shape of the birthmark. Nevertheless, the diamond shape was distinctly visible and appeared with some clarity on photographs I took of the birthmark.

The Case of Corliss Chotkin, Jr.

Summary of the Case. Victor Vincent, a full-blooded Tlingit, died in the spring of 1946 in Angoon. For the last years of his life he had felt especially close to his niece, Mrs. Corliss Chotkin, Sr., the daughter of his sister. He had often come to stay with his niece and her husband in Sitka and they had always made him feel welcome. On one of these visits, about a year before his death, Victor Vincent had said to his niece: "I'm coming back as your next son. I hope I don't stutter then as much as I do now. Your son will have these scars." He then pulled up his shirt and showed her a scar on his back. This scar was a residue of an operation he had had on his back some years earlier. It was distinctively a scar of an operation since the small round holes of the stitches remained visible. Mr. Vincent at the same time also pointed to a scar on his nose on the right side of its base as another mark by which his niece would recognize his rebirth. This scar had followed an operation at this site. In predicting his return Victor Vincent also told his niece: "I know I will have a good home. You won't be going off and getting drunk." In this he alluded to a number of alcoholics in his family. Victor Vincent believed that his deceased sister, Gertrude, the mother of Mrs. Corliss Chotkin, Sr., had been reborn as Mrs. Chotkin's daughter, Gertrude, Jr. (Gertrude, Jr. had given the family some evidence of paranormal knowledge of the life of her grandmother.) Mr. Vincent gave this as an additional reason for returning in the family of his niece, saying he wanted to grow up again with his sister.

About eighteen months after the death of Victor Vincent, Mrs. Corliss Chotkin, Sr. gave birth on December 15, 1947 to a boy named after his father, Corliss Chotkin, Jr. At birth this boy had two marks on his body of exactly the same shape and location as the scars pointed to by Victor Vincent in his prediction of his rebirth.

The mark at the root of the nose, said to have been originally at the same site exactly as the scar at the root of Victor Vincent's nose, had moved inferiorly until it lay on the right nares of Corliss Chotkin, Jr., who was fifteen in 1962. This mark, once a reddish color, then appeared only slightly more pigmented than the surrounding skin, and was definitely depressed.

The mark on the back of Corliss was much more characteristic of an operative scar. It was located about eight inches below the shoulder line and two inches to the right of the midline. It was heavily pigmented and raised. It extended about one inch in length and a quarter inch in width. Along its margins one could still easily discern several small round marks outside the main scar. Four of these on one side lined up like the stitch wounds of surgical operations. On the other side the alignment was less definite. This mark also had moved (downward) since the birth of Corliss. Moreover, it had become much more heavily pigmented since Corliss' birth. Mrs. Chotkin attributed this latter change to the frequent scratching of the mark by Corliss, who complained of much itching in the region of the mark. His scratching apparently led to inflammation and some distortion of the shape of the mark as well as to the increased pigmentation.

As already mentioned, his family noticed the marks on Corliss at his birth. This observation, however, did not lead to his being named after his uncle and instead he received his father's name.

When Corliss became able to talk, members of his family tried to instruct him in saying his name when he was asked for it. One day when he was thirteen months old and his mother applied herself to this task and was pressing the boy to say his name, he impetuously declared: "Don't you know me? I'm Kahkody." The latter name was the tribal name of Victor Vincent and the boy uttered it with an excellent Tlingit accent. When Mrs. Chotkin's aunt heard of this remark, she said that it tied in with a dream she had had. She had dreamed shortly before the birth of Corliss that Victor Vincent was coming to live with the Chotkins. Mrs. Chotkin is certain she did not tell her aunt about Victor Vincent's prediction of his return before she heard from her aunt about this dream. Mrs. Chotkin herself had expected to have such a dream, but did not. The spontaneous utterance of his uncle's name by Corliss led to his being given the uncle's tribal name which he had spoken.

When Corliss was two and being wheeled along the street in Sitka by his mother, he spontaneously recognized a stepdaughter of Victor Vincent, and called her correctly by her name, Susie. He showed great excitement on seeing her and, jumping up and down, said: "There's my Susie." This recognition took place at the docks in Sitka. Mrs. Chotkin happened to be there with her son and an older foster son (four years older than Corliss). They were not there to meet Susie and neither Mrs. Chotkin nor her foster son had noticed Susie when Corliss recognized her. After the first recognition, Corliss hugged Susie affectionately and also spoke her Tlingit name. He kept repeating: "My Susie."

When Corliss was still two he recognized William, the son of Victor Vincent. This man had come on a visit to Sitka unknown to Mrs. Chotkin and, as with Susie, Corliss spotted him spontaneously on the street and said: "There is William, my son."

When Corliss was three he recognized the widow of Victor Vincent. His mother had taken him with her to a large meeting of Tlingits which this lady happened to attend. Again Corliss picked her out of the crowd (before Mrs. Chotkin had seen her) and said "That's the old lady," and "There's Rose." Rose was the correct name of Victor Vincent's widow, and he had always referred to her familiarly as "the old lady."

On another occasion, Corliss recognized a friend of Victor Vincent, Mrs. Alice Roberts, who happened to be in Sitka and was walking past the Chotkins' house where Corliss was playing in the street. As she went by he called her correctly by her name, a pet name. In a similar way and quite spontaneously he recognized three other friends of Victor Vincent. On one of these occasions his mother was again not with him; he was alone on the street with the person in question as he had been when he recognized Mrs. Roberts. On the other two occasions his mother was with him when he accosted the persons he seemed to recognize. However, on these occasions he merely showed unusual (and for a child quite inappropriate) familiarity with these persons, who were friends of Victor Vincent from Angoon. Mrs. Chotkin stated that Corliss had recognized still other persons known to Victor Vincent and correctly called them by their tribal names, but she could not recall the details of these recognitions. All the recognitions by Corliss occurred by the time he had reached six years of age.

Corliss correctly narrated two episodes in the life of Victor Vincent about which his mother thinks he could not have acquired knowledge normally. Once he described in some detail an experience of Victor Vincent when fishing. His engine had broken down and his boat was helpless in one of the numerous and hazardous channels of southeastern Alaska. Victor Vincent changed into the uniform of the Salvation Army (in which he was a part-time worker) and rowed in a small boat to attract the attention of a passing ship, the *North Star*. (He put on the uniform of the Salvation Army to attract attention to himself; crews of passing ships might otherwise have passed by an ordinary Tlingit fisherman.) He asked its crew to deliver a message for him. Mrs. Chotkin had heard this story narrated by Victor Vincent himself when alive. She was certain Corliss had not heard the story from her or her husband before he narrated it to them one day in circumstantial and accurate detail.

On another occasion, Mrs. Chotkin and Corliss were at the home formerly occupied by Mrs. Chotkin and her family during the life of Victor Vincent. The boy pointed out a room in the building and said: "When the old lady and I used to visit you, we slept in that bedroom there." This remark seemed all the more extraordinary since the building, which had formerly been a residence, had by that time been given over to other purposes and no rooms in it could be easily recognized as bedrooms. But the room he indicated had in fact been occupied by Victor Vincent and his wife when they had visited the Chotkins.

About the age of nine, Corliss began to make fewer statements about a previous life. At the time of my interviews in 1962, when he was fifteen years old, he said he remembered nothing of the previous life.

Certain features of behavior in Corliss have impressed Mrs. Chotkin as resembling closely traits in her uncle Victor Vincent. Under this heading Mrs. Chotkin drew attention to the way Corliss combed his hair forward over his forehead in a manner exactly corresponding to the style adopted by Victor Vincent and exactly opposite to what she herself had urged on her son!

Victor Vincent stuttered severely and, as already mentioned, expressed a wish to stutter less upon his rebirth. Corliss had a severe stutter when young and it persisted until he received some speech therapy for this when he was about ten. He did not stutter at the time of my interviews.

Victor Vincent was a devoutly religious man who tried to follow the precepts of Jesus and joined the Salvation Army in which he worked industriously. Corliss showed similar devoutness and had expressed a wish to attend Bible school.

Victor Vincent enjoyed boats and living on the water. He would rather have lived on water than on land. He was skillful with boats and their engines. Corliss had a similar fondness for the water and had expressed a wish to live roaming in a boat. He also had a precocious aptitude for handling and repairing engines. He taught himself how to run boat engines without lessons. It was unlikely that he inherited this skill from his father since his father had no aptitude for engines, and Corliss easily re-paired a broken engine which his father could not mend.

Victor Vincent, according to his niece, Corliss' mother, was left-handed. So was Corliss, at least when a small child. At school a teacher more or less forced him to write with his right hand and he learned to do so. He also learned to throw a ball with either hand but preferred the right hand by the time he was seventeen years old. His mother said that at that age he still favored his left hand in chopping wood or in hitting someone in a fight. Corliss' mother and his only full sibling, a sister, were right-handed, but two of his maternal uncles were left-handed.

On the question of the congenital origin of the marks on the nose and back of Corliss, I obtained the testimony of his father, Corliss Chotkin, Sr. He stated that the marks were present at the boy's birth and I think we can take his statement as definitely confirming the fact that these marks were congenital and not acquired post-natally. Mr. Chotkin, Sr., although he had met Mr. Victor Vincent many times (the latter stayed in their house on numerous occasions), could not recall either of the scars on Mr. Vincent to which the latter had drawn attention when he predicted his rebirth. The scar on Mr. Vincent's back would not ordinarily be visible. That on his nose would be visible, but was evidently small (as was the mark on Corliss' nose) and perhaps not easily noticed or remembered unless attention were drawn to it. However, one of Victor Vincent's friends, the Rev. William Potts, did confirm the existence on Victor Vincent of a scar at the right upper corner of his nose, the result of an operation there. An official report sent to me from the U.S. Public Health Service Hospital in Seattle, where one informant said Victor Vincent had spent some time, stated that he had had there an operation for the removal of the right tear sac (dacryo-cystectomy) in 1938. The incision and scar for this operation would be at exactly the location between the right eye and base of the nose pointed out to me by the Rev. William Potts at the site of the operation on Victor Vincent and by Mrs. Chotkin as the site at birth of one of the two birth-marks of Corliss.

Mr. Chotkin, Sr. did not recall the prediction made by Victor Vincent to his wife in his house. This need not surprise us since the conversations between Mrs. Chotkin and her uncle often took place in Tlingit, which Mr. Chotkin did not understand. Moreover, Mr. Chotkin (of Anglo-Saxon extraction) affected little interest in the Tlingit customs and beliefs and seemed to have given scant attention to the relations of his wife with her relatives.

My efforts to obtain some corroborating information about an operation on Mr. Vincent's back included writing to the U.S. Public Health Service Hospital in Seattle. This hospital sent me a summary of a second admission in 1940 of Mr. Vincent. At that time he was found to have moderately advanced pulmonary tuberculosis of the right apex. No operation of any kind was recorded for that admission. It seems quite possible, however, that later Mr. Vincent did develop a right-sided pleurisy or abscess which required drainage.

I interviewed a number of persons who had known Victor Vincent, but none of them had heard of his intention to return as Mrs. Chotkin's son. But, as one of his male friends pointed out to me, he would probably not have verbalized this intention except to people of his own tribe. He may well not have told anyone but Mrs. Chotkin; or others who had heard might have paid little attention and forgotten in the intervening eighteen years before my inquiries.

When I interviewed Mrs. Chotkin's aunt with regard to the dream she was reported to have had concerning the return of Victor Vincent, I found that lady, who was ninety years old, showing serious evidence of impairment of memory. She could recall nothing of the dream. Since she dilated on the pitiful decline of interest in reincarnation among the younger generation of Tlingits, it would seem likely that her forgetfulness of this dream, if she had it, resulted from organic brain disease and not from lack of interest which seems the more probable explanation for the ignorance of Mr. Chotkin, Sr. about the case.

Unfortunately, many of the witnesses of the recognitions by Corliss, Jr. of people known to Victor Vincent were dead or unavailable. I could interview only one of the persons Corliss had recognized clearly by name. According to Mrs. Chotkin, Corliss had called her by her first name as she walked by the house. He was then a little over two years old. This person, a schoolteacher, did not recall that Corliss had ever recognized her when he was a small boy. She did, however, state that she used to walk by the house in which the Chotkins lived on her way to work. Small children did call her by her name from time to time and if one did so she would not necessarily pay attention. They usually, however, called her by her last name, seldom by her first one.

Two other witnesses were participants only with regard to the familiar behavior of Corliss; that is, he had (according to Mrs. Chotkin) recognized them by behaving in an unusually friendly way for a Tlingit child with a strange adult. Here again, the mother of the child might notice such behavior more than the other person concerned; in addition, these two witnesses were elderly and both showed a tendency to wandering of the mind. So these circumstances made me conclude that their failure to remember the alleged episodes of recognition did not necessarily discredit Mrs. Chotkin's account.

I must, however, mention that several informants did throw doubts on the reliability of Mrs. Chotkin as a witness, alleging to me that she had a tendency to embellish and even to invent stories. None of these critics challenged any particular point of the present case; they cast only general aspersions. (My informants in Alaska impugned no other witness during my visits there.) During further inquiries, I learned from still other witnesses that they had confidence in Mrs. Chotkin's accuracy as a reporter of events. And from other evidence it seemed to me possible that certain personal animosities had influenced opinion about Mrs. Chotkin and perhaps made some of my informants unreliable witnesses about her. Nevertheless, I took extra pains to check her account as far as I could with independent corroboration.

On my third visit to Alaska in 1963 I asked her to repeat the whole account for me, which she did. Although she gave a somewhat condensed account of the case and omitted some earlier details (while including a few minor items not mentioned before), her second account was in the main entirely similar to the first one which I had heard nine months earlier. The only major discrepancy occurred in her recollection of a date. Moreover, Mrs. Chotkin volunteered to furnish me with the names of other informants or witnesses who she thought could corroborate her account in various particulars. Her behavior in this respect did not seem that of someone trying to conceal a fraud. Her daughter, seven years older than Corliss, knew nothing about the case. This seemed a strange circumstance at first, but on reflection seems to speak for the genuineness of Mrs. Chotkin's account. Mrs. Chotkin's explanation is that she herself was slow to put the various events of the case together and to reach the conviction she held that her uncle was reborn as her son. Accordingly she did not speak of the matter much or at all with others at the time the events occurred. She apparently had spoken of Corliss' behavior with very few people, if any, up until the time Mr. George Hall's inquiries on my behalf induced her to tell him and me about it. And the fact that her own daughter (and some other witnesses I interviewed) did not know anything about the case until my inquiries certainly testifies to the fact that Mrs. Chotkin was not exploiting the case in the community for her own benefit in any way.

I could check some twenty-one items of details related to the case narrated by Mrs. Chotkin. For these I obtained corroboration from independent sources for sixteen items and failed to do so for five items. Of these five I have already discussed three above, these being instances of reported recognitions which other persons might not have noticed or remembered. And the same explanation might account for the failure of corroboration of the other two items not corroborated. However, I did discover that in connection with two other matters connected with other cases, Mrs. Chotkin gave information noticeably discrepant from that of other witnesses. For both the existence of a scar on the nose of Victor Vincent and a birthmark on the nose of Corliss at the same location, I obtained confirmation from other witnesses. On balance, then, I accept Mrs. Chotkin's account as reliable in its main features, although acknowledging the possibility that she may have elaborated (I think unconsciously) some of the details.

Comments. I think we should regard as established (by the corroboration of the other witnesses) Mrs. Chotkin's statement that a birthmark on the nose of Corliss Chotkin, Jr. corresponded to a scar at the same location on Victor Vincent. And it seems likely that the other birthmark (on his back) also corresponded to a scar on the back of Victor Vincent. We have then to account somehow for (*a*) the occurrence on Corliss' body of these unusual marks, and (*b*) the other features of the case which indicate that he clearly identified himself with his deceased maternal uncle.

Unlike the moles in the case of William George, Jr., we cannot explain the birthmarks of Corliss Chotkin, Jr. on the basis of heredity for three reasons. First, the marks did not resemble moles or naevi in appearance. The rather heavily pigmented mark on his back could have some resemblance to a naevus, but it was elongated rather than round, much longer than ordinary naevi I have seen, and it had in addition the peripheral marks already described which suggested stitch marks. In addition, Mrs. Chotkin asserted that when Corliss was born the mark was reddish only and lacked the heavy pigmentation it later developed. Mr. Chotkin also said it originally looked like "a small scar." Secondly, although Corliss was the nephew of Victor Vincent, he was not a direct descendant of Mr. Vincent. Thirdly, the marks allegedly reproduced on Corliss were on Victor Vincent the results of surgical operations and therefore acquired and not congenital with him. No one else in the family, according to Mrs. Chotkin, had any marks in the locations of those on Corliss.

Since the marks were definitely congenital and not hereditary, then they can have had only one of two origins. Either they arose from some intrauterine influence or from some other influence put into play before conception. But we cannot conceive of any intrauterine accident during gestation which would lead to the occurrence of a birthmark resembling the scar of a surgical wound with stitch marks along the side. The occurrence of this birthmark seems better accounted for by supposing the influence on the developing body of Corliss, Jr. of some mind. And since the birthmarks on his body when he was born corresponded (one definitely and the other probably) with the acquired scars of Victor Vincent which he had shown when predicting his rebirth, then I would think this evidence that the influence on the embryonic body of Corliss came from the deceased mind of Victor Vincent. An alternative source of the presumed psychokinetic influence would be Mrs. Chotkin herself, supposing that her wish to have her uncle return as her child was accompanied by the power to reproduce his body down to his scars.

We come next to the fact that although Mr. and Mrs. Chotkin noticed the birthmarks on Corliss, they did not regard these as conclusive evidence of the rebirth of Victor Vincent. Unlike Mr. and Mrs. Reginald George, they did not give his uncle's Tlingit name to Corliss until he said that name himself when he was thirteen months old. It would seem then that Mr. Chotkin, Sr. was uninterested and Mrs. Chotkin was at first skeptical on the question whether Victor Vincent had been reborn as her son. These circumstances make it less likely, although by no means impossible, that she imposed on Corliss an identification with her deceased uncle.

But supposing she did impose this identification on her son, we must then ask ourselves how far her influence could go in enabling the boy to acquire information known to Victor Vincent without realizing that she was passing it along to him. We must recall here that, of the seven recognitions reported as achieved by the boy, two occurred when his mother was not with him and the others occurred entirely spontaneously. No hint or suggestion was given to the boy that he should recognize someone. He called out the recognition in three cases before his mother had even seen the people he was recognizing. All this, if we believe the account of Mrs. Chotkin, implies that Corliss had somehow stored up a large body of information on the life of Victor Vincent and that he then called on this information in making his identifications of the seven relatives and friends of Victor Vincent he correctly named or behaviorally recognized. To have recognized these seven people correctly without having previously known them, he would surely have needed to retain a great deal of information about highly specific features of their faces, manners, and other appearances and behavior.

It is possible to suppose that Corliss obtained the information necessary for the recognitions he accomplished from the people he recognized by extrasensory perception. On this supposition each of them communicated to him, sometimes before they had seen him, some information about who he or she was in the life of Victor Vincent. But this theory fails to account for the fact that the recognitions were appropriate for the relationships of Victor Vincent. Why should the child recognize various people only from the point of view of Victor Vincent? Extrasensory perception does not account for the *pattern* of the recognitions. Nor does it explain the accompanying behavioral features, e.g., the enthusiasm of the child on seeing the various friends and relatives of Victor Vincent. But both the pattern of the recognitions and the accompanying behavioral features become understandable if we suppose that the mind of Victor Vincent somehow participated in these recognitions.

In summary, we can try to explain the boy's behavior by supposing that Mrs. Chotkin identified the birthmarks with the scars she had seen on Victor Vincent and then imposed an identification with his great-uncle on her son. But this does not explain how birthmarks of this shape, appearance, and location occurred in the first place. And we can explain the recognitions by imagining that Mrs. Chotkin tutored her son to recognize the various relatives and friends of her uncle. But we have to suppose that she did this unconsciously, unless we say that she was lying, for which no obvious motive has appeared. (She seemed to have obtained from the story no benefit whatever which could furnish a motive for concocting or even elaborating it.) If we think that unconscious tutoring by Mrs. Chotkin does not plausibly account for the boy's recognitions, then we must suppose that he somehow had access to the mind of Victor Vincent, that mind being either still discarnate, and "possessing" him, or reincarnated and continuous with his own personality. To these alternative possibilities I shall return in the General Discussion.

The Later Development of Corliss Chotkin, Jr. I met Corliss and his family in August, 1965, and not again until May, 1972. At that time I visited them in Sitka and had a long talk with his parents and a shorter one with Corliss himself. We discussed his further development and residual traces of the previous life in his memories and behavior. Corliss, who was born on December 15, 1947, was then in his twenty-fifth year.

Corliss had continued in high school up to the age of nineteen when he was in the eleventh grade. He had failed one year and was doing work of failing quality in his junior year. He had apparently planned to leave school and join the Navy, but before he could do this, he was drafted into the Army.

He then spent about two years in the Army in (approximately) 1968–70. During this period he was in Asia for a year and saw service in the artillery in Vietnam. An enemy shell made a direct hit on his gun, but he somehow survived this with only severe damage to one ear and lesser damage to the other. He was sent to Japan for treatment and convalescence where he passed a month in an Army hospital. He was left with what seemed to be permanent impairment of hearing in one ear and some loss in the other one. He also had an increased sensitivity to noise. Apart from this, his health was good.

After discharge from the Army, Corliss did not return to high school and in 1972 had no immediate plans for completing his education. He was then working as a semi-skilled laborer in a pulp mill on the outskirts of Sitka.

Corliss' mother said he never talked spontaneously about the previous life and that when the subject came up "he just kind of laughs about it." When I asked Corliss himself about the persistence of any imaged memories of the previous life, he said he had none. All he could remember was an event of his childhood when some old Tlingit ladies had called him "Kahkody," the tribal name by which Victor Vincent had been known and which Corliss had claimed for himself when he was a small child. In my presence, however, Corliss did *not* laugh about the subject of the previous life when it was discussed, but showed a serious interest in the matter.

Of the several behavioral traits in which Corliss showed correspondences with similar ones in Victor Vincent I was able to obtain some information about three.

His father said that he continued to have a strong interest in engines of all kinds.

In the first edition of this book I stated that Corliss had (by 1965) lost the stuttering he showed in early childhood. (Victor Vincent had expressed a wish to be reborn without the habit of stuttering by which he was severely afflicted.) It appeared in 1972 that Corliss had not in fact completely overcome the tendency to stuttering. This persisted to 1972, but only when he was excited or otherwise emotionally disturbed. His mother said that he stuttered very much less than Victor Vincent who "stuttered all the time." Corliss did not stutter at all during the hour that I spent with him in May, 1972. In this connection the remark of a man whom I met in Angoon (also in 1972) deserves mention. Victor Vincent had lived and died in Angoon and this informant had known him. I happened to mention the case of Corliss Chotkin, Jr. to him and he immediately asked, "Does he still stutter the way he did?" (Evidently Victor Vincent's stuttering was prominent enough to be closely tied to memories of him.) The answer, if the case is interpreted as one of reincarnation is: not nearly so much.

Victor Vincent was a devoutly religious person who had been active in missionary work and was a major in the Salvation Army. This interest was also remembered by those who knew him and once when I inquired about him from an older Tlingit, he specified: "Oh, do you mean the Salvation Army Major?" Corliss was interested in religion during his childhood and continued so in adolescence. His interest in religion became much attenuated by his experiences in Vietnam, and it appears that the widespread abuse of drugs and other miseries of the war were attributed in his mind to failures or weaknesses of religion. After he returned to Sitka he had a personal experience of a distressing kind with active members of a religious group there. This revolted him so much that he turned completely away from formal religion.

In 1972 I again examined the birthmarks on Corliss' nose and back. That on his nose (on the right nares) seemed to me to have become somewhat less prominent since 1965 and was barely visible. The birthmark on his back had continued to itch after 1965 and Corliss had continued to scratch it with subsequent irritation and a suspicic. or danger of malignant change in the affected tissues. Consequently he was advised to have it removed surgically and this was done about 1969. So in 1972 I could only see at this site the scar of the operation for excision of the birthmark. This had healed well.

VI

A Case
Suggestive of Reincarnation
in Lebanon

Introduction

IN THE majority of cases suggestive of reincarnation so far investigated, a regrettable delay has occurred between the development of the main events of the cases and the arrival on the scene of an independent observer. The latter, consequently, has usually to reconstruct as best he can events which happened months and sometimes years before. In accomplishing this, he has to work against two important sources of error: First, with the simple passage of time, an important loss of detail in memories of the events occurs in the witnesses; secondly, after a meeting of the two families concerned in such cases—that of the present personality and that in which he claims to have lived before—some fusion of accounts may occur. For example, the first family may erroneously report the child to have made one or some statements appropriate for the previous personality, whose life they now know something about, but which the child did not, in fact, say. The witnesses have simply imported such details into their accounts of what he said, perhaps out of an unconscious wish to have the child's statements match the details of the life of the previous personality. I do not think such errors occur very often and I believe that a careful cross-questioning of witnesses and checking of what one witness says against the account of the same events by other witnesses goes far toward reducing them. Nevertheless, one can never enjoy complete confidence in having eliminated such errors altogether or know to what extent they may have contributed in a particular case to making it seem more deserving of a paranormal interpretation than it is.

In a small number of cases already studied, written accounts of the child's statements have recorded in detail just what he said before any attempt at verification. Moreover, in some of these cases independent investigators carried out the verification so that motivated errors on the part of the families became greatly reduced or eliminated altogether.[1] Nevertheless,

---

[1] Among such cases with written records of apparent memories made prior to verification we should note the following: Case of Prabhu. R. B. S. Sunderlal. "Cas apparents de réminiscences de vies antérieures." *Revue Métapsychique*, July–August, 1924, 302–305; Case of Jagdish Chandra. K. K. N. Sahay. *Reincarnation: Verified Cases of Rebirth After Death*. Bareilly,

such cases remain extremely few compared to the total number of all cases suggestive of reincarnation now in my collection. In most of these only a delayed investigation occurred.

On a visit to Lebanon in March, 1964, I happened to find a case in which the two families concerned had not yet met. Seizing this opportunity, and exploiting the very full cooperation extended me by both families as the case developed further, I spent a week (during two visits) on its investigation. I wrote down in advance of verification nearly everything that the child had stated about his claimed previous life before attempting verification in the village where he claimed to have lived. (A few details came out after the verification began and have been noted separately.) I also had an opportunity to observe the behavior of the boy in his own family and with members of the previous family when we took him to the other village to learn whether he would recognize people and places there.

The Belief in Reincarnation Among the Druses

Before presenting the details of the case, I shall introduce the reader briefly to the religious beliefs of the Druse people.[2] The Druse (sometimes spelled Druze) religion began with the assertions of the Fatimid Islamic Caliph al-Hakim, who destroyed the Church of the Holy Sepulchre in Jerusalem, declared himself a vehicle of God's word in 1017 A.D., and several years later (in 1021) mysteriously disappeared. Al-Hakim's successors in the Caliphate persecuted his followers, but some managed to survive and develop the new religion. It became established particularly in parts of the present countries of Syria and Lebanon. The name Druse (probably) derives from that of al-Darazi, who was one of the early missionaries of the new religion in Syria. The neighboring Muslim sects and members of other

India, ca. 1927; Case of Vishwa Nath. K. K. N. Sahay. *Op. cit.;* also published with further details in I. Stevenson. "Some New Cases Suggestive of Reincarnation. II. The Case of Bishen Chand." *Journal* A.S.P.R. Vol. 66, October, 1972, 375–400; Case of Swarnlata. Reported on pp. 67–91 of this monograph. The preceding cases received verifications of the child's declarations by persons outside the families concerned. I may mention also: The case of Herr Georg Neidhart of Munich, who recorded in advance of verification what he seemed to recall of a previous life; he himself, however, carried out the verifications. See his account of his own experience included in: G. Neidhart. *"Werden Wir Wieder Geboren?"* München: Gemeinschaft für religiöse und geistige Erneuerung e.V. 1956. . . ." Several additional cases of this rare, but valuable type are now (1973) under investigation and reports of three of them will be included in I. Stevenson. *Cases of the Reincarnation Type.* In preparation.

[2] For further information about the religion of the Druses see: J. Nantet. *Histoire du Liban.* Paris: Les Editions de Minuit. 1963; . L. Dietrich. "Die Lehre von der Reinkarnation im Islam." *Zeitschrift für Religions-und Geistesgeschichte,* Vol. 9, 1957, 129–149; P. K. Hitti. "The Origins of the Druse People and Religion with Extracts from Their Sacred Writings." *Columbia University Oriental Studies,* Vol. 28. New York: Columbia University Press, 1928. For a fuller exposition of the Druse belief in reincarnation and a much more extensive bibliography of the Druse religion see I. Stevenson. *Cases of the Reincarnation Type.* In preparation.

religions harassed the Druses severely and through the succeeding centuries they practiced their beliefs secretly. The theological deviations of the Druses from other Islamic sects seem so extreme to some observers that they sometimes consider the Druses to belong to a distinct religion and not to an Islamic sect. And this is the position of the Druses themselves.

As the religious persecutions of the Druses abated, they practiced their religion more and more openly. Some Druse leaders in Beirut assured me that today the religion lies entirely open and has no secret aspects whatever. Other Druses I met, especially in the villages, showed reserve on this point and insisted that some elements of the religion continued completely secret. In any case, the Druse ideas on reincarnation are not now secret and seem never to have been. Reincarnation forms a fundamental tenet of the Druse religion.[3] To it they have also attached some other auxiliary beliefs which they maintain quite firmly.

The Druses believe that rebirth occurs instantly after death.[4] A corollary of this belief attaches great importance to maintaining calm and peace in the surroundings of a dying man to facilitate a smooth transition into his next body. This waiting body has already developed during nine or so preceding months of gestation in some woman ready at that moment to deliver a baby. In the event of an apparent interval, such as occurred in the present case, between the death of one personality and the rebirth of another personality claiming to be the previous person reborn, the Druses uniformly insist that some other intervening life must have filled the apparently empty interval. If the child has no apparent memories of any such intermediate life they assume this life contained no noteworthy events or that something else interfered with the child's memory of that life.

When deaths exceed births in number, such as occurred during the numerous wars of the Druses, they suppose a waiting period and a waiting

---

[3] Some other Islamic sects besides the Druses believe in reincarnation, although most do not. The Islamic sects believing in reincarnation support their contentions by citing passages of the Koran which, like numerous passages in the Bible, lend themselves to an interpretation supporting such a belief. For example, "How disbelieve ye in Allah when ye were dead and He gave life to you! Then He will give you death, then life again, and then unto Him ye will return" (Surah. 2, Verse 28); and "And Allah hath caused you to grow as a growth from the earth, and afterwards He maketh you return thereto, and He will bring you forth again, a (new) forthbringing" (Surah. 71, Verses 17–18). M. M. Pickthall. *The Meaning of the Glorious Koran: An Explanatory Translation.* New York: The New American Library, 1953.

[4] So far as I know, the Jains of India and some Tibetan Buddhists are the only other groups believing in reincarnation whose members also believe in immediate rebirth after death. All other groups believing in reincarnation "permit" in their beliefs a varying interval of time between death and rebirth. They often differ greatly, however, in other details of belief such as the circumstances of the person between terrestrial lives and the forces governing his return to another terrestrial life after his "intermission." The Jain belief differs from that of the Druses in that the Jains believe the soul of a dying person goes immediately to a newly conceived body, which is then born after the usual period of gestation. In contrast, the Druses believe that the soul of the dying person goes to the body of a baby born at that very instant.

place where Druse souls can be reborn in available physical bodies. This place is sometimes said to be in China. After the wars, the women again bear more children and births exceed deaths for a time. In no circumstances do the Druses admit any interval between a death and rebirth. They also believe, or did believe, that the Druses constitute a specially appointed people—almost a race apart—whose numbers God intended to keep constant. Formerly, they severely punished desertions from the sect and would not permit entrance into it from other sects. Some relaxation in these rules has occurred in recent times.

Today the Druses live in Lebanon, southwestern Syria (especially in a mountainous plateau called the Djebel Druse), northern Israel, and the adjoining sections of Jordan. In the Djebel Druse entire villages contain Druses only, but in Lebanon and Israel the Druse people live together with other Muslims and Christians. In such villages one or other religion may preponderate so that one can find villages with Druse majorities and Druse minorities. Within the villages some residential segregation into different quarters may occur along religious lines. The total Druse population of all four countries today probably numbers between 150,000 and 200,000.[5] Along with other people of the area, many Druses, especially of Lebanon, have emigrated, particularly to Brazil and the United States. Probably about a thousand Druses live in the United States today.

Once isolated in the mountains and fiercely separatist, the Druses have long since come into Beirut, Haifa, and other leading cities of their original area. There they have entered fully into the commercial, professional, and political life of the countries they now belong to. In Beirut one cannot distinguish most Druses from other people by any distinction of dress or behavior. In the mountain villages, the Druses still often practice some distinctions of clothing (women, for example, wearing black dresses and white head shawls) and of behavior, especially in the withdrawal of women from most ordinary social intercourse with strangers.

From my interviews with various members of the Druse religion, I gained the impression that the belief in reincarnation persists among them as strongly today as ever. I should say, however, that interest in the subject has perhaps diminished, especially among the Druses in the large cosmopolitan city of Beirut. Moreover, individual persons may express considerable skepticism about particular cases and it would be quite inaccurate to believe that anyone's claim to remember a previous life receives automatic credence from the people around him. On the contrary, individual cases often encounter a rather severe scrutiny, especially as regards the capacity

[5] In 1969 Hirschberg estimated the Druses of the Middle East to number approximately 300,000. (H. Z. Hirschberg. "The Druzes." in A. J. Arberry, *Religion in the Middle East: Three Religions in Concord and Conflict.* Vol. 2. Islam. Cambridge: Cambridge University Press, 1969.

of the child concerned to make accurate, unassisted recognitions of the members of the previous family he claims to have lived with. On the whole, however, the culture favors claims to remember a previous life and parents rarely discourage the narration of such claims or apparent memories by their children. These circumstances form a contrast with some other groups believing in reincarnation. The culture of the Tlingits of Alaska, for example, today stands on the defensive against the encroachments of current Western attitudes toward science and religion.[6] The belief in reincarnation has greatly diminished among the younger generation of Tlingits, something far from the case among the Druses. In India and other parts of southern Asia the belief in reincarnation remains strong today, with some erosion occurring among the educated "Westernized" people, but negligibly affecting the beliefs of the other hundreds of millions of inhabitants. But in these countries, and also in south central Turkey, where numerous cases occur among Arab Muslims, the parents often strongly discourage the child from talking. At times they even punish him by such devices as filling his mouth with filth or soap. Since among most Druses the belief in reincarnation persists strongly without any defensive attitude toward other beliefs, and since parents have little or no objection to the claims made by children to remember a previous life, we find in Lebanon and Syria almost ideal conditions for the development of cases suggestive of reincarnation.[7] (I say nothing here about the merits of any such cases; I am merely speaking of an atmosphere which enables a child to say what he wants to say about such a topic.) And we should therefore feel no surprise that the incidence of cases among the Druses is perhaps the highest in the world.[8]

Case Report

The Case of Imad Elawar

Summary of the Case and its Investigation. During a visit of investigation which I made to Brazil in 1962, a young Portuguese-English interpreter, a

[6] For information about Tlingit ideas on reincarnation, see the section above on cases among the Tlingits and references cited in that section.

[7] Yet in the Djebel Druse of Syria I heard that the belief in reincarnation has declined somewhat even there, and that sometimes parents beat children to make them stop talking about previous lives.

[8] Above (Chapter V. pp. 224–225) I have offered an estimate of the incidence of *reported* cases suggestive of reincarnation among Tlingit Indians in Alaska as approximately one case for every 1,000 inhabitants. In a population of approximately 100,000 Muslim Arabs of south central Turkey I have found more than one hundred cases, which would also give an incidence of reported cases for that area of about one for every 1,000 inhabitants. Dr. S. Makarem of the American University of Beirut, a scholar of Islamic sects, who has made some investigations himself of cases of the rebirth type in Lebanon, expressed to me his confident belief that the incidence of cases among the Druses of Lebanese villages would reach at least one case for every 500 inhabitants.

native of Lebanon, helped me greatly and also expressed interest in my investigations. He told me that numerous cases of the kind which interested me, i.e., children who claim to remember a former life, occurred in his native village in Lebanon, Kornayel. He gave me a card with a note in Arabic to his brother in this village. With this card as my sole introduction I went out to the village of Kornayel on March 16, 1964. Upon investigation, I found that my Brazilian interpreter's brother had moved into Beirut for the winter, as do many people of the Lebanese villages in the much colder mountains east of the city. When I made my interest known to the people of whom we were asking the way, some of them immediately mentioned that a child of their group had been saying he remembered a previous life. It turned out that Mr. Mohammed Elawar, the father of this child, Imad Elawar, was a cousin of the man I was looking for and of my interpreter friend in Brazil. The family of Imad invited me to hear the details of his statements about his previous life.

On that evening, March 16, I therefore made written notes of all that Imad's father and mother told me about Imad's declarations, together with some corroborating or additional testimony from other relatives present at the interview. On that occasion, however, I had with me only a chauffeur who had a defective knowledge of French and English and who, which was much worse, showed a lack of careful attention to details. I therefore decided to employ trained guides, and for each of the following four days of this visit I had excellent interpreters. These interpreters, Mr. Clement Abushdid and Mr. Wadih Rabbath, both educated in the French schools of Beirut, spoke French fluently and English somewhat less well. It seemed likely we would have a safer range of technical words if we used French, so I spoke French with them throughout the investigation. Both interested themselves in the details of the case and paid careful attention, so far as I could tell, to providing me with accurate translations of what the informants said. The latter all spoke Arabic only, with the exception of one who spoke a little French.

In August, 1964, I returned to Lebanon to recheck the case and to try to develop additional evidence from the family of the previous personality from which the testimony had been confined in March to the statements of only one witness. On this occasion I had the capable assistance of Dr. Sami Makarem, a member of the Department of Arab Studies of the American University of Beirut, who acted as my interpreter during this visit. With him I rechecked about a quarter of the items stated in the testimony of the witnesses as to what Imad had said and done, and also interviewed several additional witnesses to the life of the previous personality of the case. Thus, for many of the items I had information coming through three different interpreters on different occasions, which permitted me to compare the translations with each other. Dr. Makarem's excellent knowledge of English and Arabic also permitted me to analyze and understand some discrepancies in the testimony which I shall comment on below. On this second visit to Lebanon, Mr. Wadih Rabbath again helped me as (French-Arabic) interpreter during one day.

At the first interview with the family of Imad, I learned that he was born on December 21, 1958. He was thus a little over five years of age at the time of my first visit. When he was between a year and a half and two years old he had begun to make references to a previous life. He had mentioned a considerable number of names of people and some events in this life, as well as various items of property he claimed to have owned. Sometimes he talked to himself about the people whose names he mentioned, asking himself out loud how these people were getting along. Apart from such musings to himself, his statements about the previous life came out at odd moments here and there when something seemed to stimulate such a statement. He also seemed to speak of these matters in his sleep. He was still making statements about the previous life at the time of my visits. Imad had given the name of the village (Khriby) where he claimed to have lived and of the family (Bouhamzy) he claimed to belong to; he had importuned his family to take him to Khriby.

Imad's father told me he himself had scolded Imad as a liar for telling such stories about another life. The boy then learned to avoid the subject with his father and consequently spoke mostly to his mother and paternal grandparents, who lived with Imad's father and mother.

One day a resident (Salim el Aschkar) of the village of Khriby, where Imad claimed to have lived, came to Kornayel and Imad, seeing him in the street, recognized him in the presence of his paternal grandmother. (For details of this recognition, see Tabulation 1, item 57.) This unexpected recognition increased the credibility for his parents of Imad's declarations about the previous life. But still his family took no steps to verify his statements. Somewhat later they happened to meet a woman from Maaser el Shouf, a village near Khriby, who had come to Kornayel to visit. She confirmed to Imad's parents that some people having the names mentioned by Imad did in fact live, or had lived, in Khriby. Finally, in December 1963, about three months before my visit, an announcement and invitation to the funeral of a prominent Druse of Khriby, Said Bouhamzy, reached Kornayel. An uncle of Imad's father, himself a prominent man in the Druse community, decided to attend this funeral and Imad's father, out of curiosity to learn what he could in Khriby, went along also. In Khriby he met some people who pointed out to him two men with names corresponding to two of those given by Imad. Even at this visit to Khriby, however, Mr. Mohammed Elawar did not actually meet any member of the family Imad claimed to have belonged to. This visit was, moreover, the first visit either he or his uncle had ever paid to Khriby. They furthermore denied all other acquaintance with anyone knowing the other family beyond those mentioned above.

Since Imad had mentioned a considerable number of names, his family had tried to fit these names into a pattern of family relationships. The first words he had ever spoken were "Jamileh" and "Mahmoud" and he had repeatedly mentioned Jamileh and compared her beauty to the lesser attractiveness of his own mother. He also spoke of an accident in which a truck had driven over a man, breaking both his legs and causing other injuries which led to his death shortly after the accident. Imad had spoken of a quarrel between the driver of the truck and the injured man and he was thought to believe that the driver had meant to kill the injured man by deliberately running over him with his truck. Imad had also spoken of a bus accident. He said that he belonged to the Bouhamzy family of Khriby. And he had further expressed a most unusual joy in being able to walk, saying over and over how happy he was that he could now walk.

His family had put all these statements together as follows. They believed that he was claiming to have been one Mahmoud Bouhamzy of Khriby who had a wife called Jamileh and who had been fatally injured by a truck after a quarrel with its driver. It turned out later that Imad had never actually said the fatal truck accident had happened to him; he had merely described it vividly. Nor had he specifically said that Jamileh was his wife; he had simply often referred to her. Imad's family had assigned other places in his "previous family" to some of the other people whose names he had mentioned. Thus they had assumed that two of the persons he had mentioned were "his" sons. They further made some other inferences which proved erroneous and the details of which I shall note in the summarizing tabulation and discussion below. Although I tried to learn exactly what Imad had himself said, his parents passed on to me as having been said by Imad some of these inferences which they themselves had made in their effort to find some coherent pattern in his statements. As it turned out, however, the errors of inference made by Imad's family add considerably to the evidence of their honesty and also to the improbability that they themselves could have provided a source or a channel for the information given by Imad.

After my first talk with Imad's family, I proposed to them that on the following day a small group of us should go with Imad himself to the village of Khriby to verify there, if possible, the statements Imad had already made and to observe whether he could recognize any people or places of that area. This they readily agreed to, and on March 17 I returned to Kornayel and had a second interview with the members of Imad's family with a new interpreter. The uneasiness which I already felt about the accuracy of the details I had recorded on the previous evening led me to go over all the main points again with the family and the qualified interpreter before we set out for Khriby. When we left for Khriby I had a corrected version of everything the parents could then remember that Imad had said about the previous life. On the way to Khriby, to which in the end only Imad and his father accompanied me and the interpreter, Imad made a few more statements about the previous life and his father also mentioned some additional items. All these I recorded in the car before we reached Khriby. Still a few other items came out later, after the verifications began, as Imad's family remembered some detail of his statements or behavior which they had earlier forgotten or omitted to mention. I have noted these various differences in the time of recording the data in Tabulation 1 below.

Before resuming the narrative of my inquiries, I shall offer a prefatory digression about the villages concerned and communications between them.

Relevant Facts of Geography and Possible Normal Means of Communication Between the Two Families. The village where Imad and his family lived, Kornayel, lies in the mountains about fifteen miles east of Beirut. The village of Khriby, where Imad claimed to have lived before, lies about twenty miles southeast of Beirut. The two villages are separated by fifteen miles of direct distance, but the extremely winding mountain road between them takes more than twenty-five miles. Both villages lie on moderately good, hard-surface roads with bus connections to Beirut. No regular direct traffic, however, links the two villages. Another village, Baadaran, which figures prominently in the testimony, lies near Khriby about three miles away.

The Druses have the custom of inviting members of other villages to attend funerals. The survivors of the deceased send around messengers to villages where members of their family may live, or have relatives by marriage, inviting them to the funeral. Only the members of another village having some connection with the deceased man's family would ordinarily be invited to such funerals, unless the deceased happened to be a person of unusual prominence. In that case the inhabitants of every village might receive invitations. As already mentioned, a more or less public invitation to the funeral of Said Bouhamzy of Khriby in December, 1963, had instigated the first visit of Imad's father and great-uncle to Khriby. It seems most unlikely that any intercourse would occur between the two villages except for such funerals or occasional marriages between members of the villages. These details as to possibilities for contacts between the villages acquire importance in evaluating how Imad came to acquire the information that he demonstrated about the people and places of Khriby.

Searching for persons who might have some acquaintance with both families (although each of the families denied acquaintance with the other), I learned of the two persons already mentioned who knew something of the Bouhamzy family in the Khriby area and who had visited

Kornayel and met the Elawar family. I discovered one other person who knew both families and so will describe the details of his relationships with each as I learned them.

Mr. Kassim Elawar, paternal grandfather of Imad, had a third cousin, Mr. Faris Amin Elawar, who had heard of a bus accident corresponding to an accident narrated by Imad. This accident occurred in the village of Baadaran, near Khriby (see item 23 of Tabulation 1 below). Mr. Faris Amin Elawar visited Baadaran from time to time on business and had some acquaintance, but not an intimate one, with the Bouhamzy family of that area. He also frequently visited the Elawar family in Kornayel. Imad's father was quite definite that Mr. Faris Amin Elawar had never mentioned the Bouhamzy family or the bus accident on any of his visits to the Elawar family. After my first visit to Kornayel in March, 1964, the Elawar family told Mr. Faris Amin Elawar about Imad's narrations of the bus accident and he was said to have confirmed the correspondence of various details with an actual accident occurring many years earlier in Baadaran. But he could not give them any verification of other matters spoken about by Imad concerning the previous life. Prior to March, 1964, the Elawar family had not mentioned any of Imad's statements about the previous life to Mr. Faris Amin Elawar. Mr. Faris Amin Elawar lived some of the time in Kornayel, but was away at the time of my visit and I could not interview him to learn further details of his knowledge of the Bouhamzy family.[9]

The First Visit to Khriby. On my first visit to Khriby on March 17, I interviewed two informants of the village, Mr. Kassim Mahmoud el Aschkar and Mr. Khalil Lateif. They had some acquaintance with the Bouhamzy family and verified that one Said Bouhamzy of Khriby had in fact died (in June, 1943) after being run over by a truck. This Said Bouhamzy was a friend of the Said Bouhamzy (also of Khriby) who died in December, 1963, as already mentioned. They also verified the existence of various people in the village with names corresponding to those given by Imad. They placed Jamileh, incorrectly as it turned out, as the wife of Mahmoud Bouhamzy (a relative of Said Bouhamzy) rather than as the wife of Said Bouhamzy, the man killed by the truck. For some other items, their testimony seemed deficient or inaccurate as checked against that of the son of Said Bouhamzy, whom I interviewed the following day. This informant, Mr. Haffez Bouhamzy, had gone into Beirut on the day of our first visit. The only other person I could interview on that occasion was Mr. Yousef el Halibi, an elderly gentleman bedridden for many years and with a very marked impairment of memory. He confirmed having been a friend of Said

[9] See, however, the report given later (pp. 315–316) of my interviews with Mr. Faris Amin Elawar and his son, Saleem, in 1968.

Bouhamzy, but could provide no other verifications of details in the narrations of Imad about the previous life. On this occasion Imad pointed correctly in the direction of the house he claimed to have lived in, and made a couple of other statements suggesting paranormal knowledge of the village, but did not meet any members of the Bouhamzy family.

The Second Visit to Khriby. On the following day, March 18, I returned to Khriby with Mr. Abushdid, who acted as interpreter, but without members of the Elawar family. Mr. Haffez Bouhamzy had returned to Khriby and provided me with much detailed information about the Bouhamzy family. I had learned the day before that not Mahmoud Bouhamzy but Said Bouhamzy had been the person killed by the truck. Now I heard two further complicating pieces of information. First, the Said Bouhamzy who was killed by the truck had had no connection with a woman called Jamileh; moreover, descriptive details of "his" house given by Imad did not pertain to the house of Said Bouhamzy in Khriby. Secondly, I learned that there already existed a claimant to be Said Bouhamzy reborn. This man, Sleimann Bouhamzy, had been born a few months after the death of Said Bouhamzy as the son of Said's sister, who had married a relative of the same name and lived in Syria in the Djebel Druse. Sleimann had visited Khriby when a young boy and had given evidence completely satisfying to the family of Said that he was in fact Said reborn. I shall later summarize this case briefly, because of its relevance in certain details to the case of Imad. Here I may say, however, that the investigation of the case of Imad encountered at first baffling complexities and on two occasions it seemed to dissolve into unrelated and irrelevant fragments: once when I learned that Mahmoud Bouhamzy had not been killed by a truck, and again when I learned that the life of Said Bouhamzy, who *had* been killed by a truck, did not match in other details the statements made by Imad. Moreover, someone else had already come forward as a claimant to be Said Bouhamzy reborn.

Mr. Haffez Bouhamzy, however, tried the fit of Imad's statements to other members of the family, e.g., Mahmoud Bouhamzy, and one Salim Bouhamzy, both residents of Khriby. Mahmoud Bouhamzy became disqualified because he was still alive; moreover, details of his house did not match the descriptions given by Imad. These details did match the house in which Salim Bouhamzy had lived and he had died before Imad's birth, but events in the life of the previous personality described by Imad did not fit the events in the life of Salim. However, *both* the description of the house *and* the events of the life described by Imad exactly fitted (with corrections for the parental inferences) the details of the house and life of one Ibrahim Bouhamzy, a cousin of Said Bouhamzy. Ibrahim Bouhamzy had lived in the same house as his uncle Salim Bouhamzy and not far (300 feet) from the house of Said Bouhamzy. In particular, Ibrahim had a beautiful mistress called Jamileh.[10] They had never married, but Jamileh married after Ibrahim's death and moved to another village. Ibrahim Bouhamzy had died of tuberculosis on September 18, 1949. The detailed list of items in Tabulation 1 below shows how closely the statements of Imad matched the related items in the life of Ibrahim Bouhamzy. Moreover, a remarkable correspondence occurred between several behavioral features shown by Imad and character traits of Ibrahim, as testified to by Mr. Haffez Bouhamzy.

I shall later review these behavioral features as a group, but here will mention again Imad's repeated expressions of pleasure over being able to walk. On March 18 I learned from Mr. Haffez Bouhamzy that the death after the truck accident of Ibrahim's friend and relative, Said Bouhamzy, which had occurred June 8, 1943, had much affected Ibrahim Bouhamzy. But this did not help me to understand why, if there was some relationship between the personality of Ibrahim and that of Imad, he (Imad) should express such joy in being able to walk. Ibrahim Bouhamzy, whose life seemed to match the declarations of Imad, had not had *his* legs broken. He had, in fact, died of tuberculosis as a young man of about twenty-five after spending about a year in a sanatorium. Some mention having been made of a malady in the back of Ibrahim, it occurred to me to ask the next day if Ibrahim had happened to have tuberculosis of the spine. Mr. Haffez Bouhamzy then stated that Ibrahim had had tuberculosis of the spine and had experienced great difficulty in walking during his illness. He said that Ibrahim had not been able to walk at all for the last two months of his life. In this pitiful state Ibrahim complained of being ill, seeming to sense some injustice in the fact that one so young and formerly so strong should be thus disabled. Mr. Haffez Bouhamzy once heard him declare that if God would heal him he would become a sheikh. Mr. Fuad Bouhamzy, brother of Ibrahim, when interviewed later, did not confirm Haffez' statement that Ibrahim had had tuberculosis of the spine or had been unable to walk. The tuberculosis affected his lungs and pericardium only, according to him. Ibrahim had been able to walk until shortly before his death, he said. He was, however, enfeebled and spent the last six months of his life in the hospital, much of this time being bedridden. He returned from the hospital to the family home just before he died.[11] Imad's joy in being "up and

---

[10] I have concealed the real name of Ibrahim's mistress behind the pseudonym "Jamileh" which, appropriately, means "beautiful girl" in Arabic.

[11] The marked discrepancy in the testimony of Mr. Haffez Bouhamzy and Mr. Fuad Bouhamzy concerning the last illness of Ibrahim Bouhamzy led me to discuss this with two of the interpreters. Unfortunately, they were present at different interviews. But it seems likely that the discrepancy about whether Ibrahim Bouhamzy was only bedridden or actually was unable to walk arose from a mistranslation probably occasioned by double meanings in other languages for an Arabic phrase. On the other hand, Mr. Wadih Rabbath recalled (as did my notes) that

around" (as he learned to walk) thus accorded with the last illness and attitudes of Ibrahim Bouhamzy.

The Third Visit to Khriby. After finally finding a person with details of life, attitudes, and property corresponding closely to those described or shown by Imad, it seemed important to observe whether Imad would make any recognitions of surviving members of the family of Ibrahim Bouhamzy or recognize the inside of the house in which Ibrahim Bouhamzy had lived and to which he was brought back to die just two days before his death. So on March 19 I returned to Kornayel and persuaded Mr. Mohammed Elawar to accompany me with Imad to Khriby again. Imad, I may mention, required no persuasion as he had been asking his parents for years to take him to Khriby and the proposal of another journey there illuminated his face with delighted smiles.

At Khriby, Imad became shy and even disturbed upon entering the home of Said Bouhamzy, where we went first. He showed no sign of recognizing any features of this house and failed to recognize any of several photographs of the family of Said Bouhamzy in a book which he was shown. He gradually relaxed, however, and while at this house did show very great interest in two caged partridges which he wanted to take home and would have taken if his father (or their owner!) had permitted. We then walked over to the nearby house of Ibrahim Bouhamzy. I had hoped to arrange for a serial presentation to the boy of members of Ibrahim's family under conditions which would exclude the passing of any hints or suggestions to him. Unfortunately, when we reached the house matters passed out of my control, because three ladies who resided elsewhere in the village appeared unexpectedly and took the boy with them around the house. They were the mother and sister of Ibrahim Bouhamzy and a neighbor. Under these circumstances, the interpreter and I followed the small group which included otherwise only Mr. Haffez Bouhamzy and Mr. Mohammed Elawar. The interpreter (on this day Mr. Wadih Rabbath) made every effort to monitor everything that was said to Imad as questions were put to him. He then reported the exchanges to me and I made notes on the spot. Imad made thirteen recognitions or further correct statements related to the life of Ibrahim Bouhamzy in this situation. For most of these Mr. Rabbath felt confident that he heard all the relevant exchanges between Imad and the women questioning him and that they had offered no hints or suggestions of the answer to him. For the remaining items, Mr. Rabbath was out of ear-

---

Mr. Haffez Bouhamzy had definitely said Ibrahim Bouhamzy had tuberculosis of the spine. On this point it seems almost certain that Mr. Fuad Bouhamzy would be the more reliable witness. He was Ibrahim's brother (Haffez was his cousin) and moreover he had had some medical training and worked in the Lebanese Army Medical Corps. These two witnesses gave concordant testimony on other matters for which they both furnished information.

shot (perhaps describing the just preceding item to me) and we only heard afterwards from the informants what Imad had said. I have indicated these differences in the observations in Tabulation 2 below.

The Visit to Raha, Syria. At the end of the third visit to Khriby I had related nearly all the names mentioned by Imad to persons known to Ibrahim Bouhamzy. But three names remained unplaced. These conveyed nothing to Mr. Haffez Bouhamzy. My informants attributed these names to the intermediate life which they insisted the personality of Ibrahim must have lived between his death in 1949 and the birth of Imad in 1958. They considered these names the traces of this intermediate life which was for them a certainty, not a hypothesis. But it seemed to me possible that these names also might have a place in the life of Ibrahim and that Sleimann Bouhamzy, who claimed to be Said Bouhamzy reborn, could perhaps provide information either out his stock of information as a nephew of Said Bouhamzy or from what he claimed to remember from the previous life of Said Bouhamzy himself. It also seemed important to learn more about his own claims to memories of a previous life even though he (born December 3, 1943) was by this time a grown man. Accordingly, on March 20 I went with Mr. Wadih Rabbath and Mr. Mohammed Elawar to the village of Raha in the Djebel Druse of Syria. This village lies southwest of Damascus in Syria and about ninety miles southeast of Beirut. The roads from Beirut and Damascus reach it in a rather roundabout way and by direct distance it lies only about thirty miles east of Khriby.

At Raha Sleimann Bouhamzy described to us what he remembered of his experience in seeming to remember the life of Said Bouhamzy. And he did contribute to the verification of Imad's statements. I shall return to his account in a later section of this report.

The Fourth Visit to Khriby and Environs. At the end of my stay in Lebanon in March, 1964, the verifications of the statements attributed to Imad Elawar had come largely from only one witness, Mr. Haffez Bouhamzy. Although I had met the sister and mother of Ibrahim Bouhamzy and they had participated, as I have already explained, in Imad's second visit to Khriby, I had not interviewed them. I had no reason to doubt Mr. Haffez Bouhamzy's testimony, but believed that I ought to check it against that of other witnesses. I therefore decided to return to Lebanon again and did so in August, 1964. On this occasion, in addition to rechecking some of the details with Imad's family in Kornayel, I returned to Khriby. There I was able to interview Mr. Nabih Bouhamzy (brother of Haffez Bouhamzy), who spoke English, Mr. Fuad Bouhamzy (brother of Ibrahim Bouhamzy), who spoke English and French, and (briefly) Ibrahim's sister, Mrs. Huda Bouhamzy. I also talked with some less important witnesses. These new witnesses corroborated, with the exception of some minor details, the testimony of Mr. Haffez Bouhamzy and also clarified some previously obscure or apparently discrepant items. A few completely new (i.e., previously untold) items of statements by Imad emerged and were verified on this last occasion also.

Persons Interviewed During the Investigation. In Kornayel I interviewed:

Imad Elawar

Mr. Mohammed Kassim Elawar, father of Imad

Mrs. Mohammed Kassim (Nassibeh) Elawar, mother of Imad

Mr. Ali Hussain Elawar, cousin of Mr. Mohammed Elawar

Mr. Kassim Elawar, paternal grandfather of Imad

Mrs. Naileh Elawar, paternal grandmother of Imad

Mr. Majeed Toufic Elawar, cousin of Imad's paternal grandfather

In Khriby I interviewed:

Mr. Haffez Bouhamzy, son of Said Bouhamzy and cousin of Ibrahim Bouhamzy

Mr. Nabih A. Bouhamzy, son of Said Bouhamzy and cousin of Ibrahim Bouhamzy

Mr. Fuad Bouhamzy, brother of Ibrahim Bouhamzy

Mrs. Huda Bouhamzy, sister of Ibrahim Bouhamzy (married to a person of the same name)

Mrs. Lateife Bouhamzy, mother of Ibrahim Bouhamzy

Mr. Kassim Mahmoud el Aschkar, neighbor of Ibrahim Bouhamzy

Mr. Khalil Lateif, neighbor and cousin of Ibrahim Bouhamzy

In Baadaran (near Khriby), I interviewed:

Mr. Yousef el Halibi, friend of Said Bouhamzy

Mr. Daukan el Halibi

Mr. Milhem Abouhassan, friend of Said Bouhamzy

Mr. Ali Mohammed Abouhassan, cousin of Milhem Abouhassan

In Raha, Djebel Druse, Syria, I interviewed:

Mr. Sleimann Bouhamzy, nephew of Said Bouhamzy

Mr. Assad Bouhamzy, father of Sleimann Bouhamzy

Verification of the Original Statements Made by Imad Elawar about the Life in Khriby. In the two tabulations below I have set out the details of all the statements made by Imad concerning his claimed previous life in Khriby, together with comments on the verifications of the statements or other aspects of them. Imad made nearly all these statements before we left Kornayel for Khriby on our first visit there, but a few came out on the way or later, and a few others his family only remembered later. I have noted these differences in the tabulation.

Of the fifty-seven items in the first tabulation, Imad made ten of the statements in the car on the way to Khriby, nearly all on the first visit to Khriby before we reached that village. But of these ten, three were incorrect. Of the remaining forty-seven items, Imad was wrong on only three items. It seems quite possible that under the excitement of the journey, and perhaps sensing some expectation of hearing more statements on our part, he mixed up images of the "previous life" and memories of his "present life." In any case, his "score" for this group of statements definitely fell below that for the forty-seven made before we left Khriby.

Statements and Recognitions Made by Imad Elawar in Khriby. On my first visit to Khriby, as already mentioned, Mr. Haffez Bouhamzy was unavailable and I did not go to either the house of Said Bouhamzy (now occupied by his son, Mr. Haffez Bouhamzy) or to that of Ibrahim Bouhamzy. Imad did make two statements on this occasion which indicated some recognition of the area. But he certainly did not positively identify the house of Ibrahim Bouhamzy, which we passed on the road. From a point beyond the house, looking back toward it across a small valley, someone asked Imad to show where "his" house was. He pointed in the general direction quite accurately. While pointing, Imad drew attention to a house with bright green shutters near, but not adjoining, the house of Ibrahim; Ibrahim's house, however, did not have green shutters. If Imad meant to indicate that the house with the green shutters was the house of the previous life, he was right about the general direction, but wrong about the exact house.

On this visit, we drove beyond Khriby to the next village of Baadaran, where Mr. Yousef el Halibi lived. On the way, Imad commented that this was the way to Baadaran. A sign at the edge of Baadaran announces the village, but we had barely left Khriby for the journey of three miles when Imad made his statement, so he could not have read this sign. Conceivably, however, he might have read some sign we had not noticed and he might also have overheard someone saying we would go to Baadaran in the hope of seeing Mr. el Halibi. I therefore do not consider this statement by Imad suggestive of any paranormal knowledge.

As already mentioned, on Imad's second visit to Khriby we went to the houses of Said Bouhamzy and Ibrahim Bouhamzy, which again Imad did not seem to recognize from the outside. Mr. Haffez Bouhamzy did not think this surprising as, according to him, the village had greatly changed in the fifteen years since the death of Ibrahim Bouhamzy, especially as regards the streets. Inside the courtyard and the house of Ibrahim Bouhamzy (which

Summary of Statements Made by Imad Before Arriving at Khriby

NOTE: Unless otherwise stated, Mr. and Mrs. Mohammed Elawar were singly or together the informants for all the statements made by Imad. However, for many of the statements one or several other members of the Elawar family, chiefly Imad's paternal grandparents, were present as vocal or tacit witnesses of the statement made by Imad's parents. For some items I have indicated the vagueness of Imad (or his parents) about a particular relationship by using quotation marks around the indicated relationship, e.g., "brother."

Item	Informants	Verification	Comments
1. His name was Bouhamzy and he lived in the village of Khriby.	Mohammed Elawar, father of Imad Nassibeh Elawar, mother of Imad	Haffez Bouhamzy, cousin of Ibrahim Bouhamzy	Several families of the name Bouhamzy lived in Khriby. There is another village called Khriby near Kornayel, but when asked about this, Imad said his village was "far away." Imad seems never to have mentioned the first name of "Ibrahim."
2. Mahmoud (name mentioned by Imad).		Haffez Bouhamzy Nabih Bouhamzy, cousin of Ibrahim Bouhamzy	Mahmoud Bouhamzy was an uncle of Ibrahim Bouhamzy.
3. He had a woman called Jamileh.		Haffez Bouhamzy Nabih Bouhamzy Fuad Bouhamzy, brother of Ibrahim Bouhamzy	The mistress of Ibrahim Bouhamzy was called Jamileh. Mr. Milhem Abuhassan gave discrepant testimony on this item, but he changed his statement on the item twice and boasted of an intimate knowledge of Ibrahim which was not supported by his answers to questions put to test this knowledge. Two other peripheral witnesses, not members of the family, also gave discrepant testimony about Jamileh's relationships.
4. Jamileh was beautiful.		Haffez Bouhamzy	Jamileh was famous in the district for her beauty. The opinion of Mr. Haffez Bouhamzy was supported by the testimony of a woman of the village, Maaser el Shouf, where Jamileh had lived, who had mentioned Jamileh's beauty to Mr. Mohammed Elawar. In a land of beautiful women like Lebanon, this detail may seem to lack specificity, but did not seem so to those who had known Jamileh.

Item	Informants	Comments
5. Jamileh dressed well and wore high heels.	Haffez Bouhamzy	Wearing high heels would distinguish a Druse woman in the villages. Even today this is unusual.
6. Jamileh wore red clothes. He would often buy her red things to wear.*	Haffez Bouhamzy	Mr. Haffez Bouhamzy remembered Jamileh as wearing a red scarf around her head.
7. He had a "brother" called Amin.	Haffez Bouhamzy Nabih Bouhamzy	Amin Bouhamzy was a close relative of Ibrahim Bouhamzy. Close relatives and good friends may be referred to as "brother." It is also possible that Imad's parents inferred the relationship of brother as they did that of son for other persons named by Imad. See comments on items below.
8. Amin lived at Tripoli.	Haffez Bouhamzy	Tripoli is a coastal town north of Beirut.
9. Amin worked in the court-house building in Tripoli.	Haffez Bouhamzy Nabih Bouhamzy	Amin was an official of the topographical bureau of the Lebanese government. His office was in the courthouse building of Tripoli. He was living, but had retired in 1964. An error of inference on the part of Imad's parents occurred here. They first stated that Imad had said Amin was a "judge" in Tripoli. Mr. Mohammed Elawar later said that Imad had actually only stated that Amin worked in the courthouse building and they had therefrom inferred that Amin was a judge.
10. There was someone called Mehibeh.	Nabih Bouhamzy Sleimann Bouhamzy, cousin of Ibrahim Bouhamzy (obtaining information from his mother, not directly interviewed by me)	Mehibeh was the cousin of Ibrahim Bouhamzy. Imad's parents had thought that Mehibeh was the daughter of the previous personality.

* This item not recorded in writing prior to its verification.

Item	Informants	Verification	Comments
11. He had a "son" called Adil.		Sleimann Bouhamzy Nabih Bouhamzy	Ibrahim had a cousin called Adil. Another error of inference on the part of Imad's parents. Imad, they later said, had mentioned "Adil" and "Talal" or "Talil" and they had assumed these were the sons of the previous life.
12. He had a "son" called Talil or Talal.		Haffez Bouhamzy Nabih Bouhamzy	Ibrahim had another cousin called Khalil. (Khalil as a relative of Ibrahim also verified by Sleimann Bouhamzy* and Mr. Assad Bouhamzy, father of Sleimann Bouhamzy.) See comment for item 11 as to the question of the relationship with Talil. The family of Imad could not recal precisely whether Imad had said "Talil" or "Talal." If the former, he could well have been trying to say "Khalil" of which the first consonant is gutteral and might be heard as a "T" sound. Imad's grandparents supported this supposition by mentioning that when he was first beginning to talk about the previous life, Imad had said he was from "Tliby" (Khriby) before he could pronounce the name of the village correctly.
13. He had a "brother" called Said.		Haffez Bouhamzy Nabih Bouhamzy	Ibrahim knew two persons called Said Bouhamzy. One, his cousin, was killed by a truck in 1943. The other, a friend, died in December 1963. (See comment for item 7.) At the time of the death of the second Said Bouhamzy in December, 1963, some inhabitants of Kornayel were invited to his funeral which was announced in Kornayel. (Imad had been talking about the previous life for several years before this event.) When Imad

...heard the news of the death of the second Said Bouhamzy he expressed great interest in the event.

Item	Informants	Comments
14. He had a "brother" called Toufic.	Haffez Bouhamzy	Toufic was a cousin of Ibrahim Bouhamzy. (See comment for item 7.)
15. He had a "son" called Salim.	Haffez Bouhamzy Nabih Bouhamzy	Ibrahim's uncle with whom he lived was called Salim Bouhamzy. (See comment for item 7.) Imad's parents afterwards said he had never specifically mentioned anyone as his "sons." They had inferred these relationships.
16. He had a "son" called Kemal.	Haffez Bouhamzy Nabih Bouhamzy	Kemal was a brother of Toufic and Khalil Bouhamzy, hence another cousin of Ibrahim Bouhamzy. (See comments for items 7 and 15.)
17. He had a "sister" called Huda.**	I met Huda Bouhamzy, sister of Ibrahim Bouhamzy, in Khriby. Kassim Elawar, paternal grandfather of Imad	Witnesses did not recall whether Imad had specifically used the word "sister" in mentioning Huda. But the informants made a correct inference about the relationship of the person mentioned to the previous personality. Possibly they were helped because when a sister was born, Imad asked the family to name this baby Huda.
18. He had a friend called Yousef el Halibi.	Not verified, but probable.	Yousef el Halibi was still living in 1964 and recalled his friendship with Said Bouhamzy. Probably he was a friend of Ibrahim Bouhamzy also, but this was not specifically verified. Mr. Fuad Bouhamzy said he knew Yousef el Halibi, so it is probable his brother Ibrahim also knew him.

* Sleimann Bouhamzy verifying as from his claimed remembrance of the life of Said Bouhamzy.
** This item not recorded in writing prior to its verification.

Item	Informants	Verification	Comments
19. He had a friend called Ahmed el Halibi.		Not independently verified, but see Comment.	Not verified independently. In August, 1964, Mr. Mohammed Elawar told me that the son of Mr. Yousef el Halibi had confirmed in March that his father had a brother called Ahmed el Halibi; but I did not hear this interpreted at the time.
20. A truck ran over a man, broke both his legs, and crushed his trunk.		Haffez Bouhamzy Fuad Bouhamzy Sleimann Bouhamzy *	True of Said Bouhamzy whose accident and death were known to Ibrahim Bouhamzy.
21. He went to the "doctor's place" where he had an operation.		Haffez Bouhamzy Sleimann Bouhamzy *	After the accident Said Bouhamzy was taken to a hospital where he had two operations, one cerebral, one abdominal, but nevertheless died a few hours after the operations.
22. The accident happened after a quarrel and the chauffeur meant to kill him.		Incorrect	Incorrect, but it is not certain that Imad himself connected the quarrel and the accident. It seems possible that Imad or his parents confused or fused images of the fatal truck accident to Said Bouhamzy and the bus accident to Ibrahim's bus. (See items 23 and 24 and discussion in text.) Imad never specifically said the truck accident happened to him. The driver was tried and sentenced lightly for negligence, but not judged guilty of assault. This would be a likely suspicion. Ibrahim, who had a quarrelsome nature, could characteristically have attributed a hostile motive to the chauffeur. Sleimann Bouhamzy * stated that as he was dying Said Bouhamzy pleaded with those around him to handle the chauffeur gently as he was afraid the chauffeur would be falsely accused of malice.

290

23. His bus had gone off the road and there had been an accident. But he himself was not driving at the time of the accident. People were killed in the accident.**

Nabih Bouhamzy
Ali Mohammed Abouhassan
Fuad Bouhamzy
Mohammed Elawar (reporting verifications of Yousef el Halibi's son)

Once Ibrahim Bouhamzy alighted from the bus he was driving while it contained passengers. His assistant was in the bus and presumably in control. The emergency brake failed, the bus rolled backwards onto a slope, and passengers were injured. A crowd assembled (virtually the whole village) and the police came. One informant, Mr. Nabih Bouhamzy, said that after this accident Ibrahim became very anxious and did not drive the bus again. Not long afterwards he developed his ultimately fatal illness.

In March, 1964, I understood that the accident involved a truck (not a bus), but in August it became clear that this was a bus accident both as stated by Imad and as verified to have happened to Ibrahim's bus, not truck. No one was killed in the accident.

24. There had been a quarrel because the driver had insulted his sister. He had struck the driver, knocked him down, and the police and his friend Ahmed el Halibi had arrived.

Mohammed Elawar (quoting Yousef el Halibi's son)

No informant could confirm the details of such a quarrel between Ibrahim and the driver of the bus, but the story seemed characteristic of Ibrahim's quarrelsome nature. After the accident the police came to enquire into claims for damages. In August, 1964, I learned that in March the son of Mr. Yousef el Halibi had confirmed that his father and uncle had gone to the scene of the accident, but the interpreter did not tell me this during the interview. I believe (without being certain) that Ahmed el Halibi and Yousef el Halibi were brothers.

* Sleimann Bouhamzy verifying as from his claimed remembrance of the life of Said Bouhamzy.
** This item not recorded in writing prior to its verification.

Item	Informants	Verification	Comments
24. (continued)			This scene followed the bus accident of item 23.
25. The driver was a Christian.		Nabih Bouhamzy	Incorrect if referring to the driver of the truck which killed Said Bouhamzy. He was a Muslim. Imad may have mixed up the man who drove the truck that killed Said Bouhamzy and another man. Ibrahim did have a close friend who was both a bus driver and a Christian.
26. He was a friend of Mr. Kemal Joumblatt.		Haffez Bouhamzy Nabih Bouhamzy	Both Ibrahim and Said Bouhamzy were friends of this well-known Druse philosopher and politician. Mr. Kemal Joumblatt lived in a village not far south of Khriby. Imad became very disturbed when one day, to test him, a neighbor said (falsely) that Mr. Joumblatt had died.
27. He was very fond of hunting.		Haffez Bouhamzy Nabih Bouhamzy Fuad Bouhamzy	Ibrahim was passionately fond of hunting. Imad frequently asked his father to take him hunting. At the house of Said Bouhamzy Imad showed great interest in two partridges. Partridges are the chief game of the area.
28. He had a double-barreled shotgun.*		Haffez Bouhamzy Nabih Bouhamzy Fuad Bouhamzy	Correct. Imad would hold two fingers together to show what he meant in describing the double-barreled gun.
29. He also had a rifle.**		Haffez Bouhamzy Nabih Bouhamzy Fuad Bouhamzy	Correct.
30. He had hidden his gun.**	Kassim Elawar	The place where Ibrahim had kept his gun was shown to me by Ibrahim's mother, Lateife Bouhamzy.	Correct. This item presumably refers to the rifle which it would be illegal for a civilian in Lebanon to possess. Ibrahim had hidden his gun.

Item	Verification	Comments
31. He had a brown "hunting" dog.	Nabih Bouhamzy Haffez Bouhamzy	The dog was light brown, but was *not* a hunting dog. Another inference of Imad's family. Imad had referred to liking hunting, having a gun, and having a dog. The family had assumed the dog was a hunting dog, but it was in fact a kind of shepherd dog.
32. He had once himself beaten a dog.***	Nabih Bouhamzy	Correct. Another dog had fought with Ibrahim Bouhamzy's dog and he (Ibrahim) had beaten the other dog.
33. His house was in the village of Khriby.	House visited by myself.	The house was in the center of the village, not on the outskirts. On the first day of inquiries Imad was reported as saying the house was on the outside of the village, but this was corrected before we reached Khriby and was probably an error of translation.
34. Just before the house there was a slope.***	House visited by myself.	The road slopes rather steeply just before it reaches the house of Ibrahim.
35. There were two wells at the house, one full and one empty.***	Nabih Bouhamzy Fuad Bouhamzy "Wells" seen by me at the house.	During the life of Ibrahim there had been two "wells" whose sites were pointed out to us. The "wells" had been closed up since the death of Ibrahim. They were not spring wells, but rather concrete concavities or vats used for storing grape juice. The wells would be used alternately. During the rainy season one of these vats became filled with water, but the other shallower vat did not, because the water evaporated from it. Thus one would be empty while the other was full.

* Recorded after verification had begun, but before this item had been verified.
** This item not recorded in writing prior to its verification.
*** Mentioned by Imad during journey from Kornayel to Khirby.

Item	Informants	Verification	Comments
36. They were building a new garden at the time of his death.		Haffez Bouhamzy Fuad Bouhamzy	At the time of Ibrahim's death they had been rebuilding the garden of the house.
37. There were cherry and apple trees in the new garden.		Haffez Bouhamzy Fuad Bouhamzy The apple and cherry trees were pointed out to me on my visits to Khriby.	
38. The truck was full of stones, which they were using in the construction work on the garden.		Haffez Bouhamzy Nabih Bouhamzy	Incorrect or doubtful. Mr. Haffez Bouhamzy recalled they were using and replacing the stones of the existing terraces of the garden. He did not recall that they were bringing in new stones in a truck. Imad might have been referring to the truck which ran over Said Bouhamzy, but this apparently was empty and not full of stones at the time of the accident.
39. He had money, land, but no other regular business.		Haffez Bouhamzy Nabih Bouhamzy	On the whole true, but Ibrahim Bouhamzy did have a truck with which he worked commercially. He also drove a bus for a time.
40. He had a small yellow automobile.		Haffez Bouhamzy Nabih Bouhamzy Fuad Bouhamzy	Correct.
41. He had a bus.*	Kassim Elawar	Fuad Bouhamzy Nabih Bouhamzy	Correct.
42. He had a truck.		Haffez Bouhamzy Nabih Bouhamzy Fuad Bouhamzy	Correct. Ibrahim Bouhamzy did not use these vehicles simultaneously, but successively. In fact, he did not "own" them, as they belonged to the family, but the family held much property in common.

Kassim Elawar	Nabih Bouhamzy	Correct.
43. He used the truck for hauling rocks.*		
44. He himself did not drive the truck.	Incorrect	He did drive the truck himself. It seems likely that this item refers to the bus accident mentioned in items 23 and 24. Imad apparently wanted to emphasize that he (Ibrahim) was not in the bus (i.e., driving) when it went off the road and that his assistant (chauffeur) was responsible for the accident. There was some confusion as to whether Imad referred to a bus or a truck.
45. There were two garages at the house.**	The two sheds probably referred to were inspected by me.	Incorrect, but perhaps partially right. Ibrahim kept his vehicles in the open. Below the house there were two sheds and Imad was probably trying to refer to these. This seems all the more likely in that Imad had earlier referred to "rooms with round roofs" apparently in the same context and these sheds beneath the house did have round ceilings, as I found when I examined one myself.
46. The key to the garage was in the attic.**	Unverified	The house had an attic and it is possible that Ibrahim kept a spare key there. His sister could not verify this point. This would have been a key to the sheds of item 45.
47. There was an entrance with a sort of round opening.**,***	This opening was examined by me.	Above the main door to the house from the courtyard, there was an opening to the attic which was almost semi-circular and closed with a window. This apparently could be removed to give access

* This item not recorded in writing prior to its verification.

** Mentioned by Imad during journey from Kornayel to Khriby.

*** Recorded after verification had begun, but before this item had been verified.

Item	Informants	Verification	Comments
47. (continued)			to the attic which could also be reached by a small trap door behind the front door of the house. Although correct, attic openings of this kind also occur on other houses of the area.
48. The tools for the cars were at this place with the round opening.*		Huda Bouhamzy, sister of Ibrahim Bouhamzy Lateife Bouhamzy	Mr. Haffez Bouhamzy, Ibrahim's cousin, did not know that Ibrahim kept his tools in the attic. It is possible that item 46 was an attempt at the same reference and a misunderstanding may have arisen from the fact that the French word for both key and wrench is "clef." Arabic also, which has taken over many technical words from French, uses the same word "clef" in both senses. In any case, on item 48 Imad was quite correct; on item 46 the detail could not be verified, but may have been correct also.
49. There was an oil stove at his house.	Majeed Toufic Elawar, cousin of Imad's paternal grandfather	Fuad Bouhamzy	Imad was asked if they had a wood stove at the house of the previous family and he replied that they did not, but had an oil stove. His remark shows he was not misled. The detail itself is not specific since many houses, in Lebanon, including Imad's, have oil stoves.
50. He had one goat and the goat had a baby goat (kid).*		Fuad Bouhamzy	When Ibrahim was young the family had had a flock of goats.
51. He had a sheep.*		Fuad Bouhamzy	Ibrahim's family also had sheep when he was young.
52. He had five children altogether.		Nabih Bouhamzy	Unverified. Ibrahim had no publicly identified children. He never married, but he did have at least one child. Mr. Nabih Bouhamzy heard him admit to

52. (continued)

this parenthood. When Imad was talking about children he held up five fingers to indicate the number of children in reply to a question. Possibly he was referring to the five sons of his friend and cousin Said Bouhamzy, of whom Ibrahim had been very fond.

53. He was "well to do."

Haffez Bouhamzy
Nabih Bouhamzy

Not a very specific point, but compared to many of the families in the village Ibrahim would have been considered prosperous.

54. He had a farm.

Nabih Bouhamzy

55. "I can speak English." *

Incorrect

Incorrect for Ibrahim, who could speak French well, but English not at all. Mr. Abushdid said Imad made this remark in the car after hearing Mr. Abushdid and myself exchange a few sentences in English. His father, riding in the car at the time, did not hear Imad make a remark like this, but did hear him say at about the same time: "I can talk like you," referring to the French which Mr. Abushdid and I usually talked. Imad in his first year at school had been learning French and counted up to twenty in French quite correctly. There exists therefore some doubt about this item and in any case it is possible that Imad was not then referring to the previous life. Imad's father had not heard him claim to be able to speak English on any other occasion.

* Mentioned by Imad during journey from Kornayel to Khriby.
** Recorded after verification had begun, but before this item had been verified.

Item	Informants	Verification	Comments
56. You go to Khriby by Hammana.	Naileh Elawar, paternal grandmother of Imad	Roadmaps of Lebanon	Correct. Hammana is a village southeast of Kornayel and one passes through it on the way to Khriby from Kornayel. Imad's father insisted that Imad had not previously been out of Kornayel on that side of the village. It is odd that, since Hammana is not near Khriby, the "Ibrahim personality" would seem to remember this relationship. It would be a more characteristic orientation for someone living in Kornayel who had looked up Khriby on the map and seen which road to take to get there from Kornayel. It therefore seems possible that Imad picked this information up from hearing his father mention it. Perhaps what is important is that he picked it up from his great interest in Khriby and his frequently expressed wish to go there. (See discussion in text on evidence about whether Imad had visited Khriby earlier.)
57. Recognition of Salim el Aschkar of Khriby.	Naileh Elawar		Salim el Aschkar, a native of Khriby, had married a girl from Kornayel and sometimes visited the latter village. When Imad was about two years old he was on the street with his grandmother when Salim el Aschkar came along. Imad ran to him and threw his arms around him. "Do you know me?" asked Salim, to which Imad answered: "Yes, you were my neighbor." This man *had* been a neighbor of Ibrahim Bouhamzy's family, but was not then living close to their house.

was opened up for us), Imad made fourteen other declarations or recognitions which I have listed, together with two just mentioned from the first visit to Khriby, in Tabulation 2 below.

Of the sixteen items of declarations or recognitions occurring in Khriby, Imad was quite correct on fourteen, somewhat vague on one (recognition of the outside of the house), and failed on one test of recognition (Ibrahim's mother). We should perhaps set aside two other items in which the testimony was discrepant (episode of injury to finger) or the possibility of normal sources of information strong (road to Baadaran). That still leaves twelve items, some of a highly personal nature, concerning the house and life of Ibrahim Bouhamzy. In assessing what knowledge of the house Imad showed before going to Khriby and inside the house when we were there, readers should remember that the house itself had been shut up for some years. Most of the information which Imad had could only have come normally from some person who had known the house itself, not from an inspection of the outside terrain.

The scene of Imad's visit to the house of Ibrahim and recognition of members of Ibrahim's family did not evoke in the participants as much emotion as some other "reunions" of this kind have done.[12] Ibrahim's mother and sister seemed much interested in seeing Imad and received him most cordially, but they did not shed tears. Imad for his part did not cry either. He was, however, evidently happy to be in Khriby and with these people. He showed the strongest emotion toward a small photograph of Fuad, Ibrahim's brother, which someone had found and given him to keep. This he clung to rather tenaciously and kissed affectionately. Upon being taken away from the house and relatives of Ibrahim he did not resist or show any grief of separation.

Ibrahim had particularly liked his mother, his sister Huda, and his brother Fuad. The recognitions by Imad of Huda and of Fuad's portrait accorded with these preferences of Ibrahim. Ibrahim's mother had perhaps changed more in physical appearance (being in 1964 a distinctly old lady) than had Huda.

During the scene in the house when Imad did not know the answer to a question, he did not guess and if he did not recognize some object shown him, he simply said nothing. We may consider this also a further point against his having been given any suggestions or hints of recognitions which, if floating around, would perhaps have led to many more statements —either correct or not—than he actually made.

Relevant Reports and Observations of the Behavior of the People Concerned. In addition to recording, before we went to Khriby, the statements

---

[12] See, for example, reports of emotions expressed during such "reunions" in the reports of cases in India and Ceylon given elsewhere in this monograph.

TABULATION 2

Summary of Statements and Recognitions Made by Imad in Khriby

NOTE: The following recognitions or statements all took place either in the presence of the interpreter or myself or we were told of them within a few minutes. Mr. Haffez Bouhamzy, Mrs. Huda Bouhamzy, and Mrs Lateife Bouhamzy verified the accuracy of what Imad said or did. Items followed by an asterisk (*) were witnessed by the interpreter directly; other items only reported later by witnesses.

Item	*Comments*
58. Recognition of location of previous house. (*)	House of Ibrahim Bouhamzy seen later. Imad definitely pointed in the correct general direction of the house from a distance of about 300 yards. But he failed to identify the house specifically.
59. Recognition of the road to Baadaran from Khriby. (*)	Statement made during drive from Khriby to Baadaran. Not a significant item since Imad may have seen a sign pointing the way or perhaps heard someone mention the direction.
60. Recognition of place where Ibrahim Bouhamzy kept his dog. (*)	In the courtyard of the house, Imad was asked, "If you had a dog here, where did you keep it?" He correctly indicated the place in the yard.
61. The dog was held by a cord. (*)	Asked how the dog had been held, Imad said, "By a cord." Many dogs of this area are held by chains, not cords.
62. Recognition of bed of Ibrahim Bouhamzy. (*)	There were two beds in the bedroom. Imad pointed out Ibrahim's.
63. Statement about former position of this bed. (*)	Imad was asked: "How was the bed arranged when you slept in it?" He then indicated that the bed used to lie in a position cross-wise from its present position, in a completely different position. (See next item.)
64. Statement about how friends talked with Ibrahim. (*)	During his infectious illness, his friends could not enter Ibrahim's room so they talked with him through a window, the bed being arranged so he could see and talk with his friends through the window. When Imad was asked, "How did you talk with your friends?" he pointed to the window and said, "Through there."
65. Recognition of place where Ibrahim Bouhamzy kept his gun. (*)	Imad, when asked where he kept "his" gun, pointed to the back of a closet fitted into a partitioning wall. He did not point to the doors of the closet, but was quite right about the closet itself. Ibrahim's mother said only she and Ibrahim knew where the gun was kept. Mr. Haffez Bouhamzy, Ibrahim's cousin, did not know this fact.

Item	Comments
66. Failure to recognize mother of Ibrahim Bouhamzy.	In the presence of Ibrahim's mother, Imad was asked: "Do you recognize that old lady?" He then said, "No." He was then told to go and say "Hello" to her, which he did. Then when asked if he liked her, he replied, "Yes, a great deal."
67. Recognition of sister of Ibrahim, Huda.	Ibrahim's sister asked Imad, "Do you know who I am?" and he replied, "Huda."
68. Recognition of a portrait of Ibrahim's brother Fuad.	Imad was first shown a rather small photograph of Fuad in a military uniform. He did not recognize this photograph. But when asked of whom was a large oil painting hanging on the wall he correctly said, "Fuad."
69. Recognition of portrait of Ibrahim Bouhamzy.	When shown a moderately large photograph of Ibrahim Bouhamzy and asked who it was of, Imad said, "Me." In this case prompting was offered that it was of his brother or uncle, but no one had hinted it was of Ibrahim.
70. Statement of last words spoken by Ibrahim before dying.	Imad was asked by Mrs. Huda Bouhamzy: "You said something just before you died. What was it?" Imad replied, "Huda, call Fuad." This was correct because Fuad had left shortly before and Ibrahim wanted to see him again, but died immediately.
71. Fuad and Ali were brothers of Ibrahim. (*)	Imad was asked, "Who are your brothers?" and he replied, "Fuad and Ali," both correct. He seemed not to recall a third brother, Sami, the youngest.
72. Statement of where Jamileh lived. (*)	Imad correctly pointed with his finger in the direction of the village of Maaser el Shouf, where Jamileh used to live.
73. Ibrahim's mother had once crushed her finger in the door leading to the courtyard.	For this item I heard conflicting testimony as to what Imad had said and as to what actually had happened during the life of Ibrahim. One witness said Imad recalled an injury to "his" (Ibrahim's) finger. Mrs. Huda Bouhamzy stated Imad recalled that Ibrahim's mother had crushed her finger in the door. This did in fact occur and Ibrahim's mother still had a flattened end of her finger when I saw her during one of my visits to Khriby.

about a previous life attributed to Imad, I noted also several items of Imad's behavior reported by his parents or grandparents as presumably deriving from the experiences and attitudes of the previous personality.

Under this heading we should note first of all Imad's interest in Khriby and the people there. He repeatedly asked his parents to take him there and he talked much of the various people he claimed to have known there. On my last visit to Kornayel in August, 1964, Imad asked me to take him to Khriby since his parents, he said, would not do so. A noteworthy manifestation of his interest in Khriby occurred when he encountered Salim el Aschkar in the street of Kornayel and threw his arms around him; another happened when a woman sought to test his reactions by falsely stating that Mr. Kemal Joumblatt (the Druse statesman whom Imad claimed to have known and whom Ibrahim did in fact know well) had died. On hearing this statement, Imad became extremely angry and tried to chase the woman from the house. And still another episode of this type occurred in December, 1963, when news reached Kornayel that Said Bouhamzy (the second citizen of Khriby with this name) had died. Imad showed great interest in this news. Afterwards he said reflectively: "I still have another brother left." (This last comment presumably referred to Amin or Kemal, surviving members of the circle of close friends and cousins of Ibrahim who called each other "brother.") I myself saw the smile of pleasure on Imad's face when we proposed our trip to Khriby. In Khriby itself, except for the two occasions when something—I am not sure what—upset him, he showed constantly the greatest signs of happiness.

Of all the people mentioned by Imad as related to the previous life, Jamileh occupied the most prominent position. Her name was the first word he clearly uttered when he began to speak and it was thereafter often on his lips. He spoke of buying red clothes for her and he compared her beauty and her clothes to those of his mother who, for example, did not wear high heels as did Jamileh. Imad's longing for Jamileh reached its most advanced expression when one day he was lying on a bed with his mother and asked her suddenly to behave as Jamileh would. I do not know how he said this in Arabic, but his sentence translated into French as: "Maman, faites comme si vous étiez Jamileh." This episode occurred when Imad was about three to three and a half years old.

On the visit to Khriby, Imad did not ask to see Jamileh, who had anyway long since married and moved away from that area. This, however, need not occasion surprise if we recall that Jamileh had been Ibrahim's mistress only and the relationship a considerable scandal in the community. One would not expect Ibrahim therefore (or Imad if influenced by the experiences of Ibrahim) to have dwelt upon the relationship with Jamileh when in the presence of his female relatives. In Khriby, Imad did correctly indicate the direction of the village Jamileh had lived in, but did not spontaneously mention her name as he had done so often in Kornayel. In August, 1964, I learned that Imad could be made to react with strong emotion if told teasingly that Jamileh had died.

Imad's parents commented on a notable phobia of large trucks and buses which Imad showed even when an infant. He would run and hide from these vehicles before he could talk and verbalize his fear. Gradually Imad lost this fear and by the age of four or five it had left him completely. Imad's parents accounted for this phobia of large vehicles by supposing that in the previous life he had been run over by a truck and killed. But as we have seen, Said Bouhamzy, not Ibrahim, met his death in this manner. Ibrahim, however, was still living at the time of Said's death in the truck accident and the death of his cousin and friend had bothered him greatly. Moreover, Ibrahim had driven both a truck and a bus himself. On one occasion, when he had stepped out of the bus, the brakes slipped and the bus went on down a slope, turning over with his (Ibrahim's) assistant in it (item 23, Tabulation 1). (One informant testified that Ibrahim had become anxious after this accident, although another did not confirm this development.) Although Ibrahim was not himself hurt, this dangerous accident together with the death of Said, could well account for a fear of large motor vehicles in Ibrahim. Apart from this accident, Ibrahim had also been in an automobile accident. So the behavior of Imad toward vehicles seemed appropriate to that expected from Ibrahim's experiences.

Imad's parents and grandparents commented on the surprise and joy shown by Imad when he first began to walk. He would make such remarks as: "Look, I can walk now," as if surprised that he really could walk. Here again his parents, during the years of thinking the previous personality of Imad had had his legs broken and been killed by a truck, accounted for his pleasure in walking on the grounds that he could scarcely believe the broken legs had healed. But as we have seen, Ibrahim had been disabled also and not just before his death, but for a long period of incapacity from tuberculosis. Imad, who had said nothing of Ibrahim's vow to become a sheikh if God would heal him, himself seemed not to understand how and why he could walk around as he did. One day he asked his mother: "Mother, have you had an operation which made you so you could walk again?" Now Said Bouhamzy, after the truck accident which crushed his trunk as well as broke his legs, did have an abdominal operation after the accident, but died nevertheless a few hours later. Ibrahim would have known of this and Imad also showed knowledge of this operation after the truck accident. It seems possible, therefore, that he developed the idea that he himself had been made whole by a surgical operation. Also worth considering is the possibility of a fusion of images in Imad's mind of "memories" related to the illness of Ibrahim and the fatal accident of his friend Said. As I have already noted, Imad seems to have had various images presented to his consciousness and would then sometimes articulate these in words to himself or others. His parents did quite certainly in *their* minds fuse the scenes of the death of Said Bouhamzy with other declarations of Imad and they assigned Said's violent death to the previous personality of

Imad. Some similar fusion may have occurred in the mind of Imad himself.

The foregoing supposition receives support from the detail of a quarrel before the truck accident between the driver of the truck and the man injured and killed by the truck (item 22, Tabulation 1.) As Imad's parents told this item, Imad had accused the truck driver of voluntary murder in deliberately running down and over the injured man. Imad had also described a quarrel in which he claimed that he (in the previous life) had knocked down a truck (or bus) driver. In fact, the driver of the truck which killed Said Bouhamzy had not quarreled with him and Said Bouhamzy on his deathbed (according to Sleimann Bouhamzy) had expressly exonerated the driver of blame. But as Ibrahim himself had a quarrelsome nature, his character could readily have attributed the cause of the accident and the death of his friend to malice on the part of the driver. Other people also had such suspicions, but a trial court found the driver guilty only of negligence. Therefore Imad's inclusion of the incorrect detail of the quarrel before the truck accident could have arisen from a fusion in his mind of images about the truck accident and about a quarrel of Ibrahim with a chauffeur; or it could have arisen as an interpretation of the truck accident made by Ibrahim, incorrect but harmonious with Ibrahim's own belligerent character, and carried into the mind of Imad. And as still a third explanation, we must consider the possibility that Imad's parents themselves connected the quarrel as described by Imad and the accident as described by him. According to them, Imad talked much more of the quarrel than of the accident.

Imad showed a great interest in hunting and frequently asked his father to take him hunting. He correctly stated that Ibrahim had owned both a shotgun and a rifle and correctly pointed out where Ibrahim had kept one of them in the house. I have already mentioned Imad's great interest in the caged partridges at the home of Said Bouhamzy. (Partridges are the chief game of the area.) According to Mr. Haffez Bouhamzy, Ibrahim Bouhamzy had an intense interest in hunting and participated in this activity whenever he could. But we should note that Mr. Mohammed Elawar, Imad's father, had a gun and went hunting, so Imad's interest may have derived from knowing of his father's activities. More noteworthy was the *intensity* of the boy's interest in hunting.

I noted the foregoing features of Imad's behavior before verification of his statements began. Imad's family mentioned some other noteworthy items of his behavior *after* I learned about similar traits in Ibrahim Bouhamzy. In the course of sketching for us the life and attitudes of his cousin Ibrahim, Mr. Haffez Bouhamzy mentioned that Ibrahim frequently became embroiled in quarrels with other men, usually about women. He had once shot a man during a quarrel. (I have already mentioned the emphasis given by Imad to quarrels in his statements.) When Imad's father heard that

Ibrahim had a reputation for belligerence, he immediately laughed and said that Imad himself showed a very quarrelsome character and would nourish injuries. Imad was sensitive and cried easily when offended. He disliked being young and became angry if told he was young. At a children's dance in 1964 he complained of being with children of his own age and asked for costumes appropriate to older children. Imad assumed a dominant attitude toward other children, wanting always to be the leader. His paternal grandfather stated that when Imad was about two years old he drank maté tea as a grown man would and showed a particular fondness for bitter tea and coffee. Maté tea is particularly drunk by the Druses in the area around Khriby, but also elsewhere throughout Lebanon, including in the Elawar family. The important point of Imad's interest in tea is again the strength of his interest at such a young age.

Imad, according to his family, was precocious in school and especially advanced for his age in French. No one else in the family could speak French, but Imad had been learning it rapidly and correcting his older sister. Ibrahim Bouhamzy could speak French well (having served in the French Army), but could not speak English.

The Case of Sleimann Bouhamzy

Summary of the Case and a Comparison of the Behavior of Sleimann Bouhamzy and Imad Elawar as Children. Before a further discussion of the case of Imad Elawar, I wish to present a summary of the related case of Sleimann Bouhamzy. As I mentioned above, on my second trip to Khriby I learned that Sleimann Bouhamzy had already come to Khriby many years earlier, and often since, and had there satisfied everyone concerned as to his claim to be Said Bouhamzy reborn after being killed in the truck accident. Unfortunately, the main events of this case had occurred some sixteen years before my visit and I cannot present the case as being anything like as well witnessed by recent testimony as is the case of Imad Elawar. Nevertheless, the first account of the case given me by Mr. Haffez Bouhamzy in Khriby matched in general outline, and in nearly all details, the independent account given in Syria by Sleimann Bouhamzy himself. I gained the strong impression that if I had been present in Khriby at the time of the main events of the case, I might have thought the case even more important than that of Imad Elawar. As things stand now, however, I can present only a summary of the case, and do this chiefly to compare certain details of behavior in Imad Elawar and Sleimann Bouhamzy when they were small children.

Said Bouhamzy died on June 8, 1943, following the truck accident which crushed his trunk and broke both his legs. In the hospital, he had two operations on his head and abdomen; after this he recovered consciousness long enough to send for his wife and sons, but died a few hours later. Said Bouhamzy had only one sibling, a sister of whom he was very fond. On December 3, 1943, this sister, then living in Syria where she had married a relative of the same name, gave birth to Sleimann Bouhamzy.

In the spring of 1964, Sleimann Bouhamzy was a young man of twenty years who willingly recounted what he still remembered of the previous life and of his own behavior related to it as a child. He stated that memories of the previous life as Said Bouhamzy had very largely faded from his mind. Moreover, he disclaimed being always sure whether he actually recalled something that he had earlier remembered from the previous life or merely recalled what other persons, his parents, for example, had later told him he had said with regard to this life. Even in confirming certain details about the life of Ibrahim Bouhamzy, he could not always assure himself whether he remembered as from the life of Said Bouhamzy or remembered what he, as Sleimann Bouhamzy, had heard from his mother who was, after all, a sister of Said Bouhamzy and a cousin by marriage of Ibrahim Bouhamzy. In short, Sleimann Bouhamzy presented his account of what he remembered of the life of Said Bouhamzy with marked diffidence and freedom from claims as to the exact provenance of the apparent memories he narrated. With these candid reservations, then, I present the following account.

Sleimann Bouhamzy recalled of the life of Said Bouhamzy an occasion when he had come from Lebanon to Syria to visit his sister. In those days the journey took very much longer than it did in 1964. He recalled that he traveled on horseback and wore a distinctive Syrian costume, different from the one of Lebanon. He also recalled a time when Said Bouhamzy, stationed at Homs (west central Syria) in the French Army, heard the news of the birth of a son. A good friend of Said who was with him at Homs gave the son the name of Hassan. He recalled the marriage of a cousin, Nejip Bouhamzy, and how he (as Said) had conducted the bride from the village of Mouktara to Khriby. He recalled some details of the fatal truck accident of Said Bouhamzy, including how the latter had been taken to the hospital and how he had there revived before dying and asked for his wife and also exonerated the driver of malice in the accident. He could recall nothing of a quarrel preceding the truck accident, which he believed truly unintentional on the part of the driver.

Sleimann Bouhamzy recalled some details of his own behavior as a child related to the life of Said Bouhamzy. As a very small child he had found five eggplants and two potatoes and gave them respectively the names of Said's five sons and two daughters. He would get angry if anyone touched these vegetables and wanted to keep them indefinitely. The names of the seven children of Said were almost the first words he spoke.

He recalled a very marked fear of motor vehicles of all kinds. When small he would not even go near an automobile. At the age of eleven or twelve this fear began to diminish, first with regard to smaller vehicles and finally with regard to large ones such as trucks and buses. In 1964 he had no residue of fear of vehicles.[13] He still preserved, however, a marked fear of blood and of cotton bandages. He once fainted when he visited a friend in a hospital and saw him with his head swathed in a white bandage. According to Sleimann Bouhamzy, Said Bouhamzy had been wrapped in white cotton bandages after the truck accident. Mr. Fuad Bouhamzy saw the body of Said Bouhamzy just after he died and it was then bandaged.

Sleimann Bouhamzy further recalled a great longing for Khriby and pleasure in being there. He still visited Khriby frequently and Mr. Haffez Bouhamzy confirmed the pleasure Sleimann Bouhamzy had in staying at Khriby, which he visited at length every summer and left to return to his village of Raha in Syria with great reluctance. In fact, Sleimann Bouhamzy's pull toward Khriby would probably have caused him to move there if the educational opportunities had matched those of Raha, where he was attending a junior college.

When Sleimann Bouhamzy was a small child he visited Khriby for the first time [14] and there recognized and correctly gave the names of all the surviving members of the family of Said Bouhamzy, as well as of some other residents of the village. He further correctly pointed out boundaries of land owned by residents of the village in the surrounding farms and vineyards. Mr. Haffez Bouhamzy witnessed the recounting by Sleimann Bouhamzy when he was a child of the details of the accident and death of Said Bouhamzy; he also witnessed the recognitions by Sleimann of Said Bouhamzy's children (including himself) and other members of the family and village; he further recalled that the boy Sleimann, set down in the center of Khriby, found his way unaided to Said Bouhamzy's home, where he recognized not only various persons but also called for or recognized items of property belonging to Said Bouhamzy, such as his revolver and a special kind of cloak he had. Sleimann, then a small boy, adopted a paternal attitude toward Said's sons, who at that time were much older than he. He called his own mother (sister of Said Bouhamzy) "sister" instead of "mother." Mr. Haffez

[13] Two details of psychological interest emerge in the decline of the strength of phobia for motor vehicles in Sleimann Bouhamzy. First, he preserved his fear of them much longer than did Imad Elawar, who had lost his fear by the age of four or five. This accords with the claims of the two children to have been respectively someone killed by a truck and someone who had a friend killed by a truck, and who was involved, but not injured, in a bus accident. Secondly, the loss of the fear for stimuli to which generalization has occurred (e.g., a small vehicle) before the loss of the fear for the original traumatic agent (e.g., a large vehicle), accords with experimental observations of extinction after traumatic avoidance training. See, for example, M. Fleshler and H. S. Hoffman. "Stimulus Generalization of Conditioned Suppression." *Science*, Vol. 133, 1961, 753–755. But some other experiments have given discrepant results.

[14] A discrepancy occurred in the testimony as to Sleimann Bouhamzy's age at the time of his first visit to Khriby. Mr. Haffez Bouhamzy said Sleimann was "three to four years old" and Sleimann Bouhamzy himself said he was "six to seven years old" at this time.

Bouhamzy, the second youngest son of Said Bouhamzy, was then about eleven years old.

Sleimann Bouhamzy told me he had recognized on his visit to Khriby Mr. Milhem Abouhassan, a good friend of Said Bouhamzy, who lived in the village of Baadaran, near Khriby. Mr. Haffez Bouhamzy corroborated this recognition. So did Mr. Milhem Abouhassan himself, who said that Sleimann Bouhamzy gave his name correctly when they first met and under circumstances (which he described to me) which precluded, in his opinion, any prior suggestion of his name to the boy. Sleimann Bouhamzy was still feeling a great fondness for Mr. Abouhassan, one which we can hardly explain on the basis of shared experiences or friendships in the life of Sleimann Bouhamzy and which was, as he himself acknowledged, rather unusual anyway, considering the forty-year gap in their ages.

The family of Said Bouhamzy fully accepted Sleimann Bouhamzy as their father returned. They welcomed his visits, gave him gifts, and planned to support his further education. The interest of Said Bouhamzy's sons in him extended far beyond what one might expect in attitudes toward a cousin.[15]

I return now to a further discussion of the case of Imad Elawar.

Comments on the Evidence of Paranormal Knowledge on the Part of Imad Elawar. In this case we can firmly exclude one possibility which enters into many cases suggestive of reincarnation. I refer to retrospective errors of memory in reconstructing later (after the two families have met and compared information) exactly what the child said before verification of the statements attributed to him. Before attempting any verification, I noted in writing all but an unimportant few of the declarations attributed to Imad. And the interpreter and I both witnessed most of the events which occurred when Imad visited the house at Khriby and I made notes of these immediately. In the few exceptions not directly observed, I still noted down within a few minutes what the witnesses said had happened. Whatever else the case may be, I am confident it is not a retrospective reconstruction of imagined statements and events.

I wish to draw attention also to the fact that Imad's father, my first interpreter, and I all went to Khriby on the first visit with the expectation that the statements of Imad would relate to the life of a person called Said Bouhamzy. But in fact this proved a wrong supposition. It therefore can-

15 In May, 1972, I met Sleimann Bouhamzy again in Aley, Lebanon. He had moved to Aley from Syria in 1965 and in 1972 was teaching in a school there. He said that he thought he had preserved all or most of the memories of the previous life that he had at the time of our first meeting in 1963. He visited Khriby often and had continued to have strong attachments to the family of Said Bouhamzy. He continued also to have a marked fear of large motor vehicles such as buses and trucks.

not be said, I think, that the case was elaborated by forcing the boy's remarks to apply to a particular deceased personality.

But we must next consider the possibility that the parents of Imad somehow themselves distorted or even falsified the information attributed to Imad. Among the Muslims and Christians who surround them, the Druses have an extraordinary reputation for honesty, a reputation indeed difficult to credit in cultures which value this virtue less highly. Nevertheless, we must examine the hypothesis of fraud closely. For this hypothesis we must immediately suppose a conspiracy involving both of Imad's parents, as well as his paternal grandparents and two cousins, all of whom gave testimony as to some or many of the statements or behavior attributed to Imad. We should further have to conceive some extensive preliminary training of Imad to carry out the recognitions he accomplished at the house of Ibrahim Bouhamzy.

We might also consider a more localized conspiracy on the part of the interpreters. But this hypothesis encounters two serious objections. First, each of the first three interpreters, counting the chauffeur who helped me on the first evening, were selected for the work at the last moment and without any chance for "preparation" unless they were all consummate actors. And when I first came to Lebanon in March, 1964, I met Dr. Makarem but did not then know that he would be willing and able to act as my interpreter in August. So far as I know, he had not then, or before August, met any of the interpreters who worked with me in March. Secondly, any conspiracy on their part would have had to have included some seventeen members of the two families concerned in two villages of Lebanon and one in Syria.

Apart from these considerations, however, the case includes some other features which render the hypothesis of fraud improbable in the extreme.

First, and least important, comes the position of the Elawar family in their community. Various members of the family have held responsible positions in Lebanon as professional persons, journalists, and business men. One member of the family represented the district in the Parliament of Lebanon. The Bouhamzy family in Khriby enjoyed a similar position in that community. Both the Elawar and Bouhamzy families had nothing to gain and much to lose by contriving a case of this kind. Both knew that I had become acquainted with leading members of the Druse community in Beirut. They knew further that I was trying to corroborate and cross-check testimony and that any exposure of dishonesty through my questioning would have rocked the Druse community. Nevertheless, rank, position, and reputation offer no infallible guarantees of honesty and I pass therefore to other factors which seem to me even weightier in establishing the authenticity of the case.

Among these we should note first certain details of the case which hardly reflect credit on the family of Imad and which would not have found inclusion in a contrived case. I refer in particular to the role of Jamileh. Imad's parents stated they thought Jamileh the wife of a respectable Druse sheikh, but as identified by the witnesses in Khriby, she had only the status of mistress to Ibrahim Bouhamzy, who himself had the reputation of being a quarrelsome village playboy and chaser of women. (Upon my return to Kornayel after the second trip to Khriby, I had the duty of telling Imad's mother that Jamileh, far from being the wife of a distinguished sheikh, had been the mistress only of his cousin. This news brought an expression of mingled pain and amusement to the face of Imad's mother, which convinced me she then heard this fact for the first time.) Imad narrated a quarrel and fight he claimed to have had in the previous life, an event hardly creditable to him or his family and yet, although not specifically confirmed, entirely characteristic of Ibrahim.

Further than this, the very mistakes of Imad's parents in their inferences testify to their ignorance of actual details of the life of Ibrahim Bouhamzy. Apart from their error in the social position of Jamileh, they made further errors in declaring the dog owned by the previous personality to have been a hunting dog; in declaring that Amin was a judge in Tripoli when he only worked as an employee in the courthouse there; and in assigning the fatal truck accident to the previous personality. If they had had any previous acquaintance with the true facts related to these details they would not have passed on to me the statements they attributed to Imad about them. Finally, they would not have seemed to believe, and taken Imad to Khriby while seeming to believe, that the previous personality related to him had died after being run over by a truck, if they had know that another person (Sleimann Bouhamzy) had already laid claim to being Said Bouhamzy reborn. If Imad's parents had made sufficient secret inquiries in Khriby to learn the private facts correctly stated by Imad (or attributed to him), they would inevitably have heard of this other person claiming to be Said Bouhamzy reborn. Any contrived case relating to a Bouhamzy in Khriby would have focused on one person and would not have mingled the data from two quite distinct lives.

Finally, the fraud hypothesis has to tell us how Imad's family could have acquired the correct information Imad showed—or had attributed to him—about the life of Ibrahim Bouhamzy. According to the mother of Mr. Haffez Bouhamzy, widow of Said Bouhamzy (as reported to me by Mr. Haffez Bouhamzy), no newspaper report of the fatal truck accident in 1943 had appeared. Neither the parents of Imad (who were then young and might not have remembered) nor his paternal grandparents could recall hearing about the death of Said Bouhamzy at that time. (Possibly people of Khriby had been invited to the funeral, but they could not recall this if so.) But even supposing that some word about the death of

Said Bouhamzy had reached Kornayel, there still remains much detail of a very personal nature about the life and house of Ibrahim Bouhamzy attributed to Imad. The house of Ibrahim Bouhamzy had been long since shut up and uninhabited, the "wells" closed up and abandoned. The women of Ibrahim's family, his mother and sister, had survived, but Druse women remain quite inaccessible to questioning by strange men. Further, the details known to Imad spread out over some period of time. Imad knew not only the last words of Ibrahim before he died, but also that he had beaten a dog, an event which must have happened at least six months before his death since he spent that long in the tuberculosis sanatorium before returning home to die. Imad knew also that Ibrahim had a small yellow automobile, a bus, and a truck, but Ibrahim had owned these vehicles at different times in his life, not simultaneously. Imad knew details of the fatal truck accident which killed Said Bouhamzy, and this happened six years before the death of Ibrahim himself. He knew about Jamileh, Ibrahim's mistress during his health, and also about the new garden being constructed with cherry and apple trees at the time of Ibrahim's death. In short, he had more than a cross-sectional knowledge of one period in Ibrahim's life; he had an awareness of various events spread out over some period of time during that life. I do not think I exaggerate in insisting that such detailed and extensive knowledge could only have been acquired through normal means by lengthy questioning of the Bouhamzy family or perhaps a few close friends and neighbors. Even close neighbors and friends, such as Mr. Haffez Bouhamzy himself, did not know that Ibrahim Bouhamzy kept tools in the attic of his house or where he kept his gun in the house. I can assert with confidence that any conspiracy to contrive the case would have had to include the Bouhamzy family. But this family, as I have already stated, enjoyed *bona fides* no weaker than those of the Elawar family. Nor did they have any motive for proposing that a boy living in a village twenty-five miles away was Ibrahim Bouhamzy reborn and returning to publicize his somewhat scandalous behavior in the community.

Both families insisted they had never previously met or even known of each other's existence prior to my bringing them together in Khriby. Mr. Mohammed Elawar told me he had first gone with his uncle to Khriby in December, 1963, to attend the funeral of the second Said Bouhamzy partly to satisfy curiosity about what his son had been saying for some years previously. At that time he had, he said, visited and met Mr. Kassim el Aschkar, whose home is at the northern edge of Khriby. At the funeral he had had pointed out to him two persons named Talal and Adil, who were identified as related to the man killed in the truck (the first Said Bouhamzy). He had not actually met these persons or anyone else in the families of Said Bouhamzy or Ibrahim Bouhamzy. (The people pointed out to him were not, in fact, immediate members of either family, although related.) I must now present some observations bearing on the question whether or not Mr. Mohammed Elawar had visited Khriby before this visit of December, 1963.

As I have already mentioned, on the way to Khriby Imad made a number of remarks apparently related to the previous life. In addition to these remarks, the interpreter (Mr. Abushdid on this occasion) heard Imad say:

"You can get Coca-Cola at Barouk." (Barouk is a village on the way from Kornayel to Khriby, but much nearer Khriby.) Imad's father had, not long before this remark, told us that Imad himself had never before left Kornayel on the side going toward Khriby, and also Barouk. Imad's remark, however, suggested some previous familiarity with Barouk which would contradict his father's assertion. As stated in Tabulation 1 (item 56), Imad knew that another village, Hammana, lies on the way from Kornayel to Khriby. His knowledge of these two villages between Kornayel and Khriby may have derived from the information related to the previous life, or he may possibly have picked up the information from hearing his parents refer to them.

The possibility arose, however, that Imad had in fact traveled to Khriby before with his father. Previously the interpreter had asked me whether he should put only questions I posed or whether he could interrogate the witnesses himself if he thought of some point worth pursuing. Thinking that more information might come out in a more spontaneous exchange, I authorized him to add such additional questions as he thought would contribute to the study of the case. However, this did not prepare me for a question which Mr. Abushdid put to Imad when Imad's father left the car at the edge of Khriby to ask directions. Mr. Abushdid then turned to Imad and promised him a very large bottle of Coca-Cola if he would say that he had been in the village of Khriby before. To this Imad then replied that he had once before been there in an automobile with his mother and father. The circumstance of offering a rather thirsty small boy such a large bribe makes it quite possible that Imad simply replied falsely to please Mr. Abushdid. Mr. Abushdid, himself, nevertheless, at first regarded Imad's statement as contradicting his father's assertion that Imad had never been to Khriby before.

At this time, however, Mr. Mohammed Elawar, who had got out of the car to make inquiries, showed what seemed to be entirely genuine signs of puzzlement and confusion as to his orientation in the village. He could not be sure if he correctly recognized the house of Mr. Kassim el Aschkar which, by his own account, he had visited only three months before at the time of the funeral of the Said Bouhamzy who had died in December, 1963. Neither Imad nor his father showed any sign of recognizing the houses of Ibrahim or Said Bouhamzy, although we drove right by one and near the other. From across the small valley on the other side of the village, Imad correctly pointed in the direction of the houses, but Mr. Mohammed Elawar showed no hint of familiarity with the houses even after this indication. On the next day, when Imad and his father met Mr. Haffez Bouhamzy, they all behaved as if they met there for the first time. Mr. Abushdid, speaking Arabic, was in a much better position than I to assess as genuine the puzzlement which Mr. Mohammed Elawar showed in finding his way around Khriby. Mr. Abushdid expressed himself completely satisfied that Mr. Elawar had no sure knowledge of the village and that he could not have visited it other than on the occasion of the funeral in December, 1963. But if this were true, then Imad's remark about having been in Khriby before in an automobile with his mother and father could not possibly have referred to Imad's "present" life. Among the Druses, women do not attend funerals in other villages. Therefore, Imad's mother could not have gone to the funeral in December, 1963. And if that occasion was the only one on which Mr. Elawar had visited Khriby, Imad's remark was perhaps an invention made to earn the bottle of Coca-Cola offered by Mr. Abushdid. Or perhaps Imad in this remark also referred to the previous life, since it is quite possible that Ibrahim Bouhamzy had been with his parents in an automobile in Khriby. I do not think we can decide between these two possibilities with regard to a remark elicited in this way, but I do feel confident that Mr. and Mrs. Elawar told the truth when they said that Mr. Elawar had only come once before to Khriby in December, 1963, that Mrs. Elawar had never come, and that Imad had never come before our visit in March, 1964.

It remains to consider whether Imad might have acquired some or all of the information he showed about the life of Ibrahim from some person other than his parents who had come to Kornayel. I have already mentioned the only three persons I was able to learn about who might have provided such information. The first was Mr. Salim el Aschkar, a native of Khriby, who had married a girl from Kornayel and who also had an uncle living there. From time to time he visited his uncle's or his wife's family in Kornayel. He was slightly acquainted with Imad's family and had been in the Elawar house once before Imad's birth, but not since. Moreover, Imad's family said they had not seen him since then, except on the one occasion when Imad spotted him on the street and ran up to him and embraced him (Tabulation 1, item 57). Imad's family also became acquainted with a woman who resided in Maaser el Shouf, the village near Khriby where Jamileh had lived. This woman sometimes visited her daughter, who lived with her husband in Kornayel. Mr. and Mrs. Elawar had met her for the first and only time in the autumn of 1962. At that time she verified for them a few of the statements made by Imad, but her limited information still did not lead to an accurate identification of the correct related previous personality nor to verification of all the statements made by Imad. Moreover, since Imad had by that time been talking for about two years of the previous life, she could not have furnished a source of information to him if we believe his parents' statement that they had never met her before this one occasion.

The third possible source of normally transmitted information was Mr. Faris Amin Elawar, who was well acquainted with Imad's family, being one of their distant relatives. He had visited Baadaran and in that area developed some slight acquaintance with members of the Bouhamzy family. But he and Imad's family had not discussed the Bouhamzy family or Imad's statements prior to my first visit to Kornayel in March, 1964, and when they did, Mr. Faris Elawar could verify what Imad had said about a bus accident, but no other items of his statements.

In the foregoing I have taken some pains and space to present details of the witnessing of this case. The reliability of the people concerned and the fact that the child's statements were recorded before any verification make the case seem more authentic than many cases of this type. And this further justifies our taking trouble to consider all remaining possibilities with regard to the communication by normal means of information about Ibrahim Bouhamzy to Imad Elawar.

But if one believes, as I do, in the honesty of the people concerned, then the main other normal hypothesis remaining is that of cryptomnesia combined with a personation by Imad of the previous personality. Here it seems to me that the errors of inference made by Imad's parents in putting together his statements weigh not only against fraud, but equally against cryptomnesia. In view of the fact that Imad began talking about the previous life when he was between a year and a year and a half old (prior to which he would have been almost continuously in the company of his mother or grandmother, or both), we cannot imagine that he could have acquired the relevant information directly from someone outside the family without his parents knowing who this person was. In short, the theory of cryptomnesia in this case, as in most other cases involving very small children, has to suppose that the parents had the information, passed it on to the child somehow, and then themselves completely forgot that they ever had known the information which emerged after an incubation period from the lips of the child. Now some people have read books and afterwards insisted that they have not and still later have found notes or other evidence which showed clearly that they had nevertheless read these books. In the present case, the information shown by Imad did not exist in books or newspapers, but nevertheless his parents might have heard it from some acquaintance or others whom they afterwards forgot. It seems most unlikely, however, that Imad's parents could have known all this information, amounting to some seventy details, at one time and not have recognized any of it upon its re-emergence from Imad a year or so later. And the proof of their not recognizing it later lies in the various incorrect assumptions they made in piecing Imad's story together. If, for example, they had once known that not Mahmoud, but Said Bouhamzy had been killed by a truck, they would surely have corrected Imad instead of passing on to me the inference they made on this point. Similarly, they would have noted alterations in the details in the relationship of Jamileh, in the placing of Amin as a "judge," and in stating that the dog was a "hunting" dog. These errors, we must note, are not errors of imagery (as some others may be) on the part of Imad. His parents afterwards stated that they had inferred relationships in their efforts to make sense of his statements.

Apart from these details, I have already explained why I think it virtually impossible for the Elawar family to have acquired such detailed and intimate information about the life of Ibrahim Bouhamzy as Imad showed unless they had made deliberate inquiries. This line of thought pursued returns us from cryptomnesia to fraud, which I have already rejected as an unreasonable hypothesis.

If we can then reject both fraud and cryptomnesia as hypotheses for the case, we have left as serious contenders to explain it either some kind of extrasensory perception plus personation, possession, or reincarnation. I shall consider these contending hypotheses at length in the General Discussion to follow.

Two Later Interviews with Additional Informants. In March, 1968, I succeeded in meeting Mr. Faris Amin Elawar and also his son, Saleem, in Kornayel. Mr. Faris Amin Elawar went to Khriby from time to time and was acquainted there with a first cousin of Ibrahim Bouhamzy, but could not remember (if he ever knew) how he had died. He denied any close acquaintance with the Bouhamzy family in Khriby. And specifically he denied, contrary to the testimony mentioned above of his cousin, Kassim Elawar, any knowledge of the bus accident in Baadaran.

Saleem Elawar recalled the death of Said Bouhamzy and said he, along with four or five other members of his family, had gone from Kornayel to attend the funeral of Said Bouhamzy in Khriby. He remembered meeting members of the deceased's family at the funeral, but could not recall Ibrahim specifically. He could give the name of only one other member of the family, Selhab Bouhamzy who, however, did not figure in Imad's statements. He had never heard of Jamileh.

These last two interviews left me with the impression that there had been rather more visiting between Kornayel and Khriby than I had previously thought. At the same time they reinforced my conclusion that persons known to Imad's family did not have knowledge of the details of the intimate life of the Bouhamzy family.

I am unable to explain the discrepancy between the statement by Imad's grandfather that Faris Amin Elawar had verified some details of the bus accident in which Ibraham Bouhamzy had been involved and Faris Amin Elawar's own denial, four years later, that he had any knowledge of such a bus accident. Possibly during the intervening four years he had forgotten what he knew and forgotten that he had known about this bus accident. And possibly Imad's grandfather attributed the verification he received about the bus accident to the wrong person.

The Later Development of Imad. I did not meet Imad or his family between 1964 and 1968. But in the latter year, I visited them again and also met them on subsequent visits to Lebanon in 1969, 1972, and 1973.

In March, 1968, Imad was a few months more than nine years old. I met only him and his mother that year; his father was absent. Imad was doing well at school. His mother said that he was still talking about the previous life and, in her opinion, talking "even more than before." (This disagreed with the impression I had earlier that he had passed the peak of talking about the previous life at about the time of my visits in 1964.) Imad expressed disappointment that Ibrahim Bouhamzy's older brother, Fuad, had never been to Kornayel to visit him.

Imad mentioned Jamileh frequently at this time and expressed a wish to see her. (She had married and was living in Aley, about eight miles from Kornayel.) He reminisced about Ibrahim's relationship with her and said that he (as Ibrahim) had been ready to elope with her and actually had a license, but his family found the license and tore it up. Imad said that Ibrahim's family would not let him marry Jamileh because her family belonged to the party of Druses opposed to that of the Bouhamzy family. The Bouhamzys belonged to the Joumblati moiety of the Druses, whereas Jamileh was of the Yazbaki moiety, as are, incidentally, the Elawars. (Imad's maternal grandfather, who was present for part of this interview, gave his opinion that Ibrahim was not allowed to marry Jamileh because she was of a lower class than he, the Bouhamzys of Khriby being prominent and well-to-do persons; but as he was from Kornayel and not from Khriby, I think he could only have given a second-hand opinion on this point.)

Imad also kept asking for Ibrahim's rifle, which he said belonged to him. He said he had bought it himself! He enjoyed hunting as much as ever. He had completely lost the fear of trucks he had shown previously.

Imad's family were trying to let him forget the previous life and did not bring it up with him. He himself would start talking about Jamileh, not they. Imad's mother gave examples of his continuing identification with Ibrahim Bouhamzy. One such incident occurred when Imad expressed sorrow over the death of a member of the Joumblati group. On another occasion, when someone in his family spoke against Kemal Joumblat (the leader of the Joumblatis), Imad exploded: "Damn *your* Bashir Elawar." (Bashir Elawar of Kornayel was a deputy in the Lebanese parliament and a prominent politician who later became a cabinet minister.) By emphasizing "your" Imad clearly separated himself as a Joumblati from his family, who were Yazbakis. A third example indicating persistence of Imad's memories occurred in my presence during this same visit. There was talk of taking him again to Khriby where he had not been since I had taken him there in 1964. When Imad heard this he added, "And to Aley, too!" He meant to see Jamileh there.

When I met Imad and his family again in February, 1969, his mother said that he was still talking about the previous life and especially about Jamileh, whom he wished to see. He had still not met her. Imad had shifted his plans for her somewhat and was now saying that he would like to marry her daughter! He still wanted to hunt and continued to ask his father to buy him a gun.

At this time his family were trying to discourage him from talking about the previous life, but apparently with little success.

In February and March, 1972, I had two further meetings with Imad and his family. During this visit to Lebanon I also met again some of the earlier informants on the Bouhamzy side of the case, Mr. Haffez Bouhamzy and Mr. Fuad Bouhamzy, and one new informant, Mr. Mahmoud Bouhamzy, Ibrahim's maternal uncle.

By this time Imad was about thirteen years and three months old. He was in the fifth class at school and said he stood fifth or sixth in the class of twenty-five pupils. His parents said he was still talking "all the time" about Khriby. When I put a direct question to Imad about the fading of his memories, he insisted that he had forgotten nothing. (In fact, as will become clearer below, he was at this time forgetting much or had already done so.)

He also claimed that he still remembered some details of the "intermediate life" which he said he had passed at Dahr el Ahmar between the death of Ibrahim and his own birth. Mr. Fuad Bouhamzy told me in 1969 that Imad had mentioned this intermediate life during his first visit to Khriby in 1964. He was not himself present when Imad visited Khriby then and so was a secondhand witness of this. But I mention what he said to show that Imad did not put forward details of the "intermediate life" for the first time only in 1972. Imad now associated the names of Adil (item 11 of Tabulation 1) and Talal (item 12 of Tabulation 1) with this "intermediate life." He said they were his brothers in that life. These are not uncommon names in Lebanon and conceivably there could have been persons with such names associated both with the personality of the "intermediate life," if it occurred, and with the life of Ibrahim Bouhamzy. Imad could not remember the name he had had in the life at Dahr el Ahmar nor how he had died. The details he gave were insufficient to justify any attempt to trace this "intermediate life" further.

In the summer of 1970 Imad met for the first time Mr. Mahmoud Bouhamzy, Ibrahim's maternal uncle. When Mr. Mahmoud Bouhamzy was shown to Imad he was asked if he could recognize him, but he could not. He was then shown an old photograph of Mr. Mahmoud Bouhamzy taken at a time when he wore a moustache which he had since shaved off. Imad said the photograph was "of my Uncle Mahmoud." Mr. Mahmoud Bouhamzy then invited Imad to spend a few days with him in Khriby. He had still not been back there since I had taken him in 1964. In Khriby Imad made himself at home and went hunting with Mr. Fuad Bouhamzy's sons, using Ibrahim's old hunting gun! He showed a strong attachment to Mr. Fuad Bouhamzy and stayed close to him much of the time, even when he (Mr. Fuad Bouhamzy) was ill in bed.

One episode which occurred during this visit to Khriby had particularly impressed Mr. Mahmoud Bouhamzy, who was my informant for it. On the street one day Imad had recognized a man and he asked permission of Mr. Mahmoud Bouhamzy to talk with him. Mr. Mahmoud Bouhamzy asked Imad: "What do you want to talk to that man for? He is a former soldier." Imad replied that this was precisely why he wanted to talk with the man. He mentioned the man's name, but Mr. Mahmoud Bouhamzy had forgotten what the name was in 1972. Imad and the man then had a long talk and the man declared himself satisfied with what Imad told him. He confirmed to Mr. Mahmoud Bouhamzy that he and Ibrahim had entered the (French) army on the same day and had been close companions during their army service.

The above incidents tend to confirm Imad's claim of preserving at least some memories of the previous life. But other items of this period showed that he was losing clarity and getting details mixed up. His parents described two other items—a statement and a recognition—made by Imad at Khriby in 1970. Imad was in the room when they credited him with these and I thought he gave tacit approval to what his parents reported he had said and done. But Mr. Fuad Bouhamzy, who was at Khriby during Imad's visit, did not confirm the account of Imad's parents.

The blurring of some of Imad's memories became further apparent from a third item which I sought to verify myself. Imad's parents (again with Imad in the room and listening) said they had heard that one Abu Naim had recently died in the village of Maaser el Shouf. (Maaser el Shouf is in the Shouf district of Lebanon in which Khriby lies and is therefore in the Joumblati and Bouhamzy "territory.") When Imad heard the announcement of the death of this man, he said: "Oh, the poor fellow. He was a grocer who had broken a leg and used a wooden one." Imad's family had not verified these details, but I decided to try to do so.

Mr. Haffez Bouhamzy, whom I saw first in Khriby, seemed to remember having heard of the recent death of one Abu Naim in Maaser el Shouf and said that he had had a broken leg. Another informant at Khriby, himself a grocer, said he also had heard that a grocer called Abu Naim, who had had a leg broken, had died at Maaser el Shouf. But when I went to Maaser el Shouf I could find no trace whatever of Abu Naim or a grocer with another name who had died there recently with or without a broken leg. There had been a death in the village a month or two before, but the deceased was not a grocer and had not had a broken leg.

Mr. Mahmoud Bouhamzy, when I asked him about these statements, said he remembered that in the time of Ibrahim there had been a grocer with a wooden leg living at the village of Mrasti. (Mrasti is not far from Khriby in the direction of Baadaran.) Mr. Fuad Bouhamzy mentioned yet another person who might have entered into this item. He was a grocer named Abu Hassan Naim who lived in Goiedih, another village of the Shouf district. He had been murdered the previous summer. He did not have a wooden leg. Mr. Fuad Bouhamzy also knew of a shoemaker called Lebien (I am not sure that I took down this name correctly) who lived in Maaser el Shouf and had a wooden leg, but he was still living.

I have gone into this item in some detail to show that the ingredients of Imad's statement could have derived from actual persons known to Ibrahim. Possibly when Imad heard of the death of the man who lived in Maaser el Shouf a train of associations was started off in his mind. And he then fused and muddled the images coming into his consciousness. This had happened to some extent much earlier, especially in his confusion of the death of Said Bouhamzy (in a truck accident) as if this had happened to Ibrahim. (But in fairness to Imad, I must add that with some at least of the items about which he seemed to be mixed up in 1964, his parents had introduced the confusion by making faulty inferences from what Imad had told them.)

In summary of the evidence bearing on the preservation of Imad's memories to the age of nearly fourteen in 1972, I would say that he had provided rather good evidence of still having some imaged memories by his ability to make recognitions of persons known to Ibrahim Bouhamzy. This is rather unusual even among Druse cases where the memories of the previous lives (for reasons that I do not pretend to understand) seem to fade more slowly than they do with subjects of other cultures. At the same time, the evidence did not support Imad's claim to have retained all memories perfectly. He was, so to say, a conforming party to his parents attributing to him three items that I could not verify. Considering his remarkable accuracy on details of the previous life in 1964, his overall success had fallen considerably.

In April, 1973, I went to Kornayel for another visit with Imad and his family. Imad was then in the first class of secondary school. He was still standing among the first five pupils in a class of twenty-two. He still wanted to visit Khriby (and remain there longer than he had on his last visit in 1972) and still talked of marrying Jamileh's daughter. (He had still not met either Jamileh or her daughter.) Some months before, Lateife Bouhamzy, Ibrahim Bouhamzy's mother, had died. Imad had not received an invitation to the funeral. (The funerals of Druse women are often minor affairs with few invitations issued to persons outside the immediate family of the deceased.) He felt sad over her death and vexed at not being invited to the funeral. As we talked of the death of Lateife Bouhamzy a wave of grief came over Imad and he became momentarily tearful, showing us the persisting strength of attachment to the previous family.

Apart from having memories of a previous life, not a significant deviation or point of distinction among the Druses since so many of them have such memories, Imad in 1972–3 was, so far as I could tell, developing along entirely normal lines for a boy of his age.

VII

Discussion of Results
Obtained in Follow-up Interviews

BEFORE coming to a general discussion of alternative interpretations of these cases I shall here first consider the contributions which the follow-up interviews can make to the understanding and evaluation of the cases. Follow-up interviews can no doubt assist in a variety of ways, but I shall draw attention to only three aspects of the cases which I think they helped to clarify, although I do not claim that the follow-up interviews have resolved all problems connected with these topics.

First, there is the question of the confidence that we can place in the testimony of the witnesses. It may be wondered—and some readers have—whether in the rather brief periods of my initial investigations I could make a sufficient appraisal of the integrity of the informants and, assuming their integrity, of their freedom from grave errors of memory or bias in presenting their information to me. Almost invariably during initial interviews there is a certain reserve on both sides. Also, on the side of the informants, a wish to please me may in various ways have colored the testimony. This may have happened even though I do not think many of the informants could tell what I was looking for, and there were times when I was not sure myself.

In the early interviews also, the informants often showed hesitancy or stronger reservations in discussing the less admirable aspects of the subject's behavior or that of the related previous personality. The latter particularly was likely to be depicted more favorably than candidly. In later interviews I have usually found all the informants more at ease. They may bring out details they had previously forgotten and they seem to me to be usually more open and frank in discussing the behavior of the subject or the previous personality concerned in the case.[1]

The later follow-up interviews have also contributed additional information about the reliability of the informants. The reader of these reports has

[1] I had more than one interview with many of the subjects and their families before publication of the first edition of this book. Such repeated or multiple interviews before publication occurred with three of the Indian cases, three of the Alaskan cases, and in the case of Imad Elawar of Lebanon.

to depend upon my appraisal of this factor. It may be of some additional value for me to add, therefore, that nothing emerged in the later interviews to cause me to revise my earlier judgment, which was that the informants, although sometimes inaccurate about details, had given me information which was to the best of their knowledge true and which could be relied upon in essentials.

Secondly, the follow-up interviews permit some further appraisal of the personalities of the subjects of these cases. Some readers of the first edition of this book expressed a wish to have more information about the subjects. It was not always clear just what additional information they thought would be helpful, but the commonest request was for data bearing on the mental health of the subjects. Some critics of these cases believe that anyone who imagines that he has lived before must be—almost by defi-nition—mentally ill. They think he should at least show signs of a dis-sociated state, if not of schizophrenia. On the other hand, some persons inclined to accept the cases as best interpreted by reincarnation have ex-pressed concern about the effects on the subject of recalling a previous life. They ask if these memories are not sometimes terrible burdens that slow down the maturation and adaptation of the subjects.

During my initial investigations of these cases I never obtained any data which made me think the subjects were mentally ill. To be sure, a small child who acts as if someone else's past is its present and makes remarks such as "I wonder who is feeding my children—perhaps they are hungry" could be considered at least to some extent to be in a dissociated state when making such remarks; for at these times the child seems almost oblivious of its present situation. But at other times, and indeed most of the time, the subjects are perfectly well aware of their present situations, even when they complain about their families in comparing them with those of the previous life. We could call such children to some extent emotionally disturbed, but this would in no way explain or explain away their verifiable statements and other related behavior that correspond to the previous lives they claim to be remembering.

This is not to say that I am content with the information I obtained concerning the personalities of the subjects of these cases or have obtained in subsequent studies of other cases. In particular, I hope with additional funds and assistance to begin some systematic psychological testing of some of the subjects in fresh cases that await study. Yet I think the most valuable of all information we can have about another person comes not from our immediate observations, but from watching the course of his later life. If these children were mentally ill during the peak period of their talk about the previous lives—usually between the ages of three and seven —then this fact should become obvious in the failure of their adaptations later, if not in overt clinical illness. How then do the subjects of these cases emerge in this respect? Taking the course of a whole life eight to ten years provides only a short period of observation, but it can offer some useful data for considering this point further if not for settling it. (Some of the subjects were adults when I first met them, so we already had some record of how they had developed to that point.) I am glad to report that fifteen of the eighteen subjects whom I could see in follow-up interviews were developing well and had shown no signs of overt mental illness. Of those who were children when I first met them, the youngest had reached adolescence and the others had moved into their twenties. Various of them had had the usual troubles of these age periods, but in general they were adapting as well as the average person to their situations and some seemed to me to be doing rather better than average. One (Parmod) credited his memories of a previous life with giving him a broader view of life and a greater detachment and wisdom in coping with its vicissitudes than the ordinary person with a "one life view" of his destiny could have; and I think some of the other subjects had profited similarly.

Three of the eighteen subjects did develop clinical mental illness in later life. These were Wijeratne of Ceylon and Paulo Lorenz and Marta Lorenz of Brazil. I have given details about their illnesses in the reports of the follow-up interviews. The question to consider in this place is: Was there a significant connection between the mental illnesses they developed and the previous lives they remembered or the fact that they remembered previous lives? I think there is no evidence that they remembered previous lives because they were mentally ill; they were not mentally ill when, as children, they remembered the previous lives, unless we revert to the assumption, unjustified to me, that the mere fact of remembering a previous life defines one as mentally ill. And I do not think they became mentally ill because they had remembered previous lives. But I do see in each case a relevant connection between the previous life remembered and the subsequent mental illness.

In the case of Paulo the connection lies in the mode of adaptation to life stresses. The person (Emilia) whose life he remembered had commited suicide and so did he.[2]

Marta suffered in middle age from a depression severe enough to require her hospitalization for three weeks. This illness was precipitated by the suicide of her brother Paulo. I do not think it had any direct connection with the previous life Marta remembered beyond the fact that Sinhá had been depressive and suicidal and Marta showed the same

---

[2] In several other cases in which the related previous personality had committed suicide the subject has shown an inclination to contemplate and threaten suicide. See the information from the follow-up interview with Marta Lorenz in this volume and the report of the case of Faruq Faris Elawar (I. Stevenson. *Cases of the Reincarnation Type.* In preparation.).

tendencies as I mentioned earlier in my report of the follow-up interview with her.

In Wijeratne's case a somewhat different connection occurred between his mental illness and his memories of a previous life. This arose from the fact that a precipitating factor in the schizophrenia he developed in his early twenties was the real (or fantasied) rejection of him by a girl to whom he had become strongly attracted. The previous personality whose life he remembered (Ratran Hami) had been rejected by a woman (Podi Menike) and had then murdered her after which he was arrested, tried, convicted, and hanged.

On the question whether having memories of a previous life hinders the maturation of a subject I think I can give in general a negative answer. Most of the subjects forget the memories of the previous lives between the ages of five and ten, although wide variations in this occur, as I shall discuss next. As this happens the child has left (in consciousness) only his memories of his own childhood, although residues of behavior related to the previous life often outlast the imaged memories. Since the fading of the imaged memories usually begins at about the time the child starts school (and in my opinion this event accelerates it), he is not usually handicapped in his adaptation to school or other social occasions that occur during the years from five to ten. But occasionally one notes that the subject's preoccupation with the memories of the previous life does interfere with his adaptation. I mentioned above Parmod's opinion that remembering a previous life had helped him toward some serenity, but his mother had earlier taken a rather different view of its value to him. She blamed Parmod's later academic difficulties on the fact that during the years between four and seven he had been so lost in the memories of the previous life— busy playing with toy shops selling biscuits and soda water—that he had paid insufficient attention to what he should have been learning at school and elsewhere. In one other case (not of this volume) a mother reported a similar observation about the subject who seemed to be daydreaming at school, presumably wrapped up in her memories of the previous life. But such instances seem to comprise only a small minority of all cases.

Thirdly, the follow-up interviews have cast a little light on the processes influencing the fading or preservation of imaged memories of the previous lives. A study of the information I have furnished on this aspect of the subjects' later developments will show that many subjects say, at the time of the later interviews, that they have completely forgotten the previous lives they earlier remembered, but other subjects claim to have preserved their memories more or less intact. The tabulation below provides a summary of data for sixteen of the subjects concerning the duration of imaged memories and of personation by the subject of the related previous personality whose life he remembered.

The subjects' statements on this point require careful evaluation but I think we should not always take their assertions at face value and without further inquiry and information from other persons. In general, if a subject says he no longer has any conscious memories of the previous life we can believe this to be true. But even here we find occasional exceptions or cause for hesitation. A child of three to five generally feels no inhibition (at least in Asia) about claiming to have a spouse and children. But as the subject reaches later childhood and puberty, feelings of modesty or a fear of being teased may lead him to stop talking about the previous life even when it remains in consciousness. He may then say he has forgotten about the previous life simply to ward off inquiries that have become embarrassing or vexatious. I have known cases where this happened and in the present volume that of Sukla perhaps affords an example, although I am uncertain of the correct evaluation of her statement that she had forgotten in her mid-teens all memories of the previous life she formerly remembered.

On the other hand, a claim by the subject that he has preserved the memories intact also requires thoughtful assessment. Some subjects can provide independent evidence of preserving at least some memories beyond early childhood. For example, Gnanatilleka satisfied me when she was fourteen that she had correctly recognized a person known to the previous personality, Tillekeratne. And Imad Elawar at the age of twelve recognized a photograph and a person connected with the previous life he said he still remembered. On other details which he claimed to remember he was wrong, showing that although he preserved some memories he had lost others.

If the subject or his family present no independent evidence bearing on the persistence of the memories I find it difficult to evaluate a claim that they have not faded. One should not reject summarily the subject's claim, and yet one would like some additional support for it and for the following reason. A number of subjects who have reached adulthood have told me in words that vary, but carry the same sense: "At this time I do not myself remember anything of the previous life directly; all I remember is what my family told me I said when I was young." What happens then is that with repeated rehearsing by the family in the child's presence of what he said when young, the original memories may become layered over and forgotten while the memories of the reports of what he said remain. These are then memories of the subject's own childhood, not of the previous life he originally remembered. Some subjects can evidently distinguish the two types of memories, but others may think they can without really being able to do so.

I have already indicated that fading of the memories when it occurs often coincides (or at least begins) with the child's attendance at school, which usually starts between the ages of four and six. I think we should

TABULATION

Duration of Imaged Memories and Personation

Subject	Beginning Age of Declarations and Behavior Related to Previous Personality	Age at which Major Informational and Behavioral Features of the Case Ceased or Began to Diminish (Data of 1961–64)	Duration of Major Signs of Personation	Fading or Persistence of Memories at Latest Follow-up Interviews (Data of 1969–72)
Prakash	4½	Still continuing at 10	5 years	Claim of no fading at age 20 in 1971
Jasbir	3½	Still continuing at 10	7 years	Claim of no fading at age 20 in 1971
Sukla	1½	Still continuing at 7, beginning to fade	5 years	Complete amnesia claimed at age 16 in 1970
Swarnlata	3½	Continuing at 13	10 years	Claim of no fading at age 23 in 1971
Ravi Shankar	2½	Almost completely ceased at 11	7 years	Complete amnesia claimed at age 18 in 1969
Mallika	4	Ceased at 6	2 years	No follow-up information obtained
Parmod	2½	Spontaneous mention of previous life much diminished by age 12, but ability to recall persisted after	10 years	Some memories continuing at age 27 in 1971
Gnanatilleka	2	Ceasing at 6	4 years	Memories almost, but not entirely faded at age (nearly) 15 in 1970
Wijeratne	2	Details of information began fading at 5½, but personation persisting still at 14	12 years	Memories largely faded, but some persisting at age 21 in 1968

Ranjith	2	Persisting at 18	16 years	Claim of no fading at age 26 in 1968
Marta	2½	Some continuing into adulthood (age 44 in 1962) but with much fading by age 10	7 years	Partial fading of memories, partial retention claimed at age 54 in 1972
Paulo	2	Residues of behavior persisted to age 39 in 1962, but major behavioral incidents ceased by age 5	3 years	No additional follow-up information on persistence of memories
Jimmy	2	Began to diminish at 3; faded completely at 9	4 years	No return of imaged memories since early fading by age 19 in 1972
William	3½	Faded by 11	7 years	No follow-up information obtained
Corliss	1½	Largely faded by 9	7 years	Complete amnesia claimed at age 25 in 1972
Imad	1½	Continuing but diminishing at age 5½ in 1964	4 years	Persistence of memories claimed but some fading evident at age 14 in 1972
Average	2.6 years		6.9 years	
Median	2.3 years		7.0 years	

NOTE: Data on the other cases were not included in this tabulation because they were not available or not considered adequately reliable.

expect this. Up to that time the child has been largely confined to his own home physically and to his own family socially. He has lived in his own situation—to be sure, with varying degrees of freedom—and has had comparatively few demands to conform to other people. He can, if he wants, drift back into memories of another life without much interruption or interference. But school sets different requirements—of regular attendance away from home, of disciplined attention to what the teacher is saying, and of social adaptation to a swarm of strange fellow pupils quite different from the usual persons of his family. These changes force, if they do not jerk, the subject into a better grasp of his current position in life. The new and various experiences that come to the child at this time gradually (or rapidly) cover over, I believe, the memories of the previous life.

Other factors may also influence the child toward preserving the memories. One is their frequent repetition to interested persons within or outside the family. I have an impression that one encounters more claims to preservation of the memories in adulthood among subjects who, in childhood, received a good deal of attention from members of their family, curious observers, and newspaper reporters. These persons would ask the child to say again and again what he had already repeated many times and such reviews would tend to fix the memories. But this inference of mine has no support from a systematic comparison of such cases with those which were not accompanied by such attention. Moreover, such frequent repetition in childhood could just as easily tend to preserve the pseudo-memories (derived from what the child said he remembered when he was a child) as the original imaged memories of the previous life.

Repeated visits between the two families concerned provide another factor which can preserve the memories—and again, also any pseudo-memories—from fading. I think I can detect at least a loose connection between the claim to have preserved the memories and repeated visits between the families. We can see a trend in this direction by considering the eight Asian cases of this volume in which the previous personality was identified and belonged to a family different from that of the subject. In four of these cases the subject at the follow-up interviews said the memories had faded partially or completely (Sukla, Parmod, Ravi Shankar, and Gnanatilleka). In three of these four cases visits between the two families concerned had been discontinued or had become very infrequent. The exception was Parmod, who said his memories had partially faded, but who continued to visit the previous family rather often. In contrast, four other subjects claimed to have preserved the memories more or less intact or completely so (Swarnlata, Jasbir, Prakash, and Imad). In three of these four cases the subjects were still regularly visiting the previous families. In this group Imad was the exception for the families concerned in his case did not exchange any visits between 1964 and 1970. And Imad provided some evidence of preserving at least some of his memories of the previous life up to the age of twelve in 1970.

We should draw conclusions from this small series, or even from a much larger one, with the greatest caution. Many other factors must enter into the processes which govern the fading or persistence of these memories. Among these we should certainly attach special importance to the attitude of the subjects' parents. Many parents try to suppress their children from talking about the previous life, others encourage them to do so, and still others say they do neither. In each case such attitudes almost certainly have some influence, even if it may be less than the parents sometimes think, on the fading or preservation of the memories. Even more important I think is the content of the memories themselves. I have published elsewhere data which show a high incidence in these cases of previous personalities who died violently.[3] A man being led to execution once remarked: "This is going to be a great lesson to me." If he had survived death perhaps it would have been. It seems to me reasonable to suppose that the intensity of an experience such as a violent death can in some way strengthen or "fixate" memories so that they are more readily preserved in consciousness or remain accessible to it. This conjecture agrees with what many psychologists consider an important factor in ordinary learning —the intensity of an experience to the subject.[4] The only new feature introduced here is the application of this principle to memories that may be carried over from one life to another. The principle could still apply if it seems best to interpret these cases not as instances of reincarnation but as examples of extrasensory perception on the part of the living subject. In either case the subject might have readier access to memories of events accompanied by intense emotions such as violent deaths.

To summarize what the follow-up interviews have taught me about the fading or preservation of the imaged memories, I can repeat that some subjects say they have forgotten all about the previous lives and in most instances I think we should believe them; other subjects say they continue to remember the previous lives and in most instances I think we should treat such claims with caution, but not reject them offhand. The processes influencing forgetting or preservation of the memories are much

---

[3] I. Stevenson. "Cultural Patterns in Cases Suggestive of Reincarnation among the Tlingit Indian of Southeastern Alaska." *Journal A.S.P.R.*, Vol. 60, July, 1966, 229–243; I. Stevenson. "Characteristics of Cases of the Reincarnation Type in Turkey and their Comparison with Cases in Two other Cultures." *International Journal of Comparative Sociology*, Vol. 11, 1970, 1–17.

[4] For an old, but for me still valid statement of this principle, see E. L. Thorndike. *The Elements of Psychology*. New York: A. G. Seller, 1905: "The likelihood that any mental state or act will occur in response to any situation is in proportion to the frequency, recency, *intensity and resulting satisfaction* [my italics] of its connection with that situation or some part of it and with the total frame of mind in which the situation is felt" (p. 207).

more complicated than I at least had previously realized. We need now a much more systematic study of other, fresh cases with long-term follow-ups and evaluation of as many of the multiple factors as we can. Only then shall we obtain information justifying more confident conclusions.

In the above I have considered the fading of imaged memories in the subject's consciousness or in his ability to recall them into consciousness. But equally important questions, possibly even more important ones, derive from the little information we have about the recession, or persistence, as the case may be, of what I call the behavioral memories—the unusual behavior that often accompanies the subject's statements about the previous life and that, with rare exceptions, seems appropriate for the person whose life the subject is remembering. The intensity and persistence of such related behavior are only loosely connected with the abundance and persistence of the subject's statements about the previous life. Sometimes the subject has much to say about the previous life, but shows little or no unusual behavior; and, at the other extreme, some subjects make few or even no statements about a previous life and yet their behavior shows unusual features from a very early age—features that seem inexplicable on the basis of heredity or environmental influences but which might derive from a previous life. As to the persistence of the behavioral features, I have observed that in some cases, e.g., that of Ravi Shankar, residues of behavior apparently related to the previous life remain after a total fading of imaged memories. In other cases, the two types of memories—images and behavior—fade away together.

VIII

General Discussion

Introduction

ALTHOUGH proposing to take account in this discussion of all twenty cases here reported, and some others when appropriate, I do not believe that we must find one hypothesis which will account for all of them. I think that we should allow for the possibility that different hypotheses will best account for different cases. But we must find some satisfactory explanation for *each* of the cases. If we find that fraud accounts for one case, we must go on to the next and find some explanation for it, perhaps cryptomnesia. But then we must deal with the next case and the next. Also, in considering each case we must account for *all* of its accepted phenomena, not merely for some.

While weighing each case separately we can also look for patterns of similar characteristics in the various cases.

Normal Hypotheses

Fraud

Fraud seems the first serious theory requiring exclusion in these cases. I have already alluded to the possibility of fraud in presenting the data of the individual cases and I will therefore only summarize briefly here my opinions on the likelihood of fraud having occurred. We must consider both motives and opportunities for fraud. So far as I could learn, none of the children or their parents of these cases have gained any monetary reward as a consequence of the children's claims to have lived before and whatever publicity these have brought them. Occasionally children and parents of some of the cases, e.g., Swarnlata, have achieved some favorable publicity not displeasing to them, but most other children and families have found the publicity vexatious. Such favorable publicity as has occurred has never seemed sufficient to compensate for the effort required in staging a hoax. Moreover, if the parents developed the cases fraudulently they must have been willing to wait many years for the rewards of publicity since in some cases, e.g., Prakash and Wijeratne, other witnesses testified that they knew of the case years before news of it reached the public or press.

Critics of these cases sometimes suggest that children compensate for the poverty or maltreatment they experience in their own families by imagining themselves to belong to another family of greater wealth, superior caste, or more benevolent parents. This theory by itself does not account for the acquisition by the child of the information he shows about the previous personality. But if we overlook for the moment this aspect of the matter, the theory could have some merit if applied to the motivation of the children in the present cases alone. It happens that in several of these, the family of the alleged previous personality *did* enjoy circumstances of position, wealth, or housing that surpassed those of the child claiming the memories. However, I have studied a number of cases (as yet unpublished) in which the claimed previous life occurred in less favorable circumstances than the present one. Moreover, in most of the present cases the differences in circumstances between the two families seem slight and hardly sufficient to account for a fraud on the part of the child. In the case of Swarnlata a considerable difference existed between the affluence of the Pathak family of Katni and the relatively humble circumstances of the Mishra family in Chhatarpur. Swarnlata at times thought longingly of the happy and prosperous life led by Biya among the Pathak family. But she did not struggle to return to them and knew that in her (present) home she enjoyed the greatest affection from her parents and siblings. Moreover, Sri M. L. Mishra, her father, declined proffers of financial aid from the Pathak family which could have helped in the education of Swarnlata.

Nor can we identify other motives besides money as more reasonable explanations for getting up a fraud. A few children in Asia have received local attention from villagers who credulously believe that a child who remembers a previous life must also possess powers of healing and future-telling. Such adulation, however, occurs sporadically and transiently and it does not occur at all in Alaska or Brazil. It does not seem likely that it alone would justify the trouble of composing a fraudulent case. In the rare cases with actual direct evidence of fraud, the conspirators sometimes take no chances on the possibility of veneration by the public and arrange for the simulated return of a well-known figure, e.g., Mahatma Gandhi or some prominent saint. The previous personalities of the present cases, and of the great majority of other cases suggestive of rebirth with veridical features, lived obscure lives. Moreover, the lives and behavior of some of these personalities, e.g., Ratran Hami, the executed murderer in the case of Wijeratne, could hardly command the respect of their fellows or bring credit to their families.

Apart from the general lack or insufficiency of motives for fraud in these cases, the opportunities for it seem slight indeed. Knowing the towns and villages of India, Ceylon, and Alaska as I do, I think we can exclude the possibility of a child getting up a hoax on his own. He could only achieve a successful fraud with the assistance or the instruction of his parents. And someone in the trick—whether parents or child—would have had to gather a great deal of detailed information about the lives and circumstances of the other family. Some of the claimed memories could be inferred or derived from information in the public domain; but another, larger portion concerned intimate matters or details of family life not likely to be known outside the family circle. A successful fraud including such information would almost certainly have had to involve members of the ostensible previous family in the conspiracy. Moreover, the recognition tests (referring here only to those that did not include leading questions or other suggestions) would require for success either much coaching in advance or the participation of the many apparently recognized persons as confederates.

To these difficulties we must add those of directing and staging some of the highly emotional scenes I myself witnessed in the villages. I cannot believe that simple villagers would have the time or inclination to rehearse such dramas as occurred in Chhatta when the family of Prakash thought—or said they thought—I favored his returning to the other family. The complexity of the behavioral features of these cases alone seems to make fraud virtually out of the question, and I prefer to pass on to other more plausible explanations of them.

Cryptomnesia

Of the normal hypotheses which may account for these cases, cryptomnesia seems to me far more plausible than fraud. According to this theory, the child would somehow have known a person or other source having the information he later "remembered" about the alleged previous family. The child would somehow come in contact with this person or information and would later forget both the source of his information and the fact that he had ever obtained it, although he would remember the information and later present it dramatically as derived from a previous life. His parents would have known nothing about the person or object furnishing the information at the time or they would later have forgotten their earlier knowledge, thus genuinely expressing surprise at the statements of the child.

Now for almost all the cases in the present group, only a *person* would have sufficed to furnish the information to the child for this process. First, in the villages of Asia and Alaska, there occurred (with rare exceptions) no printed (or broadcast) records of the lives and deaths of the previous personalities. In Asia newspapers are unknown for the most part outside the large cities. Secondly, if public records had existed, the children would not have known how to read these at the age (usually under three) when they first began their main declarations of the previous lives (see tabulation pp. 326–327). Radios were almost completely unknown in villages of India and Ceylon and television was just beginning, even in Delhi, in the 1960's.

In some of the cases, e.g., Wijeratne, Marta, William George, Jr., Norman Despers, and Corliss Chotkin, Jr., members of the child's family already knew most or all of the facts stated by the child. Cryptomnesia may suffice in these cases as an explanation for all, or nearly all, of the *informational* aspects of the cases, although it will not, I think, suffice to explain other features of some of these cases, e.g., the behavioral features or the birthmarks.

In other cases, however, cryptomnesia does not adequately account even for the informational features involved unless we can imagine how the information could have reached the child. The circumstances of life in the villages of Asia and Alaska virtually exclude the possibility of contact between a small child and a strange adult without knowledge of this on the part of the parents. Asian children especially, live under extremely close surveillance by their parents. They play with their siblings usually within a courtyard of the house. Small boys rarely, and girls almost never, leave the area of the house unaccompanied by an adult. The hypothesis of cryptomnesia as applied to cases of small children in Asian villages almost requires some knowledge at one time by the parents of the person conveying the information about the previous life to the child.

If we reject fraud as a satisfactory explanation then we must believe that the parents and other witnesses are telling the truth when they assert a complete ignorance of the relevant family in the other village or town. When the witnesses number a few persons only, as in the case of Mallika, we may imagine that errors of memory have led to the forgetting of previous contacts between the families. But in other cases, the witnesses interviewed number several or more in each family; it is unlikely all would have forgotten about acquaintance with persons from the other family or village.

Some critics may argue that a brief, almost casual acquaintance between child and stranger would suffice to communicate the information later allegedly remembered by the child. But such brief contacts would not suffice, I feel sure, for two reasons. First, the information communicated is often rich in quantity and minute in detail. Also, as already mentioned, it frequently includes items of a highly intimate nature concerning the family of the previous life, information not likely to be communicated by an adult of one family to a child of a strange family, least of all in India where a wide social gulf separates children and adults, especially of different families.

Secondly, the mere passing of information casually would not explain the more satisfactory recognitions by these children of people and places of the previous life. Leaving aside those recognitions prompted by leading questions, recognitions of two other kinds occurred in these cases. Some recognitions occurred spontaneously, the child spotting someone on a street or in a crowd and addressing him by name. Such spontaneous recognitions occurred, for example, in the cases of Gnanatilleka, Imad, Corliss Chotkin, Jr., and Swarnlata. Other recognitions occurred when someone asked the child a question which did not give any guidance or permit any cues from other persons for the answers, e.g., "Do you know who I am?" or "How were we related in your previous life?" Recognitions of this type occurred, for example, in the cases of Gnanatilleka, Imad, Swarnlata, Sukla, and Marta. If we can exclude *sotto voce* whisperings in the hearing of the child, recognitions of this sort, and of the spontaneous kind, require either (a) very considerable prior rehearsal of the information necessary to effect the recognition instantaneously (which most of the children accomplished), (b) very considerable powers of extrasensory perception, or (c) some prior familiarity with the persons or places recognized. (Such familiarity could arise from either simple reincarnation or from possession and this feature would not permit a choice between these two hypotheses. I shall discuss this further below.)

In the future understanding of these cases, I believe that great importance will attach to recognition tests properly carried out. When recognitions occur under circumstances warranting confidence, I doubt if we can explain them by the mere passage of information from witnesses to the subject whether through normal means of communication or through extrasensory perception. To recognize someone requires a reservoir of information from which the recognizer makes an appropriate selection in response to a particular stimulus. I do not think we know the limits of accomplishment in rehearsing and achieving recognition without actual acquaintance with the subject later recognized. The closest similar situation known to us occurs in the efforts made by investigators of a crime to recognize a criminal fugitive from the verbal descriptions of the alleged criminal given by witnesses. In the attempts at this which I have seen, an artist first renders the verbal description of the wanted criminal into a sketch which the newspapers publish and other police departments study. I think it well known that this method throws a very wide net over many suspects whom the police must then scrutinize by other means. Exceptions no doubt occur when the criminal and suspect each have some prominent, unique mark on the face, e.g., a large scar.

Polanyi [1] has interpreted recognitions of other people as instances of

---

[1] M. Polanyi. "Tacit Knowing." *Reviews of Modern Physics*, Vol. 34, 1962, 601–616.

tacit knowing comparable to skills in their complexity and tacitness. He describes the difficulties of recognizing another person from a verbal description or even a photograph of that person and states:

> Any description we can give of a person will usually apply equally to millions of other people, from all of whom we could distinguish him at a glance [if we knew him]. The number of elements involved in such discrimination can be illustrated by the way in which the British police construct the likeness of a person whom a witness has seen. They use a slide file of 550 facial characteristics, such as different sets of eyes, lips and chins. The witness picks the individual features that most closely resemble his idea of the criminal's face, and from this selection a composite picture is assembled. Even so, such a picture can merely serve as one clue among others. For the identification of a person is such a delicate operation that even a genuine photograph of him may not suffice. . . . A witness may fail to recognize a person by a photograph, but pick him out at an identification parade (p. 603).

The task of recognition becomes easier if the person to be recognized does have markedly deviant features. Jasbir, for example, recognized a cousin of Sobha Ram who had prominent ears and for this reason was nicknamed "Gandhiji." We would not rank this recognition so high as Jasbir's recognitions of other persons who lacked any such prominent feature.

In everyday life we confess the difficulty we have in recognizing strangers by arranging to limit the circumstances when we plan to meet them. We identify a person we have never previously seen by his dress, e.g., wearing a blue suit, and we restrict the place where we will meet him, e.g., under the clock in the railroad station. Even with more cues than these, we can have difficulty, as I have had, in "recognizing" a stranger and would often fail altogether but for the additional cue of looking for someone who looks as if he expected to meet someone. In these situations, too, we know the name of the person we are meeting. The children of the cases under discussion have to recognize the face or other attributes of the person and furnish the name or state a relationship with the person.[2]

I have dwelt on the tests of recognition because I think the better recognitions make difficult the application of cryptomnesia as an explanation of the cases in which such recognitions occur. Cryptomnesia may suffice to account for other cases in which the child offers a small amount of information about the previous life, but does not achieve such recognitions. Whatever the origin of the information available to the child, the recognitions require that he have a large amount of it available to him in one way or another. That this information may become available to

---

[2] The matter has sufficient importance perhaps to justify experiments which would attempt to test the limits of recognitions from verbal descriptions by other persons alone.

him through extrasensory perception is another possibility which I shall discuss later. At this point I want only to emphasize that the available supply of information must be large for the recognitions.

Every student of abnormal psychology or psychical research knows of many cases demonstrating the occurrence of cryptomnesia. Persons have reproduced, often years later, fragments of books or other information which they had learned many years before and forgotten they had learned. Coleridge's case provides an instructive example both of cryptomnesia and of diligent pursuit of the sources of the information dramatically demonstrated years later.[3] Martín studied in much detail the case of Señora Adela Albertelli, who wrote during trances rather long passages in several different languages unknown to her in her waking state. Martín traced the origin of some (not all) of the written passages to books or magazine articles which Señora Albertelli may have seen at one time.[4] Myers [5] and Sidis [6] reported another case of trance writing of material probably illustrating cryptomnesia since investigators found a source for the English verses written, although not for some words in Latin tied to English words to make some doggerel verses.

Most instances of cryptomnesia with an *identified* source of the material produced include only a recitative reproduction of the previously learned content. The subject spouts it forth as spoken or written material and does not adapt his information to present circumstances such as successful recognition tests require. Possibly other examples of cryptomnesia may exhibit more range and flexibility in the use of the information acquired. Perhaps some of the present cases suggestive of rebirth may prove instances of these.

In a small number of cases of established cryptomnesia elements of personation have occurred. For example, in the case reported by Dickinson [7] the second personality of the medium gave a plausible personation of one "Blanche Poynings," a lady of the court of King Richard II. (In its main features the case is one of alleged spirit communication, not of claimed memories of previous lives, but for purposes of considering what

---

[3] S. T. Coleridge. *Biographia Literaria.* New York: The Macmillan Company, 1926, 70–72. (First published in 1817.)

[4] J. Martín. Personal communication. In 1962, in Rosario, Argentina, I had an opportunity to observe Señora Albertelli during one of her trances in which she wrote slowly, but clearly, a passage in English (the exact origin of which could not be traced). In her waking state she did not know English at all and she could not communicate *responsively* in English in her trances.

[5] F .W. H. Myers. *Human Personality and its Survival of Bodily Death.* London: Longmans, Green and Co., 1903, Vol. I, 354–360.

[6] B. Sidis. *The Psychology of Suggestion.* New York: Appleton, 1898, 285–289.

[7] G. L. Dickinson. "A Case of Emergence of a Latent Memory Under Hypnosis." *Proc. S.P.R.,* Vol. 25, 1911, 455–467.

cryptomnesia can account for, I do not consider this important.) Subsequently nearly all the information skillfully dramatized by the subconscious mind of the sensitive was found in a book, *Countess Maud*, which the subject had read when a child of twelve, but which reading she had completely forgotten. In this case some personation and dramatization occurred. The subject thus claimed to be in contact with a "communicator" whose ingredients probably derived solely from memories of a book retained and dramatized in subconscious portions of her own personality. But this case lacked something which the cases here reported demonstrate, namely, the fusion of the two personalities in such a way that the present personality remains constantly in touch with its current environment while drawing (from somewhere) on the knowledge of the previous personality. The information and behavior exhibited by "Blanche Poynings" only appeared when the subject was hypnotized or worked a planchette. We must contrast this with the complete or partial fusion of personalities in the waking state and in everyday living shown by the subjects of the cases here reported.

Pickford reported another case with personation of communicators and information probably derived entirely from normal sources.[8] The alleged medium in this case produced communications from notable composers, e.g., Weber and Beethoven, but he had (possibly in dissociated states) read extensively about the lives of these persons. Here again, personation and identification were confined to the periods of dissociation when the great composers would "communicate" during the subject's trances. The subject did not identify himself with these composers at other times.

In a case reported by Bose,[9] a child of ten claimed to recall the suicide of a woman in another village which he named. Eventually investigation traced the information which the child remembered to a newspaper clipping found in the home of relatives where the boy had stayed some years earlier. The woman's suicide had occurred several years before, but during the boy's lifetime. He did not claim he had witnessed the suicide or learned about it in a previous life, nor did anyone report altered personality in the boy. This case, in short, illustrates illusions of memory. It resembles another instructive case cited by Hyslop[10] of a man who claimed to remember the presidential campaign of William Henry Harrison, which occurred in 1840. When someone pointed out to him that he was born in 1847, he realized that what he remembered were his uncles' vivid narrations of that campaign which he had mistaken for memories of his own about it.

[8] R. W. Pickford. "An 'Hysterical' Medium." *British Journal of Medical Psychology*, Vol. 19, 1943, 363–366.

[9] S. K. Bose. "A Critique of the Methodology of Studying Parapsychology." *Journal of Psychological Researches*, Vol. 3, 1959, 8–12.

[10] J. H. Hyslop. *Borderland of Psychical Research*. Boston: Small, Maynard and Co., 1906, 372.

I do not think we can ever exclude absolutely some earlier normal communications of information to these children. I agree with Chari [11, 12] that unless we can do so there always remains some possibility that cryptomnesia accounts for the cases. But this possibility becomes reduced, I think, by the failure so far to find a case which would act as a model of how cryptomnesia could account for all aspects of the cases here reported. Such a case would have to include the following features: (a) Source of information traced to a book or to a person or persons who had the information without the child or his parents remembering the sources of the information, (b) mobilization of this information in appropriate responses to current stimuli during ordinary consciousness, and (c) dramatization of the information into a personality sufficiently plausible to impress others with the appropriateness of behavioral and emotional responses expected of the previous personality.

Judged by these criteria, the known or published cases of cryptomnesia do not match the rebirth cases in one or other requirement. Instances of recitative cryptomnesia fail to satisfy the second and third requirements and instances of mediumistic or hypnotically induced artificially created "previous personalities" do not satisfy the second criterion.

I know of only one published case suggestive of reincarnation in which the source of the information apparently remembered by the subject has been clearly identified. I refer to the case cited in an earlier article by myself [13] of an English army officer who with his wife had the experience of seeming to recognize a wayside pool in the country. Both the officer and his wife identified various details and became convinced of having lived in that area before, although they were sure they had never visited it before. Subsequently they remembered having seen in an art gallery a picture of a wayside pool resembling the one they "recognized" in the country. The case included only the experience of *déjà vu* which man and wife shared, and did not include veridical informational features. This was an instance of *fausse reconnaissance à deux*. I know of no case of the rebirth type in which the identification with the previous personality extended over years and in which the source of the information apparently remembered by the subject was clearly identified. In cases in which both personalities occur in the same family, e.g., the case of Wijeratne, or in which the present family knew the previous personality, e.g., the case of Marta, we can believe that cryptomnesia may have occurred. And it may

[11] C. T. K. Chari. " 'Buried Memories' in Survivalist Research." *International Journal of Parapsychology*, Vol. 4, 1962, 40–61.

[12] C. T. K. Chari. "Paranormal Cognition, Survival and Reincarnation." *Journal* A.S.P.R., Vol. 56, October, 1962, 158–183.

[13] I. Stevenson. "The Evidence for Survival from Claimed Memories of Former Incarnations, Part 2. Analysis of the Data and Suggestions for Further Investigations." *Journal* A.S.P.R., Vol. 54, July, 1960, 95–117. (The case was originally described by L. S. Lewis in correspondence in the *London Morning Post*, November 5, 1936.)

have occurred in the other cases in which the families of the two personalities did not know each other prior to attempts at verification of the child's statements. But to assert this is to offer an assumption only and such an assumption requires support from a specific case in which cryptomnesia has been shown to be the explanation for the informational features of a case with veridical elements.

Some cases allegedly satisfying the first criterion of established cryptomnesia have not in fact done so. Thus one can claim that the extraordinary linguistic feats and vivid personality of Patience Worth [14, 15] derived from a combination of cryptomnesia and subconscious dramatization on the part of Mrs. Curran, the subject of this case. But no one has brought forward evidence of the source of Mrs. Curran's knowledge of early English. Similarly, attempts to discredit the possible paranormal elements in the case of Bridey Murphy [16] and attribute them all to cryptomnesia failed in the opinion of Ducasse,[17] an opinion with which I agree.[18] This does not mean that *all* the obscure or recondite items communicated by Bridey Murphy necessarily had a paranormal origin. But the effort made to attribute all these items to an earlier acquaintance on the part of the subject, Mrs. Tighe, with friends and relatives from Ireland or familiar with it, did violence to some facts and ignored others. What some critics of the case provided were *suppositions* of possible sources of the information about Bridey Murphy, not *evidence* that these had been the sources. It is one thing to speculate on possible sources of information and quite another to show a specific matching between a subject's statements and a definite source of information providing the ingredients of those statements. The critics of the Bridey Murphy case did not accomplish this second task; the more serious investigators of the cases reported by Coleridge [19] and Dickinson [20] did accomplish it.

Nor do the interesting experiments of Zolik [21, 22] satisfy any better our requirements for a suitable model of cryptomnesia. Zolik elicited "previ-

[14] W. F. Prince. *The Case of Patience Worth.* Boston: Boston Society for Psychic Research, 1929.

[15] C. Yost. *Patience Worth.* New York: Patience Worth Publishing Co., 1925.

[16] M. Bernstein. *The Search for Bridey Murphy.* New York: Doubleday and Company, 1956.

[17] C. J. Ducasse. "How the Case of *The Search for Bridey Murphy* Stands Today." *Journal* A.S.P.R., Vol. 54, January, 1960, 3–22.

[18] I. Stevenson. Review of *A Scientific Report on "The Search for Bridey Murphy."* (Ed. M. V. Kline. New York: The Julian Press, 1956.) *Journal* A.S.P.R., Vol. 51, January, 1957, 35–37.

[19] S. T. Coleridge. *Op. cit.,* n. 3.   [20] G. L. Dickinson. *Op. cit.,* n. 7.

[21] E. Zolik. "An Experimental Investigation of the Psychodynamic Implications of the Hypnotic 'Previous Existence' Fantasy." *Journal of Clinical Psychology,* Vol. 14, 1958, 178–183. Also unpublished case reports presented at the meeting of the American Psychological Association, 1958.

[22] E. Zolik. "'Reincarnation' Phenomena in Hypnotic States." *International Journal of Parapsychology,* Vol. 4, 1962, 66–75.

ous life" fantasies in subjects hypnotized, regressed, and instructed to remember a "previous life." In later sessions with the subject hypnotized but not regressed, Zolik traced the origin of some of the information and some of the personality traits shown in the "previous life" fantasy to people, books, or theatrical productions which the subject had known. He further concluded that the theme of the "previous life" fantasy expressed significant conflicts identified in the subject. But these experiments do not provide the model of cryptomnesia we are seeking.

In the first place, the personalities evoked in the "previous life" fantasies were *ad hoc* constructions produced under the direction of the hypnotist, not personalities spontaneously exhibited by the subjects. However, I do not wish to emphasize this point since we shall have to consider later whether the personations by the children of these cases of other personalities might have been imposed on them by their parents in a way similar to that of a hypnotist, even if more subtly.

Secondly, the hypnotically regressed personalities (not merely those of Zolik's experiments, but all of them) show themselves only during the hypnosis (occasionally briefly afterwards) and not during ordinary everyday circumstances. This limited manifestation contrasts markedly with the identifications with a previous personality of the children here considered, which identifications these children have sometimes manifested for years.

Thirdly, Zolik did not achieve anything like an exact matching of details in the "previous life" fantasies and the alleged sources of these details in actual persons, books, plays, etc., known to the subject. A mere similarity of theme between a movie and a "previous life" fantasy does not necessarily mean that the information offered in the "previous life" fantasy necessarily derived only or entirely from that identified source. Supposing reincarnation to occur, the movie or play might have impinged forcefully on the memory of the subject because it resonated with certain actual memories of a previous life. After such impact, the subject would be likely to draw upon the material and themes on a later occasion. I am familiar, for example, with two cases in which watching a movie has served to arouse apparent memories of a previous life having veridical features. The weaving of buried memories into productions of later life, both artistic and psychopathological, has received much study. Lowes, for example, with diligence and success traced the origin of many of the images in Coleridge's poetry to books which Coleridge had read years earlier.[23] But Coleridge did not identify himself with the Ancient Mariner as did Sukla with Mana, for example.

[23] J. L. Lowes. *The Road to Xanadu: A Study in the Ways of the Imagination.* London: Constable and Company, 1927.

Fourthly, a similarity of personality between the "hero" of the previous life and current trends of the subject's personality, especially unconscious ones, is exactly what we should expect if reincarnation occurs, so such similarity does not in any way assure us that the themes of the previous life story arose only in experiences of the subject's life. I do not press these last two arguments. I put them forward, however, because we need to remember that portions of the phenomena observed may be susceptible to normal explanations, but also harmonious with reincarnation. The availability of an explanation along normal lines does not mean that it is the correct explanation. On the other hand, it does tell us that we must search out other and crucial evidence which will permit a decision between normal and paranormal explanations.

I do not mean by the foregoing criticisms to deny the possible value of hypnosis for scanning the earlier life of the subject with regard to possible normal sources of information which he might have used in the manufacture of a "previous personality." But we should interpret negative results cautiously, for our screening may miss possible normal sources of information. Some years ago I studied a "previous personality" hypnotically induced and subsequently reviewed carefully the entire life of the subject (under hypnosis without regression) for traces of the content and theme of the "previous personality." In this case, the "previous personality" lacked plausibility in many features and I believe that most of its ingredients derived from fantasy. But I could not, except in a few places, discover actual origins of the material used in the fantasy.[24]

We could profit from the opportunity of studying a case which would satisfy the three criteria suggested above, but until that happens the theory of cryptomnesia seems to me a possible but not a plausible explanation of those cases suggestive of rebirth which include (*a*) much accurate information about a previous personality (apparently inaccessible by normal means to the subject or his family) and (*b*) identification with the previous personality extending over years and during ordinary everyday living.

Genetic "Memory"

According to the theory of genetic "memory," the alleged memories of previous lives arise in outcroppings of the experiences of the subject's ancestors. He "remembers" with visual or other imagery what happened to his forefathers just as, for example, a bird may "remember" how to fly

---

[24] I have published a short account of this case in "Xenoglossy: A Review and Report of a Case." *Proc.* A.S.P.R., Vol. 31, 1974, 1–268. (Also published by the University Press of Virginia, Charlottesville, 1974.)

after being pushed out of the nest. In this interpretation, memories of previous lives become interesting curiosities because of their detail, but not more remarkable than other aspects of behavior that we attribute to inheritance and call "instinct."

This theory may account for two kinds of cases. First, it may account for cases in which the physical body of one personality descends lineally from the body of the previous personality, as in the case of William George, Jr. We might invoke the theory of genetic "memory" here to account not only for the naevi on the arm of William George, Jr., but also for his rather fragmentary memories of the life of his grandfather, supposing that he did not acquire these through normal communication from his parents. However, cases of this kind account for only a small number of all the cases suggestive of reincarnation. In most of the cases, the two personalities lived a few years apart and in genetic lines that were quite unrelated. In these cases the second personality could not have occupied a body genetically descended from the previous personality's body.

The explanation of genetic "memory" may apply also to those cases in which long periods of time, perhaps centuries, separate the two personalities. (No case of this type occurs in the group of cases here reported and they are anyway rare.) When this happens, we can speculate about genetic relationships between the physical bodies of the two personalities. But supposing such genetic descent to have occurred, we have then to ask what this theory actually explains in cases of this kind. The suggestion seems to call for attributing to inheritance far greater powers of transmission (of imaged memories, for example) than we have ever dared assign to it before.

Extrasensory Perception and Personation

Reasons for Considering Extrasensory Perception and Personation Together

When critics have failed to account adequately for cases of the reincarnation type by documenting (or imagining) normal means of communication between the two personalities, they have then often suggested that we may explain the accepted facts of the case by supposing an extrasensory linkage between the two personalities. I agree that we must consider this possibility very seriously, but no amount of extrasensory perception alone will account for *all* the features of many of the cases. I refer to the important behavioral features and the elements of personation which occur in most of them. We have to consider here much more than the mere mobilization of information somehow acquired. The subject attributes this information to a personality with which he identifies himself. I think it difficult for persons not acquainted with these cases at first hand to imagine the magnitude of these features of behavior and personation. I myself had no preparation for what I observed in this connection when I first went to India. I had imagined that the informational features of the cases alone would deserve attention and need explanation. But, having observed these behavioral elements in different cases, I have come to attribute more importance to them for two reasons: first, I think such behavioral features add to the evidence of authenticity of the cases. Secondly, as I have already mentioned above, I think they make much less plausible the explanation of cryptomnesia. In any explanation which attributes the child's information about the previous personality to extrasensory perception we must also explain the behavioral features of the cases. For this reason I prefer to consider as one theory what I call "extrasensory perception and personation."

This theory supposes that the subject in such a case acquires the information he has about a previous personality through extrasensory perception and that he integrates this information and personates it so thoroughly that he comes to believe he and that person are the same and convinces others of this identity also.

The theory of extrasensory perception and personation does not have to cope with one of the difficulties of the theory of cryptomnesia. It need not assume any personal contact between the child and some person familiar with the facts of the previous personality. It attributes to the child the capacity to acquire such information through extrasensory perception. Further, we must allow that extrasensory perception may transcend time and provide information about the past as well as the present. We have enough independent evidence of retrocognition [25, 26] to permit enlarging the hypothesis by its inclusion as a possibility. Moreover, we do not have to imagine an agent actively engaged in trying to transmit information. In some of Osty's cases, for example, the agent seems to have been passive and the percipient active. And if some kind of "link" is needed between the two families to facilitate extrasensory perception, we can often find a person who can fill this role. For example, in the cases of Sukla, Parmod, Imad, and Jasbir I eventually learned of persons who had some acquaintance with both families concerned although the two families did not know each other. In the case of Marta the two families concerned already knew each other before Marta was born. I have found persons who might serve as telepathic links in still other cases not included in the

[25] E. Osty. *La connaissaince supra-normale*. Paris: Librairie Félix Alcan, 1923. (English trans. by S. de Brath also published in 1923 by Methuen and Company in London under the title *Supernormal Faculties in Man*.)

[26] W. F. Prince. "Psychometric Experiments with Señora Maria Reyes de Z." *Proc. A.S.P.R.*, Vol. 15, 1921, 189–314.

present series. In the case of Shanti Devi, for example, which I have summarized elsewhere,[27] I have learned that the husband of the previous personality often traveled from his native city (Mathura) to Delhi to
purhase cloth for his shop. And while in Delhi he used to frequent a
favorite sweetmeat shop which was located within a few yards only of
Shanti Devi's home. She saw him there one day as she was passing by on
her way home from school. I have the impression that the more one
penetrates into these cases the more one is likely eventually to find some
person or persons who have known both families or, failing that, known
both areas and who could therefore have served as telepathic links between the family of the previous personality and that of the present personality. I am inclined to think it would be better to admit this possibility
for all the cases and consider the merits of the telepathic hypothesis not
on the question whether such possible links exist, but on the question
whether telepathy can anyway adequately account for all the phenomena
of the better cases without supposing extrasensory perception of a very
extensive and extraordinary kind. Furthermore, as I shall mention later
(see p. 355 *et seq.*), the theory of extrasensory perception plus personation does not even require such links since the supposed extrasensory
perception might occur without them. In discussing this theory, I shall
take up first its success in accounting for the informational features of
the cases and then its explanatory value for the behavioral features.

Extrasensory Perception and Personation Applied to the Informational Features of the Cases

In accounting for the informational features of a case, the theory has
several difficulties to contend with. First, it does not alone explain the
selection of the target for the information extrasensorially perceived. When
the family already know the previous personality, who was perhaps another
member of the family, selection of the target may derive from thoughts of
the deceased on the family's part and a wish for his or her return. But how
do we explain selection of the person identified with when the families have
had (by their accounts) absolutely no previous knowledge of each other?
Why should one particular deceased person become the model for such
an identification instead of another? Someone may reply that what we now
know does not any more satisfactorily explain why one personality should
be reborn as another, if this occurs. But the theory of reincarnation does
not put matters in quite this way. It merely supposes that a personality,
having shed one physical body at death, after an interval activates an-

---

[27] I. Stevenson. "The Evidence for Survival from Claimed Memories of Former Incarnations,
Part 1. Review of the Data." *Journal* A.S.P.R., Vol. 54, April, 1960, 51–71.

other body and develops further in it. The second personality of the re-incarnating entity thus develops as a "layer" around the previous personality which itself contained earlier layers. The personalities then develop like the rings of wood on a tree or the shell around an oyster. These crude analogies simplify the changes ridiculously, and it may be that at death personality persists largely unchanged or undergoes a reduction so that what persists is a collection of dispositions and aptitudes which we may call individuality rather than the actual habits and skills we call personality.[28] But the idea I wish to convey now is that according to the theory of reincarnation some organization, whether personality or individuality, persists from one terrestrial life to another, essentially in a continuous sequence. There is then no question of an abrupt change of personality and so the problem of the selection for identification of one personality instead of another does not arise. But it does arise in connection with the theory of extrasensory perception plus personation.

The case of Jasbir perhaps best illustrates the difference between these two theories. According to the theory of reincarnation [29] Sobha Ram died in a chariot accident and shortly afterwards found himself living, but a prisoner in a much smaller body whose previous occupant was called Jasbir by his parents. The personality called Sobha Ram did not become the personality called Jasbir; he occupied Jasbir's body and then further developed according to the circumstances of life previously available to Jasbir. He gradually accommodated partially to these new circumstances, including acceptance of the name Jasbir and all Jasbir's family and the people of Rasulpur. But he still retained many of the memories, attitudes, and longings of Sobha Ram. Why Sobha Ram selected Jasbir's body to enter when he might perhaps have found other available bodies or perhaps initiated a new one remains a mystery. But it is not one which requires explanation at this time according to the theory of reincarnation. For this theory does not say that Sobha Ram became Jasbir; it merely says that Sobha Ram occupied the vacated body and life situation of Jasbir. The theory of extrasensory perception plus personation, on the other hand, *does* require some explanation of the selection by Jasbir of the personality of Sobha Ram for identification. For according to this theory, Jasbir continued to occupy his body after awakening from his

---

[28] C. J. Ducasse. *Nature, Mind and Death*. LaSalle, Illinois: The Open Court Publishing Company, 1951. Chapter 21, "Some Theoretically Possible Forms of Survival," develops the distinction between personality and individuality.

[29] I am not overlooking the fact that Jasbir's body was about three and a half years old when it seemed to die and then revived with the change of personality to that of Sobha Ram following almost immediately. Accepting a paranormal interpretation of the cases, it properly speaking belongs to the group known as "prakaya pravesh" in Hindi and "possession" in the literature of Western psychical research. However, the point under discussion here is not affected by this feature of the case. Indeed, it seems a particularly appropriate example for this discussion precisely because the change of personality occurred so quickly.

apparent death; but at that time he underwent a profound change of personality which included the assumption by him of the personality of someone else who happened to have died about that time, but of whom neither he nor his family knew anything at that time.

Still another weakness of the theory of extrasensory perception plus personation arises in connection with the agency of the information apparently gathered by extrasensory perception. Certainly all the verified information of a particular child about the deceased personality with which he identified himself was available in the minds of other living people. Indeed, in many, but not all, of the cases now under discussion, all the information known to the child was available in the mind of *one* living person. However, in the case of Swarnlata and in some other (unpublished) cases of my collection, all the information known to the child did not reside in any single living mind. In such cases, according to the theory of extrasensory perception and personation, the information had to be gathered from two or more minds, each of which possessed a portion only of the available information. In short, multiple agents would be required for the explanation of such cases by extrasensory perception. We might suppose, however, that these children do not need agents, but acquire their information through clairvoyance, perhaps sometimes drawing on information in other persons' minds and sometimes on other sources.

The case of Swarnlata illustrates this difficulty better than any other case in the present collection. The Pathak brothers knew the facts about the changes in the Pathak house in Katni and nearly all the other facts apparently remembered by Swarnlata about events at Katni, although they did not remember the gold fillings in the teeth of their sister, Biya. But it is extremely unlikely that they knew anything about the latrine episode which Swarnlata told Srimati Agnihotri and it is equally unlikely that they knew anything about the money taken from Biya by her husband. He had told no one about this for obvious reasons. Now it is possible that Swarnlata derived different items of information from different persons each acting as the agent for one or a few items and no others. (This sets aside for the moment all the considerable information Swarnlata revealed before she or her family had any known contact whatever with members of the Pathak family or those who knew them.) She would then have acquired from each person through extrasensory perception something which that person knew in common with Biya. But what then becomes noteworthy is the *pattern* of the information Swarnlata thus derived. Nothing not known to Biya or that happened after Biya's death was stated by Swarnlata during these declarations.[30] We must account

---

[30] Rarely some of the subjects of these cases (Marta being the only one in the present series) have shown knowledge of events that occurred after the death of the previous personality, e.g., the death of a sibling. But even in these instances, the knowledge shown is within the orbit of interest of the previous personality.

somehow not only for the transfer of the information to Swarnlata, but for the organization of the information in her mind in a pattern quite similar to that of the mind of Biya. Extrasensory perception may account for the passage of the information, but I do not think that it alone can explain the selection and arrangement of the information in a pattern characteristic of Biya. For if Swarnlata gained her information by extrasensory perception, why did she not give the names of persons unknown to Biya when she met them for the first time? Extrasensory perception of the magnitude here proposed should not discriminate between targets unless guided by some organizing principle giving a special pattern to the persons or objects recognized. It seems to me that here we must suppose that Biya's personality somehow conferred the pattern of its mind on the contents of Swarnlata's mind.

In principle the problem considered here is not different from that posed by the successful recognition by Mrs. Piper's communicator "G.P." of so many of G.P.'s friends. From 150 people presented to the entranced Mrs. Piper, "G.P." recognized correctly thirty former friends of G.P., made no false recognitions (with one possible exception), and failed to recognize only one girl who had been quite young when G.P. had known her and who presumably had changed much in the interval of eight or nine years which had elapsed.[31] In this case, as in that of Swarnlata, it is the *pattern* of all the recognitions rather than the occurrence of any one recognition which calls for some explanation additional to extrasensory perception. Other subjects of the present collection showed similar organizations of the information available according to the pattern appropriate for the previous personality as, for example, when they would comment on a difference in the appearance of a building or person since the death of the previous personality. In addition to Swarnlata, several other children, e.g., Prakash, Parmod, Gnanatilleka, and Sukla, either made comments on changes in the appearance of buildings since the death of the related previous personality or showed puzzlement or confusion when they saw such altered buildings.

In the organization or pattern of the information given by the subjects we see how the informational and behavioral aspects of the cases become entwined. I turn next to a consideration of other behavioral features of the cases.

The Significance of the Descriptions of the Experiences as Memories

Before considering some of the other behavioral features of the children claiming to have lived before, I shall digress to discuss the significance of

---

[31] R. Hodgson. "A Further Record of Observations of Certain Phenomena of Trance." *Proc. S.P.R.*, Vol. 13, 1898, 284–582. For "G.P.'s" recognitions, see 323–328.

the claim made by these children that what they describe are *memories* of actual events in their own previous lives. In considering this question I should state immediately that I am not concerned now with the *accuracy* of the alleged memories. Errors and illusions of memory occur with regard to our recollections of our present lives and can certainly occur with recollections of previous lives, if these occur. But the occurrence of such errors and omissions does not lead us to deny the existence of something we call memory by which we can re-experience (and report to others) aspects of past events. Indeed, the collection of memories and hence of responses which each person has uniquely may ultimately prove our best definition of personality.[32] The question here, then, is to what extent, if at all, we ought to allow the claim of having memories to separate out the present cases from others not of the reincarnation type.

I believe that we ought not to accept the claim of having memories as the *only* point of differentiation of the cases, and we should look for other empirical differences between the cases which have this feature and those which lack it. But I do not think we should completely disregard the claim of memories as without some value in our assessment of the cases. If we do set aside the claim of memories as a differentiating feature of the cases, we have still to account for why only some cases of extrasensory perception of a previous personality occur in the style of a memory of a previous life and others do not. On this point some persons put forward the explanation that cultural influences account for the casting of some cases into a reincarnationist mold and other cases into a different one, e.g., in the form of discarnate communications. Now there is a high correlation between the occurrence of cases suggestive of rebirth and cultural attitudes favoring the telling of "memories" of previous lives. A full review of the data and the possible explanations for this correlation must await another occasion. Here I wish only to draw attention to the occurrence of *some* cases suggestive of rebirth in cultures quite alien to the belief in rebirth. For many cases do occur in the West and some in families which have either never heard of reincarnation or never given it any credence. For example, in my collection of cases there occur now a considerable number in the United States, Canada, and Great Britain. In these countries the culture runs hostile to reincarnation and many persons have never even heard of the idea while others may perhaps have heard of it, but only as a foolish superstition of Asians. I have myself investi-

---

[32] In *A Critical Examination of the Belief in a Life After Death* (Springfield, Illinois: Charles C. Thomas, 1961), C. J. Ducasse discussed the use of memories (not memory, but the entire collection of residues of past experiences) as signs of the identity of one personality as different from another. (Chapter 26, 304–307.) I am not suggesting (and Ducasse certainly did not) that personality consists *only* of memories. I am referring to our means of distinguishing one personality from another.

gated with personal interviews thirty-five cases of American children who
claimed to remember a previous life. Informational features of the cases
were scanty and in most of the cases no verification of the children's statements could be made, although the cases had interesting behavioral features. They therefore lacked the rich detail of the best Asian cases, but
they closely resembled them in *form*. I am confident that most of the
families concerned received the child's statements about a previous life
with surprise and even incredulity. Similarly, sporadic cases have occurred in India among Muslims who do not believe in reincarnation and
deny its occurrence. Some persons may object that isolated pockets of
people favoring reincarnation exist in Western society (undoubtedly
true) or that a family overtly unsympathetic to reincarnation may unconsciously foster stories of a previous life in one of its children. Such
explanations, however, suggest to me an extension of the concept of cultural influences beyond and even contrary to the available facts in those
cases that occur outside the cultures favorable to reincarnation. I do not
think we should stretch our theories to cover the exceptions, but should
test them with the exceptions.

If a person has verifiable information about a previous life which, so
far as we can tell, he could not have gained normally, and if he presents
this information as reaching him like a memory of a previous life, he
may in fact be having just such a memory of just such a previous life. If
rebirth does occur, then we would expect information about a previous
life to present as memories and ought to be surprised if it presented otherwise. We may, indeed, ask whether a child has ever claimed that information he has about a previous personality pertains to some then discarnate
person when other evidence suggests that he describes a personality continuous with his own. The ideal case of this hypothetical type would include birthmarks with high specificity between two persons like those of
Corliss Chotkin, Jr. But the child in such a hypothetical case would insist
that the information he has about the previous personality derived from
spirit communication, not from his own memory. Such a case, if we find
one, would severely shake confidence in the subjective experience of
memory as a guide to distinguishing one group of cases from another.

In the foregoing discussion of the experience of images of apparent
previous lives as memories, I have had in mind chiefly cases with veridical
features and grounds for believing the percipient could not have obtained
his information about the previous personality through normal means.
But we need to consider also the very much larger number of persons who
have experienced distinct images which seem to them to be memories of
a previous life, even though they contain no details which can be verified.
Such images usually occur briefly, sometimes in the waking state and
sometimes in dreams. The percipient experiences himself as participating

in (occasionally only watching) a scene of some other earlier time before his present life. And he cannot account for the images by recalling any source of them in his present life. I hope to publish later more details of such non-veridical cases suggestive of reincarnation. Here I mention them only in relation to the problem these images pose by presenting nearly always as "memories."

A small number of these cases show inconsistencies or anachronisms which may lead us to doubt or to discard them, and we may believe also that other cases derive from a vivid imagination acting on an eager expectation of remembering some romantic previous existence. But we cannot get rid of the majority of such cases in this way; or if we do, we run the risk of sacrificing data for the sake of theoretical preconceptions. For this larger number (in my collection) comes from intelligent (often, but not necessarily educated) persons who usually testify that the images came to them quite involuntarily and without effort or expectation of remembering the past on their part. (A few percipients have consciously tried to do so through introspective or meditational techniques.) Yet the percipients have always experienced the images as memories of something they had lived through. Some percipients have doubted their own experiencing of the images as "memories." They have wanted to disbelieve or reject this idea, although candidly reporting the images as coming in the form of memories; that is, as located for them in the past like images of past experiences of the "present" life.

I know that percipients sometimes become mixed up about the temporal location of images they perceive. I also know that sensitives or mediums sometimes say erroneously that they can distinguish their "memories" of their "previous lives" from "spirit communications" or from their perceptions of events in the present and "previous lives" of other persons. The case of Hélène Smith studied by Flournoy [33] illustrates lack of objective evidence to support a medium's claim to distinguish claimed memories of a "previous life" from supposedly discarnate communicators. Yet I think it important not to exaggerate the frequency of paramnesia. Temporal mislocation of images can occur during trance and hypnotic states, but it happens very rarely in ordinary waking consciousness. If the (approximately) twelve hundred cases suggestive of reincarnation (considering now the entire collection under study) are all instances of paramnesia, then this condition must occur much more commonly than psychopathologists and psychical researchers have hitherto thought. And one would expect to have found or heard of other instances of paramnesia in the lives

[33] T. Flournoy. *Des Indes à la planète Mars. Étude sur un cas de somnambulisme avec glossolalie.* Paris: Lib. Fischbacher, 1899. 4th ed. (New American edition with introduction and concluding chapter by C. T. K. Chari. New Hyde Park, New York: University Books, Inc., 1963.)

of the subjects, but I have not. Nor have the members of their families, with whom I have often talked personally, attributed such errors of memory to the subjects. We can rarely say in any one case that paramnesia did not occur; we deal in probabilities only. But it does seem extremely improbable that all or even a small number of these cases result from paramnesia.[34] And if this is so, our general confidence in reports of "memories" from intelligent, critical persons will increase. We will expect that sometimes even the wisest and clearest person may mislocate his images temporally. But for the most part we will believe that perhaps we ought to respect the conviction of many of these percipients when they describe their experiences as "memories." [35]

The Projection of Imagery

In nearly all cases with claim of memory of a previous life, the subject identifies himself with the images of the claimed memory. He says that the events described happened to him and that he remembers himself as an actor in them. But in a small number of cases, the images are projected so that the subject sees his previous self as another person external to himself whom he watches, somewhat like instances of seeing one's own body or double.[36] During experiences of this kind Hélène Smith[37] and Pole[38]

[34] Studies of mental imagery point strongly against paramnesia as a *common* occurrence. For example, images of learned verses emerge as the verses were read (in Western languages) , i.e., from left to right and from top to bottom. The rememberer can usually only get the end word of a line by first remembering the initial words. He cannot "read off" the words from back to front as he could if he were actually looking at a printed representation of the verses external to himself. A similar temporal order of imagery related to the order of experiencing occurs in panoramic memory and in memories unrolled during intoxication with drugs like lysergic acid and mescaline. The arrangement of memories in temporal relationship to the order of events they represent thus seems almost to be a property of memory. I do not wish to deny or minimize exceptions (see, for example, A. R. Luria. *The Mind of a Mnemonist*. Trans. by L. Solotaroff. London: Jonathan Cape, 1969) , but merely want to emphasize that one can exaggerate the incidence and importance of paramnesia out of proportion to the totality of our experience of memory.

[35] Readers who wish to study descriptions by percipients of the experience of seeming to remember a previous life will find excellent examples in J. Grant's *Far Memory* (New York: Harper & Brothers, 1956) and A. W. Osborn's *The Superphysical* (London: Ivor Nicholson and Watson, 1937) . Osborn discussed the status of these experiences as memories in "Correspondence." *Journal* S.P.R., Vol. 42, June, 1963, 86–91.

[36] The important subject of out-of-the-body experiences is not immediately germane to the present discussion, although significantly related in that some of the evidence from these experiences suggests the existence of a body independent of the recognized physical body, which other body might act as a structural vehicle for a personality between incarnations. The subject has been reviewed by J. H. M. Whiteman (*The Mystical Life*, London: Faber and Faber, 1961) and by M. Eastman ("Out-of-the-Body Experiences." *Proc.* S.P.R., Vol. 53, 1962, 287–309) . R. Shirley (*The Mystery of the Human Double*, London: Rider and Co., n.d., but probably about 1938) and J. Lhermitte (*Les hallucinations*. Paris: G. Doin et Cie., 1951) give examples of the experience of seeing one's own double.

[37] T. Flournoy. *Op. cit.*, n. 33, 260–264.

[38] W. T. Pole. *The Silent Road*. London: Neville Spearman, 1960.

had the experience of first perceiving a person seemingly independent of themselves. Then the percipient seemed to blend with this other person so that it then seemed to the percipient that he was reliving a previous life directly.[39] Similar projections of aspects of the subject's personality occur in some mental illnesses, e.g., in some cases of schizophrenia and multiple personality. The form of the claimed memories as to whether or not they are projected does not seem to provide a distinguishing feature for separating cases.

In summary, the claim of a memory of a previous life by itself tells us nothing about veridicality. And if the claim of a memory accompanies evidence of authenticity and veridicality, this experience alone cannot distinguish extrasensory perception from a "true" memory of a previous life. Nevertheless, the fact that many coherent experiences of previous personalities seem to occur in the form of memories of a previous life merits respect. Our present knowledge of cultural influences cannot account for the occurrence of this form of experience in many parts of the world where reincarnation is alien to the culture. Nor is it likely that all or even many cases of apparent memories of previous lives are instances of paramnesia since we have no other evidence of such serious mislocation of events in time by these subjects.

After the above digression, I return to consider the question of whether the children who claim to remember a previous life differ in their characteristics or behavior from other persons who exhibit extrasensory perception, but do not make this claim. If we can find similarities and no important differences between the two groups then our confidence in the theory of extrasensory perception plus personation should increase despite some of its weaknesses.

Other Evidence of Extrasensory Perception in the Subjects

I have found a little evidence that some of the children have shown extrasensory perception outside the area of the previous personality. The evidence furnished by the families of these children consisted usually of accounts of precognitive or telepathic awareness of events happening to relatives or friends at a distance. The families of Gnanatilleka, Sukla, and Marta reported incidents of this kind. But most other families have denied that they observed anything of this sort and emphasized that the declarations of the previous life constituted absolutely the only evidence of extrasensory perception in the child.

[39] During one of my own experiments with hypnotic regression, the subject first experienced a "previous personality" evoked with images of a small boy whom she watched playing and in other activities. Initially the images of the boy were separate from the narrating self. Later, the subject identified herself with the boy and continued the narration of the "previous life," talking in the first person about what was happening to this boy, supposedly herself in a previous life.

The family of Marta credited her with impressive mediumistic powers prior to her marriage, but I did not obtain the evidence for this belief. In a case cited by Delanne,[40] Blanche Courtain of Pont-à-Celles, Belgium, showed apparently veridical information about a previous life and also exhibited mediumistic behavior, that is, she claimed to communicate with discarnate spirits. In summary of the evidence that the children have capacities for extrasensory perception outside the area of the memories of the previous life, we can say that most show no evidence of such powers, a few show some slight evidence of them, and an even smaller number show behavior quite similar to that of ordinary adult mediums. So far as I know, no child, with Marta a possible exception, has shown evidence of acquiring substantial information about another person (living or dead) not connected with the personality of the previous life. In short, if these children had gathered their information through extrasensory perception, they showed an extreme localization in the targets they could perceive or at least reported perceiving.

But we must next consider an even more important question bearing on this matter. Do any "ordinary" adult mediums exhibit such restricted knowledge gained by extrasensory perception? Is it not most unusual for them to exhibit their powers only in connection with one person or group of persons as would these children if they had gathered information about the previous personality through extrasensory perception? Most "ordinary" mediums shift the focus of their attention and the source of their information so that they demonstrate their capacities over a wide range of sources of information. Nevertheless, a small number of persons do exhibit a capacity for extrasensory perception with regard to only one person or group of persons. Mrs. Claughton, described by Myers, illustrates this type of medium.[41] We can say that such persons occur rarely in the annals of psychical research, but they do sometimes occur and perhaps the children who remember previous lives really add to this number.

Circumstances in Which the Subjects' Declarations Occur

Turning to the circumstances in which the children make their declarations, we encounter a similar difficulty in asserting that these differ absolutely from the conditions for ordinary mediums. Certainly most mediums

[40] G. Delanne. *Documents pour servir à l'étude de la réincarnation.* Paris: Editions de la B.P.S., 1924, 315–316.

[41] F. W. H. Myers. "The Subliminal Self: The Relation of Supernormal Phenomena to Time." *Proc. S.P.R.,* Vol. 11, 1895, 547. (Chapter 9, Precognition.) Myers does not give much information about Mrs. Claughton apart from her perceptions connected with one house she lived in and its inhabitants. She may then have had other similar experiences unknown to Myers, or not reported by him.

furnish information about a distant person only when they come in contact either with someone who knows that person or with an object which has been in contact with him. But only a slight contact may suffice. Osty's sensitives often adduced astonishingly accurate information about a distant person from holding a scarf or a letter sealed in an opaque envelope.[42] In some of the cases reported in this monograph, slight contact had occurred between the two villages concerned, and in a few cases the families concerned, although ignorant of each other, had common acquaintances. If we take Osty's experiments as justifying our looking on almost anything or any person as a potential "psychometric" link charged with information about those who have come in contact with it, we might imagine that travelers between the relevant villages could have carried with them and left behind them some such objects which served as foci of extrasensory perception about previous lives for the children concerned. Since in every one of the cases I encountered some evidence, albeit often extremely slight, of such traffic between the villages (not between the families), we cannot completely exclude this possibility. But in fact we do not even need to postulate a psychometric link or personal acquaintance for the communication of information. Some mediums have brought out accurate information about absent persons when no one present, either themselves or the sitters, even knew of the existence of the person described by the information communicated. The literature of psychical research contains a number of reports of these communicators who "drop in" at sittings uninvited but are afterwards identified. A number of single case reports of such "drop ins" have been published.[43, 44, 45, 46] The A.S.P.R. published one rather long series of such communications which lasted over a period of several years (from 1929-35).[47] The S.P.R. has also published a group of such cases investigated by Gauld.[48] In my opinion authentic cases of this kind make an important contribution to the evidence for survival since we cannot easily account for them on the basis of extrasensory perception from the living. In most of these cases there exists no proxy or other person or "psycho-

---

[42] E. Osty. *Op. cit.*, n. 25.

[43] G. N. M. Tyrrell. "Case: A Communicator Introduced in Automatic Script." *Journal* S.P.R., Vol. 31, July, 1939, 91–95.

[44] E. B. Gibbes. "Have We Indisputable Evidence of Survival?" *Journal* A.S.P.R., Vol. 31, March, 1937, 65–79.

[45] I. Stevenson. "A Communicator Unknown to Medium and Sitters: The Case of Robert Passanah." *Journal* A.S.P.R., Vol. 64, January, 1970, 53–65.

[46] I. Stevenson. "A Communicator of the 'Drop In' Type in France: The Case of Robert Marie." *Journal* A.S.P.R., Vol. 67, January, 1973, 47–76.

[47] J. M. Bird. "A Series of Psychical Experiments." *Journal* A.S.P.R., Vol. 23, April, 1929, 209–232. (Continued in the succeeding volumes under the title of "Le Livre des Revenants.") But see also a criticism of this series in W. F. Prince. "A Certain Type of Psychic Research." *Bulletin* Boston Society for Psychic Research, No. 21, 1933, 1–30.

[48] A. Gauld. "A Series of 'Drop-In' Communicators." *Proc.* S.P.R., Vol. 55, 1971, 273–340.

metric object" which can serve as a link between the medium and the communicator.[49] But if they contribute to evidence of survival, these "drop in" cases also make it more difficult to evaluate cases of the reincarnation type since they make it possible for us to suppose that the children might have acquired the information they had about the previous personalities through extrasensory perception without any linkage of persons or objects whatever.

With this possibility in mind we should consider next the behavior of the children in comparison to the behavior of other people who apparently obtain information about deceased persons through extrasensory perception. Age alone will not separate the rebirth cases from instances of mediumship, since apparent mediumistic communications from deceased personalities do occur among children, albeit rarely. Myers cites examples [50] and Westwood has described one in considerable detail.[51]

I turn next to consider the differences in the state of consciousness of sensitives as they give information about other people with a view to noting whether regular differences occur between such persons who claim to recall a previous life and those who do not. If we take only the spontaneous cases of claims to remember a previous life (setting aside hypnotic cases), we find that the persons with such claims make their declarations, with rare exceptions, during ordinary consciousness and under ordinary circumstances of life. By "ordinary consciousness" I mean that to other observers the person seems his regular self behaving in a normal way and that in their judgment and experience he would, if he were called by his name or asked a question, respond immediately and appropriately. Most of the children of the cases suggestive of rebirth behave in this ordinary way nearly all the time. They talk about the past lives sporadically here and there without interrupting their habitual play or work. Something which reminds them of some event in the previous life stimulates a brief flow of talk about the life and then it ceases. And apart from the behavior connected with the claim to remember a previous life, the parents noted nothing markedly abnormal about the behavior of the children then or at other times. A tendency to seriousness and to precocity of knowledge were often remarked upon, but nothing that could be identified as grossly psychopathological. This general normality of behavior contrasts obviously

---

[49] In a case of this kind described by J. A. Hill (*Psychical Investigations*. New York: George H. Doran Co., 1917), the communicator, "Ruth Robertshaw," was quite unknown to the sitter (Hill) and apparently equally so to the medium (Wilkinson). But a friend of Hill (a Miss North), who had recently visited him, did know Ruth Robertshaw (who was her cousin) and verified the information communicated. Miss North may therefore have acted as a connecting link or possibly left a "psychometric object" at Hill's house where the sitting took place. But in other cases no such linkage of persons or objects has turned up or can be reasonably supposed to have occurred.

[50] F. W. H. Myers. *Op. cit.*, n. 5, 484–486.

[51] H. Westwood. *There is a Psychic World*. New York: Crown Publishers, 1949.

enough with that of most mediums who, on entering a trance, show a more or less complete change of personality and do not usually answer to the call of their regular names, much less go about their ordinary business in an intelligently responsive way.

Our task would remain simple if all the relevant cases fell at one of these extremes. Unfortunately many do not. Occasionally some of the children become somewhat abstracted when in the surroundings of the previous life or when seeming to recall that life. Such changes never extended to a complete dissociation of personality, but amounted to a degree of it, perhaps. We have to ask ourselves whether the degree would be greater than what anyone would show when he concentrates intently on recalling emotionally charged events of the past and reliving them in his mind. Then we have to consider the rather unusual cases of mediums like A. Wilkinson [52] and Mrs. Willett,[53] who communicated information of astonishing accuracy about deceased persons when in states little different (if at all) from ordinary consciousness. Such differences as exist between these sensitives and the subjects of the present cases would seem to lie not in their respective states of consciousness, but in the identification of the subjects with the deceased personalities and the duration over which they sustain this identification. I shall therefore discuss this identification next.

The Identification of the Subjects With the Previous Personalities

A comparison of the identification of the subjects with the personalities about whom they exhibited information provides no clear distinction between the cases with claim of rebirth and those without, provided we view the cases only over a *brief* period of time.

The strength of the identification of persons who claim to remember a previous life with the previous personality varies. Some children use the past tense to describe the previous life. They say, in effect, "I was called so and so," but accept also their present names. Other children battle against the identity of the present life and say, for example, "Don't call me Fred. My name is John. You are not my parents. My father and mother live away from here." Even children with strong identifications with a previous personality, such as the last statement expresses, will usually still distinguish the events of the previous life as past. Thus they will say: "Such a thing happened to me when I was big." They do not often relive the past as if it were now happening. This, however, does happen in many dreams with suggestions of a previous life. Characteristically, in these dreams the subject

[52] J. A. Hill. *Op. cit.,* n. 49.

[53] G. Balfour. "A Study of the Psychological Aspects of Mrs. Willett's Mediumship." *Proc.* S.P.R., Vol. 43, 1935, 43–314 .

experiences himself with a different identity living a scene in some past time and different place. For the duration of the dream, and sometimes for a little longer, he experiences himself as a different personality. Subjects experiencing these "previous life" dreams sometimes examine themselves in a mirror upon awakening to make certain that they do or do not have a beard, for example.[54] Similar vivid apparent reliving occurs in hypnotically induced regressions to a previous life and occurs also often in the process of abreaction in which a person recalls some past event with the experience of actually living through the event as it happened originally, although he behaves as if it is happening in the present.[55]

Among spontaneous cases suggestive of rebirth this reliving occurs sometimes. Readers will recall that Prakash during the night when sleeping would apparently revert to the personality of Nirmal and, half asleep, run out of the house in Chhatta on his way back to Kosi Kalan. And Sukla's first signs of identification with Mana consisted in cradling a block of wood like a baby and murmuring "Minu" over and over again. In these acts both Prakash and Sukla might seem to be reliving a past experience in the present.

However, some sensitives or mediums also experience a kind of identification with the persons living or deceased about whom they receive information. They may use the first person in describing the experiences of the person cognized. A vivid example of this occurs in the autobiography of Joan Grant.[56] She held an old medal to her forehead and seemed then to relive a naval battle scene of the Napoleonic wars, e.g., "I go up on the poop, give the order to lie to, and send a boat to accept their surrender . . . Their captain is Don Phillipo de Rodriguez . . . He bows and hands me his sword. I take him to my cabin and offer him drink." (The medal had belonged to one of Nelson's captains.) Prince [57] and Osty [58] reported other instances of the use of the first person and present tense in describing the experiences of other persons. In one of Osty's cases, physical aspects of a severe illness (cancer of the liver) cognized by a sensitive persisted for ten days afterwards in the sensitive. In cognizing death from a mountaineering accident, Mrs. Willett blended past and present when she said: " 'Oh! I fell down, I fell down. Oh! my head, my head, my head, Oh, oh, oh. (Groans)

---

[54] I have collected and am analyzing many such dreams suggestive of a previous life. A few contain verifiable and verified information; most do not. But certain features of these dreams recur in many of them and justify a careful study of the patterns they show.

[55] For examples of the reliving of past experiences as if the subject were experiencing the previous events in the present see P. G. Dane, and L. H. Whitaker. "Hypnosis in the Treatment of Traumatic Neurosis." *Diseases of the Nervous System*, Vol. 13, 1952, 67–76; and J. M. Schneck, "Hypnotherapy in a Case of Claustrophobia and its Implications for Psychotherapy in General." *Journal of Clinical and Experimental Hypnosis*, Vol. 2, 1954, 251–260.

[56] J. Grant. *Far Memory*. New York: Harper & Brothers, 1956, 173–174.

[57] W. F. Prince. *Op. cit.*, n. 26.   [58] E. Osty. *Op. cit.*, n. 25.

Oh, oh, oh, I bumped my head. Oh, it's all here' (putting her hands to her head below and behind the ears) ." [59]

In another instructive example, the percipient (evidently not habitually liable to psychical experiences, but on this occasion in a state of moderate emotional disturbance) experienced an apparent partial possession with veridical communications from a deceased lady.[60] The percipient used the first person to describe part of her experience, yet also preserved awareness of her own identity. The perceptions might have been experienced as memories of a previous life of the percipient, but were not. I suggest that this was because, although some blending of personalities seems to have occurred, it stopped short of a *fusion* of personalities with a sense of continuity and unity between them.

In general, however, we find no differences between the identifications claimed in the rebirth cases and those experienced by sensitives apparently describing other persons, if we view the cases over a short interval of time. Most persons with claim of memory of previous lives differ, however, in the long duration, usually extending over years, through which they maintain the claim of identification with the other personality, and in the restriction of the identification to one (rarely to two or more) other personality.

This brings me to consider in greater detail the personation by the subject of the previous personality. I shall first review just what this consists of in the average case of this sort.

Characteristics of the Identification in Cases Suggestive of Reincarnation

First, the child (or adult less often) claims (or his behavior suggests) a continuity of his personality with that of another person who has died. As already mentioned, in a few cases the identification with the previous personality becomes so strong that the child rejects the name given him by his present parents and tries to force them to use the previous name. But in most cases, the subject experiences the previous self as *continuous* with his present personality, not as substituting for it. The substitutive kind of identification does, however, occur occasionally in spontaneous cases suggestive of rebirth; and it occurs usually in hypnotically induced regressions and nearly always in mediumistic trances. It also occurs more or less in "ordinary" cases of multiple personality without claim to a previous life.

I say nothing here about completeness of fusion or of substitution of one personality for another. Certainly in cases of multiple personality, substitution of one personality for another may be much less complete than the subject himself or those observing him think. For example, psychological

---

[59] G. Balfour. *Op. cit.*, n. 53, 103.

[60] C. Green. "Report on Enquiry into Spontaneous Cases." *Proc.* S.P.R., Vol. 53, 1960, 83–161. (Case E. 687, 156–158.)

tests in one case of multiple personality with amnesia between components showed the persistence of important similarities as well as differences between the two "selves." [61] The same lack of total substitution occurs in hypnotically induced regressions to "previous lives" and in many (if not most or all) appearances of "communicating" personalities during mediumistic trances. However, the point of importance here is that in cases of "ordinary" multiple personality, the division and subsequent point of fusion when it occurs between personalities lies "vertically" between two aspects of the present personality; on the other hand, in nearly all spontaneous cases suggestive of rebirth, the division and subsequent fusion of the personalities seems to lie along a "horizontal" or temporal line. Thus, for the majority of subjects the sense of continuity between present and previous personalities fully resembles the sense of continuity each of us has about the relationship between his present personality and himself when a child.

Behavioral Features of the Cases

The outward signs which lead me to apply the words "personation" and "identification" to the child's behavior and to ask that this behavior be included in any comprehensive explanation of cases of the rebirth type with veridical statements are the following: (a) Repeated verbal expressions by the subject of the identification; (b) repeated presentation of information about the previous personality as coming to the subject in the form of memories of events experienced or of people already known; (c) requests to go to the previous home either for a visit or permanently; (d) familiar address and behavior toward adults and children related to the previous personality according to the relationships and social customs which would be proper if the child really had had the relationships he claims to have had with these persons; (e) emotional responses, e.g., of tears, joy, affection, fear, or resentment appropriate for the relationships and attitudes shown by the previous personality toward other persons and objects; and (f) mannerisms, habits, and skills which would be appropriate for the previous personality, or which he was known to possess.

For the most part, I do not regard these features of behavior (to the extent that observers may suppose they match similar ones in the previous personality) as *evidence* of paranormal acquisition of information about the previous personality. Such evidence usually derives from the informational aspects of the subject's behavior only. It is all too easy for relatives to decide that the tears or laughter of a child "exactly" resemble those of the previous personality when this is what they expect or want. (The same hazards await those who accept the identity of communicators during

[61] M. H. Congdon, J. Hain, and I. Stevenson. "A Case of Multiple Personality Illustrating the Transition from Role-Playing," *Journal of Nervous and Mental Disease*, Vol. 132, 1961, 497–504.

mediumistic trances on the basis of behavioral features, e.g., "a voice just like Uncle John's.") Some other behavioral features, e.g., special skills, are more objectively identifiable as being or not being part of the previous personality. And I hope that future investigations into correlations between the personality traits of the present and previous personalities of cases of this type will make some such traits objectively identifiable and correlatable. But for the present, I regard the behavioral features not as evidence of an identification with *the* previous personality, but as evidence of an identification with *some* previous personality and this requires an explanation. We should note in passing, however, that observers nearly always say that the personation matches what they remember of the previous personality. I have rarely encountered a case in which witnesses said that the child's behavior was *not* like that of the previous personality or was generally inappropriate to what they would have expected of the previous personality if it had survived.

Secondly, this sense of identification in the cases suggestive of rebirth usually lasts for many years. In the tabulation on pp. 326–327 I gave the durations, so far as known, of the major features of the subjects' behavior, including their identifications with the previous personalities. The average duration of the main features of personation was almost seven years. Since some of the major behavior of the subjects still continued at the time of my observations, the true average duration is certainly longer than the figure derived. Study of the data from a much larger series of cases (including those of the present series and others) shows that the phenomena of personation usually extend through early childhood, with fading of the apparent memories beginning in the school years under ten. At first the child usually stops talking spontaneously about the previous life, but will still talk about it to some persons if asked; later he usually says he remembers nothing more, or only fragments. The behavioral features usually end by late adolescence. Informational and behavioral features often diminish together, but by no means always. For example, Ravi Shankar retained a marked fear of Munna's murderers into his later childhood when he could no longer remember why he feared them or that he had once claimed that these men had murdered him in his previous life. And a definite tendency toward a feminine identification persisted in Paulo Lorenz many years after the brief period of his statements about Emilia.

Personation and Extrasensory Perception in Other Kinds of Cases

Few cases of extrasensory perception in children have received careful study. The examples cited by Burlingham [62] give only fragmentary data, but in any case the children mentioned by her seem to have exhibited only

[62] D. Burlingham. "Child Analysis and the Mother." *Psychoanalytic Quarterly*, Vol. 4, 1935, 69–92.

slight flashes of extrasensory perception. More extensive investigations of several other children who exhibited evidence of extrasensory perception with a parent as agent have been published from time to time. In the cases of Ilga,[63] Bo,[64] and Lisa,[65] the reports gave no evidence of identification by these children with persons other than their parents.

Instances of children exhibiting both extrasensory perception and personation, including alleged communications from discarnate personalities, occur even more rarely. The cases cited by Myers [66] showed the most scanty "communications." The richest case of this kind known to me is that reported by Westwood, who studied "mediumistic" behavior in his foster daughter, Anna, over a period of some years.[67] Westwood's report does not provide all the details we could wish, but it does indicate that he was an attentive and not uncritical observer sensitive to many of the common errors in interpreting evidence of apparent extrasensory perception. I therefore think that we can draw on his account of what he observed and compare Anna with the children of the present cases. Anna began to show a capacity for extrasensory perception when she was eleven and the phenomena observed extended over several years. (Westwood does not mention exactly how long.) Anna underwent personality changes similar to those of most adult mediums. Westwood describes her personation of six "communicators" and states that there were others not described in his report. Some of these communicators were known to the Westwoods, others were not. Anna's personation of one communicator, a child with whom Westwood had been acquainted, seemed vividly realistic to him.

Several aspects of the phenomena exhibited by Anna deserve comparison with the corresponding features of children who claim to remember a previous life. The number of personations is considerably greater than that of any child claiming to remember a previous life. This, however, is not likely to prove an important point of differentiation. Nor is Anna's state of consciousness. For Anna, who began her "mediumship" at a planchette, passed rather rapidly to a condition in which the communicators used her voice.

[63] H. Bender. "A Phenomenon of Unusual Perception." *Journal of Parapsychology*, Vol. 2, 1938, 5–22. The main phenomena of this case apparently derived from acoustic hyperesthesia, but some of the phenomena, at least, seem to have been paranormal.

[64] R. M. Drake. "An Unusual Case of Extrasensory Perception." *Journal of Parapsychology*, Vol. 2, 1938, 184–198.

[65] B. E. Schwarz. "Telepathic Events in a Child Between 1 and 3½ Years of Age." *International Journal of Parapsychology*, Vol. 3, No. 4, 1961, 5–47. In response to an inquiry, Dr. Schwarz wrote me that Lisa never made a claim to a memory of a previous life. In her case we have also the additional information that the family had not recently lost by death a relative with whom Lisa might have identified. Also her identification with her parents proceeded normally. For more and later information about instances of telepathy between Lisa and other members of her family see B. E. Schwarz. *Parent-Child Telepathy: Five Hundred and Five Possible Episodes in a Family.* New York: Garrett Publications, 1971.

[66] F. W. H. Myers. *Op. cit.,* n. 5, 485–486.   [67] H. Westwood. *Op. cit.,* n. 51.

But unlike most adult trance mediums (and resembling in this respect Mrs. Willett and Mr. Wilkinson), Anna did not lose consciousness of herself during these personations. She remained "aside," as it were, and able to resume as her ordinary personality almost instantly. Westwood describes this as follows: "While accent and intonation varied according to the entity allegedly speaking, the register and timbre of Anna's voice never changed. Moreover, she had as much control over herself as before. She could, so to speak, shut off the current instantly, in order to make any comment she desired. Likewise she could instantaneously throw in the switch in order to resume the interrupted experiment" (pp. 71–72). With regard to the persistence of essentially normal consciousness and at least potentiality for her ordinary behavior, Anna's behavior during this period resembled that of the children who claim to have lived before. Where it differed, and I think significantly, was in her lack of identification with any of the communicating personalities. However rapid the changes in personation, Anna never "mixed" herself with them or claimed at times when they were not manifesting that she, Anna, was in fact the same person as any such communicating personality, or a continuation of that personality. But this identification of the present with a previous personality (with continuity between the personalities) is exactly what the children of the present cases do claim and also express in their behaviors.

The case of "the Boy," [68] although occurring in an adult, showed behavioral features similar to those of Anna. "The Boy" could show the most dramatic personality changes almost instantly, being one moment quite himself and the next one of "the Brothers," the distinctly different communicators who manifested through "the Boy." We are not concerned here with the status as communicators of "the Brothers," but only with the sudden and rapid changes of personality shown by "the Boy." The emergence from the change occurred much more slowly in "the Boy" than in Anna, and even the entrance to the change occurred a little more slowly, although still often quickly. ("The Boy" was usually amnesic for what happened during the period of "control," whereas Anna often remembered.) But "the Boy," like Anna, never claimed that his identity joined with that of any of "the Brothers." Here again a substitution of personalities, not a fusion, seemed to occur.

We must note that transitional states occur in which both personalities may seem to mingle and manifest some aspects of each personality together. This was reported in the case of Lurancy Vennum during the re-emergence of Lurancy's personality after the main manifestation of "Mary Roff." [69] It

[68] Swami Omananda Puri. *The Boy and the Brothers.* English Edition. London: Victor Gollancz, 1959. American Edition, New York: Doubleday & Co., 1960.

[69] R. Hodgson. In Report of Meeting of S.P.R. *Journal S.P.R.*, Vol. 10, 1901, 99–104.

occurred also at times with "the Boy." Communicators through mediums such as Mrs. Leonard have sometimes complained that the medium's voice did not do justice, so to speak, to the sound of their voices when alive, as if a blending of vocal qualities had occurred.[70] In the quotation cited above, Westwood refers to the definite, but still partial change in Anna's voice during the manifestation of one of her communicators, "Blue Hide," who purported to be a male American Indian and showed much of the knowledge of one. But apart from the transitional stages, and allowing for the fact that the communicator still had to use the vocal apparatus of the medium, the personality changes of Anna, "the Boy," and Lurancy Vennum seemed quite complete. By this I mean that to other observers all, or nearly all, the habitual responses and fund of information upon which such responses lay seemed to vanish and another quite different set of responses apparently organized around a different group of experiences took the place of the first set. As already mentioned, it is this different organization of responses (based on different and for each person unique experiences and their memories) which provides our everyday empirical means of differentiating one personality from another.

Such a complete substitution of one personality for another does not seem to occur in the cases suggestive of reincarnation in which the death of the previous personality took place before the birth of the physical organism of the second personality. (The case of Jasbir lies outside this group and in this case a rapid, virtually total, and persisting change of personality seems to have occurred.) Brief and apparently total substitution of one personality for another occurs in cases suggestive of reincarnation in (*a*) some instances of hypnotically induced regression, and (*b*) some instances (mentioned above) of alterations in identity during dreams. I am therefore referring here to complete substitution of personality in ordinary circumstances of waking life.

There remains a possibility that the subjects *acquire* their information in some trance-like condition of dissociation (or even in dreams) but only later *communicate* it to others when they have resumed their normal personalities. I cannot exclude this possibility and something of this kind may very well have happened in some cases. For example, Marta described how she had *remembered* the saddle Sinhá had owned when by herself, but she had not *told* anyone about this until one day when she was watching the saddling of a horse. However, in most cases the witnesses described the sudden "popping out" of some comment by the subject when something in the conversation or something going on at the time apparently reminded him of an incident of the previous life which he then told to those present.

---

[70] M. Radclyffe-Hall and U. Troubridge. "On a Series of Sittings with Mrs. Osborne Leonard." *Proc. S.P.R.*, Vol. 30, 1920, 339-554. (See p. 480.)

The main point of differentiation which I detect, then, between the usual cases suggestive of reincarnation and other cases of comparable degrees of extrasensory perception is the sustained identification with one personality over years with claim of continuity and unity between the previous and present personalities. And to this we must add that during these years the subject seems to other observers not abnormal outside the area of his claim to identification with the previous personality; and specifically, he does not show marked alterations of personality during these years.

Motives in the Subject for Identification With the Other Personality

We now have to ask ourselves (and answer if we can) how this kind of sustained identification would begin and continue over years granting that somehow the child acquires (normally or with extrasensory perception) the information needed to sustain the personation. In other words, suppose the child *can* personate a previous personality continuously over several years, why *would* he do it? A tenet of modern psychology (with which I agree) is that most behavior, especially that continued over a long time, requires some motivation to sustain it. Where is the motivation for these extended personations by these children?

We may look for such motivation within the child himself. We have already done this in considering the possibility of fraud and cryptomnesia. In that connection I said I did not know of any evidence to indicate that the possible rewards from such identification justified the difficulties and complexities which the personation brought to the life of the child. One might suppose some anxiety-reducing power in the fantasies of a previous life lived in better circumstances. But these children do not stop with fantasies. They act upon their beliefs and become heavily involved in complicated relationships with both families. Swarnlata, for example, would have had an easier time if she had simply imagined that she had once had wealthy parents than she has had with thinking this to be a fact (as she believed) and knowing the previous family, yet remaining separated from them. And yet Swarnlata enjoyed her present life compared to some of the other children. Jasbir and Ranjith made themselves outcasts within their families by their claims to previous lives; Prakash and Ravi Shankar earned beatings for such claims; and Wijeratne did not increase the esteem with which his village regarded him by claiming to be the murderer Ratran Hami returned to live among them.

Yet other motives besides a wish to improve a material situation may underlie identification with the previous personality. It seems likely that we learn much through identification with older people; perhaps in order to mature, all children must identify to some extent with an older person or persons. Then if the way to identification with parents becomes blocked, the child may reach out for identification with some other person who seems more emotionally available for his needs. And if the child happens to have a capacity for extrasensory perception, he may choose a person from a distance of whom perhaps he has never heard before. Unfortunately, the available data of the present cases do not fit this interpretation. Although a few of the children, e.g., Jasbir and Prakash, seemed unhappy in their present homes, excellent relations appeared to prevail between most of the other children and their parents. Sometimes I had limited opportunities for observing the interaction of parents and children, but in other cases, e.g., Swarnlata and Imad, I could observe (over a day or several days) a loving relationship between the children and other members of the family.[71] Moreover, since many children become alienated from their parents both in Asia and the West, we ought, on this theory, to find that many of these children attempt identifications with deceased people; but in fact this occurs extremely rarely even when ample materials for the identification lie around as in portraits or other mementos of dead grandparents. Furthermore, as already mentioned, some children who give evidence of extrasensory perception, e.g., Ilga, Bo, and Lisa, cited earlier, show no evidence (or are not reported as showing any) of significant identification with any adults other than their parents.

I do not think we can find sufficient motivation for these personations in the children alone, although I think we should go on looking. But we ought also to look for other influences, most obviously in the attitudes of the children's parents.

Motivation and Capacity of Parents to Impose a New Identification on Their Children

Many studies have shown the power of parents to influence the behavior of their children. Sometimes parents influence them openly and crudely toward behavior they desire to promote, but more often they do so only covertly, unconsciously, and yet frequently with great subtlety. Parents of children so influenced will almost invariably deny with complete sincerity

---

[71] Further evidence of a lack of serious interference with the identification of these children with their parents comes from follow-up studies of persons who when children claimed to have lived before and who have now reached adulthood. In the present series three Alaskan cases and four Indian cases provide examples. And I have studied other cases in India of persons who as children made claims of remembering a previous life, and who have now grown to adulthood. Although some of these subjects do show in adulthood some important behavioral residues of the "previous personality," they have for the most part developed along normal lines, taken their expected places in adult society, and have not shown signs of serious mental illness of any kind. The information derived from the follow-up interviews with the subjects of the cases presented in this book confirmed this opinion in all but three of the eighteen cases followed up.

that they have guided a child's behavior in the direction it took. Indeed, they may express horror and repugnance at the child's conduct and even punish him for it. Yet other evidence, sometimes extracted only after many hours of interviews, shows that the parents have nevertheless been unconsciously the responsible promoting agents of the very behavior they profess to condemn in the child.[72, 73] The chief evidence for this last statement is that the behavior in the child usually continues until the parents gain insight into what they are doing to promote it *and* stop doing so; when they do this, the behavior of the child usually ceases if he is young enough and not yet under the influence of other people who have taken over the encouragement of the undesirable behavior.

Investigations have shown that parental influences may thus initiate and reinforce a wide variety of behavioral and physical symptoms, e.g., firesetting, stealing, incontinence, and constipation. Among the cases cited by Johnson was that of a six year old boy showing transvestism, mentioned in the case report of Paulo Lorenz. Interviews with the mother elicited evidence that her hatred of males and favoring of her two year old girl had led her subtly to influence her son to prefer (or at least to wear) girls' clothes. In its clinical phenomena with regard to the wearing of clothes of the opposite sex, the case resembles that of Paulo Lorenz when he was a small boy under the age of five; in other respects the cases differ considerably and Johnson reported that her patient "really wished to be the baby of the family [which his sister was] rather than a girl." But the studies of Johnson and her colleagues leave no doubt that parents can exert a powerful influence on the behavior of their children.[74] What we do not know is how far such influence can extend and whether it ever extends so far that the child actually believes he is another person, either a person still living, such as a living uncle, or a person who has died, such as a deceased uncle, of whom he claims to be the reincarnation.

Parents may reinforce the behavior they outwardly condemn by repeatedly identifying a child with, for example, a delinquent uncle. If such a mother catches her child stealing some change from her purse, she may scold him by saying: "Do you want to grow up to be like your father's brother who

---

[72] A. M. Johnson. "Factors in the Etiology of Fixations and Symptom Choice." *Psychoanalytic Quarterly*, Vol. 22, 1953, 475–496.

[73] A. M. Johnson and S. A. Szurek. "Etiology of Antisocial Behavior in Delinquents and Psychopaths." *Journal of the American Medical Association*, Vol. 154, 1954, 814–817.

[74] Germane to the question of human influence on another person's sense of his own identity are M. Erickson's experiments ("Experimental Demonstrations of the Psychopathology of Everyday Life." *Psychoanalytic Quarterly*, Vol. 8, 1939, 338–353) which included instruction to a hypnotized subject to assume the identity of another person. The subject carried out this instruction with extraordinary impressiveness, cleverly utilizing scraps of information he had picked up about the man whose personality he assumed in a conversation the day before. Erickson stated that experiments of this kind might throw light on questions of parental influence on children.

went to prison for thieving?" Then the mother may narrate the gruesome fate, but also the adventurous escapades of Uncle Timothy. The child listens with widened eyes and a mixture of fear and admiration for Uncle Timothy which the mother herself entertains but does not admit to herself or anyone else. In the case of Ranjith Makalanda a similar ambivalent attitude of intense conscious dislike and secret admiration for the English seems to have occurred in Mr. de Silva, Ranjith's father. So he may quite unconsciously have influenced Ranjith toward more and more "Englishness."

But I revert to the question, how far can this sort of influence extend? Does a little boy under such influence ever say he *was* or *is* Uncle Timothy? And we must be clear that this kind of statement is exactly what boys like Ranjith make. For Ranjith believed fully in his identity with someone else who had lived in England. It is not a question of resembling someone else in one or more features, but of a sense of continuity between that someone else and himself. Readers may have noticed earlier that Ranjith experienced this so vividly he sometimes used the present tense in telling about the previous life. He would say: "I have a father and mother in England," or "My mother calls me 'darling' and sometimes she calls me 'sweetheart.'" These statements refer to a sense of present existence, not to past states. Other children of these cases have used the present tense with equal insistence.

In answer to the question above, I can only say that except for the children in the reincarnation type of case, I have never heard of a child who so identified himself with another personality that he claimed over a long period to believe in a unity of his personality and another one, as do many of the children who claim to have lived before. This does happen in adult psychotic patients, who sometimes make claims to other identities. But psychoses of any kind are extremely rare in children and delusional false identification with another person seems even rarer. I have discussed this question with two child psychiatrists, one specially expert in childhood schizophrenia. Neither had ever heard of a case in which a child claimed to be someone else. Children do occasionally identify briefly in play with other people or animals, and some psychotic children have identified themselves with machines. But I have not discovered a case in the literature of psychiatry of prolonged claims to another identity on the part of children outside the cases here under discussion.[75] Other psychiatrists with more

[75] L. Kanner. *Child Psychiatry.* Springfield, Illinois: Charles C. Thomas, 1957. (3rd edition.) C. Bradley. *Schizophrenia in Childhood.* New York: The Macmillan Company, 1941; H. W. Potter. "Schizophrenia in Children." *American Journal of Psychiatry,* Vol. 89, 1933, 1253–1270; J. L. Despert. "A Comparative Study of Thinking in Schizophrenic Children and in Children of Preschool Age." *American Journal of Psychiatry,* Vol. 97, 1940, 189–213; C. Bradley and M. Bowen. "Behavior Characteristics of Schizophrenic Children." *Psychiatric Quarterly,* Vol. 15, 1941, 296–315.

extensive experience in child psychiatry than I have may know of such cases, and if they can be brought forward for study they would provide interesting material for comparison with those of the children who claim to have lived before. It might then turn out that children like Ranjith Makalanda are a subtype of children with delusional misidentifications, the difference in them being that they claim to have lived before whereas in other cases the children simply claim to be someone else, not necessarily dead.

The fading of informational and behavioral features of the present cases poses another objection to attributing the identification of the child with a previous personality to the influence of his parents. For in the cases reported by Johnson and her colleagues, the symptoms induced or promoted by parents *never* ceased until the parental promotion of the symptoms stopped. Since such parental influences were nearly always unconscious, they tended to persist until intensive therapy of the parents had revealed the origins of their relevant impulses and changed their motivations for covertly

------

L. S. Kubie and H. A. Israel ("Say You're Sorry." *Psychoanalytic Study of the Child.* Vol. 10, 290–299) described a five year old psychotic girl (of New York) who for a time refused to answer to her name and insisted that her name was that of a living girl she knew, or of a boy. This denial of her identity seems to have lasted less than a year.

A. M. Des Lauriers (*The Experience of Reality in Childhood Schizophrenia.* New York: International Universities Press, Inc., 1962) described a case which seems fairly typical of the limited range of delusional ideas of different identity which occur in schizophrenic children. The patient, a boy of fourteen, claimed he was Superman and frequently imitated the stance of Superman. "Then there were moments when he was Frankenstein or Samson and he would get into fights with other patients dramatizing one of these roles."

V. K. Alexander ("A Case Study of a Multiple Personality." *Journal of Abnormal and Social Psychology,* Vol. 52, 1956, pp. 272–276) reported the case of a fifteen year old girl of south India who manifested personality changes (with amnesia) in which she assumed the personalities of two "spirits," one of whom was her deceased great-aunt. The case contained no apparent paranormal features and its *form* was of the possession, not the reincarnation, type.

Western persons who hear about cases suggestive of reincarnation for the first time sometimes immediately assume that the children of the cases must necessarily be having delusions. Such quick judgments betray ignorance not only of the cases, but of child psychiatry. The fact is that psychoses of any kind are very rare in childhood, and delusions even rarer. Potter (*op. cit.*) stated: "Children do not possess the facility to fully verbalize their feelings, nor are they capable of complicated abstractions. Consequently, delusional formations seen in childhood are relatively simple and their symbolization is particularly naive" (p. 1253). And Bradley (*op. cit.*), after quoting other authors on the subject, stated: "Practically all authors agree that paranoid forms of schizophrenia are very rare during the childhood years, a further indication of the lack of delusions at this age" (pp. 35–36). The rarity of delusions of identity in childhood does not preclude the cases of the present group (or other similar cases suggestive of reincarnation) from being instances of such delusions. If we can best explain these cases by cryptomnesia or by extrasensory perception with paramnesia and personation, then the children do indeed suffer from delusions of identity. But this we must decide from close inspection of the data of the individual cases, not from *a priori* judgments made at a distance (theoretical and geographical) from the cases themselves.

influencing their children. In short, if parental influence is strong enough to promote the occurrence of symptoms, it is strong enough to persist for many years. But the hypothesis that the parents in the present cases have imposed an identification with a previous personality on the children suggests also that the motivations of the parents have spontaneously shifted after some years, thus permitting the fading of apparent memories and personation in the children to occur.

In my investigations of the present cases, I have often asked the parents of the children about their attitudes toward the claim or, as they usually see it, the actuality of a rebirth in their family. In some cases, I could easily detect motives for shaping the behavior of the child in the style of the deceased personality. The mother of Jimmy Svenson and both parents of William George, Jr. grieved for a deceased close relative and wanted him back. We may suppose that they may readily have reinforced the behavior of their children toward greater resemblances with the deceased persons they longed to have return. One can feel almost certain also that after a time, if not initially, they began to make comparisons between the child and the deceased relative openly and in front of the child. We have seen that, in the case of Norman Despers, his family did try to promote an identification with his deceased uncle, giving him the uncle's name and often talking about the uncle in his presence. They evidently believed that this uncle had reincarnated as Norman. But Norman resisted this pressure since his apparent memories related to his grandfather, not his uncle.

In any event, a quite different development must have occurred in other cases in which the two families had never met. The last thing the parents of Prakash, Sukla, Parmod, Imad, and Jasbir wanted was a child threatening or trying to go off to another village. Does it make sense, for example, to think that Jasbir's father would grieve for his apparent death from smallpox one day and then a few weeks later begin (even unconsciously) to reinforce the refusal of his son to eat with the family because he really belonged to a higher caste? And what interest would he have anyway in the rebirth of a complete stranger from another village? The deceased was not one of his loved ones whom he might wish to see again, but a complete stranger. And even if we decide that the parents did reinforce the children's behavior not consciously, but unconsciously (which latter assumption enables us to disregard their denials of intention), we still have to decide how they acquired the knowledge they would need in order to shape the child's behavior so convincingly as to impress the other family. In short, to sustain this theory we must revert to the idea of fraud or assign to the parents powers of extrasensory perception as great as those we have already considered attributing to the child. And if the parents have this much extrasensory capacity why do they not give other evidence of it? And why do not *they* imagine a previous life fashioned out of the information available to them?

Chari [76] has proposed that a *combination* of paranormal cognition and paramnesia, with perhaps also some cryptomnesia and precognition, can account for cases suggestive of reincarnation where one of these mechanisms alone does not seem adequately explanatory. We must not neglect this theory just because it seems complex and contains different ingredients. But to the extent that it includes extrasensory perception, it encounters (in the richer cases) the objections which I have previously mentioned. The chief of these is the difficulty this theory has in accounting for the restriction of the extrasensory perceptions to information about one target person and the organization of the information into a pattern characteristic of that particular person.

The difficulties of the extrasensory perception plus personation theory seem extremely great to me for some of the cases. I admit the plausibility of the hypothesis for weak cases with little detail and the expectation of the rebirth of a deceased member of the child's family. A combination of cryptomnesia (the parents dropping more information in the direction of the child than they realize or remember), extrasensory perception, and unconscious influence by the parents toward personation of the known and loved previous personality *may* account for these weak cases. And perhaps it could account for the richer and more extended cases also. If we admit the explanation for one case, why deny it for others? To this I answer that I am not even certain it is the right explanation for the weak cases. Its application transcends what we know about the ability of parents to influence the sense of identity of children. And even if we apply the explanation to the cases in which the parents know the previous personality and mourn for him, we have to ask why such personation by children does not happen more often since such grieving and wishing for the dead to return to life occurs commonly everywhere.

When we come to the richer cases,[77] such as those of Gnanatilleka, Imad, Jasbir, Prakash, Parmod, Swarnlata, and Sukla, this explanation becomes much more heavily strained. For if we believe that the parents had no knowledge initially of the other family, how can we suppose them able to promote the behavioral features of the case unless we endow them also with

---

[76] C. T. K. Chari. "Paramnesia and Reincarnation." *Proc.* S.P.R., Vol. 53, 1962, 264–286. G. Murphy ("Body-Mind Theory as a Factor in Survival Research," *Journal* A.S.P.R., Vol. 59, April, 1965, 148–156) has stated more briefly an interpretation of cases of the reincarnation type as resulting from a combination of cultural forces and paranormal cognitions. For a later development of Murphy's views concerning these cases, see G. Murphy. "A Caringtonian Approach to Ian Stevenson's *Twenty Cases Suggestive of Reincarnation*." *Journal* A.S.P.R., Vol. 67, April, 1973, 117–129. A further discussion was published in I. Stevenson. "Carington's Theory as Applied to Cases of the Reincarnation Type: A Reply to Gardner Murphy." *Journal* A.S.P.R., Vol. 67, April, 1973, 130–146.

[77] By "richer" cases, I mean cases having more abundant detail of statements, recognitions, and behavioral features relating the child to the previous personality.

extraordinary powers of extrasensory perception? And this would still disregard our ignorance of any motivation for such influence by the parents or
for response to it in the children.

Exhibition of Special Skills

There exists still another feature of some cases which the theory of extrasensory perception and personation cannot account for. I refer to the
exhibition of a special or idiosyncratic skill which the present personality
is not known to have had the opportunity for acquiring in the present life.
In the present series of cases, no case shows completely satisfactory evidence
of such a skill. The case of Paulo Lorenz includes observations of a definite
skill (for sewing) before any instruction in the present life; in this case,
however, the possibility of the inheritance of the same skill by two members
of the same family complicates the interpretation of the skill. The Alaskan
cases of William George, Jr. and Corliss Chotkin, Jr. (showing respectively
skill with fishing nets and with engines) suggest the occurrence of skills
before instruction in the present life. So does the report of the precocious
learning of French by Imad, although in this case we are told of unusually
rapid acquisition of a skill, not of the possession of the skill before any
instruction. However, all these three cases lack adequately detailed accounts
of the witnessing of the children's exhibition of the skills. They merely give
us hints of the *kind* of case which that of Paulo Lorenz illustrates more
definitely.

In this place, therefore, and because the other cases do not provide strong
enough evidence of the exhibition of skills before learning in this life, I
shall not extend the discussion of this topic. But it deserves mention here
because in principle cases of the definite occurrence of skills before learning in this life offer an opportunity for crucial evidence of survival since,
in my opinion, they exceed the limits of what we can account for by extrasensory perception alone.[78]

Summary of Objections to the Theory of Extrasensory Perception and Personation

Extrasensory perception alone cannot account for all the features of the
richer cases, especially for the behavioral features, including sustained
identification by the subject with the previous personality. We therefore
have to consider extrasensory perception together with personation since we
must account for both informational and behavioral features of the cases.

[78] For a case illustrating this principle and further discussion of it see I. Stevenson.
"Xenoglossy: A Review and a Report of a Case." *Op. cit.,* n. 24.

Individual items of information stated by the subjects may derive from extrasensory perception with unknown travelers or members of the family of the previous personality acting as agents (or "psychometric links") for such extrasensory perception. But extrasensory perception does not by itself account for the organization of the information derived by the subject into a pattern which is characteristic of the deceased personality.

The behavioral features requiring explanation are chiefly various evidences of sustained identification with a previous personality. The two personalities are experienced as fused or continuous, not as discontinuous or substituting for each other. No motive strong enough to account for this kind of sustained identification has been discovered in the subjects concerned. The complications in the subjects' lives resulting from the identification suggest that on balance they lose much more than they gain by the unusual identifications. Motives for imposing such identification on children exist in some parents who have lost through death a close friend or relative and wish him to return and believe he can. But outside the present cases and others of the same type, no instances are known of parental influence which has extended to making a child claim another identity. Moreover, many of the richer cases suggestive of reincarnation have occurred when the families of both personalities were quite unknown to each other prior to verification. The child's parents would then have no interest in the return of the strange personality and no normal source of information about him with which to fashion the image of him they might hope to create in the child. Supposing that the parents gain this information from extrasensory perception raises the question of why they do not show other evidence of such powers.

The theory of extrasensory perception plus personation does not seem to me to account adequately for *all* the facts of the richer cases. I find myself preferring for these cases some other hypothesis which may more adequately explain the organization of the information and the behavioral features by placing the origin of these outside the child himself in his present life and his current family. This brings us to the closely related concepts of possession and reincarnation.

Hypotheses Including Survival

We should accept theories including survival of the personality after physical death only when theories along normal lines or extrasensory perception (for which we have independent evidence) fail to account for all the facts of a case. I have drawn attention in the preceding sections to some failures of theories without survival, and have indicated that for some of the cases all the facts are better accounted for by supposing a continuing influence of the previous personality after death. In the present section I shall consider chiefly whether we ought to describe that influence, to the extent that the facts point toward it in certain cases, as constituting possession or as indicating reincarnation. In the course of this, however, I shall draw attention to one kind of evidence (congenital birthmarks and deformities) which we also cannot account for on the hypothesis of extrasensory perception and which, in an acceptable case, could only be explained by some influence on the physical organism anterior to birth.

I shall start by defining the difference between possession and reincarnation. But in doing so, I shall show that we can grade the cases along a continuum in which the distinction between reincarnation and possession becomes blurred.

Differences and Transitional Cases Between Reincarnation and Possession

The difference between reincarnation and possession lies in the extent of displacement of the primary personality achieved by the influence of the "entering" personality. Possession implies either a partial influence with the primary personality continuing to retain some control of the physical body, or a temporary (if apparently complete) control of the physical organism with later return of the original personality.

The Thompson-Gifford case provides one of the best-attested examples of apparent possession.[79, 80] Thompson, an engraver, became impressed by a desire, or rather a powerful impulse or compulsion, to paint certain scenes which arose vividly in his mind. He himself had little interest or known skill in painting, but he succumbed to the impulse and painted from hallucinations, as it were, a number of scenes which closely resembled places either familiar to a deceased painter or actually painted by him. The painter was Robert Swain Gifford, who had died about six months before Thompson's experiences began. Although Thompson knew a little about Gifford and had had a slight personal acquaintance with him, he did not know of his death when his experiences began.

The similarity between the paintings of Thompson and published photographs of the scenes frequented or painted by Gifford, as well as considerable other evidence, give much support to the theory that Thompson somehow fell under the influence of the discarnate personality of Gifford. Readers can only evaluate this evidence by a careful perusal of the original data, and I allude to the case here only to draw attention to the similarities and differences between the case of Thompson (and similar ones) and the cases suggestive of rebirth. This difference lies, I would say, in the extent of

[79] J. H. Hyslop. "A Case of Veridical Hallucinations." *Proc.* A.S.P.R., Vol. 3, 1909, 1–469.
[80] J. H. Hyslop. *Contact With the Other World.* New York: The Century Co., 1919.

the identification rather than in other features. In his autobiographical summary of his experiences, Thompson wrote (with regard to his impulse to paint): ". . . during the time I was sketching I remember having the impression that I was Mr Gifford himself, and I would tell my wife before starting out that Mr. Gifford wanted to go sketching, although I did not know at that time that he had died early in the year." Thompson subsequently heard a voice from time to time urging on the work of sketching and painting. The influence extended to a serious interference with Thompson's regular occupation. He would take journeys to other parts of the country under the influence of the impulse to paint certain favorite landscapes of Gifford. Throughout most of these experiences Thompson continued aware of his own identity even when most under the influence of hallucinated voices or images of scenes he felt impelled to paint. On one occasion (and possibly more) he experienced a period of amnesia for what he had done when apparently under the influence of the Gifford personality. He never claimed he had been Gifford, nor did a communication ever come directly from Gifford to other persons through Thompson as if Gifford himself spoke with the vocal apparatus of Thompson.[81]

The case of Lurancy Vennum, mentioned above, suggests a more complete possession. In this case, for several months (and occasionally afterwards) the personality of "Mary Roff" (who died when Lurancy Vennum was a year old) entirely displaced that of Lurancy Vennum and apparently occupied the vacated body of that girl. At the end of several months, "Mary Roff" departed and Lurancy Vennum resumed control.[82, 83, 84] During her tenancy of the body, if we may call her manifestation such, "Mary Roff" never claimed to be Lurancy Vennum. She merely claimed to be herself, i.e., Mary Roff, occupying the temporarily available body of Lurancy Vennum.

The case of Jasbir of the present series lies a step closer to the usual case suggestive of rebirth. After the change of personality in Jasbir, he denied that he was Jasbir and that personality gave no further indications of itself. The "occupant" of Jasbir's body then claimed he was Sobha Ram; he behaved like Sobha Ram and only gradually accepted the body and life situa-

---

[81] The case resembles that of Mrs. H. Weisz-Roos previously reported by myself (I. Stevenson. "The Evidence for Survival From Claimed Memories of Former Incarnations, Part 1. Review of the Data." *Journal* A.S.P.R., Vol. 54, April, 1960, 51–71). In interviews which I had with Mrs. Weisz-Roos later, she told me that she had experienced several additional episodes of seeming to paint while apparently possessed by "Goya." She did not in these experiences have any awareness specifically of "Goya." The evidence that the influence came from "Goya" derived from other data. At these times, however, she painted extremely rapidly, effortlessly, and with a skill which she believed was quite beyond her usual capacity.

[82] E. W. Stevens. *The Watseka Wonder. A Narrative of Startling Phenomena Occurring in the Case of Mary Lurancy Vennum.* Chicago: Religio-Philosophical Publishing House, 1887.

[83] W. James. *The Principles of Psychology.* New York: Henry Holt and Co., 1890. (Vol. I. 396.)

[84] R. Hodgson. *Loc. cit.* n. 69.

tion of Jasbir. Eventually the new personality came to accept the situation he found himself in and took his place at the family table, literally as well as figuratively. The personality of "Mary Roff" never underwent such adaptation, but preserved her identity fully while manifesting. The ostensibly reincarnated Sobha Ram preserved his identity in the body of Jasbir for much longer, for a year and a half if we count his refusal to eat with the family, and for many years if we consider his continuing sense of alienation in the village of Rasulpur and contrasting happiness when with the Tyagi family in Vehedi.

In a small number of other cases in my collection (none included in the present series) a child has claimed to be a person who had in fact died *after* the birth of the child. In one such case (India) the interval was four and a half days; in another case (Thailand) it was eighteen hours; and in still another case (Germany) it was five weeks.

The case of Ravi Shankar illustrates a point of exchange of personalities still earlier. Ravi Shankar was born about six months after the death of Munna, whom he claimed to have been. It is virtually certain that the body of Ravi Shankar had begun embryonic development before the death of Munna.[85]

If for the moment we take all these cases at face value, we find a continuous progression between cases of partial temporary possession (Thompson), complete temporary possession (Vennum), complete permanent possession beginning years after birth (Jasbir), complete permanent possession occurring a day to several weeks after the birth of the physical organism (unpublished cases), complete permanent possession occurring after conception but before birth (Ravi Shankar), and death occurring before conception with "possession" presumably occurring at conception. The last two groups of cases comprise the usual ones in which claims of continuity with a previous personality are made, and to which we ordinarily apply the word "reincarnation." In short, if the previous personality seems to associate itself with the physical organism at the time of conception or during embryonic development we speak of reincarnation; if the association between previous personality and physical organism only comes later, we speak of possession.

But in considering the cases we must not take them at face value or allow the subjective report of experiences to become the sole criterion for distinguishing them. It may turn out that cases of the reincarnation type are in fact instances of the Thompson-Gifford type in which (*a*) the deceased

---

[85] In India, as I mentioned earlier, the recording of births and deaths often lacks public documentation or even private notation. Often we can only feel certain about the month of a birth or death without having precise information about the day. Sometimes one cannot even be sure of the exact month. Such uncertainties exist, for example, for the deaths and births of both personalities in the cases of Jasbir and of Ravi Shankar.

personality died before the birth of the "possessed" personality, and (b) the possessing influence goes farther than it did in the Thompson-Gifford case so that there occurs a complete and sustained sense of continuity with the previous personality. This hypothesis will explain nearly all the facts and it jumps over all the difficulties which the theory of extrasensory perception plus personation encounters in trying to account for the features of personation in the cases suggestive of rebirth. It does, however, encounter and stumble on other difficulties.

Limitations of the Theory of Possession in Many Cases Suggestive of Reincarnation

Although the theory of possession accounts neatly for the fact that some of the children seem to remember people and places as they were when the previous personality lived, it does not adequately explain one feature of the informational aspects of the cases. I refer to the common occurrence of an increased revival of memories when the child returns to the location of the life of the previous personality. Thus a number of the children, e g., Sukla, Jasbir, Prakash, Parmod, Swarnlata, Gnanatilleka, and Imad, upon visiting the home or village of the previous life, recognized or described people and places which they had not previously mentioned. I do not think we can fully account for this rather marked increase in items apparently remembered by (a) a greater interest in the child's statements, and (b) the questioning (and stimulating) of the child by adults on these occasions. Such greater inquisitiveness on the part of surrounding adults might explain some of the greater yield of information on these visits, but other items of information flowed out spontaneously from the child as if produced by associations of images. Now we know from many observations and experiments on memory that recognition exceeds recall and also that one stimulus activates other memories by associations which link our memories together. Accordingly, for both these reasons we should expect that true memories would come more easily upon visiting a place where one had actually lived before. We do not find ourselves surprised if we reminisce greatly about our childhoods during visits to childhood homes; the same principle may explain this aspect of the behavior of the children here considered. The possession hypothesis, in my opinion, does not cover these observations quite so well. For a discarnate personality influencing and com ·unicating through an incarnate one would surely have access to his knowledge of his own incarnate life irrespective of the physical location of the person he influenced. Why, we may ask, should a discarnate personality know more about his life in the village where he lived than in the village where the personality he influences lives? To this we may, however, bring forward an objection. We may suppose that the possessing personality resembles somewhat a haunting ghost. Now haunting ghosts, unlike apparitions, do not leave the sites of the incarnate existences with which they are connected. Moreover, they often repeat in a routine, unvarying way some act of the related incarnate existence, such as the last events leading up to a murder. They behave like living persons with obsessive-compulsive neuroses who endlessly repeat some action which partially re-enacts an event of the past. But cases of ostensible possession do not usually resemble haunting ghosts. However, perhaps an intermediate kind of discarnate personality exists. This could be one somewhat tied to the surroundings of his previous life, but capable of wandering off to influence other people at a distance from the site of his main interest. Such a personality might well increase the strength of his power when he and the person he influenced approached the main base, so to speak, of his previous incarnate existence. To add strength to this supposition we should try to find a case of ostensible possession without claim to reincarnation in which the strength of the possession increased with the return of the influenced person to favorite sites of the ostensible possessing personality. The best attested case of ostensible possession, the Thompson-Gifford case, does not support what I may call the haunt-possession theory on this point. For Hyslop (and Thompson himself in his diary) described no increase in the apparent influence of the Gifford personality when Thompson visited sites familiar to Gifford such as Gifford's studio or an island on the New England coast which Gifford loved and where he had often sketched and painted.

The haunt-possession theory seems particularly poorly qualified to account for some of the minor cases where scanty information just "pops out" from the child in response to a particular stimulus that seems to awaken associations. In the case of Mallika, for example, this theory would have to suppose that a possessing spirit, say of Devi in this case, hung around Mallika in the hope of expressing something if an occasion arose. But the opportunities for expression depended very much on other people. Similarly in the case of Swarnlata, who continued to sing Bengali songs on request when she was an adult woman. These songs were related to a claimed life in Bengal of which otherwise she showed only rather fragmentary and somewhat confused information. Allowing that these Bengali songs had *some* paranormal origin, are we to suppose that a discarnate spirit who knew them waited until some visitor happened to ask Swarnlata to sing them and then came forward for the performance, afterwards retiring? I doubt if this theory will attract many adherents for cases of this kind, though it may well apply in other cases.

In general, I have not allowed into the discussion of these cases any communications through mediums from ostensible discarnate communicators relative to the issues involved in choosing among the hypotheses relevant to these cases. However, I may here make an exception to mention some mediumistic communications reported by Wickland.[86] Some of the communicators addressing Wickland through the mediumship of his wife asserted that they had erroneously "possessed" an incarnate personality's body in the mistaken idea that they should reincarnate. When they discovered their errors they apologized and withdrew. But even supposing these communicators to be discarnate personalities who once lived, we could decide that the real mistake they made was not about whether or not reincarnation occurs, but about the time and circumstances for their own reincarnations to occur. Thus they may have fumbled or stumbled into a still occupied body, as Thompson claimed Gifford tried to do to him. Nevertheless, the possibility remains that some cases suggestive of reincarnation derive from the activities of discarnate personalities of this general kind.

A second possible difficulty for the hypothesis of possession arises from the patchiness of the information apparently remembered by the child. If the possessing spirit brings influence to bear on a personality so fully as to lead to a claim of altered identification, why does the possessing personality not seem to remember everything about the previous life? We would not expect such complete memory in the partial cases of ostensible possession such as occurred in the Thompson-Gifford case. But we would expect it in cases which included a complete change of identity and personality. The possessing "Mary Roff" did seem to have full knowledge of the affairs of the deceased Mary Roff and knew much more about them than she did of the affairs of Lurancy Vennum. The possessing "Mary Roff" knew nothing of the family of Lurancy Vennum, when she took "control." But she recognized the family and friends of Mary Roff. This contrasts with most of the present cases in which the subjects exhibited only a partial knowledge of the life and times of the previous personality. And what knowledge they did show followed the customary patterns of the organization of memories around emotionally charged events. The cases of Wijeratne, Parmod, Sukla, Swarnlata, and Imad illustrate this feature. For example, Sukla apparently recalled the previous marital family, but not (with one exception) the members of the biological family with whom Mana (the previous personality of this case) had lived most of her life. But I found evidence that the events of the life of Mana connected with the marital family carried emotional charges considerably greater than those events which she shared with her biological family. Strong emotions influence the accessibility of memories; that is, their persistence in consciousness as well as their repression. We particularly either remember or forget events whose occurrence has occasioned us strong emotion. The variations of memories in the cases suggestive of rebirth thus resemble ordinary irregularities of memory. So here again the

---

[86] C. A. Wickland. *Thirty Years Among the Dead*. London: Spiritualist Press, 1924.

psychological features of these cases seem to conform to accepted psychological processes. Now we have no reason to imagine that these psychological processes alter for an individual surviving death. He also might find lacunae in his memories and a tendency for them to cluster around events originally accompanied by strong emotion when they occurred. I think, therefore, that on this second point we cannot expect to distinguish between possession and reincarnation.

The occurrence of a definite skill which the subject could not have learned in this life likewise does not permit a distinction between possession and reincarnation. Thompson (in the Thompson-Gifford case cited above) showed an artistic skill in painting far transcending anything he had previously demonstrated or was believed capable of. Yet this was certainly *not* a case of reincarnation (since Gifford died when Thompson was an adult) and was *prima facie* a case of possession.

The theory of possession also cannot adequately explain the knowledge shown by a number of the children of how buildings were arranged or people looked during the life of the previous personality. Imad, Sukla, Prakash, Swarnlata, Parmod, and Corliss Chotkin, Jr. all showed such knowledge. If a possessing discarnate personality is "hanging around" the site of his terrestrial life, why does he not keep up to date with changes in buildings and people? Occasionally a child of one of these cases *does* show knowledge of events happening after the death of the previous personality. Marta is an example of the present series, but such cases are very rare. Perhaps, however, such possessing personalities as we are here considering have become trapped in their own memories and have not kept *au courant* with changes since the deaths of their physical bodies. We know that many mentally ill persons become thus caught in memories of painful events and the succeeding years have little or no impact on them. And we have also some evidence from other sources (e.g., mediumistic communications and observations of ghosts) that discarnate personalities may become "stuck" in time. To draw on this evidence further, however, would be to beg the present question since we are concerned here with evidence of the survival of physical death, and should not assume that it occurs.

Still another difficulty for the possession hypothesis lies in the lack of apparent motive for influencing a terrestrial personality on the part of the discarnate personalities concerned in these cases. In the typical case of possession with which I am familiar (whatever the evidence of paranormality may be), we can usually discern (or infer) some motive for the ostensible possession, either on the part of the primary personality (e.g., to express otherwise inhibited impulses) or on the part of the presumptive possessing personality (e.g., to wreak revenge, have his grave attended to, etc.). I fail to see motives of these kinds in the cases of the present group. But I freely admit that I did not have or take opportunities for a thorough probing of

motives either in the children of these cases or the related previous personalities. I can only say that motives of the kind commonly encountered in
cases of the possession type were not apparent to the scrutiny I gave these
cases.

I do not consider any of the foregoing arguments decisive as between
reincarnation and possession in explaining the usual case of the reincarnation type. Two hundred years ago Swedenborg stated that apparent cases
of reincarnation were in fact instances of influence on the living by
discarnate personalities:

> An angel or spirit is not allowed to speak with a man from his own memory,
> but from that of the man; for angels and spirits have memory as well as men. If
> a spirit should speak with a man from his own memory, then the man would not
> know otherwise than that the things which he then thought were his own, when
> yet they were the spirit's; it is like the recollection of a thing, which yet the man
> never heard or saw. That it is so has been given to me to know from experience.
> From this some of the ancients had the opinion, that after some thousands of
> years they should return into their former life, and into all its acts, and also that
> they had returned. They concluded it from this, that sometimes there occurred to
> them a recollection, as it were, of things which they never saw or heard; and this
> came to pass because spirits flowed from their own memory into their ideas or
> thought.[87]

Swedenborg's argument still has much cogency today and gains support
from the case of Jasbir, in which we can feel confident that the deceased
personality influencing the behavior of Jasbir (or his body, at least) died
several years *after* the birth of Jasbir's body. Other cases of the present
group may be instances of similar "possessing influences" in which the
previous personality just happened to die well before the birth of the present personality's body.

There remains, however, one group of cases which may permit a clear
distinction (in these cases) between possession and reincarnation. I refer
to the cases suggestive of rebirth with congenital birthmarks or deformities.
In addition to the several cases of this kind here reported, I have had an
opportunity to investigate many other cases of this type personally, including examinations of the birthmarks. In my opinion, cases of this kind point
toward an ideal case we may some day discover which could permit a firm
choice between reincarnation and possession for that case at least. In some
of these cases, the birthmark may account for the story of a previous life
invented to fit the birthmark. I am prepared to learn of such a case, although I have not done so yet. But that would still leave the task of accounting for the birthmark itself. The rebirth story may come from the

[87] E. Swedenborg. *Heaven and Its Wonders and Hell.* (First published in Latin, London,
1758). Rotch Edition. Boston: New-Church Union, 1906. (Paragraph 256, page 155.)

birthmark, but the birthmark cannot arise from the story because it represents some antenatal influence on the developing fetus. Now by definition a birthmark must have its inception before delivery of the infant. If then the birthmark and the apparent memories of a previous life match so that we could explain the birthmark if the apparent memories of the related previous life are veridical, we can rule out possession of the kind we have been considering. For the birthmark supposes an influence anterior to birth, but possession supposes such an influence after birth with attempts to displace partially or completely the personality which participated in the shaping of the physical organism antenatally. And we can also exclude the theory of extrasensory perception plus personation as accounting for all the facts, since this theory clearly cannot account for the birthmark.

A considerable literature of folklore suggests that the ideas of pregnant women may influence the tissues, especially of the skin, of their babies *in utero*. There seem to be at least a few well-authenticated cases of this kind which justify taking this concept seriously and studying it further. It might then be supposed that a woman who had heard about the death of a particular personality and his wounds or scars, could so influence a developing fetus as to reproduce the same configurations on the body of a baby who would then become the present personality related to the deceased one. This theory of "maternal psychokinesis" *may* apply to birthmark cases in which the mother of the present personality knows details of the death and marks of the previous personality. But I do not see how it could apply easily to those cases in which the mother had no normal knowledge of the deceased personality at the time her child was born with relevant birthmarks.

Summary of Conclusions

Before concluding I shall briefly summarize the main arguments of the foregoing discussion.

1. A consideration of the large number of witnesses for many of the cases and of the lack of apparent motivation and opportunities for fraud makes the hypothesis of fraud extremely unlikely for the cases here reported.

2. Cryptomnesia may account for a few of the weaker cases occurring in families having acquaintance with the previous personality. Cases attributed or actually traced to cryptomnesia have lacked the behavioral features of the richer cases in the present series. In these cases the child sustains an identification with the previous personality over an average period of seven years, but without other obvious alterations of consciousness or personality. Moreover, in the richer cases cryptomnesia cannot account for the transmis-

sion of much intimate information about one family to a child of another family without supposing that much more contact had taken place between the families than either can remember.

3. Extrasensory perception plus personation may account for some of the cases, but can only be stretched with great strain to cover all the facts of the richer cases. Extrasensory perception alone does not adequately account for the organization of the information available to the subject in a pattern characteristic of the deceased personality. And it cannot account for the exhibition of skills not learned in the present life. This theory also does not adequately account for the long duration, extending over years, of the child's identification with the previous personality. I have not discovered in the child motives for such prolonged identification. Nor have I found that the parents possessed (except in a few cases) either the motives or the necessary information for influencing the children toward such identifications with strange, unknown persons. Moreover, we may doubt whether parental influences alone can lead to an actual claim of altered identity such as is almost or entirely unknown among children (even psychotic ones) apart from the cases suggestive of rebirth.

4. Cases showing a specific or idiosyncratic skill which the subject could not have inherited or acquired in the present life require some survivalist explanation, either possession or reincarnation. But we cannot make a choice between these two possibilities from the study of the skill alone.

5. Most other features of the cases also do not permit a firm decision between the hypotheses of possession and reincarnation. The conformity of the apparent memories of many of the cases to the psychological "law" that recognition exceeds recall favors somewhat the reincarnation over the possession hypothesis.

6. Cases suggestive of rebirth with congenital deformities or birthmarks, provided they are well authenticated, decisively favor reincarnation over possession for the explanation of these cases, but not necessarily other cases suggestive of rebirth. The present group does not include any birthmark cases as well authenticated, or as free of possible avenues of normal communication, as some of the other cases suggestive of rebirth which do not include birthmarks. It does, however, contain cases which illustrate the possibilities which such cases offer for making a clear distinction between extrasensory perception, possession, and reincarnation.

Concluding Remarks

In 1960 I concluded my review of cases suggestive of reincarnation without opting firmly for any one theory as explanatory of all the cases. I still hold to this general position. We may find some cases we can best explain as due to fraud, cryptomnesia, or extrasensory perception with personation (perhaps with mixed telepathy and retrocognition). For other cases we may favor survivalist explanations such as possession or reincarnation.

So far as we concern ourselves with evidence for survival, we are not obliged to suppose that *every* case suggestive of reincarnation needs to be explained as an instance of it. Our question is rather whether there are *any* cases (or even just *one* case) in which no other explanation seems better than reincarnation in accounting for all the facts.

I am doubtful if many readers will agree about any one case for we all reach belief and conviction on these matters, as on all, at different levels of exposure to evidence; and we differ also about what we shall agree to call evidence. I believe, however, that the evidence favoring reincarnation as a hypothesis for the cases of this type has increased since I published my review in 1960. This increase has come from several different kinds of observations and cases, but chiefly from the observations of the behavior of the children claiming the memories and the study of cases with specific or idiosyncratic skills and with congenital birthmarks and deformities.

I believe that one solution to the question of survival lies in the observation of *patterns* within one personality or organism which were not or could not have been inherited or acquired in the present life of that personality.[88] If it is proposed further to show that the pattern observed in the current personality belongs to a *particular* deceased person, then we need also to demonstrate a similarity of the patterns in the present and previous personalities. Such patterns may be of several different kinds.

The "Lethe" case [89] illustrates the observation of one such pattern, that of the knowledge and use of classical scholarship possessed when alive by F. W. H. Myers and demonstrated, according to the opinion of some, after his death, through the organisms of Mrs. Piper and Mrs. Willett in one of the better cross correspondences of the S.P.R.

In the "Lethe" case the relevant pattern of information consisted of classical scholarship. But the informational pattern might have any content provided the pattern shown paranormally is not characteristic of the normal knowledge of the subject and *is* characteristic of some previous personality. We could therefore qualify under this heading the patterns of information about people and places (connected with the relevant previous personalities) exhibited by, for example, Swarnlata, Parmod, Prakash,

---

[88] C. J. Ducasse has outlined this principle in "What Would Constitute Conclusive Evidence of Survival After Death?" (*Journal* S.P.R., Vol. 41, December, 1962, 401–406). I have extended the application of the principle to include the reproduction of patterns on the physical organism. For a further discussion of this important topic see I. Stevenson. "Xenoglossy: A Review and Report of a Case. *Op. cit.*, n. 24.

[89] O. Lodge. "Evidence of Classical Scholarship and of Cross-Correspondence in Some New Automatic Writings." *Proc.* S.P.R., Vol. 25, 1911, 113–175.

Sukla, Jasbir, Imad, Gnanatilleka, and (to include a less well-authenticated case of the same general group) Corliss Chotkin, Jr. The pattern consists of information about people and places known to one deceased personality and it excludes information not known to that personality. These cases provide examples of *informational patterns* corresponding to particular deceased personalities.

We may also identify *behavioral patterns* related to deceased personalities and outside the normal behavior of the present personality. The most important examples of such behavioral patterns occur in the definite exhibitions of specific skills which the subjects could not have learned normally. In the present series of cases, the case of Paulo in Brazil provides the only reasonably well-attested example of such a skill, but some others, e.g., Corliss Chotkin, Jr. and William George, Jr., give hints of such skills and have prompted a search for better examples. Moreover, relevant behavioral patterns extend beyond skills and include the occurrence of many traits such as mannerisms, fears, special likings, and aversions. My colleagues and I plan a systematic (and objective) study of correlations of patterns of personality traits between present and previous personalities in cases of the reincarnation type.

And finally we may identify specific *physical patterns* corresponding in the previous and present personalities. Examples of such physical patterns occur in the birthmark or deformity cases. Here the pattern is imprinted on the physical organism and found at birth. In some of the present cases with birthmarks, a particular person with marks specifically corresponding to the birthmark (or marks) of the subject has not been found. Such matching, however, was reported by witnesses in the cases of Ravi Shankar and Corliss Chotkin, Jr. In the case of Ravi Shankar, the birthmark resembling the scar of a cut across the throat may be thought to resemble the scar of anyone who has had his throat cut. Some persons may therefore not consider the resemblance of the birthmark on Ravi Shankar to the wound of Munna specific for these two personalities. Such specificity does, however, exist in the case of Corliss Chotkin, Jr., for it is extremely improbable that any other person would have two scars of the same kind and at the same locations on the body as had Victor Vincent. And yet according to our informants in this case, birthmarks of the same appearance and at the same locations occurred on the body of Corliss Chotkin, Jr.[90]

[90] A case in Thailand still under investigation and to be reported later resembles that of Corliss Chotkin, Jr., although it lacks the prediction of a rebirth by the previous personality. The subject provided rather well-witnessed evidence of paranormal knowledge of the life of the previous personality. He had two birthmarks which corresponded exactly in shape and location with two lesions observed by witnesses on the body of the previous personality. As in the case of Corliss Chotkin, Jr., it is extremely unlikely that two physical organisms would have two such similar marks (the one pair acquired, the other pair congenital) by chance.

In the cases of the present collection we have evidence of the occurrence of patterns which the present personality is not known to have inherited or acquired after birth in the present life. And in some instances these patterns match corresponding and specific features of an identified deceased personality. In such cases we have then in principle, I believe, some evidence for human survival of physical death. I say *in principle*, because I continue aware of particular weaknesses in the present cases. But if the principle here adopted is correct, we are thrown back onto the question of authenticity for a final judgment of the contribution these cases make toward conviction about survival. I think that some (not all) of the present cases are well enough authenticated to permit a decision on the question whether or not the events described did in fact happen as the witnesses described them, for that is the crucial question with regard to authenticity. But at the same time the chief contribution of the present cases may lie in their illustration of the *kinds* of cases which, if we could obtain them more abundantly and study them more thoroughly, would on the basis of the principle here adopted, provide compelling evidence of survival.

Index

Index

ABU-SHAKRA, M., xiv
ABUSHDID, C., xiv, 275, 280, 312, 313
Acquired characteristics, inheritance of, 241
African elements in Brazilian spiritualism, 181
AGNIHOTRI, R., 68, 69, 71
ALBERTELLI, A., 337
Aleuts, belief in reincarnation among, 216
ALEXANDER, V. K., 369
ALGER, W. R., vii
American Society for Psychical Research, viii,
  ix, xii, xvi, 355
AMES, M., 129n
ANDREWS, C. L., 253
Animal intelligence, inheritance of, 213
"Anna" case, 362-363, 364
"Announcing" dreams, see under Dreams
ANTEVS, E., 217n
ANUDA, C., xiii, 182
Apparitions, vii, 14, 378
ARBERRY, A. J., 273n
Aroumougam family (case of Mallika), 105-
  108
Athapaskans, belief in reincarnation among,
  216
ATREYA, B. L., xii, 18, 19, 92, 93, 95, 109, 110
AURANGZEB, EMPEROR, 15-16

Bach family, 213
Baddewithana family (case of Gnanatilleka),
  131-148
BALFOUR, G. W., 357n, 359n
BANCROFT, H. H., 253n
BANERJEE, H. N., xii, 18, 68, 69, 81, 93
BARBEAU, M., xiii, 216n, 218n, 219n
BAYER, R., xi, 8
Behavioral features in reincarnation-type cases,
  3, 5, 23, 31, 48, 57, 64, 80, 101-102, 107-
  108, 120-122, 135, 142-144, 199, 212, 233-
  235, 262-263, 269, 301-305, 333, 344, 360-
  361, 384

patterns of, 385
persistence of, 324, 330, 360-361, 373
BENDER, H., 362n
BERNSTEIN, M., 340n
BIRD, J. M., 355n
Birthmarks (and deformities) in reincarna-
  tion-type cases, 16, 91-105, 149-171, 220,
  221, 222, 226, 231-245, 248-269, 334, 350,
  381-382, 383, 384, 385; see also Moles
Bishen Chand, case of, 165n, 270n
BJÖRKHEM, J., 2
BLACKWELL, A., 181n
"Blanche Courtain" case, 354
"Blanche Poynings" case, 337-338
BOAS, F., 218n
"Bo" case, 362, 366
Body size, perception of changes in during
  hypnosis and drug intoxication, 197n
BOSE, S. C., 17n
BOSE, S. K., 338
Bouhamzy family (case of Imad Elawar), 275-
  320
BOWEN, M., 368n
"Boy" case, 363, 364
BRADLEY, C., 368n
BRAUER, A., 240n
"Bridey Murphy" case, 340
BROAD, C. D., vii
Buddhism and belief in reincarnation, 128-
  130, 149n, 153n, 221, 222, 272n
Burlingham, D., 361

CARRINGTON, H., 3n
Cases suggestive of reincarnation
  in Brazil, 2, 181-215
  in Ceylon, 2, 128-180
  changes of caste in, 34-52, 57, 130
  claim of memories as a differentiating fea-
    ture in, 348-352
  and cultural influences, 2, 15, 181-182, 216-
    217, 223, 225n, 274, 349, 350, 352

Cases suggestive of reincarnation *(cont.)*
  details of recorded prior to verification, 270-271, 274-320
  geographical distribution of, 2, 171-172, 224-225, 274, 349-350
  in India, 2, 15-127
  international census of, 1-2, 17, 142, 271, 349, 351
  in Lebanon, 270-320
  non-veridical, 350-351
  patterns of recurring features in, 14, 131, 331, 384-385
  present and antecedent personalities occurring in same family, 149-171, 182, 203-215, 225, 269
  sex differences in present and antecedent personalities, 131-148, 203-215
  spontaneous, methods of studying, 4-14, 17
  telepathic links in, 49, 103, 111, 124, 344-345
  among the Tlingits, 216-269
  usual history of, 16-17
Caste, changes of in reincarnation-type cases, 34-52, 57, 130
Chakravarty family (case of Sukla), 52-66
CHANDRA, J., xiii
CHARI, C. T. K., 339, 351*n*, 371
Charles Porter, case of, 241-245, 257
Child mediums, 354, 356, 362-364
Children in reincarnation-type cases
  circumstances in which their declarations occur, compared to mediumship, 354-357
  compared with mediums, 354-359, 362-365
  dreams of, 51
  duration of personation of previous personality, 324, 359-360, 361, 362
  mediumistic gifts of, 354, 362-363, 364
  other evidence of extrasensory perception in, 90, 142, 146-147, 201-202, 353-354
  parental suppression of their memories of previous lives, 20, 90, 92, 161, 181*n*, 222, 244, 250, 274, 276, 317
  precocious language attributed to, 9
  sexual orientation in, 142-144, 146, 204-205, 210, 361
Chotkin family (case of Corliss Chotkin, Jr.), 259-269
Claim of memories as a differentiating feature in reincarnation-type cases, 348-352
Clairvoyance, 3, 163, 347
"Claughton" case, 354
COATES, W. A., xiii, 131
COCKAYNE, E. A., 240*n*
COLERIDGE, S. T., 337, 340, 341
Commonwealth Fund, xi

Communications, mediumistic, *see* Mediumistic communications
Communicators, "drop in," *see* "Drop in" communicators
"Compensation theory" as related to motivation of children in reincarnation-type cases, 332, 365-366
CONGDON, M. H., 360*n*
COOMARASWAMY, A. N., 15*n*, 129*n*
Corliss Chotkin, Jr., case of, 259-269, 334, 335, 350, 372, 380, 385
Counterhypotheses in reincarnation-type cases
  cryptomnesia, 12, 144-145, 146, 314-315, 333-342, 344, 371, 382-383, 384
  extrasensory perception plus personation, 315, 343-382, 383, 384
  fraud, 12, 31, 48, 64, 81-82, 102, 144-145, 309-311, 331-333, 384
  genetic "memory," 342-343
  "imposed identification," 172, 177, 212, 229, 235, 241, 266-268, 366-372
  normal sources of information, 331-343
  possession, 315, 335, 359, 374-377, 383
Credulity concerning reincarnation, 10
Crime, attitude toward in Ceylon, 153*n*, 161
Cross correspondences, 384
Cryptomnesia
  Coleridge's case, 337, 340
  as a counterhypothesis in reincarnation-type cases, 12, 144-145, 146, 314-315, 333-342, 344, 371, 382-383, 384
  Dickinson's case, 337-338, 340
  in hypnosis, 340-342
  Martin's case, 337
  personation in, 337-338
Cultural influences and reincarnation, 2, 15, 181-182, 216-217, 223, 225*n*, 274, 349, 350, 353
CURRAN, P. L., 340

DALE, L. A., xii, xvi
DANE, P. G., 358*n*
Darwin family, 213
DAS, T., 16*n*
DATT, I., 18
DAW, S. K., 18
DAYAL, P., xv
DE BRATH, S., 344*n*
Deformities, *see* Birthmarks
Déjà vu, 230, 245, 247, 339
DE LAGUNA, F., xiii, 216*n*, 221
DELANNE, G., 354
Delusions, rarity of in children, 368
DENARO, S. J., 240*n*
DEO, R., xii, 19
Derek Pitnov, case of, 243, 252-259

DE ROCHAS, A., 2
de Silva family (case of Ranjith Makalanda),
171-180
DES LAURIERS, A. M., 368n
Despers family (case of Norman Despers),
245-248
DESPERT, J. L., 368n
DICKINSON, G. L., 337, 340
DIETRICH, E. L., 170n
Difficulties in studying reincarnation-type
cases, 4-14
DINGWALL, E. J., 3n
Diseases, physical, possibly related to previous
lives, 67, 196-197, 201, 246, 248, 256, 259
Dissociated states, 322, 338, 356-357, 364
DORSON, R. M., 254n
Double, projection of, see Human double
DRAKE, R. M., 362n
Dreams, 51, 350, 364
"announcing," 220, 231, 232, 235, 260-261,
264
suggestive of a previous life, 350, 357-358
"Drop in" communicators, 355-356
DRUCKER, P., 254n
Drug intoxication, perception of changes in
body size during, 197n
Druses, belief in reincarnation among, 271-274
DUCASSE, C. J., vii-viii, xi, 88n, 340, 346n, 349n,
384n

EASTMAN, M., 352n
Elawar family (case of Imad Elawar), 275-320
Elkin family (case of Henry Elkin), 248-252
ERICKSON, M., 367n
Eskimos, belief in reincarnation among, 216,
220
ESTABROOK, A. H., 240n
EVANS-WENTZ, W. Y., 129n, 169n
"Exchange incarnation," 2; see also Jasbir,
case of
Extrasensory perception
in children, 361-364, 366
as counterhypothesis in reincarnation-type
cases, 49, 103, 162-163, 203, 246-247,
267, 335, 337
other evidence of in subjects of reincarnation-type cases, 90, 142, 146-147, 201-
202, 353-354
Extrasensory perception plus personation,
theory of as counterhypothesis in reincarnation-type cases, 315, 343-382, 383, 384
as applied to behavioral features, 360-361
as applied to informational features, 345-348
and birthmarks, 381-382
in other types of cases, 361-365
and the projection of imagery, 352-353

reasons for considering together, 343-345
and special skills, 372
summary of objections to, 372-373, 383

Fading of memories, see under Memories
Fantasies of the "previous life" (Zolik's ex-
periments), 340-341
Faruk Faris Elawar, case of, 323n
Fausse reconnaissance à deux, 339
FICHTE, J. G., vii
FLESHLER, M., 307n
FLOURNOY, T., 351, 352n
Follow-up interviews, 321-330; see also Later
development of subjects in reincarnation-
type cases
FRANCIS, B. A., 164, 167
Fraud as a counterhypothesis in reincarnation-
type cases, 12, 31, 48, 64, 81-82, 102, 144-
145, 309-311, 382, 384
summary of objections to, 331-333

GAEBELÉ, Y. R., xii, 19, 105, 106n, 108n
GARRATT, G. T., 15n, 129n
GARRETT, E. J., xi
GAULD, A., 355
Genetic "memory" as a counterhypothesis in
reincarnation-type cases, 342-343
Genetic transmission of skills and aptitudes,
212-213
Geographical distribution of reincarnation-
type cases, 2, 171-172, 224-225, 274, 349-
350
George family (case of William George, Jr.),
231-241
Georg Neidhart, case of, 170n
Ghosts, see under Hauntings
GIBBES, E. B., 355
GIFFORD, R. S., see "Thompson-Gifford" case
Gnanatilleka, case of, xiii, xv, 7, 130, 131-148,
202n, 325, 328, 335, 348, 353, 371, 377, 384
GOMBRICH, R. F., 129n
Gopal Gupta, case of, 169n
Gotama the Buddha, 128, 130
GOULD, B. J., 239n
"G.P." case (through Mrs. Piper), 348
GRANT, J., 352n, 358
GRAVES, R., 239n
GREEN, C., 359n
GROWSE, F. S., 16n
GUNERATNE, V. F., xv, 164, 168
GUNTHER, E., xiii
Gupta family (case of Ravi Shankar), 91-105
GUPTA, L. D., 17n

Haidas, belief in reincarnation among, 216,
220, 224

HAIN, J., 360
HALL, G., xiii, 254*n*, 256, 257*n*
HARPER, E. B., 129*n*
HARPER, R. M. J., 258
HARRER, H., 239*n*
HART, H., 14
HARWELL, C., xvi
HASSAN, N., xiv
Hauntings, vii
  "haunting ghosts," 378, 380
  "haunt-possession" theory, 378-379
HEAVENER, B., xii
"Hélène Smith" case, 351, 352-353
HENDERSON, C., xvi
Henriette Weisz-Roos, case of, 1, 375
Henry Elkin, case of, xv, 248-252, 257
Heredity and reincarnation, 213
HETTIARATCHY, N. B., 166, 170
HILL, J. A., 356*n*, 357*n*
Hinduism and belief in reincarnation, 15-16,
  52, 129-130, 221, 222
HIRSCHBERG, H. Z., 273*n*
HITTI, P. K., 270*n*
HODGSON, R., 348*n*, 363*n*, 375*n*
HOFFMAN, H. S., 307*n*
HULBERT, B., xv
Human double, 352-353
HUME, D., vii
HUMPHREYS, C., 129*n*, 222*n*
Hyperesthesia, acoustic, 362*n*
Hypnosis
  assumed identity under, 367*n*
  and cryptomnesia, 340-342
  and perception of changes in body size,
    197*n*
  regression to "previous lives" under, 2-3, 14,
    340-341, 353*n*, 358, 359, 360, 364
HYSLOP, J. H., 338, 374*n*, 378

Identification of child with previous person-
    ality in reincarnation-type cases, 5, 23,
    31, 34, 48, 120-123, 187, 198, 316-317, 341,
    357-359, 365, 373
  characteristics of, 359-360
  diminishing of with passing time, 124, 229,
    233, 234
  imposed by parents, 366-372
  motivation for, 332, 365-366
"Ilga K." case, 362, 366
Illness, possibly related to previous life, *see
    under* Diseases, physical, *and* Mental ill-
    ness
Illusions of memory, *see under* Memory
Imad Elawar, case of, 4, 7, 9, 11, 13, 17,124*n*,
    275-320, 321*n*, 325, 328, 335, 344, 366, 370,
    371, 372, 377, 379, 380, 385

Imagery, projection of, 352-353
"Imposed identification" theory, 172, 177, 212,
    229, 235, 241, 266-268, 366-372
  weaknesses of, 229, 368-370
Incas of Peru, belief in reincarnation among,
    216*n*
Incidence of reported reincarnation-type cases
  in Alaska, 2
  in Brazil, 2
  in Canada, 2, 349
  in Ceylon, 125*n*
  among the Druses, 274
  in Europe, 2, 171
  in Great Britain, 349
  among the Haidas, 224
  in India, 225*n*
  in Lebanon, 225*n*, 274
  among the Muslim Arabs of southern
    Turkey, 274
  in southeastern Asia, 2
  among the Tlingits, 224-225, 274*n*
  in Turkey, 274
  in the United States, 2, 171, 224, 349
  in western Asia, 2
Informational features in reincarnation-type
    cases, 5, 334, 335, 343-345
  patterns of, 384-387
  theory of extrasensory perception plus per-
    sonation applied to, 345-348
Intelligence, inheritance of, 213
"Intermediate lives," 68, 169, 283, 317-318
International census of cases suggestive of re-
    incarnation, 1-2, 17, 142, 271, 349, 351
Interval between death and rebirth, 47, 51,
    168, 252, 272-273
ISHERWOOD, C., 15*n*
ISRAEL, H. A., 368*n*

JACOBSON, N. P., 129*n*
Jagdish Chandra, case of, 270*n*
Jain family (case of Prakash), 19-34
Jains, belief in reincarnation among, 272
JAMES, W., 375*n*
Jasbir, case of, xii, 2, 16, 18, 19, 34-52, 53,
    80, 102, 124*n*, 130, 328, 336, 344, 346-347,
    364, 365, 366, 370, 371, 375-376, 377, 381,
    385
Jat family (case of Jasbir), 34-52
Jayatilleke, K. N., xv
JENNESS, D., 218*n*
Jimmy Svenson, case of, 225-231, 370
JOHNSON, A. M., 211*n*, 367

KANNER, L., 368*n*
KANT, E., vii

KARDEC, A., 181
Karma, 149, 160n, 163, 221, 222
KARUNARATNE, G., xv
KHALIDY, M., xiv
Kinship relations between present and antecedent personalities, 149-171, 182, 203-215, 225, 269
KLEVGARD, C., xiii
KLINE, M. V., 340n
Koran, reincarnation suggested in, 272n
KRAUSE, A., 220, 224, 243
KUBIE, L. S., 368n

LAIDLAW, R. W., xi
LAL, R. S., xii, 18, 93, 95
Later development of subjects in reincarnation-type cases, 32-34, 49-52, 65-67, 88-91, 103-105, 125-127, 146-148, 164-171, 178-180, 199-203, 213-215, 230-231, 244-245, 248, 251-252, 258-259, 268-269, 316-320, 366n
LAURENCE, J., 162n
Left-handedness, possibly related to previous life, 263
LELAND, C. G., 219n
"Lethe" case, 384
LEONARD, G. O., 364
LEVEN, L., 240n
LEWIS, L. S., 339n
LHERMITTE, J., 352n
Links, psychometric, see Psychometric links
Links, telepathic, see Telepathic links
"Lisa" case, 362, 366
LODGE, O., 384n
LOOSLI, S., xii
Lorenz family (cases of Marta and Paulo), 182-215
LORENZ, F. V., 182-212
LORENZ, W., xii, 182-215
LOWES, J. L., 341
LSD and perception of changes in body size, 197n
"Lurancy Vennum" case, 363, 364, 375-376, 379
LURIA, A. R., 352n

McTAGGART, J. M. E., vii
MAITREYA, A., xiii, 131, 150, 152, 160, 161
MAKAREM, S., xiv, 274n, 275, 309
Mallika, case of, xii, 7, 11, 19, 105-108, 334, 378
MANCHESTER, F., 15n
Marta Lorenz, case of, xiii, 9, 124n, 182-203, 256n, 323, 334, 335, 339, 344, 347n, 353, 354, 364, 380

MARTÍN, J., xi, 337
MARURI, C. A., 240n
"Maternal psychokinesis" (in birthmark cases), theory of, 266, 382
MATHUR, T. C., 17n
Mediumistic communications, vii, 204, 210-211, 337-338, 348, 351, 354-357, 359, 379
patterns in, 384
Mediumship, 354, 384
behavioral features in, 360-361
in children, 354-357, 362-365
identification with communicator in, 358-359
linkage problem in, 355-356
personation in, 361-365
range of knowledge shown in, 354
states of consciousness in, 356-357
Mehra family (case of Parmod), 109-127
MEHROTRA, L. P., xv, 35n, 104
Memories of the previous life
average duration of, 324-330, 383
fading of, 32-33, 49, 65-66, 89, 103, 122-123, 125, 142, 147-148, 160, 164-165, 185-186, 200, 225, 262, 318-320
and maturation of subject, 322, 324
parental suppression of in children, 20, 90, 92, 102, 161, 181n, 222, 329
revival of at location of previous personality, 328, 377-378
significance of in separating types of cases, 348-352
Memory
disorders of, 352
errors of on part of witnesses, 9-11, 265-266, 270, 308
illusions of, 168-169, 252, 338
and personality, 348-349
retrospective errors of, 308
unreliability of in spontaneous cases, 4
Mental illness and memories of previous lives, 165-171, 213-215, 322-324
Methods of studying spontaneous reincarnation-type cases, 4-14, 17
Mishra family (case of Swarnlata), 67-91, 332
MISHRA, M. L., 18, 332
Moles, 231-241; see also Birthmarks, inheritance of, 239-241
MOREIRA, E. B., xiii
MOSS, F. A., 213n
Motivated errors in witnesses' testimony, 9-11
Mourougassigamany family (case of Mallika), 105-108
MUKHERJEE, SUBASH, xii, 19, 110, 122
MUKHERJEE, SUDHIR, xii, 19, 110
MÜLLER, K., xi
Multiple personality, 353, 359-360

MURPHY, G., xi, 371n
MYERS, F. W. H., 337, 354, 356, 362, 384
Mysticism, physical phenomena of, 163n

Naevi, *see* Moles
NAISH, C., 224
NANTET, J., 270n
NATH, V., xii, 19
NEIDHART, G., 270n
NIKHILANANDA, Swami, 15n
Nirvana, 129
NISSANKA, H. S. S., xv, 132, 144
Non-veridical cases suggestive of reincarna-
    tion, 350-351
Normal sources of information in reincarna-
    tion-type cases, 331-343
Norman Despers, case of, 245-248, 334, 370
NYANATILOKA, 129n, 149n

OBEYESEKERE, G., 129n
Object-reading, *see* Psychometry
Oliveiro family (case of Marta Lorenz), 182-
    202
Oral traditions versus written records in
    Tlingit culture, 254n
ORIGEN, vii
OSBORN, A. W., xi, 352n
OSGOOD, C., 216n
OSIS, K., xi
OSTY, E., 344, 355, 358
Out-of-the-body experiences, vii, 352n

PACE, R., xiii
PAL, P., xi, xii, xv, 52n, 54, 56, 57, 65, 67, 69,
    71, 82, 83, 86, 88
Pandey family (case of Swarnlata), 67-91
Paramnesia, 239, 247, 351-352, 353, 368n, 371;
    see also Déjà vu
    rarity of, 352n
Parapsychology Foundation, xi
Parmod, case of, xii, 10, 16, 19, 107, 109-127,
    323, 324, 328, 344, 348, 366n, 370, 371, 377,
    379, 380, 384
Pathak family (case of Sukla), 52-66
Pathak family (case of Swarnlata), 67-91, 332
"Patience Worth" case, 340
Patterns of recurring features in reincarna-
    tion-type cases, 14, 131, 331, 384-387
PAUL, W. L., Sr., xiii
Paulo Lorenz, case of, 203-215, 323, 361, 367,
    372, 385
PECK, C., xiii
PEIRIS, Q., 164
Perception of changes in body size, 197n
PERERA, S., xiii
Personality, multiple, *see* Multiple personality

Personation, 49, 203
    in cases of cryptomnesia, 337-388
    duration of in reincarnation-type cases, 324,
        359-360, 361, 362
    and extrasensory perception, 315, 343-373
    in mediumship, 361-365
Physical patterns in reincarnation-type cases,
    385-386; *see also* Birthmarks
Physical phenomena of mysticism, 163n
PICKFORD, R. W., 338
PICKTHALL, M. M., 272n
PINART, A., 220, 221, 222
PIPER, L. E., 348, 384
Pitnov family (case of Derek Pitnov), 252-259
PIYADASSI, xiii, 129n, 132, 134, 144
PLATO, vii
PLOTINUS, vii
PODTIAGUINE, O., xiv, 220, 221
POLANYI, M., 88n, 335-336
POLE, W. T., 352
Porter family (case of Charles Porter), 241-
    245
Possession as a counterhypothesis in reincarna-
    tion-type cases, 315, 335, 359, 374-376, 383
    bearing of birthmark cases on, 381-382
    limitations of, 377-382
Possession and reincarnation, differences and
    transitional cases between, 374-377
Possible errors in data of reincarnation-type
    cases
    by interpreters and in translations, 7
    of memory on part of witnesses, 9-11, 265-
        266, 270, 308
    in recording methods, 7-8
    discrepant testimony, 5-6, 9-11, 270, 281n,
        316
POTTER, H. W., 368n
POTTS, W., 263
POUSSIN, de la V., 129n
PRABHAVANANDA, SWAMI, 15n
Praibhu Khairti, case of, 271n
PRAKASH, C., xii, 18
Prakash, case of, xii, 10, 11, 13, 16, 18, 19-34,
    53, 80, 102, 107, 328, 331, 333, 348, 358,
    365, 366, 370, 371, 376, 380, 384
PRASAD, J., xi, xii, 18, 19, 49, 93, 95, 110, 125
PRATT, J. G., xii
Precocious language attributed to children in
    reincarnation-type cases
Precognition, 344, 353, 371
Predictions of rebirth, 183-184, 185, 195, 204,
    231-232, 259-260, 385n
"Previous lives"
    evoked under hypnotic regression, 2-3, 14,
        340-341, 353n, 358, 359, 360, 364
    studied hypnotically, 342

PRINCE, W. F., 3n, 340n, 344n, 355n, 358
Pseudo-memories, 229
Psychical research, 1, 17, 354, 355
and cryptomnesia, 337-338
and the study of spontaneous cases, 4-5
and survival, vii, viii, 1
Psychokinesis, see "Maternal psychokinesis"
Psychometric links, 355-356, 373
Psychometry, 355, 358
Psychoses, rarity of in children, 368
PURI, O., 363
PYTHAGORAS, vii

RABBATH, W., xiv, 275, 276, 281n, 282
RADCLYFFE-HALL, M., 364n
RADDALGODA, E. C., xiii, 131, 164, 168
RADHAKRISHNAN, S., 15n
RAHULA, W., 129n
Ranjith Makalanda, case of, 105, 131, 171-180, 365, 368
Ravi Shankar, case of, xii, 11, 16, 17, 18-19, 91-105, 107, 149n, 328, 330, 361, 365, 376, 385
RAWAT, K. S., xv
RAWDAH, A. S., xiv
Rebirth, as contrasted with reincarnation, 129, 222
Recognition, stronger than recall, 108, 377
Recognition tests, 81-82, 335-336
importance of, 335
in reply to questions, 145-146
spontaneous, 48, 135, 145-146, 234, 239, 261-262, 267, 335
unconscious direction in, 64, 239, 267-268
Regression to "previous lives" under hypnosis, see under Hypnosis
Reincarnation
and Buddhism, 128-130, 149n, 153n, 221, 222, 272n
as contrasted with rebirth, 129, 222
counterhypotheses to; see Counterhypotheses
credulity concerning, 10
Druse ideas about, 271-274
and Hinduism, 15-16, 52, 129-130, 221, 222
Kardec's views on, 181
and possession, differences between, 374-377
skepticism about, 273-274
in subhuman animal bodies, 168-169
Tlingit ideas about, 219-223
RENOUVIER, C., vii
Retrocognition, 344, 384
Retrospective errors of memory, see under Memory
RHINE, L. E., xiii
RODRIGUEZ, L. J., 181n
ROFF, M., see "Lurancy Vennum" case

ROOS, W., 168n
"Rosemary" case, 183n
"Ruth Robertshaw" case, 356n

SAHAY, K. K. N., 17n, 270n
SALTER, W. H., 3n
SAMANERA, B., 110n
SAMARARATNE, G., xv, 164, 170, 171
Scars, see Birthmarks
SCHNECK, J. M., 358n
SCHOPENHAUER, A., vii
SCHWARZ, B. E., 362n
SCRIVEN, M., 3n
Sen Gupta family (case of Sukla), 52-66
SEN, I., 17n
SEN, K. M., 15n
Sex difference in present and antecedent personalities in reincarnation-type cases, 131-148, 203-215
incidence of, 142-143
Sexual orientation of children in reincarnation-type cases, 142-144, 146, 204-205, 210, 361
Shamlinie Prema, case of, 202n
Shanti Devi, case of, 17, 345
Sharma family (case of Parmod), 109-127
SHARMA, N. R., 17n
SHIRLEY, R., 352n
SIDIS, B., 337
SIMPSON, G., 243
SINGH, S. K., xii, 19
Skills and aptitudes
genetic transmission of, 212-213
in cases of possession, 380, 383
in reincarnation-type cases, 88, 205, 209-210, 262, 263, 372, 383, 384, 385
Sleimann Bouhamzy, case of, 305-308
Society for Psychical Research, 355, 384
SOLOTAROFF, L., 352n
Spiritism, Kardecian, in Brazil, 181-182
Spiritualism in Brazil, 181
Spontaneous case material, criticisms of, 3
STEVENS, E. W., 375n
STEVENSON, I., vii, 1n, 3n, 16n, 17n, 165n, 169n, 171n, 202n, 232n, 252n, 270n, 323n, 329n, 339n, 340n, 345n, 355n, 360n, 371n, 372n, 375n, 384n
Stigmata, 163n
STORY, F., xi, 8, 19, 131, 150, 151, 161, 164, 168, 172
Stuttering, possibly related to previous life, 259, 262, 269
Subhuman animal bodies, rebirth into, 168-169; see also Transmigration
Suicide, 324

Sukla, case of, xii, 11, 12, 17, 18, 52-66, 107, 124n, 130n, 256n, 325, 328, 335, 344, 348, 353, 358, 370, 371, 377, 379, 380, 385
SUMITHAPALA, D. V., 131, 132, 134, 135, 142-144, 146
SUNDERLAL, R. B. S., 17n, 271n
Survival of bodily death, vii, viii, 1, 181, 355
discarnate versus reincarnate form of, 373-386
Svenson family (case of Jimmy Svenson), 225-231
SWANTON, J. R., 220, 221
Swarnlata, case of, ix, xii, xv, 4, 7, 11, 13, 17, 18, 67-91, 107, 202n, 270n, 328, 331, 332, 335, 347-348, 365, 366, 371, 377, 379, 380, 384
songs and dances of, 67-68, 69, 82-86, 88, 378
SWEDENBORG, E., 381
SZUREK, S. A., 367n

"Tacit knowing," 235-236
TAGORE, R., 82, 83, 85, 86, 87
Telepathic links in reincarnation-type cases, 49, 103, 111, 124, 344-345; *see also* Psychometric links
Telepathy, 3, 49, 103, 111, 124, 163, 353, 384
Theravada branch of Buddhism, 128-129
"Thompson-Gifford" case, 374-375, 376-377, 378, 379, 380
THORNDIKE, E. L., 329n
THURSTON, H., 163n
TIGHE, V., 340
Tillekeratne and family (case of Gnanatilleka, 131-148
Tlingit ideas on reincarnation, 219-223
Tlingits, incidence of reincarnation-type cases among, 224-225, 274n
Transmigration, 220
Transvestism, 211n, 367
TROUBRIDGE, U., 364n
TRYON, R. C., 213

Tsimsyans, belief in reincarnation among, 216
Tyagi family (case of Jasbir), 34-52
TYRRELL, G. N. M., 355

Varshnay family (case of Prakash), 19-34
VENIAMINOV, I. E. P., xiv, 219, 220, 221, 232
VENNUM, L., *see* "Lurancy Vennum" case
VINING, E. P., 218n, 219n, 222n
Violent deaths, incidence of in reincarnation-type cases, 223, 329
Vishwa Nath, case of, 270n

WARD, J., vii
"Watseka Wonder," *see* "Lurancy Vennum" case
WATTEGAMA, Mr., 151
WEERARATNE, A., xvi
WEISZ-ROOS, H., 1, 375
WEST, D. J., 3n
WESTWOOD, H., 356, 362, 363
"Wheel of rebirth," 129, 130
WHITAKER, L., 210n
WHITAKER, L. H., 358n
WHITEMAN, J. H. M., 352n
WICKLAND, C. A., 379
Wijeratne, case of, xiii, xv, 7, 12, 130 131, 149-171, 323, 324, 331, 332, 334, 339, 365, 379
WILKINSON, A., 356, 363
WILLETT, Mrs., 357, 358, 363, 384
William George, Jr., case of, 11, 231-241, 267, 334, 343, 370, 372, 385
Witchcraft among the Tlingits, 217
WOOD, F. H., 183n

Xenoglossy, ix, 3, 88, 183n, 212

YOST, C., 340n

ZOLIK, E., 340-341